Ambient Intelligence
and Internet of Things

Scrivener Publishing
100 Cummings Center, Suite 541J
Beverly, MA 01915-6106

Publishers at Scrivener
Martin Scrivener (martin@scrivenerpublishing.com)
Phillip Carmical (pcarmical@scrivenerpublishing.com)

Ambient Intelligence and Internet of Things

Convergent Technologies

Edited by

Md Rashid Mahmood
Rohit Raja
Harpreet Kaur
Sandeep Kumar
and
Kapil Kumar Nagwanshi

Scrivener
Publishing

WILEY

This edition first published 2023 by John Wiley & Sons, Inc., 111 River Street, Hoboken, NJ 07030, USA and Scrivener Publishing LLC, 100 Cummings Center, Suite 541J, Beverly, MA 01915, USA
© 2023 Scrivener Publishing LLC
For more information about Scrivener publications please visit www.scrivenerpublishing.com.

Wiley Global Headquarters
111 River Street, Hoboken, NJ 07030, USA

For details of our global editorial offices, customer services, and more information about Wiley products visit us at www.wiley.com.

Limit of Liability/Disclaimer of Warranty
While the publisher and authors have used their best efforts in preparing this work, they make no representations or warranties with respect to the accuracy or completeness of the contents of this work and specifically disclaim all warranties, including without limitation any implied warranties of merchantability or fitness for a particular purpose. No warranty may be created or extended by sales representatives, written sales materials, or promotional statements for this work. The fact that an organization, website, or product is referred to in this work as a citation and/or potential source of further information does not mean that the publisher and authors endorse the information or services the organization, website, or product may provide or recommendations it may make. This work is sold with the understanding that the publisher is not engaged in rendering professional services. The advice and strategies contained herein may not be suitable for your situation. You should consult with a specialist where appropriate. Neither the publisher nor authors shall be liable for any loss of profit or any other commercial damages, including but not limited to special, incidental, consequential, or other damages. Further, readers should be aware that websites listed in this work may have changed or disappeared between when this work was written and when it is read.

Library of Congress Cataloging-in-Publication Data

ISBN 978-1-119-82123-6

Cover image: Pixabay.Com
Cover design by Russell Richardson

Set in size of 11pt and Minion Pro by Manila Typesetting Company, Makati, Philippines

Printed in the USA

10 9 8 7 6 5 4 3 2 1

Contents

4   Security in Ambient Intelligence and Internet of Things   81
Salman Arafath Mohammed and Md Rashid Mahmood

10 Healthcare Internet of Things: A New Revolution 301
Manpreet Kaur, M. Sugadev, Harpreet Kaur,
Md Rashid Mahmood and Vikas Maheshwari

Preface

Working environments based on the emerging technologies of ambient intelligence (AmI) and the internet of things (IoT) are available for current and future use in a diverse field of applications. The AmI and IoT paradigms aim to help people achieve their daily goals by augmenting physical environments using networks of distributed devices, including sensors, actuators, and computational resources. Because AmI-IoT is the convergence of numerous technologies and associated research fields, it takes significant effort to integrate them for the purpose of making our lives easier. It is asserted that AmI is able to successfully analyze the vast amounts of contextual data obtained from such embedded sensors by employing a variety of artificial intelligence (AI) techniques, and that it will transparently and proactively change the environment to conform to the requirements of the user. Over a long period of time, the long-term research goals and implementation strategies could meet the design and application needs of a wide range of modern and real-time applications.

Ambient Intelligence and Internet of Things: Convergent Technologies provides comprehensive knowledge of AmI and the IoT along with practical applications. Since this book focuses on the fundamental structure of innovative cutting-edge AmI and IoT technologies, it will be of interest and use to students, academicians, researchers and industry professionals in the domain of AI, AmI and IoT. It will be a better option compared to the majority of books that are now available on the market because older publications rarely touch on contemporary applications of AmI and IoT.

We would like to thank all of the contributing authors who made a significant contribution to the creation of this peer-reviewed edited volume by giving of their time, effort, and insightful recommendations. The editors are also thankful to Scrivener Publishing and their team members for the opportunity to publish this volume. Lastly, we thank our family members for their love, support, encouragement, and patience during the entire period of this work.

Dr. Md Rashid Mahmood
Dr. Rohit Raja
Dr. Harpreet Kaur
Dr. Sandeep Kumar
Dr. Kapil Kumar Nagwanshi
October 2022

Ambient Intelligence and Internet of Things: An Overview

**Md Rashid Mahmood¹*, Harpreet Kaur¹, Manpreet Kaur¹, Rohit Raja²
and Imran Ahmed Khan³**

*¹Department of ECE, Guru Nanak Institutions Technical Campus,
Hyderabad, India
²Department of IT, Guru Ghasidas Vishwavidyala, Bilaspur, India
³Department of ECE, Jamia Millia Islamia, New Delhi, India*

Abstract

Ambient intelligence (AmI) is the ability of technology to make judgments and act on our behalf. AmI is a cutting-edge technology that has the potential to fundamentally alter the way we interact with machines and electronics in our environment. It does not ask the user questions but rather understands the context in which the user is operating. Ambient intelligence (AmI) uses sensors and devices in our homes and offices to gather information about the environment. The AmI system then makes inferences based on proximity, intent, and behavioral patterns. It reacts to the user via a smart device's elegantly built natural interface. The Internet of Things (IoT) is a network of web-connected smart gadgets that collect data from their surroundings and use it to make decisions about their own lives. Ambient intelligence refers to what occurs when various devices connect, and more specifically, what they learn from one another. Ambient computing is a new kind of relationship between computers and employees. It gathers information for us when we ask for it, or even before we ask. Ambient intelligence aims to improve the way people and their environment interact with one another. Ambient intelligence (AI) is a subset of artificial intelligence (AI). Artificial intelligence mimics human cognitive processes such as perceiving, interpreting, and learning, among others. AmI is interlinked with the Internet of Things (IoT).

Keywords: Ambient intelligence, Internet of Things, artificial intelligence, human computer interaction

---

*Corresponding author: er.mrashid@gmail.com

Md Rashid Mahmood, Rohit Raja, Harpreet Kaur, Sandeep Kumar and Kapil Kumar Nagwanshi (eds.)
Ambient Intelligence and Internet of Things: Convergent Technologies, (1–32) © 2023 Scrivener
Publishing LLC

1.1   Introduction

Ambient intelligence, often known as AmI, is the ability of technology to make judgments and act on our behalf while taking our preferences into consideration depending on the data accessible to it from all of the linked sensors and devices surrounding the user. AmI is a highly intelligent, widespread, and intuitive system. It does not ask the user questions but rather understands the context in which the user is operating. It does not make its physical presence known but instead performs actions that are suited to the user's needs. AmI is a cutting-edge technology that has the potential to fundamentally alter the way we interact with the machines and electronics in our environment. Ambient intelligence (AmI) is a term that is frequently used in conjunction with artificial intelligence (AI), the Internet of things (IoT), big data, machine learning (ML), networks, human-computer interaction (HCI), and pervasive, ubiquitous computing. On the other hand, artificial intelligence owes its success to the amazing growth of information and communication technology (ICTs) [1].

Intelligence is defined as the capacity to acquire knowledge and use it in novel settings. "Artificial" is anything created by humans, whereas "ambience" is what surrounds us. Additionally, we prefer to think of ambient intelligence (AmI) is an artificial construct since the mechanisms underlying natural AmI are the focus of biology and sociology. Numerous artificial intelligence technologies developed by computers are based on the concept of replicating brain functioning and human intellect.

Everyday life is made up of a combination of hardware, software, user experience, and machine/human-machine interaction and learning. In other words, it is the act of employing a computer, a device having far-field communication capabilities, or an internet-enabled gadget without necessarily being aware of doing so. For example, we no longer need to use a desktop computer in order to operate a computer. They are unseen to us, function in sync with us, and provide an overall seamless experience.

AmI uses a variety of IoT sensors and devices in our homes and workplaces to gather information about the environment and user context. The acquired data is then processed by the AmI system. The processing and analysis of collected data are used to identify user proximity, state, intent and behavioral patterns in the AmI system. Thereafter, it makes inferences based on what it has learned so far, what it has seen before, and any patterns it notices. Once it has determined the appropriate course of action, it reacts to the user via the smart device's elegantly built natural interface.

There are countless ways in which ambient intelligence may improve our lives. Regardless of where we are in the office, living room, shopping mall, or driving, we should always be mindful of our surroundings. Technology will serve as a constant companion. Our health monitoring devices can measure our blood pressure, so it tells us not to eat those high-cholesterol food items. It can be inconvenient to divert the route because it knows that there was an accident on our regular way to work. As soon as we get home from work on a hot summer evening, it turns on the air conditioner to keep us cool.

Consider the following scenario: Peter returns home after a hectic day at work, and AmI systems assist him in relaxing.

- At his front entrance, Peter's car is recognized by the system, and the parking door will open to allow him to enter it.
- At the next level, Peter is recognized by a facial recognition system, which allows him to enter his house.
- Peter's facial expressions are captured by the AmI system, and the system determines that he is under stress.
- When Peter walks into the living room, the system automatically adjusts the lighting to suit his mood.
- AmI plays relaxing music from Peter's music library, according to his preferences.
- The blinds and curtains are closed by AmI to keep the light from coming in from the windows.
- As soon as Peter gets on the couch, AmI plays a very important message from his wife. She says she will be home a little later from work.
- When I look at Peter's calendar, it informs me that the conference call at 8.30 PM has been moved to 9:00 AM tomorrow.
- AmI reminds Peter that his favourite reality show is on TV tonight by reading the TV schedule and asking if he wants to set a reminder for it.

Ambient intelligence (AmI) is interlinked with the Internet of Things (IoT). IoT refers to smart lighting, smart transportation, smart homes, smart villages, smart grids, etc., among other things, and the way these items communicate. Ambient intelligence refers to what occurs when various devices connect, and more specifically, what they learn from one another.

The Internet of Things (IoT) is a network of web-connected smart gadgets that collect data from their surroundings and use it to make decisions about their own lives. Interactions between Internet of Things devices and a gateway or other cutting-edge devices transmit sensitive data that may be analyzed remotely or on-site. These gadgets communicate with one another and respond to each other's data. While people can communicate with robots, machines are capable of doing the majority of jobs without the need for human intervention.

It is expected that the Internet of Things will have an impact on society, the economy, and technology as it grows. Sensors and other ordinary items, as well as consumer devices, are becoming increasingly capable of storing and processing data. Despite this, there are a number of significant challenges that could hinder the Internet of Things from realizing its potential. The general public is well aware of the risks associated with Internet-connected gadgets, hacking, surveillance, and privacy violations. There is a new set of policy, legal, and development challenges that have evolved in recent years. The increasing use of Internet of Things (IoT) devices has the potential to transform our lives.

With the Internet of Things (IoT) devices such as Internet-enabled appliances, home automation components, and energy management gadgets, we are getting closer to having a smart house. In addition to other Internet-of-Things-enabled medical equipment, wearable fitness and health monitoring devices are transforming the way healthcare is delivered. The disabled and the elderly will benefit the most from this technology, as it will increase their freedom and quality of life while simultaneously cutting their expenditures [2].

To exchange data and manage message traffic, an Internet of Things device connects directly to a cloud service, such as an application service provider, through a secure connection. When an Internet of Things device connects to a cloud service through an application-layer gateway (ALG), the device-to-gateway model is utilized. On local gateway devices, features like data translation and protocol encoding are accessible.

Using this paradigm, smart devices can communicate with one another without using the Internet Protocol (IP). A gateway is required for IPv4 devices and services to function effectively. This strategy is most frequently used to incorporate new smart gadgets into current parental control systems. In order to conduct an analysis, data from various sources can be integrated with smart object data from the cloud service. A business can even benefit from ambient computing. It can help it work more efficiently, remove unnecessary steps in processes, and collect, analyze, and actively learn from data.

When computers are used in the workplace, a new kind of relationship between employees and computers develops. It gathers information for us when we ask for it or even before we ask. Ambient computing already delivers sophisticated services like voice-assisted systems, chatbots, etc. [3].

1.2 Ambient Intelligent System

Figure 1.1 illustrates the ambience intelligence system for some specific application areas; it exhibits several smart and intelligent systems that surround the user and make use of AI and ML technology. In this way, AmI is not a specific technology but rather a user's experience with the services

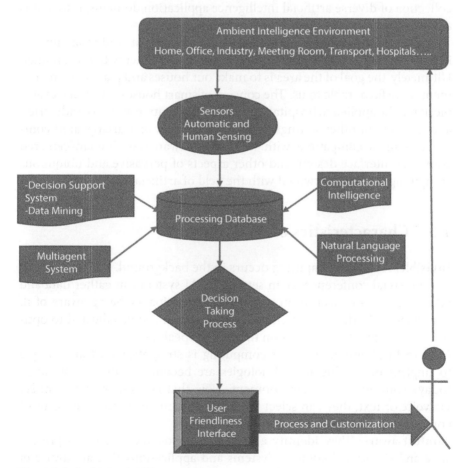

Figure 1.1 Ambience intelligence system.

supplied by such systems. Typically, the cost functions employed to optimize AmI systems are related to subjective human experience, which can be quantified only to a limited extent. As a result, in order to ensure the success of AI and AmI, we must find the optimal objective-cost functions that accurately capture the subjective human experience in AmI.

AI, also known as "machine intelligence" (MI), is the intelligence demonstrated by machines as opposed to the natural intelligence (NI) exhibited by humans and other animals. AI is a subset of artificial intelligence (AI). As a result, artificial intelligence mimics human cognitive processes such as perceiving, interpreting environmental input and learning, among others. Whenever robots demonstrate intelligence in their immediate environment, this is referred to as "ambient intelligence." Because of its emphasis on humans and the environment, AmI is much more than a collection of diverse artificial intelligence application domains; rather, it is a network of disparate areas that function together.

Ambient intelligence is an interdisciplinary topic of study that aims to improve the way people and their environments interact with one another. Ultimately, the goal of the area is to make our houses and places of employment more favourable to us. The concept of smart houses is just one example; it may be applied to hospitals, public transportation systems, industries, and a variety of other settings. Unlike the concept of a disappeared computer, AmI is compatible with it. Context awareness, human-centered computer interface design, and other aspects of pervasive and ubiquitous computing are all intertwined with the field of artificial intelligence [4].

1.3   Characteristics of AmI Systems

Invisible: Ambient computing occurs in the background. For example, in a commercial conference room setting, an AI system can gather data and take notes on a conversation without the participants' being aware of it. Simultaneously, the camera and a speaker system can be adjusted to optimize image quality and focus on the person speaking.

Easy to Implement: Ambient computing is straightforward and simple to implement. Intelligent technologies are becoming more common in today's communication environment. Now that consumers can connect via voice or text, they can select the mode of communication that is most convenient for them.

Context-aware: They identify a user and, if possible, the user's present state and situational context. Systems and applications that are aware of the context in which they work can gather and interpret information about the people, roles, activities, times, places, devices, and software that make up the current situation and then act in a way that fits the situation. Such behavior could include giving personalized or structured information, as well as taking action to avoid something that could be bad. As computers become more intelligent and more aware of their surroundings, they could change how we interact with them in the future.

Integration: Ambient computing allows for the seamless integration of tools, which is considerably more useful than information from non-integrated systems. They are completely incorporated into their surroundings; they are "invisible."

Personalized: The system can be customized by the user to match their specific requirements. They are frequently adapted to the user's specific requirements.

Adaptive: Components of the system may change according to individual requirements. AmI systems adjust to changes in the user's physical or mental condition.

Anticipatory: Capable of anticipating user wishes in the absence of cognitive mediation.

Unobtrusive: Discreet, delivering just the information essential to other devices and humans about the user.

Noninvasive: They do not need the user to take action; rather, they act on their own.

AmI is a type of future intelligent computing (IC) in which sensors and processors are embedded in everyday objects, allowing the environment to dynamically adapt to the user's needs and desires. These AI systems will employ the contextual data collected by these embedded sensors, as well as AI algorithms, to interpret and forecast the desires of their users. The technology will be simple to use and designed with the user in mind.

AmI is the capacity of technology to make judgments and act on our behalf while taking our preferences into account, based on data collected from all of the user's linked sensors and devices. AmI is a highly intelligent system that is widely distributed and intuitive. It does not pose questions to the user, but rather recognizes and understands the context in which the user is acting. It does not make its physical presence known but instead executes activities that are tailored to the demands of the individual user. An emerging technology, ambient intelligence (AmI), has the potential to profoundly modify how humans interact with machines and other devices in their surroundings. In its interdisciplinary nature, ambient intelligence (AmI) is a technology that functions at the confluence of many technologies, such as the IoT, AI, big data, pervasive-ubiquitous computing, networks, and human-computer interaction (HCI).

Intelligent digital systems put in our homes or offices, among other things, that employ sensors and gadgets from the IoT to perceive the environment and user context are used to accomplish this sensing and contextualization. This is followed by the AmI system itself processing the data it has collected from these other systems in the following step. In addition to processing and evaluating the data, the AmI system performs analysis on the data in order to ascertain the vicinity of the person in question as well as his or her condition, purpose, and behavior. Intuition follows after that, and it is produced from insights derived from current facts, previous learning, and pattern recognition. It then calculates the most suitable course of action to take and interacts with the user through a natural interface that can be readily developed on a smartphone or tablet computer.

When it comes to making our lives easier and more pleasurable, AmI opens the door to a myriad of possibilities. It makes no difference what we are doing, whether it is in our living room, kitchen, or place of employment. At the backdrop of our activities, whether we are in the store, in the automobile, or in the hospital, technology will be there to assist us with our tasks. All sorts of things have happened, from our cell phones warning us not to eat that ice cream because it can detect our blood sugar levels from health monitoring equipment to our work computers informing us that there was an accident on our regular way to work. When we go home from work on hot summer evenings, it will automatically switch on the air conditioner to chill our homes before we arrive home.

It is important to know that privacy will be a big issue with AmI, even though the technology has a lot of promise. It is possible that AmI systems will know almost everything about the lives of the people they follow. If their communications are read by people who are not supposed to be reading them, they could cause a lot of problems. When people ask about how their data is used, how it is kept private, and how it is kept safe, they need to get more detailed answers. Systems need to be built with trust at the heart of their architecture.

AmI has a lot of potentials to improve the quality of life for everyone, as well as their comfort and safety. Houses that have technology that is more focused on people will make many common tasks much easier. As the population ages, providing the right care for the elderly will become more important in this situation. Even when we are not at home, AmI will be used in a wide range of fields, including retail, healthcare, manufacturing, smart cities, and more [5].

1.4 Driving Force for Ambient Computing

A group of technologies is assisting in the development of ambient intelligence.

User Interface: The use of machines that respond to speech, touch, movement, and biometrics in place of a computer screen and keyboard (speech recognition, retina recognition, face recognition, fingerprints, etc.).

Artificial Intelligence (AI): Automated systems that can read documents, analyze data, make decisions, and translate languages are becoming more common.

Machine Learning (ML): It is the ability of electronic equipment to learn new skills and improve performance at specific tasks without being explicitly programmed to do so.

Natural language processing (NLP): Natural language processing (NLP) is a technology that allows computers to interpret and respond to human speech.

Edge Computing (EC): "Edge computing" is a term that refers to the practice of moving data processing away from a "centralized" processing center (often in the cloud) to smaller processing centers that are closer in proximity to the data source.

Maintain ongoing connectivity as users of digital devices move from one location to another. Mesh networks have the capability of facilitating smooth movement among a wide range of devices, applications, places, and individual networks, among others.

1.5 Ambient Intelligence Contributing Technologies

1. **Sensing:** This could be done through a wired or wireless connection. Sensors can be either stand-alone or integrated into an electronic device.
2. **Reasoning:** Systems will be able to "think," and they will be able to do things like help people, such as:

   - Recognizing and predicting activity
   - The ability to identify and evaluate the context of each activity.
   - Proposing a plan of action or decision

- Centralized data transmission and computation vs. distributed sensing and computation

3. **Acting:** Changing an environment's attributes. For example, a robot vacuuming or a user notification asking them to make a decision.
4. **Interacting:** Users will be able to interact with ambient intelligence in a variety of ways. The Web, mobile, and wearable gadgets, as well as home appliances and natural user interfaces, are among them.

The basic goal of AmI is to create systems that adapt the surrounding environment to the demands of users, whether expressed consciously or not, while also attaining other system-driven goals, such as reducing global energy usage. The widespread deployment of sensor and actuator devices in accordance with ubiquitous computing is an inherent necessity.

The ultimate goal of ambient intelligence is to have the user's preferences fully integrated into the system. When it comes to AmI systems, the key requirement is the presence of unobtrusive and ubiquitous sensors, which are necessary for context-aware reasoning in order to respond to user inputs and act on the environment. A ubiquitous digital intelligent environment, then, is one that puts the human user at the center by allowing them to control their surroundings.

A wireless sensor network (WSN) is made up of a lot of small computational units that can be programmed, are self-sufficient, and can communicate wirelessly with each other. These small sensor nodes can also be equipped with sensors that can measure a wide range of environmental characteristics, and ad-hoc sensors for specific tasks can be made.

A WSN can do low-level processing of sensed data, which makes it easier to choose only important data from a lot of measurements. Basically, wireless sensor networks (WSNs) are just one part of a bigger architecture that tries to figure out how to deal with a lot of data without overwhelming the person who is trying to figure out what to do with it.

The various physical or environmental conditions are monitored by WSNs, A node-to-node network enables each sensor to send data to the next terminal. Nodes in WSNs are small and inexpensive and can be put in a wide range of locations. With the help of energy harvesting, which uses energy from external sources such as kinetic and wind energy, as well as sound and electromagnetic radiation, WSN nodes can readily run on low-power batteries.

Using pervasive sensory infrastructure, it is possible to collect information about the surrounding environment, which may subsequently be utilized to run artificial reasoning algorithms on a central server.

The WSN is equipped with commercially accessible sensors that monitor temperature, pressure, humidity, ambient light, etc. [7].

1.6   Architecture Overview

Pictured in Figure 1.2 is a schematic representation of the architecture of the ambient intelligence system (AIS). The physical layer includes all of AmI functions' sensors and actuators, as well as those required by the end-user in case they are not already included in the AmI software. Exporting higher-level abstractions that identify the primary monitored components and address basic connectivity issues between gateways are two of the main functions of the physical abstraction interface. It will be possible to

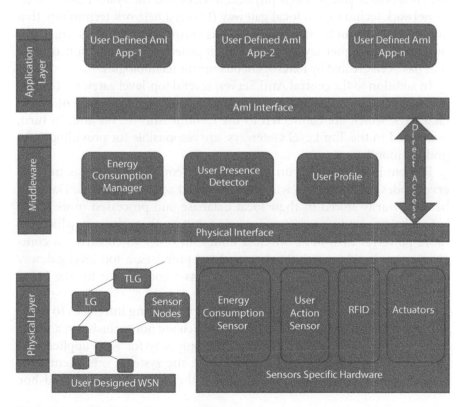

Figure 1.2 Ambience intelligence architecture.

consolidate functions such as message transmission, physical infrastructure health monitoring and control, and system reconfiguration due to physical infrastructure changes.

There are core AmI features defined in a middleware toolkit for generating intelligent services over available hardware, and these features are housed in the middleware layer where final developer AmI applications are produced.

In addition to the AMI modules and their interfaces with AMI-hosted applications, several other components contribute to the middleware in the system. There is a thin layer of middleware over distant sensor nodes that allows them to respond to system commands, but most of the services are delivered by remote gateways. There are both wireless and wired sensors and actuators in each of the remote networks that have been placed in a particular location.

According to the system, it is possible to gain access to the room through the use of a specific gateway node, referred to as the Local Gateway (LG), which acts as a link between physical devices and the system as a whole. In network technology, a local gateway (LG) is a network technology that facilitates the connection between various network technologies while also providing the higher layers with a homogeneous representation of data that has been created by heterogeneous sensor technologies.

In addition to the central AmI Server, several top-level gateways (TLGs) are connected to it, each of which handles a unique environment. Local Gateways, which are connected to the Central AmI Server and, in turn, connected to the Top Level Gateways, are responsible for providing fine-grained monitoring.

Remote LGs could be run on low-power computers, such as microserver nodes connected to a wireless sensor and actuator network. Data can be temporarily stored in their local database and processed more finely before being sent to a remote processing unit on these devices, which are more powerful than basic wireless nodes. In order to construct a communication backbone within the regulated premises, a top-level gateway collects data from all of the LGs and acts as a coordinator for the Local Gateways Network.

The Top-Level Gateway also provides programming interfaces to some components, like sensors and actuators, which are not exclusive to a single building. The Central AmI Server is the only way for AmI applications to access the physical layer's functionality; the system's intelligent software components are not directly tied to the hardware, making ad-hoc application creation easier and more generalizable. WSNs represent the proposed system's primary sensory infrastructure. Because of the standard abstraction layer, the system has been built to be easily adaptable with additional sensors.

Various connected elements rely on a variety of physically diverse media, which may be wired or wireless, to communicate with the Local Gateway, and the presence of this protocol on board of the Local Gateway prevents the data management and communication software operations on board from being constrained by information about the data formats and communication modalities specific to each of those technologies.

There are a lot of choices when it comes to the sensors and platforms for environmental monitoring. The AmI application under testing decides which sensors and which platforms to use. However, supplementary sensors are also used for specific testing purposes so that AmI applications can get more information about how to save energy so that they can make the right decisions.

Tracking energy consumption at various resolutions is possible, and the energy consumption of entire buildings or individual devices can be studied. An energy monitor that has multiple functions can be used to keep track of the overall energy use of a certain room. It was connected to the monophase power line that supplied power to the room under observation, and it enabled us to collect data on voltage, current, and active and reactive power in real-time. The energy consumption of each individual gadget is monitored by specialized "energy sensor nodes," which measure the energy consumption of every device connected to the sensor's power outlet.

A middleware layer that provides the essential functionality that enables the development of specialized modules on top of a hardware substrate is referred to as a hardware substrate. Thus, these modules were developed in accordance with the multi-tier knowledge representation schema, which classifies them as Level 0; some of them perform only low-level data processing, and as a result, they are classified as sub-symbolic in nature, while others perform a type of high-level processing, and as a result, they are classified as symbolic in nature. Several of these modules can be used in conjunction with one another to offer support for a specific AmI application.

Logically, the primary goal of middleware is to decouple the programmes from a specific choice in terms of the underlying hardware, allowing the developer to devote his or her attention solely to the challenges pertaining to AmI features.

1.7   The Internet of Things

The Internet of Things (IoT) is a new technology that establishes a global network of devices and objects that can connect and share data via the Internet. It is important to distinguish between the Internet and the IoT. The IoT can produce, analyze, and make judgments on linked items; in other words, it is wiser than the Internet. Interconnected devices include security cameras, autos, sensors, buildings, and software.

In the IoT, any object that can connect to the Internet but is not a mobile device or computer qualifies as a "thing." Wearables, digital and mechanical machines, and even animals are examples of "things." An object must have two components in order to be classified as an IoT device: the object itself and an Internet connection [8].

However, simply connecting an object to the Internet does not guarantee that it will be more useful, so manufacturers typically incorporate one or both of the following:

- sensors that collect information about an object or its surroundings,
- actuators are machines that perform physical actions in the real world.

In other words, an IoT device is a nontraditional object that is connected to the Internet and must include at least one sensor or actuator in order to profit from the connection.

1.8   IoT as the New Revolution

In the industrial industry, the use of automation and data interchange is referred to as "Industrie 4.0." In the words of the Boston Consulting Group, "Industrie 4.0" is comprised of nine major technologies: autonomous robots, horizontal and vertical system integration, simulation, the industrial Internet of things, cybersecurity, big data and analytics in the cloud additive manufacturing, and augmented reality. Using these technologies, a "smart factory" is being built in which machines, systems, and humans communicate with one another in order to coordinate and monitor progress on the assembly line. It is the networked devices that supply the sensor data, and they are controlled digitally. Microsoft has named the IoT the "fourth industrial revolution," alongside the Digital Revolution, mechanical production, mass production, and science. In 2017, IoT spending exceeded $800 billion, with the industry's impact estimated to range between $3.9 and $11.1 trillion by 2025 [9].

Since 2000, digital disruption has resulted in the loss of 52% of Fortune 500 corporations. The IoT will have a similar impact on people who are left standing in the future. By 2020, 80% of firms expect their industry to be disrupted, and it is easy to understand why: two-thirds of customers aim to buy connected gadgets for their homes by 2019, and Gartner forecasts that 95% of all electronic products will have built-in IoT technology by 2020.

As if that were not enough, the US Department of Transportation estimates 76% of car accidents can be prevented with that vehicle-to-vehicle communication. South Korea's new "smart city" has reduced per capita energy consumption by 40%, and advances in IoT healthcare are expected to prevent 50,000 preventable deaths per year in just a small area–hospital errors.

Between the late 1700s and the early 1800s, the world underwent its first industrial revolution. During this time period, manufacturing evolved, with a strong emphasis on physical labour performed by people and supplemented by work animals. This includes the use of water and steam-powered engines, as well as various other types of machine tools and other methods of production.

The introduction of steel and the widespread use of electricity in commercial companies in the early twentieth century marked the beginning of the world's second industrial revolution. Following the introduction of electricity, manufacturers were able to increase production while also making factory machinery more mobile. As a means of enhancing productivity, mass manufacturing techniques were developed during this period.

Manufacturers progressively began to incorporate more electrical and, subsequently, computer technology into their operations in the late 1950s, heralding the beginning of the third industrial revolution. The manufacturing industry began to shift its emphasis toward digital and automation software around this time period.

The fourth industrial revolution (also known as Industry 4.0) has made major advances in the last few decades, particularly in the United States. The Internet of Things (IoT), cyber-physical systems, and access to real-time data are all available in addition to interconnectivity through the Internet of Things (IoT). From past decades, Industry 4.0 has elevated the importance of digital technology to a whole new level. Manufacturers in the Fourth Industrial Revolution (Industry 4.0) will need to be more integrated, comprehensive, and all-inclusive in their operations. It serves as a transitional layer between the digital and physical worlds, allowing for improved communication and access among departmental teams and products, as well as suppliers, partners, and individuals. In the fourth industrial revolution, CEOs will have a better understanding of and control over all aspects of their organizations, and they will be able to harness real-time data to increase efficiency, streamline procedures, and drive development [10].

1.9   IoT Challenges

It is expected that the Internet of Things will get more sophisticated as the number of real-time applications that demand smart connectivity between themselves increases. A few examples of these problems are described below.

1. Smart connectivity
The Internet of Things architecture may require sensors and devices to update their trends or features to keep up with changes in their surroundings. In essence, the Internet of Things (IoT) is a data processing and decision-making system that constantly seeks to improve itself. It also has the ability to change the trends or characteristics of connected devices in order to react to changes in the environment. Smart technology, such as the Internet of Things (IoT), allows all linked devices to update themselves in response to changes in their environment, as well as adapt and perform with great precision in any unexpected situation. Because of this, smart-linked systems can be produced provided that a smart infrastructure is adequately constructed to properly treat the data acquired from devices and make the necessary decisions.

2. High security and privacy
Connecting billions of devices around the world is the primary objective of the Internet of Things. The Internet of Things is expected to connect 50 billion devices by 2020. Strong security measures are required to avoid fraud and provide high levels of data protection when connecting such a large number of devices. Getting organizations and consumers to trust the IoT enough to share their data is therefore a significant hurdle.

3. The treatment of big data
The exponential growth in data exchange between connected devices is the most important drawback of the IoT. Social media like Facebook, weblogs, and email, as well as physical equipment connections like microphones, sensors, and cameras, are all major sources of data, but databases used in

corporate processes are also important. The last 2 years have seen the creation of 90% of the world's data. Because of this, it is becoming increasingly difficult for IoT infrastructure builders to handle the exponential expansion of data.

The most major issue with utilizing IoT is the massive increase in data sent between linked devices. As shown in Figure 1.3, the three main sources of data are (1) the database used in the business process; (2) human everyday activities, such as Facebook, email, and weblogs; and (3) the connection of physical equipment such as microphones and cameras. It is worth noting that 90% of all the data on the planet has been created in the last 2 years. This makes it increasingly difficult for IoT infrastructure builders to deal with the exponential expansion of produced data.

While the IoT architecture connects a large number of devices, the amount of data sent between them grow quickly. This will cause some data delivery latency or delay among the connected devices. This introduces a new challenge for the Internet of Things: reducing latency in order to offer a stable Internet of Things infrastructure.

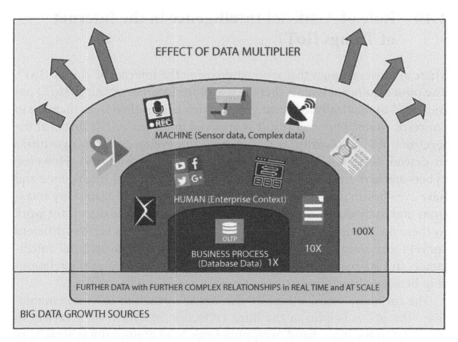

Figure 1.3 Different sources of data growth (https://www.slideshare.net/bjorna/big-data-in-oil-and-gas).

1. Lowering bandwidth and energy consumption

The number of devices connecting to the Internet of Things, speaking with one another, and sharing data with one another has expanded tremendously, as has the amount of bandwidth and electricity they consume. Therefore, while developing an Internet of Things architecture, it is important to consider both bandwidth and power usage. The current tendency is for connected devices to be smaller in size, which results in decreased power usage. Due to the high amount of data that is shared among devices, the communication data rate is still an issue that needs to be addressed.

2. Complexity

To connect devices and share data via the IoT, several layers and levels of software and hardware, as well as some standard protocols, can be employed. As the volume of shared data and linked devices grows significantly, so will the sophistication of the software, hardware, and standard protocols that are employed. As a result, as the number of connected devices grows, it becomes increasingly difficult to reduce the complexity of the Internet of Things (IoT) technology.

1.10   Role of Artificial Intelligence in the Internet of Things (IoT)

There are several issues that arise while using the Internet of Things (IoT). The most significant issue is that the use of the Internet of Things (IoT) has increased dramatically in recent years, which has resulted in an increase in concerns about cyber security. It is artificial intelligence (AI) that is at the forefront of cybersecurity, as it is utilized to develop complex algorithms to defend networks and systems (including IoT technology). However, cyber-attackers have figured out how to exploit artificial intelligence and have even begun using hostile AI to launch cyber-attacks against organizations and individuals. Aiming to present and summarise significant work in these disciplines, this review study collects data from various different surveys and research papers on the Internet of Things, artificial intelligence, and AI-based assaults and counter-attacks, as well as the relationship between these three issues.

The corporate world is rapidly altering as a result of IoT implementation. The IoT is helpful in the huge collection of data from a variety of sources. On the other hand, wrapping one's head around the avalanche of data coming in from countless IoT devices makes data gathering, processing, and analysis tough.

A lot of money will have to be spent on new technology to see the future and full potential of IoT devices. There is a chance that AI and the Internet of Things (IoT) could have a big impact on how businesses and economies work in the future. With little or no help from humans, the IoT powered by AI creates intelligent technologies that act like smart people and help people make smart decisions.

The Internet of Things (IoT) is concerned with devices talking with one another over the Internet, whereas artificial intelligence (AI) is concerned with devices learning from data and experience. The Internet of Things (IoT) is being used in a variety of applications these days [11].

1.11   IoT in Various Domains

The below-given Figure 1.4 depicts applications based on IoT. There are many more applications that can be combined with IoT.

Figure 1.4 IoT applications.

1.12   Healthcare

The Internet of Things (IoT), a new revolution, offers enormous potential in a variety of areas, including healthcare. The full use of this technology in healthcare is a common goal since it enables medical service providers to work more efficiently while offering better patient care. There are various benefits to implementing this technology-based healthcare plan, which could increase treatment quality and efficiency, as well as improve the health of seniors and other patients.

1.13   Home Automation

Home automation is indeed a notion that attempts to put management of common household electrical equipment at your fingertips, providing consumers with more cost-effective lighting options, increased energy conservation, and efficient energy usage. Apart from lights and the establishment of a centralized home entertainment system, the concept also includes complete control over your home security and much more. Home automation systems based on the Internet of Things (IoT) seek to control all of the devices in your smart home using internet protocols or cloud computing, as the name implies. IoT-based systems have numerous advantages over traditional wired systems, including simplicity of use, ease of installation, lack of complications caused by running wires or faulty electrical connections, and reduced difficulty in detecting and reacting to faults.

Three components are required for home automation: hardware connection protocols, software, and apps. Each of these components is equally crucial in providing your customers with a truly smart home experience. You can iterate on your IoT prototype and respond rapidly to technical advances if you have the right hardware. A protocol chosen after extensive testing and consideration helps you avoid performance limits that might otherwise limit sensor and IoT gateway technologies, as well as device integration options. Another factor to consider is the firmware on your hardware, which is responsible for data management, data transfer, firmware OTA updates, and other key operations that enable devices to communicate.

1.14   Smart City

Smart city projects all over the world now use Internet of Things (IoT) applications. It lets you manage, control, and keep an eye on your devices remotely. It also lets you get new insights and actionable data from a lot of real-time information. There are many important things about a smart city, like how well information technology is integrated and how many different kinds of information there are. Developing a smart city should include smart industry, smart technology, smart administration, smart life, and smart services. Smart recognition, location, tracking, monitoring, and management are all things that the Internet of Things can help with. To do this, sensors, laser scanners, GPS, infrared, RFID, and other devices must be integrated into everything and connected to the Internet through specific protocols for data exchange and communication. Smart cities, made feasible by the Internet of Things, must have three traits in order to be considered smart: they must be instrumented, networked, and intelligent in some way. As cities continue to expand and grow, smart cities are becoming increasingly crucial. In order to make a city smart, the Internet of Things is the most effective method available. It is possible to use IoT for a variety of applications, such as environmental monitoring (for example, measuring water levels in lakes, soil humidity, or gas concentrations), smart parking, waste management, autonomous driving, and CO_2 emissions reduction. In order to achieve such objectives, a huge number of interconnected items must be used. It is true that the number of connected goods is rapidly increasing, with predictions that by 2020, smart cities will have installed 50 billion connected objects in total [16]. However, having such a large number of goods poses a lot of hazards and raises questions about privacy.

1.15   Security

The term "IoT security" refers to the ways that devices that are connected to the Internet or work on a network are kept safe. People use the term "Internet of Things" to describe a lot of different things, and it will keep growing as technology gets better in the next few years. Almost every modern gadget, from watches to thermostats to video gaming consoles, includes an internet or other device connection [21]. "Internet of Things security" refers to a combination of methodologies, strategies, and solutions that work together to keep these devices safe from hackers. Ironically, due to their inherent interconnectedness, Internet of Things (IoT) gadgets are becoming increasingly vulnerable to cyberattacks.

As the Internet of Things grows in scope, the importance of IoT security grows even further. A variety of changes have occurred as a result of the Internet of Things' increased importance in security. IT managers can utilize a variety of strategies to tackle the growing threat of cybercrime and cyber terrorism posed by insecure Internet of Things devices, including API security, public key infrastructure (PKI) authentication, and network security, to name just a few [22].

At every level, the IoT infrastructure is vulnerable to attacks, posing a host of security concerns that must be addressed. Authentication and access control mechanisms are now the focus of the majority of IoT research. New networking protocols, like IPv6 and 5G, will be required as technology advances to achieve the dynamic mashup of IoT topology that is now unattainable. The most major Internet of Things breakthroughs has occurred on a small scale, such as within organizations, industries, and other similar settings. In order to expand the Internet of Things framework from a single firm to a group of companies and systems, a range of security concerns must be addressed. The Internet of Things has the potential to completely transform our way of life. Nonetheless, when it comes to developing entirely intelligent frameworks, security is the most critical factor to consider. It is not hard to imagine how the Internet of Things will change everything in the near future if security concerns like privacy and confidentiality are adequately addressed. Existing open research concerns in the Internet of Things demand new identification, wireless, software, and hardware technologies, such as standards for heterogeneous devices, key management and identity establishment systems, and trust management hubs.

1.16   Industry

The Internet of Things (IoT) is proving to be a game-changer for those in the automation industry. Industrial automation firms that make use of Internet of Things (IoT) technologies may be able to gain additional benefits. A major contribution to the Internet of Things is the development of new technologies that aid in the resolution of problems, improvement of operations, and advancement in the field of manufacturing. The Internet of Things (IoT) is the linking of indistinguishably identifiable electronic things through the Internet using "data plumbing," such as IP, cloud computing, and web services. To give a few instances, the Internet of Things (IoT) has had a tremendous impact on industrial automation, resulting in the widespread use of tablet computers, smart phones, virtualized systems, and cloud data storage, to name a few. The Internet of Things (IoT) continues to play a crucial role in industrial automation as it studies and deploys IoT concepts and technology. System architectures can be streamlined, collapsed, and made more efficient, cost-effective, and responsive thanks to the Internet of Things. By enabling frictionless communications and interaction from manufacturing field input and output such as actuators, robotics, and analyzers, the underlying goal is to improve flexibility and extend manufacturing. In crucial applications, such as replacing banks of relays with PLCs, industrial automation has adopted IoT to utilize commercial technologies.

Large volumes of data may be collected and analyzed by businesses using the Industrial Internet of Things (IIoT) system. This data can then be used to produce new services, monetize them, and improve overall system performance by improving overall system performance. This report highlights the most recent state-of-the-art research efforts in the Internet of Things (IoT) [20]. Specifically, the research is divided into three areas of interest: IIoT architectures and frameworks, communication protocols, and data management strategies. A number of IIoT-related enabling technologies were discussed during the panel discussion. There are also a number of open research problems that need to be addressed in order for IIoT to be implemented successfully. In this study, the authors identify several challenges, including effective data management schemes, robust and flexible big data analytic technologies, collaborations between heterogeneous IIoT systems, the coexistence of wireless technologies, trust in IIoT systems and protocols, enabling decentralization on edge, specific operating systems, and public safety in IIoT. It is possible to overcome these obstacles by providing appropriate responses. This research can be used as a starting point for tackling some of the most critical concerns related to the Internet of Things. The research trends in customized manufacturing are something we would like to look at in the future.

1.17 Education

As the potential for IoT applications grows, so will the benefits of IoT in education. IoT devices are now being utilized to improve educational environments for children of all ages, and there are a variety of innovative methods for IoT applications to have a positive influence on schools. IoT networks use connected devices like coloured lights, digital signage, door locks, and sensors to construct personalized security systems. Some schools use an IoT network to design a variety of programmes in response to intruders, bad weather, and other security threats. IoT technology can also be used in the classroom to provide solutions such as integrated emergency alarm buttons. IoT security tools can be used by teachers to take action and keep their students safe. It is possible to programme and automate lighting and other IoT-connected devices. Lights, for example, can be programmed to turn on and off at specific times or be connected to occupancy sensors and turned off when a classroom is empty. IoT connectivity increases building efficiency and minimizes energy waste, which saves money. The Internet of Things has the potential to shape smart campuses and classrooms (IoT). A safe and secure learning environment is one of the primary goals of implementing IoT in higher education while also ensuring that students have access to high-quality healthcare and enhancing the teaching and learning process. The authors of this paper break down how IoT can be used in higher education into four distinct categories [14]. As a result, we have also demonstrated how the Internet of Things could change the commercial model for education. According to the Canvas business model research, the IoT has a significant impact on value propositions. Individualized learning, time savings, increased safety, and improved comfort are just a few of the benefits. New client interactions and channels have emerged as a result of developing a virtual and individualized interaction with them.

1.18   Agriculture

Inadequate natural resources, such as fresh water and arable land, have exacerbated the situation, as have deteriorating production patterns in important basic crops. In addition, the changing structure of agricultural labour is a cause of concern for the farming industry. In addition, agricultural employment has declined in the vast majority of nations. A growing number of farming techniques are using internet connectivity solutions as a result of a shrinking agricultural workforce, which reduces the need for manual labour.

Farmers may be able to take advantage of the Internet of Things (IoT) technologies to help close the supply-demand imbalance by ensuring good harvests, profit, and environmental preservation while also increasing productivity and profitability. Internet of Things (IoT) technology is used in precision farming to ensure the most efficient use of resources while improving agricultural production and lowering operating costs. Precision farming is becoming increasingly popular. The Internet of Things in agriculture includes specialized equipment, information technology services, wireless connections, and software, to name a few components.

With the help of the Internet of Things technology, smart farming may assist farmers and producers in a variety of ways, including cutting fertilizer requirements, decreasing farm vehicle mileage, and increasing the efficiency with which resources such as water and electricity are utilized [13]. Sensors are used in the Internet of Things (IoT) smart farming solutions to monitor and control the irrigation system in an agricultural field (crop health, humidity, soil moisture, light, temperature, and so on). Farmers can keep an eye on their fields from anywhere in the world. Making good data-driven judgments can be accomplished through the use of either human or automated methods. For example, if the soil moisture level declines, the farmer can utilize sensors to trigger irrigation to restore the soil moisture level. Smart farming outperforms traditional agriculture in terms of efficiency by orders of magnitude.

As arable land continues to shrink, a greater emphasis on smarter, more efficient crop-producing technologies is essential to fulfilling the world's growing food needs. A few examples of the crop yield and handling methods being developed by today's technologically aware, forward-thinking youth include crop tracking, food safety and nutrition labelling, and cooperation among growers, suppliers, merchants, and customers. Innovating crop production and handling technologies such as food safety and nutrition labelling, collaborating with growers, suppliers, and merchants, and tracking crops are all examples of novel crop production and handling technologies that are currently being developed. All these elements were thoroughly explored in this essay, which emphasized the need for various technologies, namely the Internet of Things, to make agriculture smarter and more efficient in order to meet future demands. This goal is achieved through the use of wireless sensors, unmanned aerial vehicles (UAVs), cloud computing, and communication technologies, all of which are explored in detail in this book. Also included is an in-depth examination of current scientific endeavours and projects in the making. Agricultural applications can also benefit from a variety of IoT-based designs and platforms that are currently being developed. Scientists and engineers will benefit from a discussion of the industry's current issues as well as its long-term goals and objectives. Therefore, it is clear that when it comes to enhancing agricultural productivity, every square foot of field counts. It is not an option; rather, it is a must to use the Internet of Things (IoT)-based sensors and communication technologies to correctly control every inch.

1.19   Tourism

Tourism-related organizations and locales can employ IoT technology to provide clients with location-specific information, increasing visitor experiences throughout the "during-trip" stage. Tourists can get messages at the most appropriate time, based on their location, by combining smartphone capabilities with beacon technology or other sensors. This would be very helpful on city walking tours. When tourists pass by a historical ruin, for example, a message might be sent to them summarizing what they are seeing and what it means in terms of the destination's history or culture. Children may find educational courses boring while on vacation; however, incorporating a technical component into the experience via IoT may help to pique their interest.

Furthermore, location-specific information can enhance experiences by reducing alienation. Sending travellers location-based alerts when they are likely to get lost or approach a high-crime area could allow destinations to be proactive in avoiding unfavourable experiences, increasing the possibility of return visits. In recent years, a diverse range of Internet of Things (IoT) applications has been implemented. The Internet of Things (IoT) is slowly but steadily becoming standard in the hospitality industry. It is anticipated that the Internet of Things would ease a number of tasks, from enabling automatic hotel room check-ins and check-outs to assisting passengers in identifying their vacation destination and tracking people's health status. Furthermore, the Internet of Things (IoT) is critical because it provides numerous benefits, including cost savings, increased productivity, higher operational efficiency, more delighted customers or guests, and unique service offerings.

The IoT offers a great deal of promise in the tourism and hospitality industries, according to the research. The Internet of Things boosts the possibilities of the tourism and hospitality industries since it allows several devices to be connected at the same time. Tourism and hospitality applications have been discussed in detail [19]. It is important, however, to call attention to significant roadblocks and problems in the adoption of IoT, like security, "expensive" investment prices, technological infrastructure, communications infrastructure, and IoT standards.

Hotels and their employees should be ready to adopt new technologies in order to improve the efficacy and efficiency of various work processes in order to be ready for what is to come. Scholars and practitioners in the field can benefit from our research by better understanding the enormous potential of the Internet of Things (IoT), particularly in the tourist and hospitality sectors [12].

1.20   Environment Monitoring

Many environmental trends are intricate and challenging to grasp. Using traditional methods to monitor environmental conditions has a number of drawbacks. Since the dawn of the modern era and innovative management tactics, it has been easier to keep a real-time check on people's surroundings.

This Environment Monitoring System is made up of low-cost, commonly available components that can monitor a wide range of environmental data. This system is flexible for both indoor and outdoor use. The proposed approach has been tried in a variety of scenarios and has consistently proven to be successful. Finally, without requiring any design changes, this device may connect to the gateway through Bluetooth, Infrared, or WiFi, making it suitable for a range of scenarios. As a result, the system is flexible and expandable. The research will expand in the future to include a number of machine learning approaches that will deliver more information to the user [15]. Furthermore, records can be maintained in a secure, immutable digital ledger to properly manage alterations.

The Internet of Things (IoT) has a significant impact on air quality. It has clever and innovative air quality measuring and water treatment technologies that help significantly with sustainable living. Furthermore, the IoT employs a data-driven strategy to deliver actionable insights and forecasted consequences. The better your system is at monitoring, measuring, and cataloguing data, the better you will be able to understand your business and obtain insights for improvement. Many environmental trends are intricate and difficult to grasp. Using traditional methods to monitor environmental conditions has a number of drawbacks. With the introduction of the modern era and clever management tactics, it has become easier to keep a real-time check.

Smart environmental monitoring can be categorized into several categories.

- Monitoring of water quality
- Air Quality Monitoring
- Energy Monitoring
- Toxic Gas Detection

1.21   Manufacturing and Retail

The IoT is widely recognized as a new technological advancement that has a substantial impact on the manufacturing industry. It is capable of integrating the entire manufacturing sector's components, including sensors, actuation devices, processing units, and communication devices. These fully integrated smart cyber-physical systems paved the way for the new industrial revolution 4.0, opening up new business and market potential in manufacturing. It opens up a lot of possibilities in the manufacturing industry for improving system performance in globalized and distributed situations. The following are the numerous advancements in the manufacturing industry as a result of IoT adoption, as well as its challenges:

The Internet of Things enables sustainable development in a range of industries by conserving energy and water, extending the life of machinery and equipment, enhancing supply chain efficiency and such things as reducing product miles. Multiple defensive layers, encrypted communication, digital signature, and two-factor authentication are just a few of the tactics used to keep data safe and secure in a decentralized model network without an intermediary [18]. By accessing real-time data to estimate maintenance requirements at the precise moment, IoT completely eliminates the traditional approach to maintenance, which depends on guesswork based on prior data. IoT can help enhance product quality, resulting in less waste, cheaper costs, higher customer satisfaction, and more sales.

1.22   Logistics

Many benefits are possible when IoT technology is connected with transportation networks. Among the benefits are:

- The trip distance of the vehicle is optimized, resulting in reduced fuel consumption and increased revenue.
- Routes can be adjusted or redirected during harmful and dangerous conditions.
- A centrally controlled network can be used to operate a service based on demand.
- Traffic control, depending on the number of vehicles on the road, can aid in public safety [17].
- Goods and material exports and imports, as well as purchase and other shipping details, can all be tracked.

- Owners of transportation and logistics companies will see an increase in revenue.

1.23   Conclusion

Ambient intelligence (AmI) opens the door to a myriad of possibilities. It is possible that AmI systems will know almost everything about the lives of the people they follow. Privacy will be a big issue with AmI, even though the technology has a lot of promise. Ambient intelligence (AmI) aims to create a digital environment that puts the human user at the center by allowing them to control their surroundings. The key requirement is the presence of unobtrusive and ubiquitous sensors, which are necessary for context-aware reasoning in order to respond to user inputs. A wireless sensor network (WSN) is made up of a lot of small computational units that can be programmed, are self-sufficient, and can communicate wirelessly with each other. Nodes in WSNs are small and inexpensive and can be put in a wide range of locations.

References

1. Gams, M., Gu, I.Y.-H., Härmä, A., Muñoz, A., Tam, V., Artificial intelligence and ambient intelligence. *J. Ambient Intell. Smart Environ.*, 11, 71–86, 2019.
2. Khan, W.Z., Rehman, M.H., Zangoti, H.M., Afzal, M.K., Armi, N., Salah, K., Industrial internet of things: Recent advances, enabling technologies and open challenges. *Comput. Electr. Eng.*, 81, 1–13, 2020.
3. De Paola, A., Gaglio, S., Lo Re, G., Ortolani, M., Sensor9k: A testbed for designing and experimenting with WSN-based ambient intelligence applications. *Pervasive Mob. Comput.*, 8, 3, 448–466, 2012.
4. Gams, *et al.*, Artificial intelligence and ambient intelligence. *J. Ambient Intell. Smart Environ.*, 11, 1, 71–86, 2019.
5. Ramos, C., Augusto, J.C., Shapiro, D., Ambient intelligence—The next step for artificial intelligence. *IEEE Intelligent Syst.*, 23, 2, 2008, 2008.
6. Augusto, J.C., Ambient intelligence: Basic concepts and applications, in: *Communications in Computer and Information Science*, International Conference on Software and Data Technologies, pp. 6–26, vol. 10, Springer, Berlin, 2006.
7. Chen, R.-C., Hsieh, C.-F., Chang, W.-L., Using ambient intelligence to extend network lifetime in wireless sensor networks. *J. Ambient Intell. Hum. Comput.*, 7, 6, 777–788, 2016.

8. Chandrakar, R., Raja, R., Miri, R., Sinha, U., Enhanced the moving object detection and object tracking for traffic surveillance using RBF-FDLNN and CBF algorithm. *Expert Syst. Appl.*, 191, 116306, 2021, https://doi.org 10.1016/j.eswa.2021.116306.

9. Das, A., Dash, P.K., Mishra, B.K., An intelligent parking system in smart cities using IoT, in: *Exploring the Convergence of Big Data and the Internet of Things*, pp. 155–180, IGI Global, IGI Global Publisher of Timely Knowledge, USA, 2018.

10. Kishor Narang, N. and Zhao, J.K., Mentor's musings on IoT, environment and standards interplay. *IEEE Internet Things Mag.*, 4, 1, 4–8, 2021.

11. Sahu, A.K., Sharma, S., Tanveer, M., Raja, R., Internet of Things attack detection using hybrid deep learning model. *Comput. Commun.*, 176, 146–154, 2021, https://doi.org/10.1016/j.comcom.2021.05.024.

12. Lämmle, A., Seeber, C., Kogan, E., Automatic simulation model implementation of robotic production cells in a 3D manufacturing simulation environment. *Proc. CIRP*, 91, 336–341, 2020.

13. Ayaz, M., Ammad-Uddin, M., Sharif, Z., Mansour, A., Aggoune, E.-H.M., Internet-of-Things (IoT)-based smart agriculture: Toward making the fields talk. *IEEE Access*, 7, 129551–129583, 2019.

14. Bagheri, M. and Movahed, S.H., The effect of the Internet of Things (IoT) on education business model. *International Conference on Signal-Image Technology & Internet-Based Systems*, 2016.

15. Hassan, M.N., Islam, M.R., Faisal, F., Semantha, F.H., Siddique, A.H., Hasan, M., An IoT based environment monitoring system. *3rd International Conference on Intelligent Sustainable Systems ICISS*, 2020.

16. Tiwari, L., Raja, R., Awasthi, V., Miri, R., Sinha, G.R., Alkinani, M.H., Polat, K., Detection of lung nodule and cancer using novel mask-3 FCM and TWEDLNN algorithms. *Measurement*, 172, 108882, 2021. https://doi.org/10.1016/j.measurement.2020.108882.

17. Kumar, N.M. and Dash, A., The Internet of Things: An opportunity for transportation and logistics. *International Conference on Inventive Computing and Informatics (ICICI 2017)*, 2017.

18. Santhosh, N., Srinivasan, M., Ragupathy, K., Internet of Things (IoT) in smart manufacturing. *ICAMPC*, 2020.

19. Car, T., Stifanich, L.P., Šimunić, M., Internet of Things (IoT) in tourism and hospitality: Opportunities and challenges. *ToSEE – Tourism in Southern and Eastern Europe*, vol. 5, pp. 163–175, 2019.

20. Khan, W., Habib ur Rehman, M., Zangoti, H.M., Afzal, M., Armi, N., Salah, K., Industrial Internet of Things: Recent advances, enabling technologies, and open challenges. *Comput. Electr. Eng.*, 81, 1–13, 2019, 10.1016/j.com peleceng.2019.106522.

21. Mahmoud, R., Yousuf, T., Aloul, F., Zualkernan, I., Internet of Things (IoT) security: Current status, challenges and prospective measures. *2015 10th International Conference for Internet Technology and Secured Transactions (ICITST)*, IEEE, 2015.
22. Lenka, R.K., Rath, A.K., Tan, Z., Sharma, S., Puthal, D., Simha, N.V.R., Tripathi, S.S., Prasad, M., Building scalable cyber-physical-social networking infrastructure using IoT and low power sensors. *IEEE Access*, 6, 1, 30162–30173, 2018.

2

An Overview of Internet of Things Related Protocols, Technologies, Challenges and Application

Deevesh Chaudhary and Prakash Chandra Sharma*

Department of Information Technology, Manipal University Jaipur, Rajasthan, India

Abstract

The network of interconnected computers that can communicate with each other globally through communication protocol called the Internet (or Internet) started in the early 1980s. In 1999, the term Internet of Things named IoT was coined by British technologist Kevin Ashton. Internet of things transformed the consumer lifestyle to another level by enabling the various devices to become smart, transferable, and decision taking. A new era of "smart" versions of devices emerged to make people's lifestyles not only at ease but also to connect them with the latest technology. The chapter gives an introduction to Inter of things, messaging protocols, and other enabling technologies required to set up a wireless and sensor-enabled environment. It also discusses architectures and applications in real time. The chapter ends with a discussion of security issues, and challenges in the Internet of things–enabled systems.

Keywords: Internet of Things (IoT), wireless network, smart devices, sensors

Corresponding author: prakashsharma12@gmail.com

Md Rashid Mahmood, Rohit Raja, Harpreet Kaur, Sandeep Kumar and Kapil Kumar Nagwanshi (eds.) *Ambient Intelligence and Internet of Things: Convergent Technologies*, (33–52) © 2023 Scrivener Publishing LLC

2.1   Introduction

A few years back, nobody thought of receiving a notification on a mobile phone if there is a burglary in the house, thus taking timely action to avoid the same by informing the nearby police station. Measuring heartbeat rate, oxygen level, number of steps count, etc., by using wearable devices such as smartwatch encourages proactive healthcare. Autonomous farming equipment saves crops from decay by providing water as soon as soil gets dried. They are switching off your home devices remotely from any part of the world, just by mobile phones. Ordering food, paying bills, exploring the Internet just by saying to Siri or google assistant is an application that 1990s kids never thought about. These are the few applications of IoT that are currently in use. All these applications become possible because the objects (things) are connected and can communicate in a way so that the user can use them as per his requirement. With the involvement of various IoT devices, there has been seen an extensive transformation in the lives of human beings.

The IoT is an emerging technology that enables objects of daily life embedded with sensors and electronic circuits to get connected and

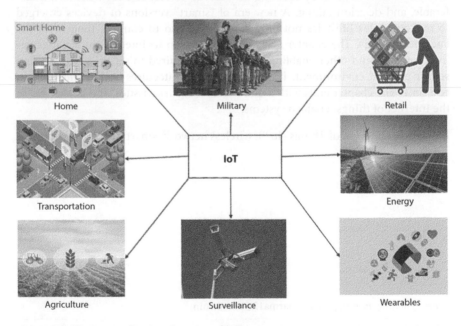

Figure 2.1 Various application domains of IoT.

communicate with each other with the help of the Internet to facilitate human lives. IoT is becoming an important part of human life throughout the world. IoT can be sensed in various fields such as businesses, public healthcare [1], security [2], home automation [3], agriculture [4], lifestyle, logistics, retail, cities, etc. [5]. IoT has shown a remarkable presence in trade, stock markets, and financial services as well [6]. Increasingly, organizations from the private and public sectors are using IoT potential to operate more efficiently, better understand user requirements, and improve decision making for delivering better customer services [7]. The potential of IoT technology can be seen in the multidisciplinary domain, as shown in Figure 2.1 discussed in detail in this chapter.

2.1.1   History of IoT

As the name suggests, the Internet is one of the core technologies in IoT, which has its origin in the Advanced Research Projects Agency Network (ARPANET) project started by the US defence department in 1969 to interconnect the computers to share information, findings, and knowledge and communicate. The IoT has not been around for very long. The term IoT did not exist till 1999. However, in early 1880, a local program team at Carnegie Melon University devised an automated machine connected online and checked to see if there was a drink or not and also if it was cold enough to drink. Kevin Ashton, the director of Auto-ID Labs at Massachusetts Institute of Technology, United States, was the first to describe the term IoT. While introducing the Procter and Gamble team of directors, he introduced IoT as a technology that connects multiple devices with the help of radio frequency identification (RFID) tags for the purposes of asset and supply chain management. He believed that installing sensors and RFID tags on products would help to generate data with the help of which product location can be tracked. He used the word "internet" as the name of his presentation to get the attention of the audience because, at that time, the Internet was beyond the concept of .dot com.

The concept of IoT started to gain popularity in 2010. The Chinese government was the first to implement IoT, which is a key component of its 5-year plans. In 2012, the organizers of Europe's online conference, LeWeb, decided the theme of the conference would be the Internet of Things. In the same year, popular magazines like Forbes, Wired started using this term. In January 2014, IoT reached the mass market when Consumer Electronics Show (CES), held in Las Vegas, was based on an IoT theme.

2.1.2   Definition of IoT

The definition of IoT changes with its application area and domain. Although many researchers, academicians, scientists, industrialists have defined the term in their way. With the common terms and goals of any IoT environment, the IoT can be best defined as: It is a dynamic global interconnected network of physical objects having unique identities and embedded with electronic circuits to sense or communicate with each other and the external environment by collecting and exchanging data to facilitate human lives. IoT can also be considered a global network of portable devices that allow communication between person, person and objects, and object-to-objects [8].

2.1.3   Characteristics of IoT

The principal behind IoT is enabling devices incorporated in large-scale wireless networks to transfer messages and communicate with each other. Figure 2.2 shows the fundamental features and characteristics of any IoT-related environment. Now we explain each characteristic separately in brief one by one as below:

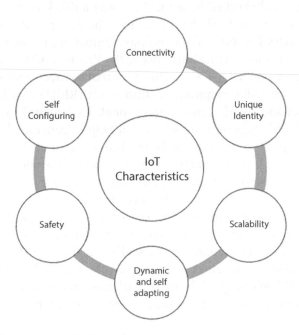

Figure 2.2 Characteristics of IoT-enabled environment.

(a) **Connectivity**—Connectivity is one of the essential aspects of IoT infrastructure. The things in IoT should be connected 24*7 without any connection issues. The connectivity among devices should be ensured.

(b) **Unique Identity**—The devices connected should have their unique identities, i.e., IP addresses, so that they can be identified throughout the network. The unique identity of devices also facilitates users to query, monitor, and control devices from anywhere.

(c) **Scalability**—The IoT environment should be scalable enough to handle the enormous amount of devices in terms of connectivity, communication, and data sharing. The IoT setup should be able to handle the expansion appropriately.

(d) **Dynamic and Self-adapting**—IoT devices should dynamically adapt to ever-changing scenarios and operating conditions. There should be minimum human intervention in maintaining the IoT environment.

(e) **Safety**—Safety is one of the major concerns in IoT. When a large number of devices are over a network, then data and device security is a major challenge. There are chances of sensitive personal information of the user being compromised or shared when all his devices are connected over the Internet.

(f) **Self-configuring**—IoT devices should upgrade themselves in case of network or software updation with minimum human intervention. IoT environment should provide authentication, authorization, and data security.

2.2 Messaging Protocols

There would be 50 billion IoT devices connected worldwide, creating a massive network of interconnected devices extending over mobile phones to home appliances by the end of 2030 [8]. The main idea behind IoT is reliable connection and efficient data transfer between various devices that can communicate when required. As the number of devices expands, the magnitude and velocity of data exchange become the major concern. The efficiency of IoT networks in a particular application domain depends upon the connection between interconnected devices and how well they can communicate with each other and the external world. Any two communicating devices to communicate requires some protocols, i.e., well-defined set of rules to follow. The functioning of any IoT system primarily depends upon messaging, and data transfer protocols for data collection and message exchange in between devices. Various messaging protocols have been used to facilitate reliable and secure communication between devices in IoT systems [9]; however, given the heterogeneous nature of IoT in terms of the computing power of devices, processing power, the energy requirement, hardware configuration, and network infrastructure, choosing a reliable, secure, interoperable, and lightweight communication protocol becomes a challenging task.

The selection of messaging protocol for expansion and implementation of IoT systems primarily depends upon the following factors: (a) interoperability, (b) secure data transfer, (c) privacy, (d) network infrastructure, (e) deployment model, and (f) device configuration. Keeping these factors in mind, this section discusses four messaging protocols majorly used for the expansion and implementation of IoT systems, i.e., Constrained Application Protocol (CoAP), Message Queue Telemetry Transport (MQTT), Extensible Messaging and Presence Protocol (XMPP), and Advanced Message Queuing Protocol (AMQP).

2.2.1 Constrained Application Protocol

Constrained Application Protocol (CoAP) protocol is a web transfer protocol similar to HTTP, mainly intended for networks consisting of constrained devices embedded with low processing power and memory, generally 8-bit microcontroller, and a limited RAM and ROM (10 kb). This protocol is designed to connect devices in the network having low bandwidth and low connectivity, usually considered constrained networks, such as IPv6 over Low Power Wireless Personal Area Network (6LoWPAN) [10]. COAP was designed by Internet Engineering Taskforce (IETF) and specified in IETF RFC7252 [11]. It is generally designed for use in M2M (machine-to-machine) applications, such as factory automation, building automation, and smart energy. It shares the same customer-server configuration or request-response model as HTTP, where the client requests and the server sends the response back. It is a RESTful (Representational State Transfer) application that operates in the application layer and works on top of UDP (User Datagram Protocol), thus ensuring end-to-end transmission and congestion control within the network. CoAP supports four methods: GET, POST, PUT, and DELETE to support CURD operations shown in Table 2.1. It uses four types of messages to communicate, i.e., confirmable, nonconfirmable, acknowledgement, and reset message.

Table 2.1 CoAP techniques.

Technique	Explanation
GET	Recollects the representation of the valid resource identified by request URI
POST	Demands the server handle the complaint and to create a new subordinate resource under the requested parent URI
PUT	Request to revise/generate a resource as marked through a request URI
DELETE	Request to remove the resource marked through request URI

The CoAP message header is of 32 bits which are shared for all CoAP messages. The first four bytes represent a header that consists of a 2-bit CoAP version number, 2 bit for the type of message, 4-bit token length, 8-bit method or response code of a message, and 16-bit unique message-id assigned by the source to match the response.

2.2.2   Message Queue Telemetry Transport

Message Queue Telemetry Transport (MQTT), an OASIS standard protocol, is designed to transport messages between IoT-enabled constrained devices and the cloud. It is a publish-subscribe lightweight protocol that is well suited for communication with the cloud server and middleware applications where an unreliable network with intermittent connectivity is a major concern. This protocol is best suited for M2M applications [12]. It is an application layer protocol that works over standard TCP/IP. The publish-subscribe model consists of two entities: broker and clients. MQTT broker is a server that receives messages from all clients and transmits them to targeted clients over the network. An MQTT client is any device (node or server) connected to an MQTT broker. The clients need to register with a broker to receive messages from other clients within the network. The client sends (publishes) a message to the broker, and then the broker filters the message and forwards it to clients who are registered with the broker and subscribed to specific topics. Clients receive a message through a broker whenever some new device publishes a message. A subscriber list is maintained at the broker end to deliver the messages to

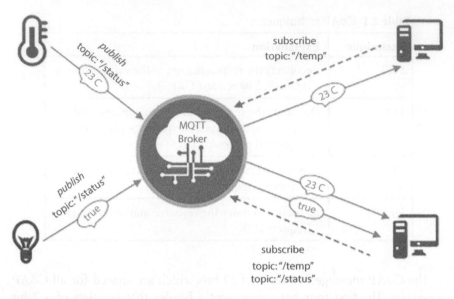

Figure 2.3 MQTT publish-subscribe model.

intended clients. Figure 2.3 represents the working of the MQTT publish-subscribe model [13].

To ensure reliable message delivery, the MQTT protocol provides three levels of quality of service (QoS) measures.

1) At most once: This is a level 0 and least reliable QoS measure. The message is sent only once, and there is no delivery guarantee. There is no acknowledgement of the message by the recipient. The sender neither stores nor retransmits the data. This level is often called "fire and forget."

2) At least once: This is a level 1 and reliable QoS measure in which the sender stores and retransmit the message until it receives any acknowledgement, thus ensuring successful delivery of the message to the intended client. A message may be sent multiple times.

3) Exactly once: This is a level 2 and most reliable QoS measure that guarantees that the intended receiver receives the message only once by engaging in two-level handshakes between the sender and the receiver.

MQTT is widely used in applications related to industries, such as automotive, telecommunication, energy, and public safety.

2.2.3 Extensible Messaging and Presence Protocol

This is an open communication protocol, originally called Jabber, and was designed for instant messaging capabilities applications. This protocol supports multiple applications such as video and voice calling, multiparty chat, file transfer, telepresence, routing of XML data, etc. [14]. The architecture of Extensible Messaging and Presence Protocol (XMPP) is similar to email. Anyone can run their XMPP server, enabling individuals to control communication without any central master. In 2004, IETF had formalized the XMPP protocol as an approved instant messaging standard and has been continuously updated to newer standards. The IETF published the XMPP specifications as RFC3920 and RFC3921. In terms of security, XMPP provides end-to-end encryption (TLS) build into core XMPP specifications.

2.2.4 Advance Message Queuing Protocol (AMQP)

It is an open standard lightweight application layer protocol designed specifically for financial and corporate environments [15]. It encourages equally the request-response and publish-subscribe model to ensure interoperability while using message-oriented middleware (MOM). It also supports three levels of QoS (at most once, at least once, and exactly once) to maintain reliable and trustworthy communication between clients. Queuing, orientation, switching, routing, security, and privacy are some of defining characteristics of AMQP. It utilizes TCP as the underlying transport layer protocol. For security, it uses TLS- and SASL-based encryption/decryption algorithm.

2.3 Enabling Technologies

IoT is all about communication between devices and monitoring of data gathered from these devices. It is enabled with multiple technologies to generate data, transfer data between devices, analysis of data, security, and maintenance. This section discusses various enabling technologies for IoT.

2.3.1 Wireless Sensor Network

WSN is a network of devices embedded with sensors to detect the environment and physical phenomena such as light, air quality, heat, pressure, etc. A WSN consists of three main entities: nodes, router, and gateway coordinator, as shown in Figure 2.4. Nodes are embedded with various kinds of

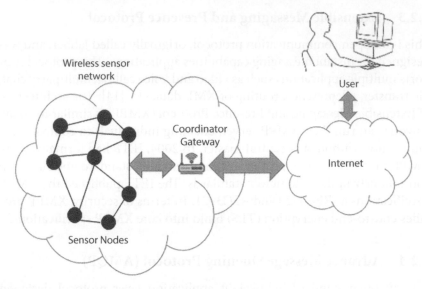

Figure 2.4 A wireless sensor network model.

sensors depending upon the application of IoT. One of the nodes acts as a router to route all the data packets from nodes to the gateway coordinator. The coordinator is responsible for collecting all the data and also connects the WSN to the Internet. Users can access the data using the Internet.

2.3.2   Cloud Computing

Cloud computing is responsible for delivering various computing services, tools, and specific applications such as databases, servers, networks, Software, analytics, etc., to users that are otherwise not available on local machines. It also facilitates on-demand delivery of computing

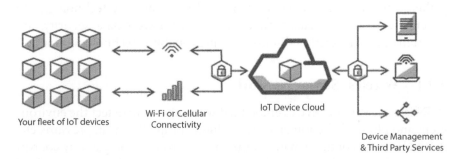

Figure 2.5 Cloud computing-enabled IoT.

infrastructure. Users can remotely use these services on a "pay as you go" basis. A cloud computing-enabled IoT platform makes it flexible and more scalable by adding more IoT devices. Also, data stored on cloud servers can be easily accessed from any part o the world independent of hardware configuration. Cloud computing provides three services, namely, Software as a service (SaaS), Platform as a service (PaaS), and Infrastructure as a service (IaaS). Figure 2.5 [16] represents a cloud computing-enabled IoT system.

2.3.3   Big Data Analytics

Big data analytics refers to collecting, organizing, and analyzing the huge amount of data collected from various IoT devices to extract some useful information from it. As IoT grows, a large amount of unstructured data is being created by IoT devices. A big data system is a shared distributed database where this data is stored for further processing by using specialized analytics tools such as Hadoop, spark, apache storm, etc. Examining the data reveals new data trends, finds unseen data patterns, finds hidden data correlation, and reveals new pieces of information, thus helpful in making decisions. Figure 2.6 shows an IoT environment based on a cloud computing model. Big data can analyze a large volume of heterogeneous data quickly to get insights into any helpful information.

2.3.4   Embedded System

An embedded system is a small device or machine having some processing power, memory, and has some dedicated function for input and output. An embedded system can be independent or part of a large system. IoT is a

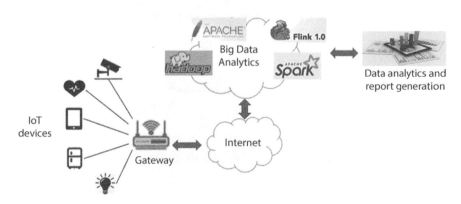

Figure 2.6 Cloud computing in IoT.

combination of several embedded devices connected over the Internet that can sense the external environment and communicate with each other. It plays an important role in any IoT-enabled system due to its unique features, such as low power consumption, real-time computing, low maintenance, and high availability.

2.4 IoT Architecture

IoT has a wide area of applications. Depending on the area of application, devise configuration, network management, etc., IoT comprises various technologies. There is no single reference architecture that is universally accepted and can suit all application areas. This section discusses the most basic and widely accepted four-layered IoT architecture shown in Figure 2.7 that defines the physical components, network configuration, data operational procedures and suits almost all application areas ranging from industrial to home automation. The four layers, namely, perception layer, network layer, data management layer, and application layer, are discussed in this section.

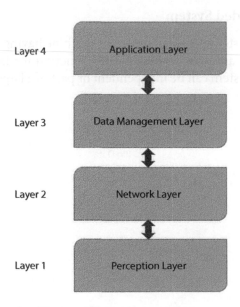

Figure 2.7 Four-layered architecture of IoT.

Layer 1: Perception Layer—This layer, also known as the sensory or physical layer, consists of all the devices, things, actuators embedded with sensors, microcontrollers, memory, etc. This layer is responsible for sensing the environment and gathering data by using various kinds of sensors. Various sensors available for IoT-related projects are soil moisture sensor, temperature sensor, infrared sensor, UV sensor, humidity sensor, gas sensor, etc. Figure 2.8 illustrates various devices in the perception layer.

Layer 2: Network Layer—This layer is also known as a transmission layer, responsible for carrying data over the network from device to device, device to the network, network to network. The connectivity model may be wired or wireless, depending upon the application. This layer consists of routers, gateways, bridges, majorly responsible for transmitting data. This layer is extremely sensitive to attackers and has security issues related to authentication and integrity of personal data. Various transmission technologies work in this slayer, such as Wi-Fi, Bluetooth, Ethernet, NFC, ZigBee, LPWAN, etc. Figure 2.9 represents the Network layer.

Layer 3: Data management Layer—This layer is also known as a middleware layer, responsible for capturing, storing, and processing the data. This layer mainly deals with data analytics and decision units. This layer performs two major functions: data accumulation and data abstraction. In data accumulation, the unstructured data received from millions of devices is converted into meaningful and structured data. In data abstraction, it separates the essential data from structured data so that it can be

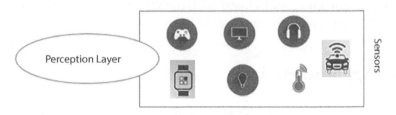

Figure 2.8 Perception layer.

Figure 2.9 Network layer.

Figure 2.10 Data management layer.

Figure 2.11 Application layer.

converted into business intelligence. Figure 2.10 represents the data management layer.

Layer 4: Application Layer—This layer consists of domain-specific applications meant for end-user. This layer can be considered an interface between the end-user and the IoT system. It provides application-specific services to users. Smart home applications, car diagnostics applications, health monitor applications installed in mobile phones are a few examples. Figure 2.11 represents the application layer.

2.5   Applications Area

IoT has wide multidisciplinary areas of application ranging from home to industrial automation. IoT enables the embedded devices to become smart by allowing them to sense the environment and communicate with each other. In a very short period, IoT has covered a large part of the market in various domains, including medical, transport, retail, agriculture, education, healthcare, etc. [17]. The power and potential of IoT be able to look at almost every field. Figure 2.12 demonstrates the share of the top 10 application areas of IoT in 2020 [18]. It can be seen that the industrial and manufacturing sector has wide applications of IoT, followed by transportation, energy, and retail. This section discusses the role of IoT in various domains.

Manufacturing/Industry—Various manufactures are discovering new ways of applying IoT inside and outside the factory. Floor monitoring, connected machinery, augmented reality, automated quality control systems, are a few industrial applications of IoT that not only minimizes the operational time but also cost-saving. Various technology giants such as Google, Microsoft, AWS have collaborated with industrial automation players like Siemens, Rockwell automation to bring digital transformation in industrial and manufacturing processes.

Transportation—Smart route planning, fleet management, car diagnostics, self-driving cars, telematics, traffic management are a few application areas in the transportation and mobility domain to facilitate human lives. In the future, cars may connect to share information about traffic, road conditions, congestion, etc., for smart route planning. It will result in low fuel consumption and a greener environment for the future generation. Driverless cars are currently in use in developed countries like America. Big giants like Tesla, Apple, BMW are into developing new generation intelligent and interconnected cars. Driver behaviour tracking is another important feature in future generation cars with the help of which IoT embedded sensors and devices track the driver behaviour and connect to the central server if there is any abnormality in driver behaviour.

Energy—With the increase in population, the overall energy consumption is expected to increase by 40% in the next 20 years. There is a need for a smart energy saver solution to meet the ever-increasing energy demand. The IoT sensors make it possible to monitor and gather grid data that can be analyzed to improve grid efficiency. With the help of data provided by

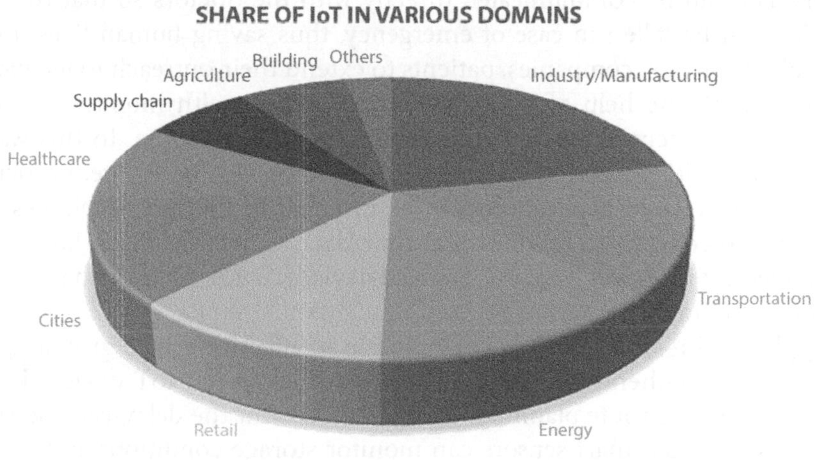

SHARE OF IoT IN VARIOUS DOMAINS

Figure 2.12 IoT application areas.

sensors, statistical models can be designed to forecast energy consumption. Smart meters, grid optimization, remote asset monitoring, predictive maintenance are a few IoT-related applications in the energy sector.

Retail—The retail sector uses the potential of IoT in improving the customer experience by creating smart shopping solutions. A voice-assisted digital assistant helps the customer with a smart selection of cost-effective products and time saviours also. Smart digital kiosks not only automate customer experience but also analyze customers' demands. Companies study this data to identify norms and trends and create plans to increase productivity. Customer tracking, goods monitoring, inventory management are applications in the retail sector where IoT can be useful.

Cities—Smart city planning is the need for the hour, which includes smart lighting, smart parking, traffic management, waste management, video surveillance to give ease life, safety, and decreased power utilization. Smart homes are one of the trending and growing application areas of IoT. It consists of IoT-enabled home appliances, such as air conditioners, refrigerators, various video streaming devices, CCTV cameras that can communicate with each other and provide a digitized use experience. A user can control all home appliances through an application installed on his mobile phone from any part of the world. A smart waste management system may connect to government officials to inform in which part of the city there is a need for waste management.

Healthcare—In the current scenario of the COVID-19 pandemic, there is a need for smart digital health solutions. IoT-enabled smart wearable devices to help collect and analyze real-time data such as the number of steps, heartbeat rate, blood pressure, oxygen level, glucose monitoring, etc. This data can be communicated directly with the doctors so that timely action can be taken in case of emergency, thus saving human lives. IoT enables hospitals, companies, patients to extend their outreach to its maximum. With the help of IoT patients, real-time health monitoring can be done remotely by doctors, thus saving money and time. In this way, medical facilities reach to maximum population. In the future, particular ailment-related applications can be installed in the mobile phones of patients to collect and monitor real-time data. Currently, many hospitals and medical institutes have IoT-enabled devices that remind them to wash hands and sanitize.

Supply Chain—In the supply chain, IoT is an effective way to give unique identities to authenticate the products and track them. IoT devices help to plan effective route planning taking into account the delay-causing situations. Various smart sensors can monitor storage conditions and location of products throughout their journey, which facilitates the company to ensure quality delivery to consumers. With the help of IoT devices and GPS, it is easier to monitor goods, where they are, how they are stored at different locations and their expected delivery to consumers. Goods are tagged with RFID to make it easier to find the location within a large warehouse. With IoT, there is the least chance of goods being lost or destroyed. **Buildings**—An IoT-enabled smart building consists of automated air conditioning, ventilation, fire management system, security, surveillance, etc. With the help of smart sensors and devices, such kind of infrastructure helps reduce energy consumption, efficient space utilization, and minimize the building's environmental effects, thus easier to maintain building assets. Connected homes will ensure overall security and improve the comfort and productivity of occupants. Real-time indoor air quality monitoring is possible with the help of IoT to improve people's lifestyles.

2.6   Challenges and Security Issues

IoT technology and related applications are broadly accepted in society. There are still many challenges and technical issues in the deployment of IoT that needs to be researched. Efforts are required to address these challenges to ensure a good fit of IoT devices into a human-centric environment. This section discusses major challenges and technical issues in an IoT-enabled environment.

a. Interoperability—IoT is an interconnected network of various devices communicating with each other. This brings the complexity in devices communicating through various communication technologies, which leads to delayed and nonstandardized transfer of data [19]. Also, these devices have different types of hardware and software components; providing them unique identities and addressing them is still a big challenge.
b. Data—A large amount of data from real-time communication between various devices is an issue for the current database management system. The current technology of storing and monitoring real-time data is insufficient. The proper solution for IoT-based data-centric database system needs to be devised.
c. Standards—IoT is still an emerging technology. Security standard, architectural standard, and addressing standard needs to be evolved with the growth of technology that will bring a unified approach for efficient implementation of IoT.
d. Security and Privacy—With the wide range of applications and connectivity among different devices, security will always remain a major

concern. The vulnerability of data increases with the number of devices and connections. The security architecture must ensure end-to-end encryption, confidentiality, authentication, and integrity of personal data.

e. Scalability—As IoT grows, millions of devices add up to the Internet. These devices generate a huge volume of data to store, monitor, analyse, and extract useful information. The system that stores and monitors this data needs to be scalable to achieve the highest level of efficiency. The raw data generated by billions of devices need big data and cloud storage [20].

f. Design—With the increase in popularity and usability of IoT-related technologies, a unified design is a major concern for researchers and manufacturers. There have been design-related issues that manufacturers have to cope up with, such as limited computational power, limited memory, hardware, Software maintenance, etc.

g. Testing and Updating—Currently, over 23 billion IoT devices are connected, and this number is assumed to grow up to 60 billion by the end of 2025. With this much number of devices its become very difficult for manufacturers and firmware to undergo proper testing and updating of devices, which makes them prone to various security issues such as malware attack, phishing, credential theft, etc.

h. Device Management—A study [21, 22] reveals that currently, there are over 5 million IoT devices and unmanaged connected devices in the healthcare, retail, industry, and manufacturing sector. Any hacker can easily breach and acquire confidential information from these devices. These connected but outdated devices need proper device management and security updates [23].

2.7   Conclusion

IoT is a massive network of connected things that senses the environment, communicates, and shares data and valuable information with each other. Experts estimate about 30 billion IoT objects connected by 2025. IoT is not a standalone technology. To manage the huge network of heterogeneous devices connected over the Internet, IoT is facilitated by other leading technologies such as cloud computing, big data analytics, embedded devices, etc. From large-scale industrial applications to small-scale home automation, IoT brings a transformation from physical to digital operations in every field. With that much popularity and a wide area of application, there come some challenges also. IoT brings a new era and wide area of research for academicians, scientists, scholars, and researchers to overcome various challenges such as devise management, privacy, networking, design, etc. However, the idea of IoT is emerging and growing rapidly in our modern society, filling the gap between humans and technology by connecting many devices and aiming to improve quality of life. In the near future, IoT will allow automation of almost everything around us.

References

1. Baker, S.B., Xiang, W., Atkinson, I., Internet of things for smart healthcare: Technologies, challenges, and opportunities. *IEEE Access*, 5, 26521–26544, 2017.
2. Gulve, S.P., Khoje, S.A., Pardeshi, P., Implementation of IoT-based smart video surveillance system, in: *Computational Intelligence in Data Mining*, vol. 556, H.S. Behera and D.P. Mohapatra (Eds.), pp. 771–780, Springer Singapore, Singapore, 2017.
3. Majeed, R., Abdullah, N.A., Ashraf, I., Zikria, Y.B., Mushtaq, M.F., Umer, M., An intelligent, secure, and smart home automation system. *Sci. Program.*, 2020, 1–14, Oct. 2020.
4. Ayaz, M., Ammad-Uddin, M., Sharif, Z., Mansour, A., Aggoune, E.-H.M., Internet-of-Things (IoT)-based smart agriculture: Toward making the fields talk. *IEEE Access*, 7, 129551–129583, 2019.
5. Kumar, S., Tiwari, P., Zimbler, M., Internet of Things is a revolutionary approach for future technology enhancement: A review. *J. Big Data*, 6, 1, 111, Dec. 2019.
6. Chandrakar, R., Raja, R., Miri, R., Patra, R.K., Sinha, U., Computer succored vaticination of multi-object detection and histogram enhancement in low vision. *Int. J. Biom. Special Issue: Investigation of Robustness in Image Enhancement and Preprocessing Techniques for Biometrics and Computer Vision Applications*, 1, 2, 1–12, 2022.
7. Sfar, A.R., Chtourou, Z., Challah, Y., A systemic and cognitive vision for IoT security: A case study of military live simulation and security challenges, in: *2017 International Conference on Smart, Monitored and Controlled Cities (SM2C)*, pp. 101–105, 2017.
8. Sinha, C.S., Patra, R.K., Raja, R., A comprehensive analysis of human gait for abnormal foot recognition using neuro-genetic approach. *Int. J. Tomogr. Stat. (IJTS)*, 16, W11, 56–73, 2011, http://ceser.res.in/ceserp/index.php/ijts.
9. University of Baltimore, Baltimore, MD, USA, Johnson, D., Ketel, M., IoT: application protocols and security. *IJCNIS*, 11, 4, 1–8, Apr. 2019.
10. Tukade, T.M. and Banakar, R.M., Data transfer protocols in IoT-An overview. *Int. J. Pure Appl. Math.*, 118, 121–138, Jan. 2018.
11. rfc7252. The Constrained Application Protocol (CoAP) Community Name: Internet Engineering Task Force (IETF), Document Name: Request for Comments (RFC-7252) Year: 2014 [Online]. Available: https://datatracker.ietf.org/doc/html/rfc7252. [Accessed: 23-May-2021].

12. Soni, D. and Makwana, A., A survey on MQTT: A protocol of Internet of Things (IoT). *International Conference on Telecommuncation, Power Analysis and Computing Techniques (ICTPACT - 2017)*, pp 1–5, Apr. 2017.

13. Al-Masri, E., Kalyanam, K.R., Batts, J., Kim, J., Singh, S., Vo, T., Yan, C., Investigating messaging protocols for the Internet of Things (IoT). *IEEE Access*, 8, 94880–94911, 2020.

14. Chen, Y. and Kunz, T., Performance evaluation of IoT protocols under a constrained wireless access network, in: *2016 International Conference on Selected Topics in Mobile & Wireless Networking (MoWNeT)*, pp. 1–7, 2016.

15. Yassein, M.B., Shatnawi, M.Q., Al-Zoubi, D., Application layer protocols for the Internet of Things: A survey, in: *2016 International Conference on Engineering & MIS (ICEMIS)*, pp. 1–4, 2016.

16. How to choose the right IoT cloud platform, DZone IoT, Durham, NC, 2019, [Online]. Available: https://dzone.com/articles/how-to-choose-the-right-iot-cloud-platform. [Accessed: 26-May-2021].

17. Khanna, A. and Kaur, S., Internet of things (IoT), applications and challenges: A comprehensive review. *Wireless Pers. Commun.*, 114, 2, 1687–1762, Sep. 2020.

18. Chandrakar, R., Raja, R., Miri, R., Animal detection based on deep convolutional neural networks with genetic segmentation. *Multimed. Tools Appl.*, 73, 2, 1–14, 2021, https://doi.org/10.1007/s11042-021-11290-4.

19. Bandyopadhyay, D. and Sen, J., Internet of things: Applications and challenges in technology and standardization. *Wireless Pers. Commun.*, 58, 1, 49–69, May 2011.

20. Cabre, J.A.C., Precup, D., Sanz, R., Horizontal and vertical self-adaptive cloud controller with reward optimization for resource allocation, in: *2017 International Conference on Cloud and Autonomic Computing (ICCAC)*, pp. 184–185, 2017.

21. Threat highlight: Analysis of 5+ million unmanaged, IoT, and IoMT devices, Help Net Security, Croatia (European Union), 2021, [Online]. Available: https://www.helpnetsecurity.com/2020/07/24/analysis-of-5-million-unmanaged-iot-and-iomt-devices/. [Accessed: 25-May-2021].

22. Sahu, A.K., Sharma, S., Tanveer, M., Raja, R., Internet of Things attack detection using hybrid deep learning model. *Comput. Commun.*, 176, 146–154, 2021, https://doi.org/10.1016/j.comcom.2021.05.024.

23. Lenka, R.K., Rath, A.K., Tan, Z., Sharma, S., Puthal, D., Simha, N.V.R., Raja, R., Tripathi, S.S., Prasad, M., Building scalable cyber-physical-social networking infrastructure using IoT and low power sensors. *IEEE Access, Special Issue on Building Scalable Cyber-Physical-Social Networking Infrastructure Using IoT and Low Power Sensors,* 6, 1, 30162–30173.

Ambient Intelligence Health Services Using IoT

Pawan Whig[1]*, Ketan Gupta[2], Nasmin Jiwani[2] and Arun Velu[3]

[1]Department of Information Technology, Vivekananda Institute of Professional Studies, New Delhi, India
[2]Department of Information Technology, University of the Cumberlands, Williamsburg, Kentucky, USA
[3]Department of Information Technology, Equifax and Researcher, Atlanta, USA

Abstract

Ambient intelligence refers to the combination of pervasive ubiquitous computing, big data and artificial frameworks, IoT, sensor networks, and human-computer interaction (HCI) technologies. This technology paves the way for a futuristic world in which sensors incorporated into everyday devices create a smart environment that is seamlessly adapted to customer requirements and wishes. With patient health status records and patient electronic medical record (EMR), updates can help to provide a better and more straightforward narrative for the healthcare sector. It can assist healthcare workers, such as physicians and nurses, in providing quality care by analyzing patient data, such as prior treatments, allergic reactions, and more. Ambient intelligence helps the elderly in countries with a higher population of senior citizens by remotely monitoring their health and enabling them to live independently through ambient assisted living (AAL) technology. In this chapter, a case study related to the COVID disaster will be discussed with the help of ambient intelligence and new technologies.

Keywords: Ambient assisted living (AAL), human-computer interaction, IoT, artificial intelligence

*Corresponding author: pawanwhig@gmail.com

Md Rashid Mahmood, Rohit Raja, Harpreet Kaur, Sandeep Kumar and Kapil Kumar Nagwanshi (eds.) *Ambient Intelligence and Internet of Things: Convergent Technologies*, (53–80) © 2023 Scrivener Publishing LLC

3.1   Introduction

The new information technology paradigm in ambient intelligence (AmI) aims to empower human skills through digital surroundings that are perceptive to human needs, behavior, gesture, and emotion [1–4]. This idea of the daily surroundings will allow novel human-machine relations that are enveloping, modest, and defensive [5]. Amy promises to successfully interpret the wealth of appropriate order obtained from implanted sensors by relying on a variety of artificial intelligence (AI) techniques and will become accustomed to the surroundings to the user requirements in a clear and preventative manner [6, 7].

Intelligence means knowledge in new conditions and their capacity to learn and use it [8]. Artificial is anything created by people, and Ambience is the atmosphere that surrounds us [9, 10]. We tend to think that environmental intelligence (AmI) is an artificial element; biology and sociology are the themes of natural AmI [11].

Several characteristics distinguish an AMI system:

- exploits contextual and situational information
- personalized to the requirements

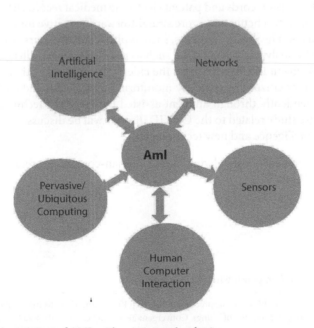

Figure 3.1 Association of AML with existing technologies.

- expect an individual's needs
- adapt to the varying needs
- We are surrounded by our everyday environment.

Recent breakthroughs in the field of sensor networks led to economic monitor systems in the domestic and residential areas, as shown in Figure 3.1 [12]. AMI systems can significantly improve the healthcare profession. AMI technology, as in the case, may be used to monitor the healthcare position of older persons or those with constant conditions, as well as to give assistive care to persons with physical or mental impairments [13–15].

3.2   Background of AML

3.2.1   What is AML?

Researchers have distinguished ambient intelligence in several ways. Table 3.1 summarizes the attributes that AmI technologies are looking for: sensitivity, responsiveness, adaptability, transparency, omnivorousness, and smartness [16]. We can observe how the field contrasts and contrasts areas of general computing, ubiquitous computing, and artificial intelligence based on these concepts and qualities [17]. These are the terms that are used to characterize ambient intelligence [18, 19]. The requirement for AmI systems to be sensitive, responsive, and adaptive emphasizes the importance of context-aware computing in AmI [20].

As observed by Mark Weiser, CTO of the Xerox Corp Palo Alto Research Centre, in 1991: "Disappearing technology is the most significant and important [21]. You tweed into the usual cloth till it is different." Weiser has shown that satellite and mobile Internet phones are examples of deep, invisible technology.

In the future, environmental intelligence will be as strong yet hidden. Just as environmental music plays behind the scenes to improve the environment, environmental intelligence is incorporated into the user's immediate environment [22]. A multitude of sensors fills the atmosphere, making the surroundings intelligent and user-friendly. Environmental intelligence, once fully developed, will have a substantial impact on many companies, including healthcare and assisted living [23, 24]. Seniors are becoming more environmentally independent, and their service providers are always aware that information is available in real time [25, 26].

Excellent Internet connection and technologies allow us to map our information about activity [27]. The notion is to move sensors and

Table 3.1 Ambient Intelligence using Sensitive (S), Responsive (R) , Adaptive (A), Transparent (T), Ubiquitous (U) and Intelligence (I).

Definition	S	R	A	T	U	I
A developing technology that will increasingly make our everyday environment sensitive and responsive to our presense [4].	✓	✓				
A potential future in which we will be surrounded by intelligent objects and in which the environment will recognize the presence of persons and will respond to it in an undetectable manner [1].	✓	✓		✓	✓	
"Ambient Intelligence" implies intelligence that is all around us [5].					✓	✓
The presence of a digital environment that is sensitive, adaptive, and responsive to the presence of people [6].	✓	✓	✓			
A vision of future daily live … contains the assumption that intelligent technology should disappear into our environment to bring humans an easy and entertaining life [7].		✓		✓	✓	
A new research area for distributed, non-intrusive, and intelligent software systems [8].				✓		✓
In an Aml environment people are surrounded with networks of embedded intelligent devices that can sense their state, anticipate, and perhaps adapt to their need [9].	✓		✓	✓	✓	✓
A digital environment that supports people in their daily lives in a nonintrusive way (Raffler) [10].				✓	✓	

computers in the background and the atmosphere and measurements that may be used by a user to help or to provide information that a user requires [28]. Environmental intelligence strives to enrich people's experiences via their daily routines and activities naturally [29].

Ambient intelligence is a multidisciplinary method to improve the interaction between surroundings and humans, as shown in Figure 3.2.

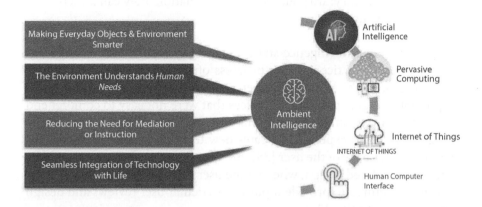

Figure 3.2 AmI features.

The ultimate objective of the area is to improve the location in which we live and work. Smart Homes are one example, but the principle may also be employed in hospitals, public transit, industry, and other areas. Ambient intelligence's achievement depends mostly on the technology employed and on the intelligence of software used to make decisions [30].

Ambient intelligence (AmI) is based on developments in sensor, sensor, computer, and artificial intelligence networks [31]. Due to the great growth in these disciplines over the previous only some years, AmI Research has strengthened and delayed. Because AmI research is growing, this technology promises the revolutionize human existence via the flexibility and adaptation of people's environment [32].

Ambient intelligence was a prediction of Eli Zelkha and his Palo Alto Ventures team for 2010 to 2020 for the expectations of consumer electronics and computers. Environmental intelligent technology would permit gadgets to job together to enable the public to intuitively move out daily behavior, chores, and rituals utilizing information and intelligence concealed from the network linking these gadgets [33]. The API example builds upon enveloping compute, everywhere computing, profile, circumstance alertness, and human-based computer communication design, which is characterized by system and technology are:

- Fixed: numerous networked strategies are incorporated into the situation
- Framework alert: these gadgets can know and context customized

- Adaptive: can modify reaction
- Anticipatory: without conscious mediation, they can anticipate your wishes.

Environmental intelligence stands out largely for the reason of its relevance to user practice and the progress of sensors and sensor network
technologies. In the late 1990s, interest in user experience became more
important as digital goods and services that were not easy to comprehend
or use became becoming voluminous and important [34]. As a result, the
design of the user experience creates new technology and media for the
personal experience of the user [35]. Environmental aptitude is inspired by
consumer-centered design, whereby the user is at the center of plan activities and is required to provide input via particular user reviews and design
improvements testing [36].

Several critical technologies are needed for environmental Intelligence.
These included discrete, user-friendly equipment including miniature,
nanoscale, and intelligent gadgets and computer interfaces focused on
humans [37]. This system and devices function through interoperability,
wired and wireless network and examine learning structural design, with
the seamless communication and compute communications [38].

Dynamic, massively distributed, controllable, and programmable device
networks to apply environmental intelligence [39]. These systems and gadgets must also be reliable and safe to ensure technology through self-test,
self-repair, and privacy [40].

3.3   AmI Future

Today, technology is all so prevalent that it is "taken as obtained." Take
our smartphones, for instance. It has become an omnipresent element
of our lives. A subtle portion of my background has become virtual personal assistants and Bluetooth speakers. While these technological breakthroughs have improved our lives, we are prepared for a far more dramatic
disturbance in our everyday lives with what we call environmental intelligence [41].

Our yearning for a better life drives the oncoming disruption, especially if you consider that by 2050, the population of the globe at the
age of 60 and above will most probably reach 2 billion. In the USA, the
number of seniors who require help will climb by 75%. Imagine a digital
home that helps people proactively yet sensibly via the use of human
center technology and offers the necessary geriatric care. The way we live

in our houses via ambient intelligence prepares us with such a significant upheaval. AmI is smart, all-around, and intuitive [42]. The user does not inquire but knows the context of the user. It does not make its presence noticed, yet it acts according to the preferences of the user. AmI is a new technology that will fundamentally revolutionize our way of interacting with machinery and objects in our environment.

Amy operates next to the crossroads of multiple technologies, including AI, big data, the Internet of things (IoT), ubiquitous invasive computing, and network and Interaction with human computers (HCI).

AmI understands the surroundings and the consumer environment via a variety of intelligent digital systems deployed in our homes or workplaces using various IoT sensors and devices. The AmI system then processes the information from these systems. The AmI system understands the vicinity, the status, purpose, and the performance of the user after data is processed and evaluated. It intuits the present facts, past knowledge, and pattern identification through insights. The next best step is taken, and the user is responded to through an intuitive, natural interface of an intelligent gadget. The connection of AmI environmental intelligence opens up enormous opportunities to facilitate and improve our lives.

Whether we are in our kitchen or living room or workstation, whether we are at the shop, lashing or in the rest home, technology is what helps us. Wait for us not to choose this ice cream, as it may be read from our health checklists to advise us to receive a different road to work since it knows that an accident was occurring on the normal course. The air conditioner is switched on to chill our houses before returning from work on hot summer evenings.

To further appreciate how it will affect our daily lives, consider the following scenario: Steve, an IT trick, returns residence after a hard day, and AmI systems assist him in relaxing. A face acknowledgement system recognizes Steve at the entrance and allows him to come into his house. The technology detects Steve's tension by capturing his facial expressions. When Steve walks into the living area, the system switches on gentle lighting that is tailored to his mood and preferences, as shown in Figure 3.3.

AmI plays calming music chosen by Steve from his iTunes library. AmI shuts the blinds and drapes to reduce glare from the windows. AmI plays an important message from Steve's wife, indicating she would be home a bit late from the workplace after he has settled down on the sofa. Also, AmI scans Steve's chart and informs him that the conference call scheduled for 8.30 PM has been rescheduled for 9:00 AM tomorrow and that he must bring a physical copy of an essential document to the assembly.

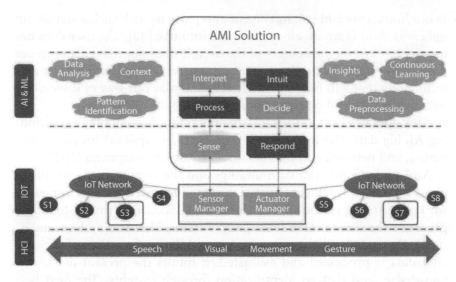

Figure 3.3 AML solution.

In the meantime, the AmI system detects Steve's father, an elderly citizen, going starting the kitchen to his bedroom and watching him ensure he is safe. AmI scans the TV agenda and reminds Steve with the purpose of there is a football match tonight on TV and asks him if he wants to set a reminder that AmI offers enormous potential for increasing people's quality of life, comfort, and safety. AmI houses equipped with human-centric technology would make daily tasks much easier. This will be crucial as long as appropriate care for the elderly, especially as the population ages. Even exterior our homes, Even outside of our homes, AmI will find applications in a variety of fields like retail, healthcare, manufacturing, smart cities, and others.

3.4   Applications of Ambient Intelligence

3.4.1   Transforming Hospitals and Enhancing Patient Care With the Help of Ambient Intelligence

Artificial intelligence (AI) is being used to transform operations in a variety of sectors. Researchers are developing algorithms to better anticipate wildfires in the western United States. An AI system uncovered an existing rheumatoid arthritis medicine earlier this year that might be repurposed to treat COVID-19 patients. In a new publication, researchers show how these technologies may be used to improve patient care in hospitals of the future.

Stanford's Engineering School published research in which they analyzed possibly catastrophic medical incidents by "ambient intelligence" in the hospitals. The article focuses on a paper coauthored by Milstein that was just published in Nature.

In one such scenario, hospital rooms may be outfitted with artificial intelligence systems and sensors to monitor adequate cleanliness practices. Other AI methods might be used to forecast possible medical emergencies based on patient behavior. These ideas, when combined, have the potential to alleviate strain on hospital staff.

"The intricacy of bedside care is afoot sprint," Milstein stated in the paper. "In a recent count, a hospital physician took 600 bedside measures per patient each day. In a hospital intensive care center. The faultless implementation of this amount of complicated actions is well beyond what even the most diligent clinical teams can reasonably hope without technological support."

AI, thermal imaging, IoT sensors, and more were employed to reduce the spread of COVID-19 during the coronavirus epidemic. There are several privacy issues with the expanding usage of such systems. They have avoided utilizing HD video sensing technology "since the video capture might inhibit clinics and patients' privacy excessively," the paper says. "Infrarot pictures can give data which is sufficiently precise to train AI algorithms for several applications of clinical importance," Haque noted in the research.

3.4.2   With Technology, Life After the COVID-19 Pandemic

The COVID-19 epidemic has already included about 5.6 million verified fatalities worldwide and more than 350,000 fatalities. This is disastrous stats per se, and at the same time, a profound recession affecting most companies and people is occurring throughout the global economy.

To improve the situation? Cognitive technology, such as ML, neural networks, RPA, bots, neural networks, and the larger area of AI, can revolutionize how critical health and safety issues such as COVID-19 are predicted, reacted, or interacted with.

The Cognize PCP provides situation sensitivity to people and crowds using AI and multisensors to recognize persons less than six feet apart or in groups of over ten individuals. Visualize an always-on autonomous sensor system that can help monitor rooms and correlate information in complicated settings far faster and more efficiently than a human mind can, as shown in Figure 3.4.

Through thermal sensor applications and biometrics at access points, the body temperature with or without masks may now be monitored, and circumstances that need additional health checks efficiently reported, as shown in Figure 3.4.

Thermographic cameras provide heat detection at an exact temperature measurement level of ±0.5°C, as shown in Figure 3.5. The presence of a virus will not be proven by infrared sensors as a heat scanner with camera systems, but it can see whether the individual is in danger. It can expose information and warn operators about possible threats that need to be further analyzed by a visibility system that comprises a camera and display.

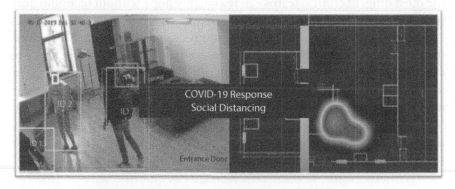

Figure 3.4 Camera sensor used to measure social distancing.

Figure 3.5 Thermographic cameras used for finding the temperature of the patient.

3.5   COVID-19

COVID-19 is a communicable infection caused by a recently recognized coronavirus as shown in Figure 3.6. Coronaviruses are a genus of RNA viruses associated with mammalian and avian illnesses. The subfamily Orthocoronavirinae, Coronaviridae family, Nidoviral family, and Riboviral kingdom are the coronaviruses. The enclosed viruses include an RNA genome with positive wisdom and a helical regularity nucleocapsid. Coronaviruses have one of the biggest genomes among RNA viruses, ranging from around 26 to 32 kilobases. The feature distinguishes club-shaped spikes that protrude from their surface, creating a picture suggestive of the solar corona, from which its name originates.

On December 31, 2019, China released a cluster of unknown pneumonia in Wuhan City in Hubei Province to the World Health Organization in China. The sickness then spread to additional provinces in China and throughout the world. It has now been labelled a pandemic by the WHO.

Most COVID-19–stained individuals will suffer from mild to harsh respiratory illness and recover without specific treatment. The risk of developing serious sickness is greater for the elderly and individuals with severe medical circumstances such as cardiovascular illness, diabetes, persistent respiratory diseases, and cancer.

It is necessary to be thoroughly aware of the COVID-19 virus, the sickness it produces, and how it distributes to avoid and slow down transmission. Wipe your hands or use a spiritual rib regularly, and do not touch your face to protect yourself and others against illness.

Figure 3.6 Corona virus.

The COVID-19 virus is mostly transmitted by saliva droplets released when a contaminated person taxes; hence it is crucial that one have to have a respiratory protocol.

3.5.1   Prevention

Do the following to avoid infection and slow COVID-19 transmission:

- Regularly wash your hands with soap, water or massage alcoholic hands with alcohol.
- Keep coughing or sneezing from you at least 1 m apart.
- Evitate your face contact.
- When coughing and sneezing, cover-up mouth and nose.
- Smoke retention.
- To physically distance oneself by preventing unneeded journeys and keeping away from larger groupings of people.

3.5.2   Symptoms

COVID-19 impacts various individuals in various ways. The majority of those infected with the infection will get mild to moderately unwell.

Most prevalent symptoms

- dry cough
- fever
- tiredness
- aches and discomfort

Less frequent symptoms

- harmlessness
- diarrhoea
- conjunctivitis
- headache
- smell or flavour loss
- skin rash, or finger or toe discolouration

Serious symptoms

- breathability problem or breathlessness
- discomfort or tension on the chest

Loss of speech or motion. If you have severe symptoms, get quick medical assistance. Talk to your doctor or health center before you visit.

3.6   Coronavirus Worldwide

Corona Virus worldwide information regarding cases deaths recovered and active cases are tabulated in Table 3.2 and represented in Figures 3.7–3.9.

COVID-19 is a tough job for experts throughout the world to detect from medical imaging. COVID-19 began in 2019 in China, and even today, it is expanding. The essential imaging procedures for the diagnosis of COVID-19 are chest X-raying and Computed Tomography (CT). All researchers strive for efficient remedies for this epidemic and rapid treatment approaches.

Fast and precise automated detection techniques are provided to eliminate the requirement for medical expertise. The DL-CNN technologies demonstrate amazing results in the detection of COVID-19 cases. Deep learning convolution (DL-CNN). In this article, the method of deep-functional concatenation (DFC) is used in two ways. The initial DFC connects a basic suggested CNN to the profound characteristics derived from

Table 3.2 Worldwide COVID-19 stats till June 2021.

#	Country, other	Total cases	Total deaths	Total recovered	Active cases	Population
	World	172,972,612	3,718,988	155,921,094	13,332,530	
1	USA	34,174,752	611,611	28,025,575	5,537,566	332,791,423
2	India	28,574,350	340,719	26,597,655	1,635,976	1,392,494,128
3	Brazil	16,803,472	469,784	15,228,983	1,104,705	213,951,414
4	France	5,694,076	109,857	5,378,299	205,920	65,406,747
5	Turkey	5,270,299	47,882	5,139,993	82,424	85,174,270
6	Russia	5,108,129	123,037	4,720,512	264,580	145,992,211
7	UK	4,499,878	127,812	4,296,244	75,822	68,214,706
8	Italy	4,225,163	126,342	3,893,259	205,562	60,379,739
9	Argentina	3,884,447	79,873	3,438,437	366,137	45,577,625

Cumulative COVID-19 tests, confirmed cases and deaths

The confirmed counts shown here are lower than the total counts. The main reason for this is limited testing and challenges in the attribution of the cause of death.

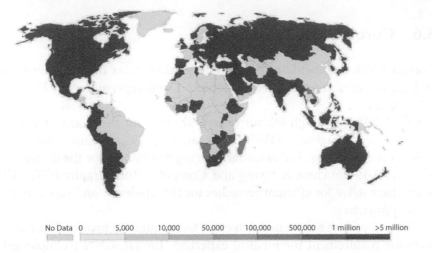

Source: Official data collated by Our World in Data; Johns Hopkins University CSSE   OurWorldInData.org/coronavirus • CC BY

Figure 3.7 COVID-19 tests, confirmed cases, and death.

Cumulative confirmed COVID-19 deaths

Limited testing and challenges in the attribution of the cause of death means that the number of confirmed deaths may not be an accurate count of the true number of deaths from COVID-19.

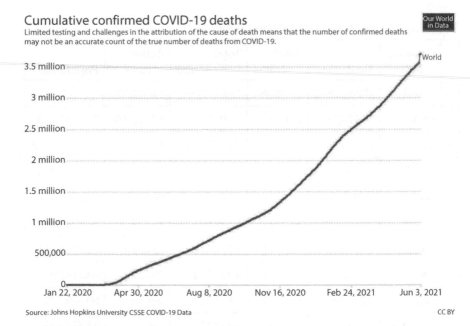

Source: Johns Hopkins University CSSE COVID-19 Data   CC BY

Figure 3.8 Confirmed COVID deaths till June 2021.

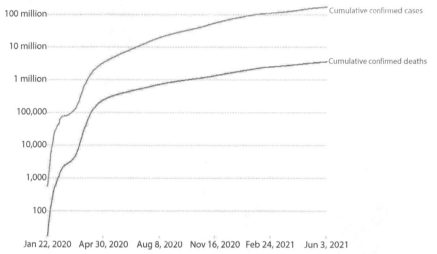

Figure 3.9 Cumulative confirmed COVID-19 deaths and cases, world.

X-ray and the CT image. The alternative option is that using the CNN's suggested design and two modern pretrained CNNs, DFC may merge characteristics obtained from both an X-ray or CT scan: ResNet and GoogleNet.

A final classification descriptor is applied to the DFC method. The suggested CNN design has three deep layers to solve the huge time consumption problem. For each type of picture, several optimization strategies and varied values for a maximum number of epochs, the LR, and small-batch sizes will be used to study the proposed CNN performance. Experiments showed the superiority of the suggested methodology in terms of accuracy, precision, reminder, and f score, compared to the other current and advanced approaches.

3.7   Proposed Framework for COVID-19

In COVID times, we have COVID-19 special centers or home arrangements to take care of patients. since COVID is extremely communicable, it is critical to quarantine COVID patients; however, doctors must also monitor the physical condition of COVID patients. Amid the rising quantity

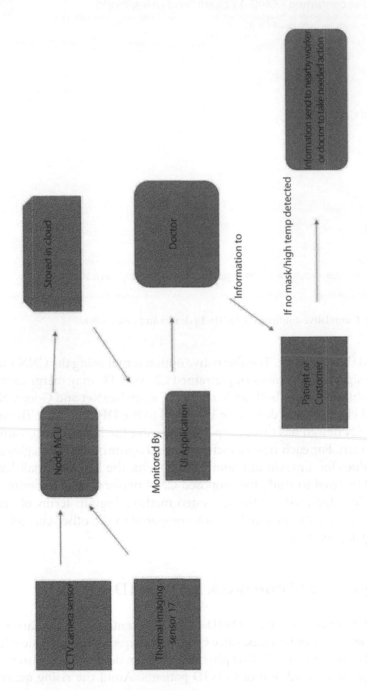

Figure 3.10 Proposed framework.

of cases, keeping track of the health conditions of so many quarantined patients is becoming increasingly difficult.

The issues are as follows:

- Doctors must regularly check patient health.
- The number of patients for doctors to check is growing.
- The doctors are in danger of illness simply for the reason of monitoring.
- Many times, patients need help related to many things like medicines, food, oxygen, and others household things.
- Wasting of time in finding help

With the aid of the sensors, the mask and body temperature of the individual are detected, and the result is communicated by MCU Node to the Doctor as shown in the framework Figure 3.10. Then the Doctor checks it and takes the essential action; if no mask or excessive temperature is discovered, it will display red colour and warn you so that you can send employees to take care of the problem. This allows the Doctor to watch a large number of individuals far less than before.

To resolve this issue, we here aim a remote AI-based health observation system that not only allows for remotely monitoring of multiple COVID patients over the internet but also helps the patient to connect with the local NGOs working day and night to help COVID patients. The arrangement monitor patient heartbeat, fever, and blood pressure by resources of a heartbeat sensor, temperature, and BP Sensor; in that order, the coordination is also connected to the NGOs available locally. In case the patient needs help, they can ask for help through the available option in the device.

3.8   Hardware and Software

The Physical material used for the construction of the device is called hardware. The typical hardware used are

3.8.1   Hardware

- Heartbeat sensor
- Temperature sensor
- Blood pressure sensor
- Node MCU board
- Mini breadboard

- Wires
- Led

3.8.2 Heartbeat Sensor

A person's heartbeat is the sound of the valves in the heart contracting or expanding as blood is moved from one location to the next. The heartbeat is the number of times the heart beats per minute (BPM), and the pulse in each artery adjacent to the skin is the heartbeat.

3.8.3 Principle

The photoplethysmographic concept underpins the cardiovascular sensor. It monitors variations in blood volume in any organ in the body that induce variations in light intensity via that organ. The timing of the pulses is especially significant in applications that monitor the heart's pulse rate. The rate of heartbeat pulses determines blood volume flow, and signal pulses are equal to heartbeat pulses because the light is absorbed by the blood.

3.8.4 Working

The fundamental heartbeat sensor shown in Figure 3.11, consists of a light-emitting diode and a sensor such as a light resistor or a photodiode. The pulses of the heartbeat cause blood to fluctuate in various parts of the body. When lit by the light source, i.e. the light emitted by the led, the tissue reflects or transmits the light. Some of the light is absorbed by the blood, and the light transferred or reflected by the light detector is received. The amount of light absorbed depends on the quantity of

Figure 3.11 Heartbeat sensor.

blood in the tissue. The detector's output is electrical and proportional to the rate of heartbeat.

3.8.5 Temperature Sensor

Temperature sensors measure an object's temperature either by contacting the object or by remotely detecting the infrared energy the object emits.

3.8.6 Principle

The voltage across diode terminals constitutes the fundamental principle of operation of the temperature sensors. Increasing voltage also causes an increase in temperature and a drop in the voltage between the base transistor terminals and the diode transmitter.

3.8.7 Working

In principle, a thermistor is a sensitive temperature sensor that precisely reacts to changes in temperature even minutes. At very low temperatures, it provides huge resistance. This means that the resistance falls quickly as soon as the temperature increases.

The Negative Temperature Coefficient (NTC) Thermistor is displayed accurately even with a small temperature change due to the big resistance change per degree Celsius. It requires linearization because of this exponential functioning principle. They usually work between −50 and 250°C. The pictorial image of temperature sensor is shown in Figure 3.12.

Figure 3.12 Temperature sensor.

3.8.8   BP Sensor

The BP sensor is a noninvasive sensor for human blood pressure measurement. It uses the oscillometric method to monitor systematic, diastolic and means arterial stress. Pulse rate is reported as well.

3.8.9   Principle

In general, blood pressure is measured by the pressure cuff attached to the mercury column. The Doctor pumps the cuff manually to boost the artery pressure. The blood noise rushing through the artery is then used with stethoscopes.

3.8.10   Working

An auto pressure sensor instead of mercury will be used to detect pressure in the artery and give output in the autoblood pressure measurement system. On the monitor, this digital output appears. A built-in monitor is equipped with an onboard processor that can process the result of the pressure sensor.

This sensor is safe to use because it is not invasive. It is easier to use and is easier for anyone to monitor. This sensor simplifies the task by providing

Figure 3.13 Blood pressure sensor module.

automatic results instead of watching the level of mercury and calculating pressure. The blood pressure module is shown in Figure 3.13.

For high blood pressure patients, this sensor is very important, as it can also be used as a solid-state Blood Pressure Monitor. This is a portable system. In remote areas where medical facilities are not available, it is easy to carry, operate, and extremely useful. The pressure sensor present in the chuff is the main sensing element of this system. This pressure sensor should be carefully selected for precise and reliable measurement.

3.9   Mini Breadboard

The building basis for prototyping electronics is a breadboard or proto-board. The word was originally a literal bread panel, a polished wood used for slicing bread. In the 1970s, the solderless breadboard was made available, also called "breadboard" as shown in Figure 3.14.

Since the breadboard without solder does not need soldering, it is reusable. That is why solder-less breadboards for pupils and technology education are also popular.

3.10   Node MCU

NodeMCU is a development board and open-source Lua-based firmware built primarily for Internet of Things (IoT) applications. It includes

Figure 3.14 Mini breadboard.

firmware based on the ESP8266 wifi SoC and hardware based on the Expressive Systems ESP-12 module as shown in Figure 3.15.

NodeMCU ESP8266 Specifications & Features as shown in Table 3.3.

- Microcontroller: Tensilica 32-bit RISC CPU Xtensa LX106
- Operating Voltage: 7-12V
- Input Voltage: 7-12V
- Digital I/O Pins (DIO): 16
- Analog Input Pins (ADC): 1
- UARTs: 1

Table 3.3 Specification of Node MCU.

Pin category	Name	Description
Power	Micro-USB, 3.3V, GND, Vin	**Micro-USB:** NodeMCU can be powered through the USB port **3.3V:** Regulated 3.3V can be supplied to this pin to power the board **GND:** Ground pins **Vin:** External Power Supply
Control Pins	**EN, RST**	The pin and the button resets the microcontroller.
Analog Pin	A0	Used to measure analog voltage in the range of 0-3.3V.
GPIO Pins	GPIO1 to GPIO16	NodeMCU has 16 general purpose input-output pins on its board.
SPI Pins	SD1, CMD, SD0, CLK	NodeMCU has four pins available for SPI communication.
UART Pins	TXD0, RXD0, TXD2, TXD2	NodeMCU has two UART interfaces, UART0 (RXD0 & TXD0) and UART1 (RXD1 & TXD1), UART1 is used to upload the firware/program.
12C Pins		NodeMCU has 12C functionality support but due to the internal functionality of these pins, you have to find which pin is 12C.

Figure 3.15 Node MCU board.

- SPIs: 1
- 12Cs: 1
- Flash Memory: 4 MB
- SRAM: 64 KB
- Clock Speed: 80 MHz
- USB-TTL based on CP2102 is included onboard, Enabling Plug n Play
- PCB Antenna
- Small Sized module to fit smartly inside your IoT projects

Software used

1. Arduino IDE for Development
2. Thinker cad for Simulation

Explanation

Heartbeat, blood pressure, and body temperature sensors of the patient, as shown in the sensor module, are sent to the Doctor via Node MCU, which is a wifi Board. Then Doctor can monitor patient health along with the sensor data on a UI application made on Thing Speak. This way, the Doctor can monitor many patients at a time. The Patients with critical conditions will be shown in red colour. The Doctor can advise the patients about their health from the portal itself. After receiving the medication from the Doctor, the patient can have the option in the APP for any help needed once the patient clicks on it, various kinds of help are opened like

Food, Oxygen, Medicines. Once the patient clicks on the particular help, the message will be sent to the concerned NGOs/Social Workers/Hospitals etc.

3.11   Advantages

The major advantage of the device is

1. Doctors may remotely monitor patients without the danger of infection.
2. A single doctor may see over 500 patients at once.
3. The Doctor receives an immediate alert in the event of a health fluctuation or an emergency.
4. Reduction in Wasting time in finding help by the patient.
5. Can be used in the healthcare center where patients are large in number.

3.12   Conclusion

In this book chapter on ambience, technology is discussed. Also, an interesting Case study with the future framework is proposed by keeping COVID-19 in mind. In COVID times, we have specially designed COVID-19 quarantine clinics to treat patients with COVID. Because COVID is extremely contagious, it is critical to isolate COVID patients; nevertheless, doctors must also monitor the health of COVID patients. With the rising number of cases, the health situations of many isolated patients are becoming harder to monitor. This device is multipurpose, which can be used not only for accosting doctors to monitor patients but also to the patients who need help in an emergency. I hope WHO must recommend this for the developing counties where the healthcare infra is not so strong.

References

1. Singh, R., Singh, R., Bhatia, A., Sentiment analysis using machine learning techniques to predict outbreaks and epidemics. *Int. J. Adv. Sci. Res.*, 3, 2, 19–24, 2018.
2. Ting, D.S.W., Carin, L., Dzau, V., Wong, T.Y., Digital technology and COVID-19. *Nat. Med.*, 9, 1–3, 2020.

3. Benvenuto, D., Giovanetti, M., Vassallo, L., Angeletti, S., Ciccozzi, M., Application the ARIMA model on the COVID-2019 epidemic dataset. *Data Brief*, 10, 105340, 2020.

4. Deb, S. and Majumdar, M., A time series method to analyze incidence pattern and estimate reproduction number of COVID-19. *Populations and Evolution (q-bio.PE)*, arXiv preprint arXiv:2003.10655, 15, 1–10, 2020.

5. Kucharski, A.J., Russell, T.W., Diamond, C., Liu, Y., Edmunds, J., Funk, S., Eggo, R.M. *et al.*, Early dynamics of transmission and control of COVID-19: A mathematical modelling study. *Lancet Infect. Dis.*, 22, 89–99, 2020.

6. Dey, S.K., Rahman, MdM, Siddiqi, U.R., Howlader, A., Analyzing the Epidemiological outbreak of COVID-19: A visual exploratory data analysis (EDA) approach. *J. Med. Virol.*, 17, 1–25, 2020.

7. Meredith, R., Azman, A.S., Reich, N.G., Lessler, J., The incubation period of coronavirus disease 2019 (COVID-19) from publicly reported confirmed cases: Estimation and application. *Ann. Intern. Med.*, 13, 1–35, 2020.

8. Sahu, A.K., Sharma, S., Tanveer, M., Internet of Things attack detection using hybrid deep learning model. *Comput. Commun.*, 176, 146–154, 2021, https://doi.org/10.1016/j.comcom.2021.05.024.

9. Awad, M. and Khanna, R., Support vector regression, in: *An Efficient Learning Machines*, pp. 67–80, Apress, Berkeley, CA, 2015.

10. De Castro, Y., Gamboa, F., Henrion, D., Hess, R., Lasserre, J.-B., Approximate optimal designs for multivariate polynomial regression. *Ann. Stat.*, 47, 1, 127–155, 2019.

11. Tiwari, L., Awasthi, V., Miri, R., Sinha, G.R., Alkinani, M.H., Polat, K., Detection of lung nodule and cancer using novel Mask-3 FCM and TWEDLNN algorithms. *Measurement*, 172, 108882, 2021.

12. Ojha, U. and Goel, S., A study on prediction of breast cancer recurrence using data mining techniques. *Proc. 7th Int. Conf. Conflux. 2017 Cloud Comput. Data Sci. Eng.*, pp. 527–530, 2017.

13. Ghosh, S., Mondal, S., Ghosh, B., A comparative study of breast cancer detection based on SVM and MLP BPN classifier. *1st Int. Conf. Autom. Control. Energy Syst. - 2014, ACES 2014*, pp. 1–4, 2014.

14. Osarch, A. and Shadgar, B., Machine learning techniques to diagnose breast cancer. *2010 5th Int. Symp. Heal. Informatics Bioinformatics, HIBIT 2010*, pp. 114–120, 2010.

15. Bazazeh, D. and Shubair, R., Comparative study of machine learning algorithms for breast cancer detection and diagnosis. *Int. Conf. Electron. Devices Syst. Appl.*, 7, 2–5, 2017.

16. Azmi, M.S.B.M. and Cob, Z.C., Breast cancer prediction based on backpropagation algorithm. *Proceeding, 2010 IEEE Student Conf. Res. Dev. - Eng. Innov. Beyond, SCOReD 2010, no. SCOReD*, pp. 164–168, 2010.

17. Gayathri, B.M. and Sumathi, C.P., Comparative study of relevance vector machine with various machine learning techniques used for detecting breast

cancer. *2016 IEEE Int. Conf. Comput. Intell. Comput. Res. ICCIC 2016*, pp. 0–4, 2017.

18. Agarwal, P. and Whig, P., Low delay based 4 bit QSD adder/subtraction number system by reversible logic gate. *2016 8th International Conference on Computational Intelligence and Communication Networks (CICN)*, IEEE Xplore, October 26 2017.

19. Chacko, J.B. and Whig, P., Low delay based full adder/subtractor by MIG and COG reversible logic gate. *2016 8th International Conference on Computational Intelligence and Communication Networks (CICN)*, IEEE Xplore, October 26 2017.

20. Sujediya, G. and Vyas, P., A robust technique for image processing based on interfacing of Raspberry-Pi and FPGA using IoT. *International Conference on Computer, Communications and Electronics (Comptelix)*, IEEE Xplore, August 18 2017.

21. Schaffers, H., Komninos, N., Pallot, M., Trousse, B., Nilsson, M., Oliveira, A., Smart cities and the future internet: Towards cooperation frameworks for open innovation. *Future Internet Lect. Notes Comput. Sci.*, 6656, 431–446, 2011.

22. Cuff, D., Hansen, M., Kang, J., Urban sensing: Out of the woods. *Commun. ACM*, 51, 3, 24–33, Mar. 2008.

23. Dohler, M., Vilajosana, I., Vilajosana, X., Llosa, J., Smart cities: An action plan. *Proc. Barcelona Smart Cities Congress*, pp. 1–6, Dec. 2011.

24. Whig, P. and Ahmad, S.N., Impact of parameters on the characteristic of novel PCS. *Can. J. Basic Appl. Sci.*, 3, 2, 45–52, 2015.

25. Chandrakar, R., Miri, R., Sinha, U., Kushwaha, A.K.S., Raja, H., Enhanced the moving object detection and object tracking for traffic surveillance using RBF-FDLNN and CBF algorithm. *Expert Syst. Appl.*, 191, 116306, 2022, https://doi.org/10.1016/j.eswa.2021.116306.

26. Mulligan, C.E.A. and Olsson, M., Architectural Implications of smart city business models: A perspective. *IEEE Commun. Mag.*, 51, 6, 80–85, Jun. 2013.

27. Whig, P. and Ahmad, S.N., Simulation of linear dynamic macro model of photo catalytic sensor in SPICE. *Compel, the International Journal of Computation and Mathematics in Electrical and Electronic Engineering*, 33, 1/2, 1–22, 2014.

28. Lynch, J.P. and Kenneth, J.L., A summary review of wireless sensors and sensor networks for structural health monitoring. *Shock Vibr. Dig.*, 38, 2, 91–130, 2006.

29. Whig, P. and Ahmad, S.N., A novel pseudo PMOS integrated CC-ISFET device for water quality monitoring. *J. Integr. Circuits Syst.*, 8, 2, 1–6, October 2013.

30. Al-Ali, A.R., Zulkernain, I., Aloul, F., A mobile GPRS-sensors array for air pollution monitoring. *IEEE Sens. J.*, 10, 10, 1666–1671, Oct. 2010.

31. Maisonneuve, N., Stevens, M., Niessen, M.E., Hanappe, P., Steels, L., Citizen noise pollution monitoring. *Proc. 10th Annu. Int. Conf. Digital Gov. Res.: Soc. Netw.: Making Connec. Between Citizens Data Gov.*, pp. 96–103, 2009.

32. Li, X., Shu, W., Li, M., Huang, H.-Y., Luo, P.-E., Wu, M.-Y., Performance evaluation of vehicle-based mobile sensor networks for traffic monitoring. *IEEE Trans. Veh. Technol.*, 58, 4, 1647–1653, May 2009.

33. Whig, P. and Ahmad, S.N., Novel FGMOS based PCS device for low power applications. *Photonic Sens. (Springer)*, 5, 2, 1–5, 2015.

34. Kastner, W., Neugschwandtner, G., Soucek, S., Newmann., H.M., Communication systems for building automation and control. *Proc. IEEE*, 93, 6, 1178–1203, Jun. 2005.

35. Lenka, R.K., Rath, A.K., Tan, Z., Sharma, S., Puthal, D., Simha, N.V.R., Building scalable cyber-physical-social networking infrastructure using IoT and low power sensors. *Cyber-Phisical-Social Computing and Networking, IEEE Access*, 6, 1, 30162–30173, 2018.

36. Whig, P. and Ahmad, S.N., Simulation and performance analysis of low power quasi floating gate PCS model. *Int. J. Intell. Eng. Syst.*, 9, 2, 8–13, 2016.

37. Whig, P., Nadikattu, R.R., Velu, A., COVID-19 pandemic analysis using application of AI, in: *Healthcare Monitoring and Data Analysis Using IoT: Technologies and Applications*, vol. 1, pp. 1–25, 1, 1-25, 2022.

38. Li, Y. *et al.*, IoT-CANE: A unified knowledge management system for data-centric internet of things application systems. *J. Parallel Distrib. Comput.*, 131, 161–72, 2019.

39. Atzori, L., Iera, A., Morabito, G., The internet of things: A survey. *Comput. Netw.*, 54, 15, 2787–2805, 2010.

40. Whig, P. and Ahmad, S.N., Controlling the output error for photo catalytic sensor (PCS) using fuzzy logic. *J. Earth Sci. Clim. Change*, 8, 4, 1–6, 2017.

41. Nadikattu, R.R., Mohammad, S.M., Whig, P., Novel economical social distancing smart device for COVID 19. *Int. J. Electr. Eng. Technol. (IJEET) - Scopus Indexed*, 11, 4, 204–217, 2020.

42. Jupalle, H., Kouser, S., Bhatia, A.B. *et al.*, Automation of human behaviors and its prediction using machine learning. *Microsyst. Technol.*, 10, 1, 1–9, 2022. https://doi.org/10.1007/s00542-022-05326-4

Security in Ambient Intelligence and Internet of Things

Salman Arafath Mohammed[1]* and Md Rashid Mahmood[2]

[1]Electrical Engineering Department, Computer Engineering Section, College of Engineering, King Khalid University, Abha, K.S.A.
[2]Department of ECE, Guru Nanak Institutions Technical Campus, Hyderabad, India

Abstract

Many paradigm-s have shifted from the realm of computer networks to the world of Ambient Intelligence and IoT. The network's and its deployment's perspective has shifted. A 60-year-old computer expert and a kid have quite different views on networks. The former considers a network to be a collection of linked computer devices, whereas the latter considers networks to be a collection of connected things! Whatever the case may be. Changes in the paradigm lead to changes in the ways security is being accomplished in AmI and IoT. Because IoT is nothing more than the connectivity of things, the way security must be achieved reliant on the "things" due to which a network is formed. The sensor network serves as the foundation for every IoT application. The difficulties and challenges that occur in AmI and IoT are the same as those that arise in the course of sensor networks; plus, in order to make the network intelligent, a new set of challenges will emerge from the domain of artificial intelligence. Thus, in the researcher's opinion, AmI and IoT are nothing more than intelligent sensor networks that route data, provide security, enforce privacy, enable authentication, and give identity. As a result, the aim of this chapter is to shed light on the privacy and security problems, as well as the identification and authentication issues that must be addressed in wireless sensor networks in order to achieve smart, secure IoT.

Keywords: Ambient, ambient intelligence, wireless sensor network (W.S.N.), opportunistic sensor network, ad-hoc sensor network, Internet of Things (IoT)

**Corresponding author*: salmanphdcse@gmail.com

Md Rashid Mahmood, Rohit Raja, Harpreet Kaur, Sandeep Kumar and Kapil Kumar Nagwanshi (eds.) *Ambient Intelligence and Internet of Things: Convergent Technologies*, (81–124) © 2023 Scrivener Publishing LLC

4.1   Introduction

Opportunistic sensor networks (O.S.N.) or wireless sensor networks (W.S.N.) are the backbones of Internet of Things (IoT) [1]. Ambient Intelligence (AmI) refers to research advancements in the O.S.N., artificial intelligence, sensors and Everyware computing. Sensors are usually tiny, making them suitable for use in nearly any AmI or IoT application. Smart homes, health monitoring, and military applications are just a few examples of AmI and IoT applications [2]. In AmI and IoT systems, tracking and identifying individuals in a hostile environment (a war zone) is a major concern. If a person's location is known, the system can better serve them by predicting requirements based on their preferences and delivering services at times when they are most frequently needed. Motion sensors are a type of technology that is frequently used to track people. For decades, motion sensors have served as the foundation of security systems. While they can detect movement, they cannot identify who (or what) caused it. For example, troops and commandos in the military safeguard their whole country at the country's border. Here, communication between officials must be kept safe, which necessitates a high level of Confidentiality when transferring information from one person to another. Routing between nodes should be focused as well, ensuring that data arrives at its destination on time. Paper [3] focused on the development of a security framework with the help of cryptographic algorithms for military Security. Many studies have shown that it is best suited for military use [4–6].

Because of the ad hoc nature of the network, it is possible to include networks with minimal infrastructure. The sensor improves the ability to locate and identify neighbors in the immediate vicinity. AmI adds intelligence, responsiveness, and every-ware computing to the network; The IoT ad-hoc communication network is a network that connects mobile devices such as sensor nodes. In emergency scenarios in distant locations when there is not enough internet access, and the situation necessitates the establishment of a temporary network, such as in the event of floods, where establishing internet connectivity is time-consuming, infrastructure-dependent, and expensive. The AmI with IoT network can be deployed on the fly. It is not enough to just construct network infrastructure in order to protect our country from adversaries; secure communication between soldiers is essential. In the context of emergency preparedness and response, an AmI with an IoT network is utilized (E.P.R.). Ad-hoc networks that were not originally employed as nodes of an Oppnet, but that joined it dynamically in order to accomplish particular activities in which they had been requested to engage are referred to as "opportunistic networks" [7]. AmI and IoT networks have restricted communication options. Due to the fact that mobility and disconnections are the norms in these networks, they are naturally delay-tolerant. The absence of an end-to-end link is a fundamental contrast between such networks and mobile ad-hoc networks [8]. However, because of the inconsistent connectivity, defining a complete path between source and destination is not always possible. As a result, routes are constructed "on the fly" in the IoT network as messages are transferred. Routing considers a path to the destination hop by hop rather than an end-to-end approach.

Most of the early work in this field for routing does not focus on privacy and security methods. This might be due to the fact that the problems of routing in this environment are so fascinating that designers' full emphasis is drawn to routing rather than Security. Traditional routing techniques such as OLSR [9] or AODV [10] are not applicable to AmI and IoT networks or Wireless ad hoc sensor networks. The shortest path routing protocol is typically used in classical routing algorithms to get the end-to-end route. Recent research has sparked interest in constructing opportunistic routing systems, in which the next relay for each packet and hop is picked dynamically [11]. In the first look, it appears like removing the need to design end-to-end pathways will simplify network routing, yet problems remain that are distinct from traditional network routing approaches. Time-space opportunistic routing [12] is an example of an opportunistic routing strategy in wireless ad hoc networks [13]. Each relay is chosen based on not just the local topology but also the current M.A.C. channel conditions. Geographic routing [14] strategies optimize geographic criteria by determining the route to the destination based on node locations. All of the aforementioned protocols were designed just to obtain the optimal routing decision, with no regard for privacy, Security, or intelligence. To build a safe routing protocol, however, designers must think right from its inception.

The rest of the chapter is organized as follows: Section 4.2 delves into some of the most hotly debated research topics in the AmI and IoT networks. Section 4.3 discusses security threats and requirements arising from the network's ad hoc, intermittent nature, as well as the presence of sensors in the network, as well as associated threats, security loopholes in existing non-secure routing protocols, and detailed classification of the IoT based on sensor networks and respective secure routing algorithms. Section 4.4 includes the algorithms and approaches that do not take Security into account. The methods and approaches utilized to provide privacy and secure routing in the network are listed in Section 4.5 in tabular form, along with security remarks. The majority of algorithms are addressed here, and Security is taken into account right from the beginning. It is concluded that working on a hybrid model is the best way to make significant progress. One of the hybrid models was addressed in Section 4.6, which uses the PPHH protocol and demonstrates that the solution is significantly superior to previous approaches. Finally, Section 4.7 brings the chapter to a conclusion.

4.2   Research Areas

The current state of the art in security-critical ambient systems falls well short of ideal: Almost every day, new security flaws are discovered. To help ameliorate this scenario, a lot of effort has lately been made on approaches and tools that assist the creation of reliable security-critical software in security-critical ambient systems. On an almost daily basis, new security flaws are uncovered. To help ameliorate this scenario, a lot of effort has lately been made on methodologies and tools that enable the creation of a secure algorithm. Certainly, routing and Security in AmI and IoT is the most studied aspect; however, still, many issues remain open which deserves appropriate attention. Following are the open areas that attract a lot of researchers to put their work and come up with new ideas.

- Robust security solutions
- Quality of service
- Scalability
- Mobility models in active environments (such as office, war field etc.)
- Reduction of driver stress while driving (using AmI technology and IoT)
- The integration of ad hoc networks and infrastructure-based networks
- The integration of ad hoc networks and Internet Protocol (I.P.) networks
- Efficient Broadcasting schemes and coverage problems.

4.3   Security Threats and Requirements

Security and privacy are two concepts about which most security professionals from various organizations have differing viewpoints. Many of them feel that privacy and security are identical terms, while others believe that they are not and that both are necessary to secure our data. The distinction is taken from the publication [16]. To protect privacy, you must establish security. The sealed envelope is the symbol of security. The essence of privacy is the successful delivery of the message contained in the envelope.

4.3.1 Ad Hoc Network Security Threats and Requirements

As we know that ad hoc networks are infrastructure-less and they are formed on the fly without any base station. Ad hoc networks use wireless connectivity to connect devices within their own communication range. As the network is formed on the fly, it is possible that a device leaves the communication range of other devices (move out) or enters in the communication range of other devices (move-in), which results in a change of topology, and this change is all the time whenever to move in or move out happens. A consequence of this is that ad hoc networks are particularly vulnerable to attack, and security issues become incredibly hard to deal with. The use of sensor nodes in ad-hoc networks can make use of powerful devices such as laptops, but they also come with a new set of constraints to contend with. These include limited battery life, restricted processor capacity, and limited memory storage. Adversaries (intruders) may exploit a sensor network's inherent nature may be exploited by adversaries (intruders). These traits should be able to be tolerated by the method used by secure routing protocols (S.R.P.s). The perception of sensor networks can be divided into two categories: wireless sensor networks with fixed infrastructure and wireless sensor networks without fixed infrastructure. Wireless sensor networks with established infrastructure are more common. Ad hoc wireless sensor networks are examples of ad hoc wireless sensor networks, which are wireless sensor networks that do not have an established network architecture. Because of the ad hoc nature of sensor nodes, security methods are constrained in two ways. The first constraint is owing to the network's ad hoc nature, whereas the second category is due to the features of the sensor nodes. The designer must take these limits into consideration throughout the design stage in order to construct an algorithm for it. Alternatively, the designer can take current algorithms and determine which technique favours a particular component of the network, then assemble and apply the results as a new algorithm.

The following are the requirements that ad hoc networks must satisfy for maintaining Security in AmI and IoT based on their ad hoc nature.

4.3.1.1   Availability

The term "availability" relates to ensuring that network services are always available because an ad hoc network relies on each other to send messages, a rogue node could try to jam or impede the flow of data. By supplying the network with reliable information, a secure routing protocol should be able to accommodate changes in topology as well as withstand attacks from malevolent users. Router protocol adaptability is good, but no routing protocol can withstand all attacks [17–19]. This kind of attack on availability is referred to as Denial of Service attacks (DoS).

To deal with node separation in these networks requires that the network is adequately connected. Not connected to the network at the time of creation, the message is rejected, assuming nonexistence. It is also a type of availability attack caused by network disconnection.

4.3.1.2   Confidentiality

Ensuring that message sent can be understood by only intended recipients or authorized personnel. With proper authentication, we can ensure confidentiality; however, ensuring authentication is difficult but once authentication is ensured, achieving confidentiality by securing the connection with appropriate keys is not a big deal.

4.3.1.3   Integrity

Ensuring that message sent by the sender is received by the receiver without any modification. Messages in ad hoc networks may be corrupted as a result of a malicious attack or inference from radio waves on the network; this attack on integrity is known as a modification.

4.3.1.4   Key Management and Authorization

The purpose of the authorization is to verify the identification of the communication partner. Distributing keys and attaining integrity and non-repudiation are both possible with the help of public key infrastructure. Through secret key methods, nodes authenticate and create a secret session key for future communication [15, 20, 23]. These networks have concerns with trusted third-party schemes. Multiparty Diffie-Hellman key exchange with password protection can be used for ad-hoc networks' authentication.

4.3.2   Security Threats and Requirements Due to Sensing Capability in the Network

Sensor networks must meet the following requirements to ensure IoT security.

4.3.2.1   Availability

Ensuring that the necessary network services are always available. Since the sensor nodes are either directly or indirectly connected to another network sensor node through a data link. In order to conserve battery power, employ energy-saving strategies so that energy is not wasted when the gadget is not being used. Attackers or foes can interrupt network connections by sending out a powerful signal that consumes a lot of energy and eventually kills the devices [21]. A Denial of Service (DoS) attack is the technical term for the availability attack.

4.3.2.2   Confidentiality

Ensure that no one other than authorized personnel can understand the message. In a sensor network, data is wirelessly exchanged between sensor nodes within range of each other's communication ranges. Because data is exchanged across the air, a malevolent node may easily sniff it. It violates confidentiality and is referred to as interception or eavesdropping.

4.3.2.3   Integrity

Cryptography is employed in wireless sensor networks to avoid data packet tampering (modification). Hardware cryptography support improves computing efficiency while increasing system costs.

4.3.2.4   Key Distribution and Management

Direct usage of public-key cryptography is not permitted in AmI and IoT networks owing to its limited battery power, limited storage, and limited computing power. Each sensor node in this sensor-based network must establish a key with its neighbor to ensure the privacy of data relayed via multihop mode [22]. The Diffie-Hellman key agreement is unsuitable for application because of the poor computing and energy resources of sensor nodes.

4.3.2.5   Resilience to Node Capture

An attacker can easily get to the cryptographic secrets in the sensor node and replace the compromised node with a malicious node. Tamper-evident hardware can provide additional protection, but it is costly.

4.3.3   Security Threats and Requirements in AmI and IoT Based on Sensor Network

In a network with inconsistent links and limited capabilities, most of the existing security-enabled protocols are impractical. Therefore, to be efficiently applicable, all security solutions for IoT based on opportunistic sensor networks or ad hoc wireless sensor networks should be lightweight, decentralized, reactive, and fault-tolerant. The aforementioned requirements are specific to the application.

4.3.3.1   Availability

Ensuring that the network nodes are working correctly and available all the time needed. The hardware platform for IoT based on wireless sensor network comprises of embedded microcontroller, radio transceivers, batteries, and operating system. Radio transceivers are the transmission medium; an attacker may jam the network by sending high energy jam signals or with energy starvation attacks. An attacker at the physical layer can disrupt radio communications by broadcasting indefinitely. The "hidden terminal" problem, which asserts that even when a node is present, it is not accessible to the network's services, can be exploited by attackers to produce collisions. This is an attempt to disrupt service, which is also known as an outage. One solution to the "hidden terminal problem" is clear-to-send/receive (CTS/RTS) frames. As a result, the attacker can make several C.T.S. requests with extended time fields, blocking the channel. It is sabotage of availability.

IoT networks are mobile wireless networks. These networks are delay tolerant in nature. The intermittent connection is a rule here rather than an exception. It is usually assumed that there is no "continuous" sender-to-receiver path. Because the networks are considered to be very dynamic, the topology is exceedingly unstable and occasionally entirely unpredictable. An attacker may send packets that have no destinations, and those packets travel in the network, creating traffic and congestion, which results in an attack on availability on the entire network.

4.3.3.2 Confidentiality

It is possible to achieve confidentiality using any of the encryption techniques accessible. However, these encryption techniques should not be computationally costly (heavyweight), i.e., they should use less memory and less computational power. More complex methods of concealing a user's identity or location are needed to protect their privacy when using encryption alone [24]. For encryption, public-key cryptography is not a good idea because it requires a lot of computational power that in turn lowers the battery life. Many researchers are working to enhance the energy efficiency of wireless sensor networks by using public key algorithms, such as elliptical curve cryptography; however, the results are not encouraging [25–27]. For security, however, encryption using public keys from Elliptic Curve Cryptography is recommended in Gupta *et al.* [28], which uses less memory but takes longer to encode and decode. HyperElliptic Curve Cryptography saves time [29], which is ideal for military applications because communication delays are a major concern in battle. Symmetric key cryptography, although the use of these approaches to sensor networks appears promising, these protocols are vulnerable to blackmailers. Paper by Perrig *et al.* [30] demonstrates with a simulation that two protocols are designed and optimized for use in sensor networks, namely SNEP and μTESLA. SNEP ensures the confidentiality of data, two-way data authentication between parties, and data freshness [18].

4.3.3.3 Confidentiality of Location

In some cases, such as military applications, routing information is as critical as, if not more crucial than, the message content itself.

4.3.3.4 Integrity

It protects the recipient's message from being corrupted during transmission. The term "integrity" refers to two things in military applications: first, guaranteeing that the communication received is correct, and second, verifying that the sender has been verified. The former is accomplished through the use of digital signatures or one-way hashes, while the latter is accomplished through the use of trust computation.

In IoT based on sensor networks in the context of Security, attacks are classified as direct attacks and indirect attacks. To safeguard guards from direct attack, we use cryptography which is discussed above, but to safeguard from indirect attacks, i.e., attacks within the network, ensuring trust is important. Trust is the mechanism that ensures the sender's identity and helps in avoiding Sybil attacks. It is possible that any node in the network may get compromised and start sending modified messages or any intruder node may be recruited by the network as a nonintruder node and start sending/receiving the messages. Therefore, it is important not only to ensure that the message is not modified but also to ensure it comes from the authenticated node. With point-to-point communications, Sirios and Kent propose using encrypted one-way hash functions with windowed sequence numbers to assure data integrity [31]. A stronger feature known as SPINS is used to ensure data integrity [32].

4.3.3.5   Nonrepudiation

Make sure the sender cannot deny sending the message. Systems that are lightweight, decentralized, reactive, and fault-tolerant are recommended. In certain cases, this is crucial, but in others, it is not. Nonrepudiation can be relaxed, but there should be a system in place to identify the intruder node jamming. In combat (military), non-repudiation may not be as vital since if we win, there is no need to verify the origin of the communication, but if we lose, there will be no one to ask for verification of the message's source. In opportunistic sensor networks, this feature can be relaxed. Rather than focusing only on proving the origin of the message, designers should make authentication procedures so stringent that fabrication attack is avoided. Authentication is a must in military applications.

4.3.3.6   Fabrication

If there are two communication partners, namely node "A" and node "B" in an IoT based sensor network, node "A" has not sent any message to node "B" but node "B" receives the message from node "A." It is feasible that an intruder node "C" is capable of sending a message to node "A" while pretending to be node "B," i.e., node "C" is impersonating node "B." This is an authentication attack.

4.3.3.7   Intrusion Detection

Finding out which node on a network is compromised is a challenge. Hence, it is a good idea that any node in opportunistic sensor networks can operate in a model in which it does not trust any peer. The study categorizes attacks into passive and aggressive categories. Passive attacks aim to steal data from the target network's sensor nodes. For example, an attacker can eavesdrop and compromise secrecy, although encryption helps miti-gate this. Encryption and authentication can only reduce the risks of pas-sive attacks, not guarantee that the information stolen is safe [33]. Another example of passive attack is intruders may do traffic analysis or traffic monitoring, and this analysis/monitoring may reveal a lot of information in turn. An active attack generally alters the function of the network or may change the system resources with the intent of overloading the sensor node in the network. To carry out this attack, the attacker must be able to inject packets into the network (fabrication, i.e., an authentication attack), change the message (i.e., an integrity attack), message replays, message fabrication, and a denial of service attack (i.e., the attack on availability). Intrusion detection is also one of the hot topics of research in IoT-based sensor networks.

4.3.3.8   *Confidentiality*

All key-based cryptographic techniques necessitate the use of a key man-agement service (K.M.S.). It guarantees to keep track of key-to-sensor-node bindings and assists in the development of secure communication and mutual trust between sensor nodes. The majority of academics believe that public key infrastructure is preferable in terms of key distribution. Once nodes authenticate each other and to make further communication secure private key schemes are used as already mentioned in Section 4.3.3.2. However, because of resource constraints, all K.M.S. for Oppnet are not similar to conventional wireless approaches. Its primary setup approach must be authentic, secret, secure and scalable [68]. While developing a key establishing strategy for sensor nodes, the following limits must be taken into account:

- Bandwidth,
- Memory,
- Battery life,
- Prior deployment knowledge,
- Transmission range.

The evaluation metrics for efficiency in key management are as follows:

- Scalability,
- Resistance,
- Revocation, and
- Resilience.

4.3.3.9   Trust Management

Mobile users can participate in social interactions in IoT-based sensor networks. However, open interactions are banned in the military; therefore, we must discover ways to participate in interactions discreetly. Building trust in an IoT-based sensor network is critical for secure interaction. A certification authority (C.A.) establishes trust in conventional networks by utilizing a public key architecture [35]. In an ad hoc or opportunistic network, nodes are the C.A.s and must establish their own credentials and sign certificates from others [36]. The author's suggests three ways to build trust, namely social trust, environment trust and similarity trust. The abovementioned trust evaluation approach, on the other hand, concentrates on communication behavior when creating pathways while ignoring transmission activity in the detection environment. In the study of Ashif and Rahman [69], the authors present a dynamic trust evaluation technique based on the direct and indirect trust factors. The direct trust factor is calculated by multiplying the value of the communication trust factor by the value of the transmission trust factor. The indirect trust factor is derived from other node suggestions, which are classified as either safe or hazardous. It necessitates the frequent computation of confidence factors, which complicates transmission route selection. Trusts are classified as static and dynamic trust mechanisms in [37]. Static trust mechanisms create the relationship from the start of the network structure, and it cannot be changed afterwards. PolicyMaker [37] and REFEREE [38] are two instances of static trust management systems. This form of trust mechanism is unsuitable for military use. The dynamic trust assessment method [39] continues to monitor the trust assessment factor in order to quickly update the connection tie. Because trust connections can alter over time, context, and other unpredictable circumstances, dynamic trust evaluation looks to be a preferable choice for IoT-based sensor networks. As previously stated, the trust factor must be calculated many times.

4.4   Security Threats in Existing Routing Protocols that are Designed With No Focus on Security in AmI and IoT Based on Sensor Networks

Secure routing in an IoT-based sensor network is a challenge because the global topological information is not available, the development of the topology is not known, or the knowledge of the topological development is not readily available. It is possible to separate IoT-based sensor networks into two categories, depending on the routing technique that is used, namely infrastructure-less IoT-based sensor networks and infrastructure-based IoT-based sensor networks [40]. Therefore, whenever the AmI and IoT network is mentioned, it may be any one of the following classifications shown in Figure 4.1 below. Therefore, this chapter proceeds with the first existing protocols that were designed focusing only on routing without considering the security issues that intruders enjoyed with the loopholes in existing protocols; it is neither the mistake of designers nor the talent of Intruders to misuse loopholes because designers were not concerned about Security at design time. However, this chapter also throws light on the area where unintentionally designers created doors for Intruders. Next, it will

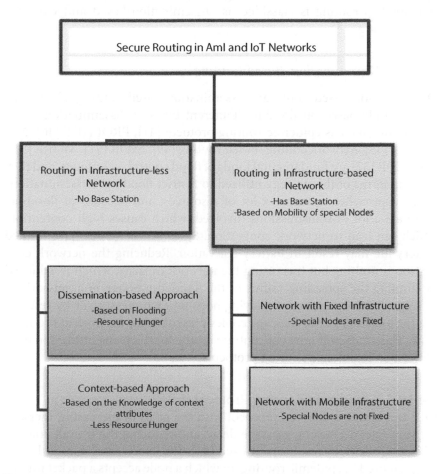

Figure 4.1 Classification of routing techniques in the network.

present the protocols that were designed, keeping the focus on security also mentioning which protocol addresses what security issues.

4.4.1   Infrastructureless

Routing in the absence of infrastructure is fully ad hoc, with all nodes equally responsible for routing and forwarding activities. Hence, we can say that an opportunistic infrastructural sensor network is an ad hoc wireless sensor network. In routing without infrastructure, the destination/target node is known directly to the source through flooding messages, or it is not directly known to the source, but rather the source knows the context attributes of the destination/target, i.e. the identity of the target is replaced by its context attributes. Depending on the above two approaches, infrastructureless routing is classified as Dissemination-based and Context-based routing.

4.4.1.1   *Dissemination-Based Routing*

Dissemination-based routing: Dissemination-based routing algorithms are generally based on flooding. Different types of dissemination-based algorithms, such as epidemic routing protocol [41], PROPHET [46], MV Routing [48], network coding–based routing [49], ExOR [51], MORE [53], and EEOR [52] are fundamental kinds of flood control techniques, and they differ in terms of the strategy utilized to restrict flooding. Dissemination-based approaches consume a lot of resources, and because of flooding, there are a lot of transmissions involved, which causes high contention, which can lead to network congestion. Since sensor nodes have limited battery life may result in battery starvation. Reducing the network congestion is nothing but increasing the network capacity, which is achieved by limiting the spreading radius of the flooded message in a network by setting a limited number of relaying hops on each message or by restricting the total number of message copies present in the network at the same time. This study will now concentrate on the mechanisms utilized in each of the aforementioned routing protocols.

4.4.1.1.1   Epidemic Routing Protocol (ERP)

ERP is a message delivery protocol with the goals of increasing message delivery rate, decreasing message delay, and reducing the overall amount of message delivery resources utilized [42]. The "store-carry-forward" paradigm is used in epidemic routing, in which a node accepts a packet into its local buffer, carries it while travelling, and then sends the packet on to the next node encountered in the epidemic network. As a result, the packets proliferate around the network in a similar manner to how viruses spread throughout the network. In order to exploit this trade-off between delivery delay and resource utilization, several variations of epidemic routing have been developed in recent years. These include K-hop systems [43], probabilistic forwarding [44], and spray-and-wait [45]. Because every node in IoT-based sensor networks is ready to forward packets for others, this ability of individual nodes may be readily misused by malevolent nodes or selfish nodes, which may result not only in a reduced ratio of packet delivery but also may be a victim of wormhole attack and bad-mouthing attack. It is an indirect attack on availability.

4.4.1.1.2   PROPHET

PROPHET: It is a probability-based network routing protocol that does not ensure the existence of a fully connected path between source and destination at any given time (such as IoT based sensor network). Messages are exchanged during pairwise interactions in these protocols, much like in epidemic routing. The mechanism for selecting a message to forward is based on the likelihood of the encountered nodes successfully delivering the messages to their final destinations. The likelihood of delivery is based on observations of node meetings [25]. PROPHET can send more messages with less communication overhead than epidemic routing [46]. PROPHET considers that nodes in the network are trustworthy and work together to forward messages. In the presence of malevolent nodes that might drastically hamper the transmission, accuracy, and timeliness of situational messages, this assumption proves to be incorrect [47]. It is regarded as a denial of service (DoS) attack against the integrity of the system.

4.4.1.1.3   MV Routing Protocol

MV Routing: Messages are also sent in this protocol for paired contacts, just like with epidemic routing. When a node makes contact with another node, the message is forwarded based on the chance that the nodes encountered will successfully deliver the message to its final destination. The delivery probability here is based on the most recent node meetings and the most recent node visits in geographic regions. It also implies that network nodes are trustworthy and cooperative in forwarding messages; however, for malicious nodes, this assumption proves to be incorrect. It is considered as a lack of trust or an attack on integrity.

4.4.1.1.4 Network Coding–Based Routing

IoT sensor networks and sensor networks based on ad-hoc wireless networks with no infrastructure can both benefit from network coding–based routing, which lowers the cost of probabilistic routing methods (IoT is a subclass of the delay-tolerant network because communication opportunities are intermittent). Congestion control and dependability are only two examples of the many difficulties that network coding has been shown to simplify and alleviate. Network coding is based on the assumption that intermediate nodes actively mix (or code) input packets before transmitting the resulting coded packets. Both the source and the intermediary nodes encode data. You will have significantly better protection against both packet and route loss by using this method. Aside from providing new and more dangerous attacks, the use of coding techniques also makes previous attacks more difficult to combat. Except for packet pollution, network coding security concerns are mainly unknown, providing intriguing potential for academics to investigate security issues [50].

4.4.1.1.5 ExOR

ExOR: The ExOR routing is bound with M.A.C. This method uses hop-by-hop routing choices for packet routing. The sender sends a batch of packets to the nodes, each with a list of priority forwarding nodes. Each node in the list buffer that hears the transmission buffers properly received packets and waits for the batch to finish. The packet is then broadcast by the highest priority forwarding node along with its batch map, which identifies the portions it has received and may thus forward. Following lower priority nodes, the remaining packets are forwarded until 90% of the packets are transmitted, at which point the remainder is sent using standard routing. The malicious node may inject superfluous packets, preventing high-priority packets from being transmitted.

4.4.1.1.6 MORE

MORE: ExOR binds the M.A.C. to the routing and defines a rigid schedule for router access to the medium. Therefore, it may underutilize the wireless medium. MORE is a MAC-independent opportunistic routing protocol. The problem is that numerous nodes can hear a packet and forward it unnecessarily. A malicious node may knowingly forward redundant packets, thereby reducing the lifetime of the network i.e. attack on availability. MORE, on the other hand, uses randomization to alleviate this problem. Before the packets are transmitted, they are combined at random.

In contrast to ExOR, it does not require a special scheduler and simply works on 802.11 [52]. Because routers that hear the same broadcast do not forward the same packet. The security threat is that a malicious node may act as a router that will drop packets without forwarding them, i.e., node selfishness attack, and the user may think that these are redundant packets that are dropped for forwarding.

4.4.1.1.7   EEOR

EEOR: With random forwarding lists and traditional distance vector routing protocols, EEOR is much lower than ExOR. Some exciting and difficult questions remain unsolved here. Creating efficient techniques for finding the optimal forwarding list for multicast and broadcast is a fascinating question. While we need to incorporate in the additional overhead of sensor nodes to agree on a unique node on the forwarding list to forward the data when numerous nodes might conceivably have received the data correctly, calculating the estimated cost appropriately becomes a difficulty [52]. This can be attacked on battery energy, which in turn attacks on availability. The security challenge here is any malicious node can act as a forwarder list and drop the packets or be flooded with packets in the network.

4.4.1.1.8   Epidemic Routing for Mobil Ad-Hoc Network Using Dijkstra's Algorithm

The purpose of this study [66] is to identify the shortest path between any two nodes so that message delivery is maximized and message delivery latency is minimized. It uses flooding. In this implementation, each node maintains generated messages and received messages tagged with unique identifiers and stores the entered messages I.D.s in a bit vector called the summary vector. As when any two nodes come in the communication range of each other, they exchange messages to update each other this process is referred to as antientropy. Since each node maintains a local buffer, exchanging messages may result in redundant connections. However, this protocol maintains a list of all recently met nodes to avoid redundant connection, but it has the following problem. As each node can independently decide whether to accept or reject messages based on buffer size, a malicious node may keep on rejecting the messages and try to overflow other nodes buffers, which may be an attack on availability or may result in a denial of service attack. This algorithm assumes sufficient buffer space and time, which is a threat to security because the threat comes from assumptions and weak points.

4.4.1.1.9   Stable Geographic Forwarding With Link Lifetime Prediction in Mobile Ad Hoc Networks for a Battlefield Environment

This paper [67] is a step to defend against an attack on availability by avoiding communication interruptions, which is a critical security problem for defense applications. Communication disruption is avoided by proposing a link stability metric (to ensure connectivity) to forward packets from a pair of communicating nodes using a distance metric (to assure continuity). In addition, this algorithm/scheme employs a backup node in addition to the next forwarding node to minimize communication disruption even if the connection is broken. This protocol is based on a greedy forwarding technique in which the source node only forwards packets to its nearest neighbor node in the destination's progress area.

As a result of the foregoing, we may infer that all of the abovementioned dissemination-based approaches are developed solely for routing purposes, with no regard for security or privacy concerns. Intruders will be able to show off their skills as a result of this. As a result, it is critical that while building routing protocols for IoT-based sensor networks, the designer considers not only routing but also security and privacy concerns.

4.4.1.2   Context-Based Routing

In an IoT-based sensor network, context-based routing is one of the protocols that does not rely on flooding and instead transfers packets from the source to the destination using contextual information or context knowledge. As a result, they use fewer system resources. Privacy is the largest threat to security in these systems. Reduced network congestion, delays, and message loss can be achieved through the use of context-based routing methods. Privacy is sacrificed for the abovementioned perks. Context-based techniques, on the other hand, are used to some extent to ensure security.

4.4.1.2.1   Context-Aware Routing (C.A.R.)

The important part of this protocol is delivery probabilities. Each network node is responsible for calculating the probability of delivery to each known destination host. They are exchanged at regular intervals so that each node may identify which carrier is most appropriate for each destination. Depending on the context's attribute information, such as battery level and degree of mobility, the best carrier is determined [20].

This context attribute information gives enough courage to the malicious node to exploit. It may find the battery level of nodes that are running short of power and start starving it.

4.4.1.2.2   MobySpace Routing

MobySpace Routing: MobySpace routing, like C.A.R. routing, requires complete information or the knowledge of all possible destinations in order to fulfill the forwarding [54]. This knowledge of nodes context is a threat to security and privacy.

4.4.1.2.3   The History-Based Opportunistic Routing Protocol

In this protocol, it is not required for all nodes to be aware of one another. In HiBOP, each node remembers context information that they have got from previous interactions in touch. When using HiBOP, the delivery probability is estimated based on whether or not the context information about the destination contained in a message matches the context information kept by the encountered node [55, 56]. This routing protocol also lacks in privacy if the concept of community is not implemented, as context information can be seen by any node while interaction and the malicious node may only interact to extract the context information to use it in tampering with the network connectivity. The good news is that it enforces privacy by including the notion of community. This protocol assumes that exposing context information to the same community is not a security threat. Therefore, it tries to select the intermediate node only from the same community, but the threat here is that only a limited forwarder will be selected. Clearly, such a security mechanism will have a negative impact on routing performance [64].

4.4.2   Infrastructure-Based

Unlike in traditional sensor networks, where messages are routed on the basis of flooding, in IoT-based sensor networks, a particular infrastructure is responsible for routing messages on the basis of opportunity. Due to the presence of a fixed base station, there is intermittent connectivity here, but not ad hoc. Because they have a bigger energy budget and storage capacity than conventional network nodes, infrastructure-based network nodes are more powerful than typical network nodes. Opportunistic networks can be divided into two types depending on node mobility: fixed infrastructure and mobile infrastructure. For example, in the first situation, certain nodes are immovable and stuck in place. Depending on the situation, special nodes move across a network in predefined or random paths.

4.4.2.1   Network with Fixed Infrastructure

A base station is a special type of fixed node that is found in a network with a fixed infrastructure. Based on their geographic location, base stations are used to gather messages from the network. When the source node is within range of the base station, the message is forwarded to that node. This process is repeated for every message sent to a destination node. Base stations act as entry points, making it easier to locate the desired location after you have reached it. Asynchronous and synchronous protocols can be used in an opportunistic network with fixed infrastructure.

4.4.2.1.1   Protocol 1
The sender node desires to send a message to the destination node but must first reah the base station. The base station sends data to the destination node. It is used in the Infostation model [57].

4.4.2.1.2   Protocol 2
The sender node intends to send a message to the destination node. If the transmitter node is within range of the base station, if the sender node is not connected to the base station, it sends a message to a neighboring node, which relays it to the base station, which then delivers it to the target node. One such protocol is Shared Wireless Infostation Model (SWIM) [58].

4.4.2.2   New Routing Strategy for Wireless Sensor Networks
to Ensure Source Location Privacy

A static sensor plus a base station make up this system [68]. All static sensors have the same communication, processing, storage, and energy capabilities. Sensor nodes interact with one another using the symmetric key system, and private keys are preloaded onto sensors prior to deployment. Because the attacker's listening radius coincides with the communication radius of the sensors, the attacker cannot compromise Confidentiality. Base station flood operation enables each sensor node to report the shortest possible hop from node to base station. It employs a three-stage routing technique that promotes source location anonymity by dispersing packet delivery among zigzag routing pathways. Because power consumption is directly proportional to the number of hops, when packets travel more hops, they may consume more energy.

The sensor network with mobile nodes: When a new node joins an AmI or IoT network with fixed infrastructure, expanding the infrastructure is a costly business. Therefore, the use of a mobile infrastructure instead of a permanent infrastructure offers an enormous opportunity to create a cost-effective, adaptable infrastructure. Carriers or supporters, freight forwarders, MULEs, or even ferries are called the special nodes [59].

4.4.2.2.1 Protocol 1

It is the responsibility of the special node to ensure that messages are delivered when only node-to-carrier communication is permitted.

4.4.2.2.2 Protocol 2

The responsibility of delivering a message to the destination is on a special node or ordinary nodes. The types of communications allowed in this protocol are node-to-node or node-to-carrier.

AmI and IoT networks relying on fixed infrastructure are vulnerable to fabrication because of a lack of authentication (attack on authentication). The malicious node may join the network or may hire a helper, which is a malicious node, due to a lack of initial authentication. Another challenge is that we cannot guarantee that a malicious node may not join the network. If it joins, we cannot rate the device as malicious until we detect its notorious behavior. MITM, packet dropping, I.D. Spoofing (masqueradation), DoS, and other attacks are even more dangerous [59].

4.5 Protocols Designed for Security Keeping Focus on Security at Design Time for AmI and IoT Based on Sensor Network

4.5.1 Secure Routing Algorithms

4.5.1.1 Identity-Based Encryption (I.B.E.) Scheme

It is a fully operational identity-based encryption approach that is based on a natural approximation of the Diffie-Hellman assumption. It employs basic threshold cryptography methods to ensure that the master key is never available in a single location. The fundamental identity-based encryption technique provided by the author here is not safe against adaptive chosen-ciphertext attacks. In the random oracle model, another variant of I.B.E. is the concrete functional identity-based scheme or completely functional identity-based system that has selected ciphertext security. Building chosen-ciphertext-safe identity-based systems that are secure in the conventional computational model rather than the random oracle model is an open problem [60]. The primary advantage of this method is that a node's public key serves as the node's identification, and the node does need not know the destination public key to send an encrypted message [61].

4.5.1.2   Policy-Based Cryptography and Public Encryption with Keyword Search

Privacy-preserving context-based forwarding [62]: It employs two types of ID-based cryptography refinements: Policy-based cryptography and Public Encryption with Keyword Search (PEKS). In context-based forwarding, if the context of the destination is known, then there will be no privacy; therefore, to guarantee destination privacy, the intermediate node should be able to find the matching characteristics with the destination while not learning any other attributes related to a destination or any other further information on other attributes [62]. PEKS allows an intermediary node to seek a match on encrypted data if the node contains a trapdoor that has been modified. The node learns nothing except whether or not a match happened [61]. In PEKS to avoid giving private key to the destination, the destination is replaced with trusted third party (TTP). TTP computes the trapdoor for authorized nodes. TTP cannot be accessed by nodes except during the setup phase since TTP only has to be called once before nodes join the network and are offline during the operation, which is appropriate for the opportunistic network.

4.5.1.3   Secure Content-Based Routing

In this networking, the sender and receiver are completely decoupled. In this type of communication, receivers advertise their interests and messages are simply published by senders without a destination specified. Since advertisements and published contents are simply forwarded by the intermediate nodes that may not be trusted by advertisers and publishers moreover, receivers do not want any untrusted node to know its interest for security and privacy reasons. However, the intermediate node should be able to build a routing table using encrypted advertisements and be able to forward the encrypted content correctly using forwarding tables.

To achieve this, a goal multiple-layer commutative encryptions (MLCE) technique is used. The concept behind MLCE is that receivers advertise their encrypted advertisements with r layers based on the following r hops using r distinct keys. As previously stated, the sender also discloses the encrypted message. To create their routing table, the intermediary node N can remove just one layer of encryption, and data is always secured by r-1 layers. The intermediate node N adds a new encryption layer that corresponds to the rth next-hop without destroying the other levels [63].

4.5.1.4   Secure Content-Based Routing Using Local Key Management Scheme

Secure content-based routing using local key management scheme: In the abovementioned protocol, the problem of key management is overlooked. The problem is addressed with topology dependent key management. It uses a local self-organized mechanism that prevents sybil attacks. Identity manager (IM) plays a very important role here. I.M. is a lightweight security server that generates a key on the fly. Only during the setup phase node contact I.M., but during network operation, I.M. is offline [14]. Despite the lack of end-to-end connection, a local key agreement mechanism achieves end-to-end secrecy.

4.5.1.5   Trust Framework Using Mobile Traces

Mobile traces are being used to generate trust for data forwarding in opportunistic networks [64]. This article describes a trust framework for opportunistic networks using the trace-based mobility paradigm. The next-hop to which data packets are routed is determined by the node's trust value and its direction towards the destination. The data forwarding node's trust mechanism determines the trust value. In this context, a trust value is the same as human trust. The network nodes' movement trace files are used to establish the destination direction. The message is encrypted in this design to secure both the data and the route. Article [64] uses simulation to show the proposed framework's efficacy.

4.5.1.6   Policy-Based Authority Evaluation Scheme

To address the prevalent issue of data recipients' lack of confidence and concern about their privacy, the Policy-Based Authority Evaluation Scheme (PAES) was developed. To gain access to the information, recipients must provide their credentials to a policy evaluation authority they have no control over and may not be able to trust. The data may also be unavailable to recipients if their internet connection is unstable or if they have been unplugged. Data security and policy evaluation were combined in PAES, a Policy-based Authority Evaluation Scheme [68], to address these issues. It guarantees data secrecy, but it may be a target of a DoS assault.

4.5.1.7   Optimized Millionaire's Problem

The essential method suggested in the paper [70] is an extension of the well-known protocol for solving the Millionaire's problem, which allows determining if user interests regarding a specific topic are comparable enough without exposing their private interest value. If Alice is interested in books, she sets her interest profile, turns on the WiFi/Bluetooth interface, and starts walking when another device discover an interest in the same topic they share knowledge [70]. It employs a privacy-preserving interest-casting primitive, which is described as a set of N users, and whenever any user S creates a Message M, the message must be given to all nodes in the set with comparable interest topics provided the relevance threshold is fulfilled. Thanks to the protocol using Millionaire's problem, collusion attack is avoided, and according to the author, this attack was not considered so far in the Opponents.

4.5.1.8   Security in Military Operations

Wireless Sensor Network Security in Military Operations [71]: The primary goal of the work [71] is to offer effective security for military applications by deploying sensor nodes. The session key serves as the foundation for the whole cryptography approach. Elliptic Curve Cryptography is used in this security approach (E.C.C.). This is a kind of public-key cryptosystem. When compared to the R.S.A. cryptography approach, it gives the same degree of Security. E.C.C. has a key length of 160 bits, which is quite short when compared to R.S.A. When employing E.C.C., communication overhead is decreased, costs are lowered, and deployment is simplified. It addresses problems to node capturing, node replication and various other attacks [71].

4.5.1.9   A Security Framework Application Based on Wireless Sensor Networks

A Military Security Framework for infrastructure-based wireless sensor networks [3]: The numerous cryptographic techniques used for security are described in depth in this work. The study [3] focuses on achieving the necessary level of Security in Wireless Sensor Networks. It covers the mode of operation, M.A.C. address, and key management. The chosen cryptographic algorithm is MISTY 1, with a key size of 128 bits. Because utilizing this with A.E.S. takes so long, the M.A.C. chose to utilize HMAC with MD5 as a hashing method. The trustworthy base station, which has numerous authentication keys, is used to manage keys. Because the number of keys is determined by the key length, the memory capacity can be lowered in this case. Data confidentiality, data integrity, and data authentication are all major criteria that are being handled [28].

4.5.1.10   Trust Evaluation Using Multifactor Method

Dynamic Trust Evaluation of Wireless Sensor Networks Based on Multifactor [69]: The trust factor for each node is evaluated to offer security. In this case, the trust factor is calculated using direct and indirect trust. The communication trust element and the transmission trust factor combine to form direct trust. The suggestions of other nodes provide an indirect trust factor. On combining both the direct trust and indirect trust, the weights of each node change dynamically. It requires the repeated computation of the trust factor. Here the security is maintained, but in case many numbers of nodes actively participate, then it becomes difficult to estimate the trust factor for each node and then they have to select the path for transmission. Thus, the trust mechanism addresses the problem that arises from insider attacks [69].

4.5.1.11   Prevention of Spoofing Attacks

Prevention of Spoofing Attacks in Wireless Networks [72]: The prevention of spoofing attacks is illustrated in the paper [72], which focuses on two primary processes, including the attackers' ignorance of data requests and the server's traffic reduction. By estimating the Received Signal Strength parameter, the attacker nodes may be identified. After that, the k-means method is used to cluster the data. The Generalized Attack Detection approach uses the RSS value to identify attacker nodes. An intermediate dummy node is used to choose the path for packet delivery. The selection of dummy nodes is to overcome the attackers if present in the path. Thus, it addresses identity compromise and injection attacks [72].

4.5.1.12 QoS Routing Protocol

Quality-of-Service Routing Protocol for Wireless Sensor Networks [73]: Routing is the main focus of this paper, which is completely based on the quality of service in the network. This paper proposed a new algorithm, namely high quality of service routing (HQSR). This algorithm focuses on predicting the near optimal path with reduced energy consumption and maintained reliability. The proposed routing algorithm is based on the estimation of the reliability of the selected path. If high reliability, then the packet transmission will be effective, and so the path with high reliability is selected. The algorithm proposed here improves the lifetime of wireless sensor nodes [73].

4.5.1.13 Network Security Virtualization

The first step toward Network Security Virtualization: From Concept to Prototype [65]: From Concept to Prototype: A First Step towards Network Security Virtualization [65]: This study introduces four distinct techniques for secure packet transmission and route selection. This paper's suggestion begins with the network's security device selection. The first algorithm starts packet transmission after selecting all accessible pathways. The second approach, which is a bit simpler, transmits packets along all possible shortest pathways. The shortest pathways are then chosen, together with the existence of a security device, in the third method, and the packets are then transferred. Finally, in the final process, the packets are sent via the single path that the security device is available on, as well as the shortest way that is accessible. However, each of the four methods described has its own set of drawbacks when it comes to performance.

4.5.2 Comparison of Routing Algorithms and Impact on Security

We compare all the algorithms discussed in Section 4.5.1 and mention routing approaches used by them in tabular form Table 4.1, followed by the techniques used in the algorithms and mentioning security achievements or security gaps.

In Table 4.1, routing protocols and the approach used in the routing protocol is listed. The above table also shows the level of Security achieved by the different techniques as well as security loopholes if exists. All the algorithms/protocols in Table 4.1 above are listed in chronological order.

Table 4.1 Techniques and approaches for routing and their impact on security.

Routing approach	Technique	Security remarks
HYBRID (2018) [76]	It uses the PPHH protocol. This model is discussed in detail in section 4.6.	- Malicious node is detected (secured) - Less packet overhead (with stand Denial of Service attack) - Low energy consumption (Achieved availability) - High reliability
Dissemination-based Approach (2016) [67]	- It employs a mechanism that avoids interruption if the communication channel is steady. - It makes use of two metrics: link stability and distance. - Makes use of a greedy forwarding mechanism	- Defend against a denial-of-service attack, i.e., no downtime. A hostile node may enter the advancing region and promise connection and continuity due to the greedy forwarding mechanism, but this protocol has no means for distinguishing the untrusted node.
Dissemination-based Approach (2016) [66]	- Using Dijkstra's Algorithm, a buffer named as summary vector keeps track of received and inputted messages. - Using anti-entropy and flooding techniques	- Install a flaky mechanism to prevent redundant attacks that could result in a denial-of-service attack, which is a type of availability attack.
Fixed Infrastructure (2015) [3]	- MISTY1 is the cryptographic algorithm utilized. - HMAC with MD5 is used for the hashing function - Counter (C.T.R.) is the block cypher mode	- Data Integrity and Authentication are handled as primary security needs. - Proposed distributed key management approach.

(Continued)

Table 4.1 Techniques and approaches for routing and their impact on security. (*Continued*)

Routing approach	Technique	Security remarks
Fixed Infrastructure (2015) [69]	- The Direct and Indirect trust factors are used to calculate the trustworthiness of nodes. - The Direct Trust Factor is made up of two components: transmission and communication. - An indirect trust factor based on neighbor recommendations.	This increases network packet overhead, regarded as necessary for network security.
Mobile Infrastructure (2015) [72]	- Allow the server to communicate with the users via a dummy node. - To identify attackers, the K-Means Algorithm and GADE (Generalized Attack Detection Model) are used. - IDOL detects and locates attackers (Integrated Detection and Localization System)	- Detection and prevention of M.A.C. spoofing attacks. - Avoid injection attacks caused by compromised identity.
Fixed Infrastructure (2015) [73]	- The HQRA (High Quality of Service Routing Algorithms) algorithm is employed.	- Assuring a certain level of reliability. - Minimizes energy to find near-optimal pathways in W.S.N.s. As a result, the network lifetime is extended, resulting in increased availability.

(*Continued*)

Table 4.1 Techniques and approaches for routing and their impact on security. (*Continued*)

Routing approach	Technique	Security remarks
Fixed Infrastructure (2015) [65]	- NETSECVISOR, a new prototype system, is being implemented, and four algorithms are being used.	- If a host or virtual machine is discovered as malicious, it can be isolated.
Fixed Infrastructure (2013) [28]	Pre-key distribution Scheme for Public Key Cryptography	- Node capture resiliency - Doesn't allow nodes duplication. - Anti-replay attack protection, and much more.
Context based (2012) [70]	- Developing an interest-casting mechanism that does not divulge any sensitive data.	- Prevents collusion attacks - Ensures privacy
Controlled flooding using the trust threshold idea is used in dissemination-based research (2012) [64]	- Source, destination, and seed nodes all have access to the same secret key for Encryption and decryption.. - A trust-value-based trace-based mobility model. - Trust value is obtained from the trust framework; mobility, or the movement of nodes toward their destinations, is assessed using the trace files maintained by network nodes.	- Data is safe - The path is safe - Confidentiality has been achieved
Context-Based forwarding (2010) [62]	TTP is used to implement policy-based cryptography and Public Encryption with Keyword Search (PEKS) (Trusted third party)	- Allows context-based forwarding while maintaining privacy.

(*Continued*)

Table 4.1 Techniques and approaches for routing and their impact on security. (*Continued*)

Routing approach	Technique	Security remarks
Context based (2010) [68]	Authority Evaluation and key distribution	- Provides Confidentiality to disseminate data - May have been a victim of a Dos attack.
Context-Based forwarding (2010) [8]	Local Key Management (L.K.M.) and multiple-layer commutative encryption (MLCE) approaches are employed.	- Allows for content-based routing, which protects recipients' privacy. - There will be no Sybil attack.
Context-Based forwarding (2009) [63]	M.L.C. methods (multiple layer commutative encryptions) are utilized.	- Allows for content-based routing, which protects receiver privacy. - The victim of Sybil's attack.
Context Based (2008/2007/ 2006) [20, 54, 55]	Based on Context, Attribute information	- Priority was given to routing rather than Security. - HiBOP enforces privacy if the community idea is implemented.
Dissemination Based (2005/2003/ 2000) [42, 46, 49]	Based on Flooding	- Routing was prioritized over Security. - Suffers from resource hunger technique
Can be used in Opportunistic network with Fixed Infrastructure (2001) [60]	Uses Identity-Based Encryption	- It inhibits context-based forwarding while also establishing an end-to-end secure connection between the source and destination.

4.5.3 Inducing Intelligence in IoT Networks Using Artificial Intelligence

The research community is aggressively pursuing the objective of clustering sensor nodes in order to increase the network's scalability. A leader, sometimes known as a cluster head, would be assigned to each cluster (C.H.). Fuzzy logic is utilized to make the system smarter. The focus was on fuzzy logic-based clustering methods for lowering resource consumption (energy) and extending network life. Brief information about fuzzy logic is shown in Table 4.2.

4.5.3.1 Fuzzy Logic-1

Fuzzy logic [74] is utilized to make the system smarter. The focus was on fuzzy logic-based clustering methods for lowering resource consumption (energy) and extending network life. For the clustering process, fuzzy logic was built using the LEACH protocol. All sensor nodes were presumed to be static in this technique, while B.S. was assumed to be a mobile node. C.H. was chosen based on fuzzy logic in each phase of clustering. As membership functions in the fuzzy system, residual energy, mobility, and centrality

Table 4.2 Fuzzy-logic in clustering sensor nodes.

Existing work	Objective	Parameters	Drawback
Fuzzy logic [34]	Efficiency in energy usage	Energy, Mobility, Centrality.	Uncertainty affects the Fuzzy-1 system. Only static nodes should be used.
Fuzzy-2 logic [89]	To make the fuzzy-1 system better	Energy, Distance with B.S., Concentration of node.	Because to the standby C.H., energy consumption is significant.

were employed. C.H. was chosen as a node with high residual energy and near centrality. By integrating C.H. rotation and optimum C.H. selection, this approach enhances network lifespan. However, for C.H. selection, a type 1 fuzzy method is employed. In the presence of noise, the Fuzzy one system has poor efficiency. As a result, the fundamental goal of this technique, C.H. selection, is ineffective.

4.5.3.2   Fuzzy Logic-2

To solve the shortcomings of type-1 fuzzy system-based C.H. selection, a type 2 fuzzy logic system-based C.H. selection approach was presented. The residual energy of the node, the distance between the node and the B.S., and the node's concentration were employed as membership functions in fuzzy logic. The function of type 2 fuzzy logic was defined as follows [75]:

$$Type2FL = PrincipalMF(Type1FL) + FOU$$

FOU stands for footprint of uncertainty in this case. Fuzzifier, fuzzification module, type reducer, and knowledge base were among the four components of the type 2 fuzzy system. When the energy level of C.H. was lowered, this approach chose standby C.H. to spin C.H. Even this technique uses type 2 logic to deal with uncertainty. This technique is unable to take into account all relevant parameters for C.H. selection. The energy consumption of standby C.H. has been considerable since it was first selected.

This section discusses the security threats and requirements for routing protocols, as well as how secure routing in AmI and IoT is classified based on the sensor network and the variables that impact it. We discuss the security flaws in a few of the approaches utilized because they are not concerned with privacy and secure routing. It is possible to design a new security protocol based on existing approaches or to leverage existing infrastructure to recommend improvements to the security framework that are domain-specific for our application. The material in this part can assist researchers in developing a deeper grasp of the problem and motivate them to seek out the most effective solutions. For the next stage of study and modeling, the system in accordance with security criteria, we can consider integrating infrastructure-based and infrastructure-less solutions into a unified framework. Additionally, it aids researchers in understanding that sustaining network security requires designers to think from the outset, defining what the system requires and then combining the protocols that best meet the requirements. It is not realistic to rely solely on infrastructure-based or infrastructure-free strategies to meet actual difficulties; rather, a combination of the two approaches may yield promising results. This hybrid model is introduced in Section 4.6.

4.6   Introducing Hybrid Model in Military Application for Enhanced Security

In this model, a hybrid approach is presented, in which normal sensor nodes (light blue color in the Figure 4.2 below) and security nodes

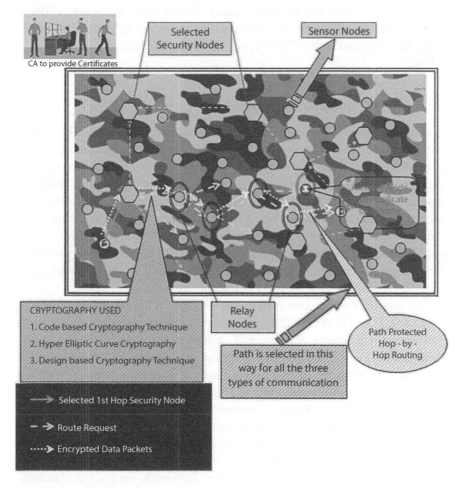

Figure 4.2 System architecture [76].

(yellow color) stationary (infrastructure-based). Total of 50 sensor nodes are taken for simulation and 4 security nodes.

4.6.1   Overall System Architecture

In military application, the troops and commandos defend their whole country in the country's border and the communication between authorities should be maintained secure which means it demands high secrecy to transmit data from one person to another. Routing across the nodes should also be focused, and so, the data will reach destination successfully within the time.

As indicated in Section 4.6, there are two types of nodes in the network: security nodes and mobility nodes. The security nodes are yellow in color and are fixed/immovable. The mobile nodes are light blue in hue. As a result of the existence of both types of nodes, the system architecture is hybrid.

4.6.2   Best Candidate Selection

In order to build a safe network, routing should be followed by secure path selection with trustworthy nodes. The present suggested approach in wireless Ad-hoc sensor networks for secure route selection and data transfer across the Military application. Because the network is made up of sensor nodes that are deployed without any centralized authority, it is referred to as a Wireless Ad-hoc Sensor Network. Communication takes place between Commando to Commando (CC), Soldier to Soldier (SS), and Commando to Soldier (C.S.). Then, for path selection, we provide a Path Protected Hop-by-Hop Routing Protocol and three different cryptographic techniques for security maintenance.

Path selection is based on Path Protected Hop-by-Hop Routing Protocol, which selects the best candidate by verifying the availability of Certificate provided by Certificate Authority (C.A.), minimum distance and higher residual Energy. Working of this protocol starts with the selection of the first-hop security node by the source node. Then the node which satisfies these constraints will be selected as a relay node. In this way, relay nodes are selected until Route Request reaches the destination. After reaching the destination, all the selected nodes with these three constraints are replied to the selected security node. The selected security node verifies whether the certificate is original or fake then further calculates the reliability of the path. Each relay node selects its best next-hop node for packet transmission. Since each hop selects their next hop, this routing is said to be hop by hop routing. The selected path details are verified by the security node; if any attacker presents with a duplicate certificate, then that node is revoked from the path. Details can be seen from [76] for better understanding.

4.6.3   Simulation Results in Omnet++

The simulation results show that this hybrid approach is far superior to the existing approach in terms of throughput, reliability, packet delivery ratio, and energy consumption. The security nodes are made intelligent by A.I. with human intervention to secure the network. The model also detects the malicious node in the network if any node has no certificate.

Throughput is defined as the total number of packets delivered successfully to each individual intended destination in a given period of time over the communication channel (as shown in Figure 4.3).

As shown in Figure 4.4, the packet delivery ratio is calculated by dividing the number of packets transmitted by the number of packets received by the node at the time of transmission. This performance metric shows the maximum amount of data transfer that the network is capable of delivering.

As shown in Figure 4.5, the sensor nodes' involvement in the network is sustained by energy, which is a significant characteristic for each node. Because this type of network has sensor nodes that demand energy for sensing, this measure should be decreased. To increase network performance, energy consumption should be decreased.

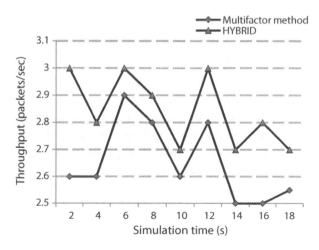

Figure 4.3 Comparisons on throughput [76].

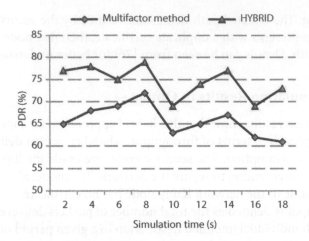

Figure 4.4 Comparative analysis on P.D.R. [76].

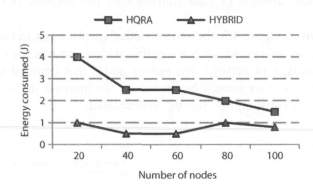

Figure 4.5 Consumption of energy comparative analysis [76].

There are security nodes as well as mobility nodes in Figure 4.6. We have no knowledge of which node in a mobile network is malicious. Some nodes have a red cross on them, indicating that they are attacking nodes. The certificate was verified using the PPHH protocols, which revealed that nodes 10 and 19 are malicious nodes.

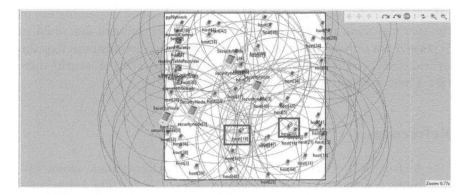

Figure 4.6 Malicious nodes 10 and 19 are found correctly.

4.7   Conclusion

This chapter presents security threats and requirements for routing protocols and clearly classifies secure routing in AmI and IoT based on sensor networks and factors that influence it. It also discusses approaches for infrastructure-less networks, as well as techniques for infrastructure-based networks, all with an eye toward privacy and safe routing as a priority. A few of the strategies employed are not concerned with privacy or safe routing, and in this section, we discuss the security gaps that exist. It is possible to design a new security protocol on the basis of existing techniques or to recommend certain adjustments to exist security frameworks in order to fit security achievements to our application area. As a result of the information offered in this chapter, researchers may obtain significant insight into the subject, which may also act as a motivator to find the best answers. For future research and modeling of the system, readers may wish to consider integrating infrastructure-based and infrastructure-less approaches into a single framework that can be customized to match their unique security requirements. Additionally, it directs researchers' thinking in the direction that imposing Security on a network needs designers to evaluate the network's origins, identify the requirements for developing the system, and then integrate the protocols that meet those requirements. However, it is not realistic to rely exclusively on infrastructure-based or infrastructure-free solutions to address practical issues; a combination of the two may yield promising outcomes. The hybrid model described in Section 6 not only verifies our conclusion but also demonstrates that the hybrid model outperforms earlier methodologies in terms of security metrics, a noteworthy accomplishment.

References

1. Arafath, M.S., Khan, K.U.R., Sunitha, K.V.N., Opportunistic sensor networks: A survey on privacy and secure routing. *2017 2nd IEEE International Conference on Anti-Cyber Crimes (ICACC)*, 26-27 March 2017, IEEE, pp. 41–46.
2. Cook, D.J., Augusto, J.C., Jakkula, V.R., Ambient intelligence: Technologies, applications, and opportunities. *Pervasive Mob. Comput.*, 5, 4, 277–298, 2009, ISSN 1574-1192, https://doi.org/10.1016/j.pmcj.2009.04.001.
3. Roy, S. and Nene, M.J., A security framework for military application on infrastructure based wireless sensor network. *IEEE International Conference on Research in Computational Intelligence and Communication Networks*, pp. 369–376, 2015.
4. Raghavendran, C.H.V., Security challenges and attacks in mobile ad hoc networks. *I.J. Inf. Eng. Electron. Bus.*, 3, 49–58, 2013, Published Online September 2013 in MECS (http://www.mecs-press.org/) doi: 10.5815/ijieeb.2013.03.06.
5. Zhou, L. and Haas, Z., Securing ad hoc networks. *IEEE Network*, November/December 1999.
6. Xiao, Y., Rayi, V.K., Sun, B., Du, X., Hu, F., Galloway, M., A survey of key management schemes in wireless sensor networks. *Comput. Commun.*, 30, 11–12, 2314–2341, 2007.
7. Lilien, L., Gupta A., Yang, Z., Opportunistic networks for emergency applications and their framework, *2007 IEEE International Performance, Computing, and Communications Conference*, pp. 588-593, 2007.
8. Shikfa, A., Önen, M., Molva, R., Bootstrapping security associations in opportunistic networks. *2010 8th IEEE International Conference on Pervasive Computing and Communications Workshops (PERCOM Workshops)*, Mannheim, pp. 147–152, 2010, doi: 10.1109/PERCOMW.2010.5470676.
9. Clausen, T. and Jacquet, P. (Eds.), Optimized link state routing protocol, IETF RFC3626, 2003, https://datatracker.ietf.org/doc/rfc3626/.
10. Perkins, C., Belding-Royer, E., Das, S., Ad hoc On-Demand Distance Vector (AODV) routing July 2003, RFC 3561, https://datatracker.ietf.org/doc/html/rfc3561.
11. Jacquet, P., Opportunistic routing in wireless ad hoc networks: Upper bounds for the packet propagation speed, *IEEE, 2008.*

12. Biswas, S. and Morris, R., Exor: Opportunistic multi-hop routing for wireless networks, in: *Proceedings SIGCOMM 05*, New York, 2005.
13. Baccelli, F., Blaszczyszyn, B., Muhlethaler, P., On the performance of time-space opportunistic routing in multihop mobile ad hoc networks. *Wiopt*, 2008.
14. Blum, B., He, T., Son, S., Stankovic, J., IGF: A state-free robust communication protocol for wireless sensor networks, 2003, http://citeseerx.ist.psu.edu/viewdoc/download?doi=10.1.1.12.2828&rep=rep1&type=pdf
15. Sánchez-Cid, F., Maña, A., Spanoudakis, G., Kloukinas, C., Serrano, D., Muñoz, A., Representation of security and dependability solutions, chapter 2, in: *Security and Dependability for Ambient Intelligence*, pp. 69–95, 2009.
16. Herold, R., What is the difference between security and privacy, Information Sheild, this article was previously published in the C.S.I., Alert newsletter, July 2002, https://privacyguidance.com/downloads/PrivacyandSecurity-Herold.pdf.
17. Zhou, L. and Haas, Z., Securing ad hoc networks. *IEEE Network*, November/December 1999.
18. Deng, H., Li, W., Agrawal, D.P., Routing security in ad hoc networks. *IEEE Commun. Mag.*, 40, 10, 70–75, October 2002.
19. Zhou, L., Securing ad hoc networks. *IEEE Network Issue*, Special Issue on Network Security, November/December 1999.
20. Anastasi, G., Conti, M., Passarella, A., Pelusi, L., Mobile-relay forwarding in opportunistic networks, chapter 13, in: *Adaptation and Cross Layer Design in Wireless Networks*, M. Ibnkahla (Ed.), C.R.C. Press, New York (U.S.A.), August 2008.
21. Stajano, F. and Anderson, R., The resurrecting duckling: Security issues for ad-hoc wireless networks. *7th International Workshop on Security Protocols LNCS*, Springer-Verlag, 1999.
22. *Ad Hoc and Sensor networks Theory and Applications*, March, 2006, Pages: 664 Carlos de Morais Cordeiro (Intel Corporation, USA) and Dharma Prakash Agrawal (University of Cincinnati, USA), https://doi.org/10.1142/6044.
23. Demers, A., Shenker, S., Bhargavan, V., Zhang, L., Macaw: A media access protocol for wireless LANs, in: *A.C.M. SigComm 94*, 1994.
24. Raghavendran, C.H.V., Security challenges and attacks in mobile ad hoc networks. *I.J. Inf. Eng. Electron. Bus.*, 3, 49–58, 2013, Published Online September 2013 in MECS.
25. Guido, B., Breveglieri, L., Venturi, M., Power aware design of an elliptic curve coprocessor for 8-bit platforms, in: *Fourth IEEE Annual Conference on Pervasive Computing and Communications Workshops*, pp. 337–342, 2006.
26. Malan, D.J., Welsh, M., Smith, M.D., A public-key infrastructure for key distribution in TinyOS based on elliptic curve cryptography, in: *First Annual IEEE Communications Society Conference on Sensor and Ad Hoc Communications and Networks*, pp. 71–80, 2004.

27. Piotrowski, K., Langendoerfer, P., Peter, S., How public key cryptography influences wireless sensor node lifetime, in: *The Fourth A.C.M. Workshop on Security of Ad Hoc and Sensor Networks*, pp. 169–176, 2006.

28. R. Gupta, K. Sultania, P. Singh and A. Gupta, Security for wireless sensor networks in military operations, *2013 Fourth International Conference on Computing, Communications Networking Technologies (ICCCNT)*, pp. 1-6, 2013.

29. Wankhede-Barsgade, M.T. and Meshram, S.A., Comparative study of elliptic and hyperelliptic curve cryptography in discrete logarithmic problem. *IOSR J. Math.*, 10, 2, 61–63, 2014.

30. Perrig, A., Szewczyk, R., Wen, V., Culler, D., Tygar, J., SPINS: Security protocols for sensor networks, in: *Proceedings of Mobile Networking and Computing 2001*, 2001.

31. Perrig, A., Szewczyk, R., Wen, V., Culler, D., Tygar, J., SPINS: Security protocols for sensor networks, in: *Proceedings of Mobile Networking and Computing 2001*, 2001.

32. Perrig, A., Security protocols for sensor networks, in: *Proceeding of the 7th Annual International Conference on Mobile Computing and Networks (MOBICOM)*, July 2001, pp. 189–199.

33. Bouam, S. and Othman, J.B., Data security in ad hoc networks using multipath routing, in: *Proc. of the 14th IEEE PIMRC*, pp. 1331–1335. Sept. 7-10, 2003.

34. Xiao, Y., Rayi, V.K., Sun, B., Du, X., Hu, F., Galloway, M., A survey of key management schemes in wireless sensor networks. *Comput. Commun.*, 30, 11–12, 2314–2341, 2007.

35. Patra, R.K., Raja, R., Sinha, T.S., Extraction of geometric and prosodic features from human-gait-speech data for behavioural pattern detection: Part II. *First International Conference on Advanced Computational and Communication Paradigms (ICACCP) will be held at Sikkim Manipal Institute of Technology (SMIT)*, Majitar, Rangpo, East Sikkim, Sikkim-737136, during 08-10 September 2017, ICACCP, 2017.

36. Trifunovic, S. and Legendre, F., Trust in opportunistic network, Computer Engineering and Networks Laboratory, TIK Report 318.

37. Blaze, M., Feigenbaum, J., Lacy, J., Decentralized trust management, in: *Proceedings of the 17th Symp on Security and Privacy*, pp. 164–173, IEEE Computer Society Press, Oakland, 1996.

38. Chu, Y.H., Feigenbaum, J., LaMacchia, B., Resnick, P., Strauss, M., REFEREE: Trust management for Web applications. *Comput. Netw. ISDN Syst.*, 2, 127–139, 1997.

39. Marsh, S.P., *Formalizing trust as a computational concept*, University of Stirling, Stirling, 1994.

40. Pelusi, L., Passarella, A., Conti, M., Opportunistic networking: Data forwarding in disconnected mobile ad hoc networks. *IEEE Commun. Mag.*, November 2006.

41. Vahdat, A. and Becker, D., Epidemic routing for partially connected ad hoc networks, Tech. Rep. CS-2000-06, Department of Computer Science, Duke University, Durham, NC, 2000.

42. Vahdat, A. and Becker, D., Epidemic routing for partially connected ad hoc networks, Technical Report CS-2000-06, Department of Computer Science, Duke University, April 2000, (Technical Report), Available online http://citeseerx.ist.psu.edu/viewdoc/summary?

43. Groenevelt, R., Nain, P., Koole, G., The message delay in mobile ad hoc networks, in: *Performance*, October 2005.

44. Kumar, S., Raja, R., Gandham, A., Tracking an object using traditional MS (Mean Shift) and CBWH MS (Mean Shift) algorithm with Kalman filter, in: *Applications of Machine Learning. Algorithms for Intelligent Systems*, P. Johri, J. Verma, S. Paul (Eds.), Springer, Singapore, 2020, https://doi.org/10.1007/978-981-15-3357-0_4.

45. Spyropoulos, T., Psounis, K., Raghavendra, C.S., Spray and wait: An efficient routing scheme for intermittently connected mobile networks, in: *A.C.M. Workshop on Delay-Tolerant Networking*, 2005.

46. Lindgren, A., Doria, A., Schelen, O., Probabilistic routing in intermittently connected networks. *A.C.M. Mobile Computing and Communications Review*, July 2003.

47. Basu, S., SAGE-PRoPHET: A security aided and group encounter based PRoPHET routing protocol for dissemination of post disaster situational data. *Proceeding ICDCN '15 Proceedings of the 2015 International Conference on Distributed Computing and Networking Article No. 20*, A.C.M. New York, NY, U.S.A., 2015.

48. Burns, B., Brock, O., Levine, B.N., MV routing and capacity building in disrupt9in tolerant networks, in: *Proceedings of the IEEE INFOCOM 2005*.

49. Widemer, J. and Le Boudec, J.-y., Network coding for efficient communication in extreme networks. *Proc. f ACM SIGCOMM 2005 Workshop on Delay Tolerant Networks*, Philadelphia, PA, U.S.A, August 22-26, 2005.

50. Dong, J., Curtmola, R., Sethi, R., Nita-Rotaru, C., *Toward secure network coding in wireless networks: Threats and challenges*, IEEE, 2008, 978-1-4244-2652-2/08/$25.00.

51. Biswas, S. and Morris, R., Exor: Opportunistic multi-hop routing for wireless networks, in: *SIGCOMM*, pp. 133–144, 2005.

52. Mao, X., Tang, S., Xu, X., Li, X.-Y., Li, X.-Y., Energy efficient opportunistic routing in wireless sensor networks. *IEEE Trans. Parallel Distrib. Syst.*, 2011.

53. Sahu, A.K., Sharma, S., Tanveer, M., Internet of Things attack detection using hybrid deep learning model. *Comput. Commun.*, 176, 146–154, 2021, ISSN 0140-3664.

54. Dewangan, K.P., Bonde, P., Raja, R., Application of group mobility model for ad hoc network, in: *Advanced Computing and Intelligent Engineering. Advances in Intelligent Systems and Computing*, vol. 1089, B. Pati, C.

Panigrahi, R. Buyya, K.C. Li (Eds.), Springer, Singapore, 2020, https://doi.org/10.1007/978-981-15-1483-8_31.

55. Boldrini, C., Conti, M., Passerella, A., Impact of social mobility on routing protocols for opportunistic networks. *Proc. IEEE WoWMoM A.O.C. Workshop 2007*, Helsinki, Finland, June 2007.

56. Boldrini, C., Conti, M., Passerella, A., HiBOp: A history based routing protocol for opportunistic networks. *Proc. IEEE WoWMoM 2007*, Helsinki, Finland, June 2007.

57. Goodman, D., Borras, J., Mandayam, N., Yates, R., INFOSTATIONS; A new system model for data and messaging services. *Proc. IEEE VTC'97*, May 1997, vol. 2.

58. Boldrini, C., Conti, M., Iacopini, I., Passarella, A., HiBOp: A history based routing protocol for opportunistic networks. *Proc. IEEE WoWMoM 2007*, Helsinki, Finland, June 2007.

59. Kaur, Er.U and Kaur, Er.H, Routing techniques for opportunistic networks and security issues. *National Conference on Computing, Communication and Control (CCC-09)*.

60. R. K. Lenka *et al.*, Building scalable cyber-physical-social networking infrastructure using IoT and low power sensors, in IEEE Access, 6, 30162–30173, 2018.

61. Shikfa, A., Önen, M., Molva, R., Privacy and confidentiality in context-based and epidemic forwarding. *Computer Communications*, 33, 1493-1504, 2010.

62. Shikfa, A., Security issues in opportunistic networks. *Extend Abstract MobiOpp'10*, Pisa, Italy, February 22-23, 2010.

63. Shikfa, A., Önen, M., Molva, R., Privacy in content-based opportunistic networks. *WON 2009, 2nd IEEE International Workshop on Opportunistic Networking*, Bradford, May 29, 2009.

64. Poonguzharselvi, B. and Vetriselvi, V., Trust framework for data forwarding in opportunistic network using mobile traces. *Int. J. Wirel. Mobile Netw. (IJWMN)*, 4, 6, December 2012.

65. Shin, S., Wang, H., Gu, G., A first step towards network security virtualization: From concept to prototype. *IEEE Trans. Inf. Forensics Secur.*, 10, 10, 2236–2249, 2015.

66. Ashif, M. and Rahman, A., Epidemic routing for mobile ad-hoc network using dijkstra's algorithm. *Int. J. Eng. Dev. Res.*, 3, 3, 2016, ISSN: 2321-9399.

67. Jaiswal, and Sinha, Stable geographic forwarding with link lifetime prediction in mobile adhoc networks for battlefield environment. *Hum.-Centric Comput. Inf. Sci.*, 6, 22, 2016, doi: 10.1186/s13673-016-0078-x.

68. Scalavino, E., Russello, G., Ball, R., An opportunistic authority evaluation scheme for data security in crisis management scenarios. *ASIACCS'10*, Beijing, China, April 13–16, 2010.

69. Raja, R., Kumar, S., Mahmood, M.R., Color object detection based image retrieval using ROI segmentation with multi-feature method, *Wireless Pers. Commun.*, 112, 169–192, 2020, https://doi.org/10.1007/s11277-019-07021-6.

70. Costantino, G., Martinelli, F., Santi, P., Privacy-preserving interest-casting in opportunistic networks. *IEEE Wireless Communication and Networking Conference (WCNC)*, April 2012.
71. Gupta, R., Singh, P., Sultania, K., Gupta, A., Security for wireless sensor networks in military operations. *IEEE Comput. Commun. Netw. Technol. (ICCCNT)*, 1–6, 2013.
72. Yadav, A.S.S., Natu, P.M., Sethia, D.M., Mundkar, A.B., Sambare, S.S., Prevention of spoofing attacks in wireless networks. *IEEE Computer Society, International Conference on Computing Communication Control and Automation*, pp. 164–171, 2015.
73. Levendovszky, J. and Thai, H.N., Quality-of-service routing protocol for wireless sensor networks. *Inf. Technol. Software Eng.*, 4, 2, 1–6, 2015.
74. Yu, F., Chang, C.-C., Shu, J., Ahmad, I., Zhang, J., de Fuentes, J.M., Recent advances in security and privacy for wireless sensor networks 2016. *J. Sens.*, 2017.
75. Nayak, P. and Vathasavai, B., Energy efficient clustering algorithm for multi-hop wireless sensor network using type-2 fuzzy logic. *IEEE Sens. J.*, 17, 14, 4492–4499, 2017.
76. Arafath, M.S., Khan, K.U.R., Sunitha, K.V.N., Incorporating privacy and security in military application based on opportunistic sensor network. *Int. J. Internet Technol. Secur. Trans. (IJITST)*, 7, 4, 295–316, 2017, ISSN print: 1748-569X ISSN online: 1748-5703.

5

Futuristic AI Convergence of Megatrends: IoT and Cloud Computing

Chanki Pandey[1], Yogesh Kumar Sahu[2], Nithiyananthan Kannan[3], Md Rashid Mahmood[4], Prabira Kumar Sethy[5]* and Santi Kumari Behera[6]

[1]*Department of Electronics and Comm. Engineering, NITK Surathkal, India*
[2]*Department of Electrical Engineering, IIT Gandhinagar, India*
[3]*Department of Electrical Engineering, King Abdulaziz University, Rabigh, KSA*
[4]*Guru Nanak Institutions Technical Campus, Hyderbad, India*
[5]*Department of Electronics, Sambalpur University, Odisha, India*
[6]*Department of CSE, VSSUT Burla, Odisha, India*

Abstract

Recent years have seen increasing curiosity among users in migrating their cloud computing and internet-of-things apps. Cloud-based and internet-of-things infrastructures require specialized hardware to enable software and advanced management strategies to improve performance. Adaptability and autonomous learning capabilities are highly valuable in facilitating the configuration and complex transition of these infrastructures to customers' changing demands and designing adaptable applications. This capacity to self-adapt is increasingly essential, particularly for nonexpert managers and autonomous device applications. Cloud Networking (CN) and the Internet of Things (IoT) have arisen as modern outlets for the ICT movement of the 21st century. In this paper, we carry out a survey of nearly 183 articles on which the latest methodologies have been applied. Also, we discuss the proposed approaches and the reported advantages and limitations. The goal of this survey paper is to offer a brief idea to researchers working in this area. In order to consider the present and future challenges of such a framework, it is important to recognize critical innovations that will allow future implementations. This article examines how three new paradigms (cloud computing, IoT, and artificial intelligence) can affect workspace and business. Also, we describe a range

Corresponding author: prabirsethy.05@gmail.com

Md Rashid Mahmood, Rohit Raja, Harpreet Kaur, Sandeep Kumar and Kapil Kumar Nagwanshi (eds.)
Ambient Intelligence and Internet of Things: Convergent Technologies, (125–188) © 2023 Scrivener Publishing LLC

of innovations that propel these paradigms and encourage experts to address the current state and perspective directions.

Keywords: Artificial intelligence, cloud computing, IoT, autonomous system, self-adaptation

5.1   Introduction

All the digital information obtained by these computers, software, and IoT sensors can be easily accessed and contextualized by AI technology in cloud computing services. The Internet is continually evolving from the Internet of People (IoP) to Internet of Machines (IoM) to the Internet of Things (IoT). Moreover, many aspects such as networks, built-in electronics, human and physical structures are assimilating mass-connected structures, also known as cyber-physical systems (CPS). What we are headed for is a massive "Internet of Everything in a Smart Cyber-Physical Planet." Internet of Things and cyber-physical systems coupled with data science may emerge as the next "intelligent revolution" [1]. Therefore, the problem is to manage the tremendous data produced with far fewer computing resources available. Research in computer science and artificial intelligence (AI) sought to react to the issue. Artificial intelligence systems and the study of insertion of intelligence content into machines (any computers) and infrastructural facilities in such a way that they execute typical and nonconventional tasks parallel to intelligent human operation. The AI or AI integrated computer will have an extensive range of applications in our everyday lives and often a professional experience, where people can utilize AI-based technology. Another factor is that human intelligence seems comparatively less effective due to the unwelcome existence of the analog world's data, as shown in Figure 5.1.

With futuristic AI-based systems, we can efficiently resolve the problems and make data more relevant, more precise, more accurate, and structured. However, the usage of AI-based technologies can be included in all the fields covered beyond human needs years to achieve excellence in them with suitable equipment, a wide variety of areas, such as economics, information science, arithmetic, statistics, genetics, physics, sociology, psychology, etc. [2, 3]. We can also see that we need methods to address the real world's obstacles and cope with data science in today's modern world. Data science is the science area where we introduce a satisfactory way of simplifying, analyzing, rearranging, and reorganizing data to fulfill our requirements [1]. With AI-based technology, precision, efficiency,

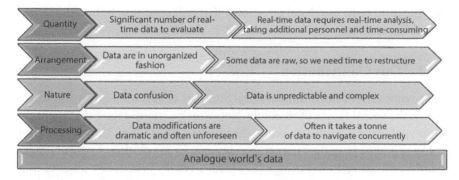

Figure 5.1 Problem and factors why human intelligence seems comparatively less significant.

speed, and adaptability in the human intellect can be accomplished [1, 4, 5]. AI can, therefore, limit workers, and the chance of mistake in return can be minimized, although it depends entirely on the quality of part of AI (AI device training). The convergence of megatrends: internet of things, artificial intelligence and cloud computing, therefore, become an unprecedented futuristic, as shown in Figure 5.2. It does not just save resources, creative stuff, minimize human effort, or hype. It is far more than that; it makes human life simpler. However, there are significant challenges, such

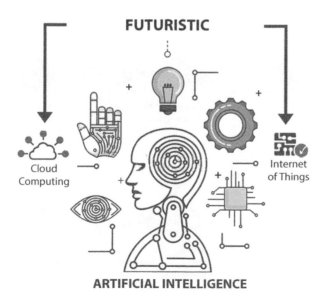

Figure 5.2 Futuristic AI—convergence of megatrends: cloud computing and IoT.

as protection risks and legal questions, that will continue to haunt IoT and Cloud Computing.

5.1.1   Our Contribution

The review covers both fundamental analyses of research and somewhere within the social facets of research. Noteworthy, many argue that there are billions of installed sensors everywhere in the Internet of Things (IoT), for instance, in house gadgets, wearable devices, smart clothes, furniture, pets, people, and other living things [6, 7]. As a result, practically all data may be kept in the cloud and analyzed in real time [8–10]. With IoT-technology evolving unimaginably, over 50 billion mobile devices are anticipated to

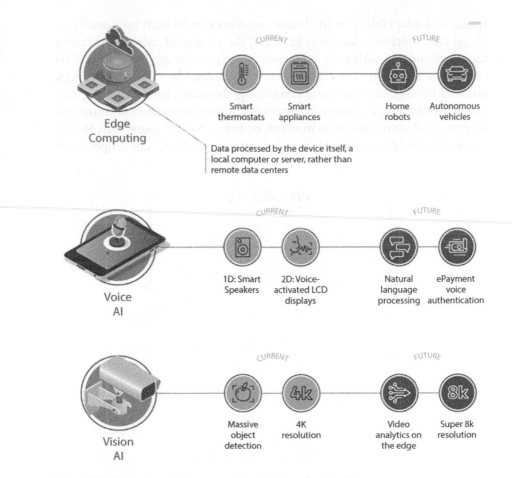

Figure 5.3 Current and future scenarios of AI-based technology.

be linked to the network and accessible at any time, as well as from anywhere [11]. This is also an outstanding chance to integrate IoT technology with large-scale data and data mining [9] to develop the intelligent areas of artificial intelligence and market intelligence. After the desired techniques have been used, AI can be used in any field like pattern recognition [12], machine learning [13], data mining [8, 9, 13, 14], information management systems [15], or big data analytics [16, 17].

This detailed review is motivated by the desire to learn about the history of computing and how IoT and cloud computing might help AI handle future problems, as shown in Figure 5.3. Also, experts from various AI research areas are coming together to address current research and possible potential research paths for scholars, professionals, and IoT and cloud computing researchers.

This review reflects primarily on the intuitions, problems, and implementations of AI in the principles of cloud computing and IoT. Here, Section 5.1 discusses artificial intelligence and its implementations. Section 5.2, research methodology, reach, literature references, screening research papers, and the final collection of articles in this review are addressed. Sections 5.3 and 5.4 analyze an overview of AI's position in Internet of Things (IoT) and cloud computing. Finally, Section 5.5 presents the conclusion.

5.2   Methodology

The bibliographic within the AI domain is analyzed to make this paper. Initially, a keyword-based search for conference papers or journal articles was performed from the scientific databases as shown in Figure 5.4. In order to find the desired articles, three digital databases were investigated.

> **IEEE Xplore** is a scholarly research database that provides the most reliable and wide-ranging articles in computer science, electronic technologies, and electrical engineering.
> **Web of Science** offers cross-disciplinary research in sciences, electronic technologies, social sciences, arts, and humanities.
> **Science Direct** is an extensive database of scientific techniques and medical research.

These three databases provide comprehensive coverage of artificial intelligence and its applications in the Internet of Things and Cloud Storage, which offer a comprehensive view of current studies in a diverse

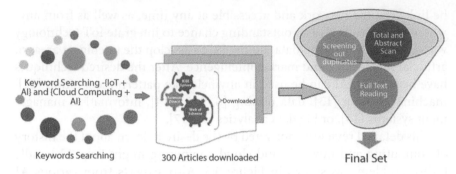

Figure 5.4 Flow for obtaining final set for writing review.

yet influential variety of disciplines. We use the search keywords to collect the research paper and filtered out the research paper, which is irrelevant to AI, IoT and CC are; {IoT + AI} and {Cloud computing + AI}. Doing so, we have downloaded almost 300 papers, including from IEEE Xplore's, Science Direct's, Web Science's, and other source article. After downloading the article, we have screened out the duplicates by carried out complete and abstract scanning and separated almost 234 papers for further consideration. For more scanning and filtering, we have performed a full-text reading and obtained 183 as a final set for articulating this survey article, which involves 106 IoT papers, 80 papers linked to CC with AI, and six papers on IoT + cloud computing- Edge of Things.

5.2.1   Statistical Information

Figure 5.5 shows the plot between number of papers in diverse fields covered by the various databases article vs years and Figure 5.6 shows percentage of papers included in various fields by IoT and cloud computing.

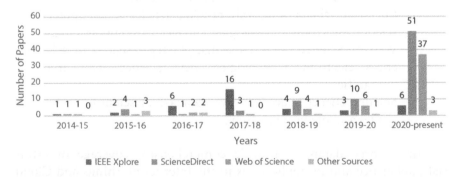

Figure 5.5 Number of articles in diverse fields covered by the database.

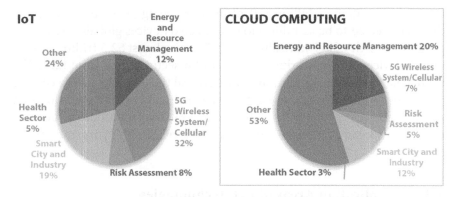

Figure 5.6 Percentage of papers included in various fields by IoT and cloud computing.

5.3   Artificial Intelligence of Things

IoT and AI technology are increasing in a rapid manner [18, 19]. Increasing cases of developing information resources utilizing sensor data were recently recorded. Artificial Intelligence and the Internet of Things combine to form the artificial intelligence of things (AIoT), which is a smart, linked network of devices that seamlessly communicate across strong 5G networks unleashing the potential of data better and faster than ever before. Digitalization has made "smart" [20] the epicenter of technical advances that have already been underway. IoT originated from merging the physical system and infrastructure with the internet or the web to benefit humankind. IoT technology is already sharpening the edge of innovation and development [21]. Some of the key characteristics of IoT, as Ghosh *et al.* [1] mentioned, are interconnectivity, heterogeneity, energetic changes and uncontrolled environment, and gigantic scale. In these technologies, the actuators and sensors connect seamlessly with the Internet of Things environment.

Also, sensed data is exchanged across networks to innovate into a standard operational image. Sensor nodes, embedded actuators, RFID tags, and readers are just some of the IoT devices that enable near-field communication technologies. The Internet of Things has risen from its infancy and has established a fully integrated future Internet [22]. The growth in IoT technology is currently extreme, and over 125×10^9 IoT devices are projected to be associated according to forecasts over the next 10 years [23]. The premise that makes IoT so common is that physical networks are required to control, reorganize, simplify, and communicate with all adjacent devices or technology surrounding it that can be more effective.

Every day, about 1 billion GB of data are being generated. "By 2025, there's projected to be 42 billion IoT connected devices globally" [24]. The predicted worth of IoT in healthcare by 2025 is almost $2.5 trillion. 30.3% of IoT devices will be working in the health sector at that time [22]. The more data sets we can obtain, the more critical the connexion between the programs and the data and the greater the likelihood of high precision that we can achieve. For the foreseeable future, AIoT integration will become more widespread as it pushes the boundaries of data analytics and intelligent learning.

5.3.1   Application Areas of IoT Technologies

IoT's technology fields are diverse and based on the latest technology solutions available; the most described technology segments where IoT is giving impressive results are shown in Figure 5.7.

The following subsection described and analyzed the different specific application of IoT technologies.

5.3.1.1   Energy Management

Rising energy prices and demand have driven many companies to find smart ways to track, regulate, and conserve electricity [25, 26]. It is worth mentioning that IoT implementations regularly need battery-based hubs that operate for long stretches without humans in venation [27]. Thus, without proper planning and a well-organized system structure, all the nodes in IoT will drain these hubs would deplete their batteries within a short timeframe to achieve our primary goal of using IoT as long as the battery remains alive. As a result, the primary goal of an energy supply and management strategy is to extend the network's life. Subsequently, energy use is one of the most fundamental and multidimensional challenges on the IoT platform. IoT Smart Energy Management Services include energy storage, electricity exchange, and exchanging facilities by interconnection and incorporation of energy supply-transfer-use structures utilizing the Internet of Things.

Yaghmaee *et al.* [28] suggested that IoT technologies be used to plan a high-vitality metering system consisting of a cloud server and shrewd plugs for gateway extension. The implementation of this system requires a judgment in terms of IoT specifications, and the outcome is deemed incorrect and inadequate. The three key techniques have been clarified in the study by Said *et al.* [25]. The first involves methods that minimize the calculation of the data sent and obtained by the so-called device nodes. The next strategy consists of a functional approach to saving the resources used

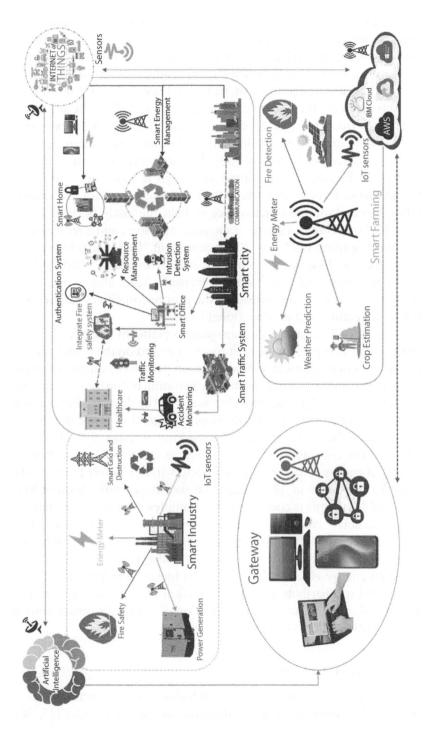

Figure 5.7 Application areas of IoT technologies.

by each device. Lastly, the third includes a fault-tolerance procedure to mitigate for energy-based node failures. However, very few relevant studies on this subject can be carried out explicitly in the IoT community, even in the heterogeneous IoT setting established to produce the required results.

Ku *et al.* [29] had suggested a smart technology service for internet of things. This service is focused on data processing of vitality. The key drawback of this service is to neglect the issue of fault tolerance in the extension to the frail tests that regard the IoT infrastructure. Energy management device was proposed by Choi *et al.* [30]. This architecture is a special-purpose structure because it is designed as though it were for a particular kind of accessible level. In expansion, the experiments are not deliberately established to include the exact source of help the analysts claim. Also, Pan *et al.* [31] presented an energy management system and a reduction in energy consumption rates in an IoT environment. This structure is called exceptional cause. Besides, the proposed IoT architecture, which utilizes mobile applications and cloud storage infrastructure, allows multiscale proportionality of resources, including the proportionality of resources at the house, consumer, and organizational levels.

The Internet of Things' energy management platform is applied to solve Intelligent City's energy management issue. Centered on the preparation of electricity costs of equipment and preparation period of equipment in the IoT context, the multiobjective machinery planning optimization equation is built in the IoT setting. The algorithm searches the device's idle time and optimizes its scheduling energy consumption model to lower the overall energy usage of the device in an IoT environment. Also, Ejaz *et al.* [32] studies show the enormous effect on the efficiency of IoT in smart cities, the impact of energy-efficient scheduling and wireless power transfer. The study by Anzanpour *et al.* [33] stated that the energy dissipation of IoT-based wearable systems is controlled via a complex multipurpose method. The proposed device can minimize power usage by 44% and avoid data failure due to battery depletion by 0.78% of the overall data collection period relative to a reference device without a target manager. Oma *et al.* [34] had proposed an energy-efficient demonstration focused on fog computation and attempted to distribute sensor information transmission across mist hubs. The analysis neglected the accumulation of vitality for sensor hubs as it extends to other IoT nodes such as RFIDs.

5.3.1.2   5G/Wireless Systems

The 5G networks are supposed to extend today's IoT significantly and to improve wireless operations, IoT reliability, and network issues [35, 36].

The 5G network also promises to offer faster quality, reduced latency, and a massive access point for numerous users by leveraging 4G advancements such as enhanced radio technologies, service-based design, and cloud computing [37]. The 5G is capable of huge IoT networking, where billions of smart devices are linked to the network. 5G networks can have versatile and quicker networks that can be introduced by identifying networking (WSDN) paradigms via wireless software. Many 5G WSDN options, like SoftAir [38], CloudRAN [39] are being arisen in recent years. The 5G wireless network will also significantly increase IoT coverage's reach and size by offering the highest connectivity and capacity. In the 5G network, IoT consists mainly of five layers of infrastructure, namely IoT Sensor Layer, Network Layer, Contact Layer, Infrastructure Layer, Application Layer, which includes data collection, processing, interpretation, and information sharing between the communication network and devices [40].

Some of the main challenges and vision of 5G IoT are as follows:

1. High Bandwidth and Spectrum Efficiency: 5G technology needs extensive transmitting capability, which can be done by utilizing MIMO radio [41] wire and mm-wave developments [42]. The range efficiency can be achieved by cognitive radio [43, 44], which enables the consumer to use both approved and unlicensed range classes
2. Low cost: IoT can have moo-fetched cameras, gadgets, and low sending costs [45].
3. More associative gadgets: In the IoT platform, about 80 billion IoT gadgets are supposed to be connected to the enterprise [46].
4. Reduced energy usage by approximately 90%: reduced vitality in 5G technologies can be done by sending renewable technologies and efficient gigantic networks and high knowledge rates [47].

Centered on the design and features of 5G wireless connectivity technology, Cheng et al. [48] suggested 5G-based IoT design and explains deployment approaches of different advanced manufacturing scenarios and manufacturing technologies under the circumstances of three traditional 5G device types, i.e., enhancing eMBB, mMTC, and URLLC. In order to address the needs of 5G-IoT service-driving applications, a contemporary heterogeneous computing architecture has been designed for them. For spectrum solutions, energy collecting and conversion have been offered [49]. An NB-SCMA approach for 5G-IoT uplink connectivity is introduced in Schinianakis and Khalfi *et al.* [50, 51]. Chen *et al.* [52] presented a wireless channel model for 5G IoT that would implement wireless broad data excavation to provide an effective, active expectation-guaranteed wireless connectivity.

Energy usage is an important concern in 5G-IoT. Zhang *et al.* [35] evaluated 5G IoT's energy consumption and suggested an optimized design that would determine the wireless and wired sections separately. Also, Clustering Strategies in WSNs were analyzed in Xu *et al.* [53], though recognizing the complexities of adapting such to 5G IoT Scenarios. Chie *et al.* [54] addressed the new developments and existing tasks to distribute cellular network connectivity services in the 5G network. They presented advice on the implementation of resource allocation. The authors assessed the newest capital distribution trends for wireless connectivity and core networks, categorizing them according to application priorities, service styles, and resource types; and addressed their merits and drawbacks. The outstanding question of the distribution of 5G services and the course of research direction for research has also been raised.

5.3.1.3   Risk Assessment

The IoT risk management platform provides software tools, controlled resources, software implementation, and consulting resources to support plan, execute, run and develop a communications services provider (CSP) through an Internet of Things risk management framework. AI and ML offer methods to fight fraud [55]. They assist anti-fraud teams process big data quantities quickly and discover fraudulent trends that can then be further analyzed by a team of anti-fraud experts. This enables cooperation on training data, the development of shared models, the effects of inferences, and the confirmation of these effects. Applied to actual data in an intuitive and low-latency way, the findings may impact market practices right when they unfold and providing real comparative advantages for companies.

In the past decades, private data spillage from embedded sensors in IoT gadgets has been widely considered, especially motion sensors based on confidential data spillage. Risk management of private data dependent on embedded sensors is extremely critical to prevent imperceptible private data spillage from customers [56]. Based on security certification, Laxmikant *et al.* [57] suggested a framework for modeling IoT to allow various stakeholders to evaluate security strategies for large-scale IoT implementations in an automated manner. It also encourages accountability at the level of IoT protection for customers, as the technique includes the mark as one of the core outcomes of the certification procedure. The qualification strategy is an overview of the risk-based safety evaluation and testing framework provided by ETSI is based on ISO 31000 and ISO 29119. It is designed on top of the diverse technologies and methods for protection testing and risk assessment applied to the IoT environment. As proof of principle, the suggested approach is extended to one of the scenarios suggested for the Horizon 2020 ARMOUR project to test certain IoT protection features' efficiency.

Identifying basic security specifications and system architecture are very complicated and costly tasks in the IoT case since they rely heavily on the actual application implementation and involve security expertise. To address these issues, Casola *et al.* [58] suggests a methodology to support an IoT system's vulnerability monitoring by an almost entirely automated threat modeling and risk management procedure, which often helps define the security controls to be enforced to mitigate current security threats. Shodan has been included in many research projects relevant to the security evaluation of internet-facing IoT applications. While several of the questions that may reveal these instruments are widely documented, subsequent evaluations also suggest the presence of instances of such vulnerabilities. Albataineh and Alsmadi [59] had proposed a remote protection evaluation focused on an expanded dataset of initial Shodan queries (known disclosure terms).

Based on the review of public Shodan queries phrases, remote backdoor access is modified. Results revealed that several public queries in the initial Shodan list would exploit many Internet-facing systems and computers. George and Tampi [60] had developed a multiattacker multitarget risk management model describing attackers, objectives, and network vulnerability relationships. Risk vectors for IoT and Medical Stuff Internet (IoMT) and the special risk rating approach are implemented in Kandasamy *et al.* [61]. The suggested rating framework initiates a risk management strategy for IoT structures by quantification of IoT risk vectors, successful risk management methodologies and procedures are contributed. The proposed unique numerical technique for predicting cyber hazard for IoT systems with IoT-specific impact factors was devised and clarified in the context of IoMT systems. In Liao *et al.* [62] survey "risk of activity sensor-based private data deduction by considering language assortment of varied input strategies, sophisticated computational intelligence strategies, and promoting the learning of personal use propensities." Accurate customer details and data processing and entertainment to include a bonafide and up-to-date risk evaluation. They are centered on the simulation outcome. They also had risky use implications and potential defense methods for IoT users.

5.3.1.4   Smart City

Smart City conceptualization, based on the development level, depending on the location and the country in which it is located. Smart City is a metropolitan environment that utilizes Information and Communication Technology (ICT) to make people's livelihoods simpler [63]. To collect and understand data, Smart Cities rely on Artificial Intelligence (AI), cloud-based services, and Internet of Things (IoT) devices, such as linked sensors, lighting, and metres. Then communities use this data to enhance roads, facilities, programs, and more. Multiple access and signal processing are huge challenges for Internet of Things systems, which are an integral aspect of the smart society. Rohit *et al.* [64] proposed a creative and scalable scheduling approach for Smart City's multiaccess channel sector. In particular, the AI-based scheduling approach can achieve better performance due to low complexity, particularly by increasing the number of devices. Additionally, smart city applications like healthcare, smart transport, retail and firefighting generate a large amount of data. There is still a question regarding how the vast amount of produced data can be handled effectively. Recently, several current studies have addressed the processing of an enormous volume of data utilizing cognitive computing; nevertheless, the scalability and flexibility of data acquired in a smart city scenario have not been addressed by these investigations.

There are numerous cognitive computing applications that can be used to implement data from millions of sensors in real time. In Park *et al.* [65], the smart city network architecture (CioT-Net), shows how cognitive computing can be used to analyse data from smart city applications, as well as the issues of scaling and adaptability. Guo *et al.* [66] suggested a new AI Semantic IoT (AI-SioT) architecture that incorporates heterogeneous IoT devices to provide smart services. Semantic and AI technologies support the proposed architecture, allowing for flexible connections between heterogeneous devices. By selecting and switching between a subset of machine learning models from a superset of models, an intelligent polynomial-time heuristic system offered by Qolomany *et al.* [67], optimizes the degree of trust in machine learning models while remaining within the reconfiguration budget/rate and reducing cloud communication overhead. Next, Industrial Internet of Things (IIoT) services are being investigated, as well as the usage of the turbofan engine deterioration simulation dataset to predict the engine's remaining usable life as a proxy. The results indicate that the confidence level associated with the chosen models is between 0.49% and 3.17% lower than that associated with the results from Integer Linear Programming (ILP). Second, according to the Smart Cities facility and as a reference, an experimental dataset to estimate the number of cars, results show that 0.7% to 2.53% lower conviction levels were obtained using the chosen model compared to the results obtained using ILP. In the polynomial-time approximation scheme for the problem, the suggested heuristic achieves an optimum competitive ratio. In addition to intelligent economics and governance, intelligent mobility, intelligent environment, disaster management and intelligent lifestyle are some of the essential characteristics of smart cities.

5.3.1.5 Health Sectors

Medical care administrations have been one of the foremost significant problems for both individuals and governments with a rapid increase in human populaces and protection utilization [68]. IoT has completely transformed how the healthcare industry operates today, as it has a lot of promise and has numerous applications, ranging from remote control to medical equipment convergence. The IoT healthcare market is projected to rise by USD 188 billion by 2024, with a CAGR of 27.6% during the forecast era [69]. In healthcare, IoT is used for integrated healthcare technology that collects real-time health data, such as tracking networks, sensor devices, and detectors. Detectors save data to a centralised cloud/server for further processing to improve healthcare.

Standard healthcare support system fails to predict correct patient health specifics and demands that reduce process accuracy. To address these concerns, an AI-enabled IoT sensor is presented by Fouad *et al.* [70] that indicates healthcare providers can choose the best way to treat a patient based on precise information like their fitness tracker or medical history, as well as their health activity, body mass, temperature, and more. Mobile healthcare infrastructure and patient awareness are used, followed by cloud universe use optimized processes to expand this knowledge. The integrated deep neural belief network (IGDBN) stores patient knowledge. AI-based prediction method develops IoT sensor output using MATLAB platform along with the excellence in the results, i.e., precision (99.87%), loss error (0.045%), matching coefficient (99.71%), correlation coefficient (99.10%), and accuracy (99.86%). In Souri *et al.* [71], an IoT-based student healthcare surveillance model is proposed to actively track student vital signs and identify biological and behavioral shifts via smart healthcare technology.

IoT sensors are used to collect the necessary data, and machine learning algorithms are used to detect possible variations in physiology and behavioral patterns. The proposed model's excellence is obtained 99% accuracy with the help of SVM. Digital healthcare networks exploit Internet of things and big data to provide a continuous digital link to the patient. These networks are now progressively related through the internet to different forms of medical technology that can be used to provide us with real-time patient details. Until digital healthcare is implemented; however, some issues must be addressed:

- Adequate data protection is needed to safeguard the privacy of the patient.
- Several systems operating with various protocols raise the difficulty and slows down the data sharing method.
- An immense volume of stored data requires effective processing and data storage.

Table 5.1 shows a brief description of various AI and IoT techniques.

5.4   AI Transforming Cloud Computing

In 1958, computer devices were developed to maximise the utilisation of available hardware resources [120] effectively. In these decades of computation, diverse forms of computing paradigms were created and developed, contributing to modern computing science. "Cloud Computing concept emerges from on-demand network access to a shared pool of configurable computing resources (e.g., server storage rooms)" [121–124]. "Cloud Computing is providing the advantage of the huge storage, computational capacities, and processing power with the many possible Cloud computing deployment methods, private, public, hybrid and community, researchers can benefit from shared and collaborative provisioned infrastructures" [125–127]. In addition to all the mentioned properties, the researcher community can have surety that all information (data) is in a highly secure place and backed up. The adaptability of these advancements and administrations, for a specific measure of cash, permits one to demand that the specialist co-ops allot more assets like processors, memory, and disks. These advantages and numerous different focal points of Cloud Computing provide researchers with better and more precise outcomes in their inspections.

According to De Donno *et al.* [128], some of the characteristics, such as on-demand self-service, fast flexibility, and measurable benefit, are particularly relevant in charge-per-use, pay-per-user, and administrations, as it offers the service provider and incredible client clarity.

Table 5.1 Highlights of some of the most well-known AI and IoT techniques.

Main goal	References	Methods and device used	Results	Pros/cons
The lifetime optimization algorithm for cellular ad-hoc IoT networks	[72]	EDTC topology control algorithm, MST as the network's backbone, and GCN.	Less energy consumption	Complex system
Secure wireless communications for IoT networks	[73]	Concave-convex procedure (CCCP) algorithm, Second-order cone programming by means of successive convex approximation (SOCP).	Higher secrecy rates at 10 dBm	Lower computational complexity
Resource Control Strategy for MULTITRAFFIC IoT communications	[74]	QoS requirements of M-M and H-H flow.	Less percentage of rejected flows, The Dynamic's success Either in heavy or low traffic, Scheduler is easier	Cost increases
Resource Optimization	[75]	MATLAB and YALMIP simulators, OFDMA system with = 64 sub-channels.	Data rate requirements = 64 bits/user, maximum interference power = 22 dBm	Not energy Efficient
Digital blind voice watermarking	[76]	FBMC	Less BER with BER % 0.99 at 5dB SNR	Less Bit Error Rate

(Continued)

Table 5.1 Highlights of some of the most well-known AI and IoT techniques. (*Continued*)

Main goal	References	Methods and device used	Results	Pros/cons
Monitoring of Real-Time Traffic Clearing for Emergency Responders	[77]	Interfacing sensors- Detection of siren sound (REES-52), wireless sensor (NRF905se), and an improved algorithm for monitoring emergency vehicles (OEVTA).	Execution time (ms) = 45.652, Accuracy % = 93.54 and Data rate = 250 kbps	The complexity of the system increased
Detection of vehicle accident	[78]	RFID sensors, ESP8266 Wi-Fi Module, Axis accelerometer (MPU6050), Arduino IDE software.	Detection of road accidents quickly	Reduced the lead time between accident occurred and information received by the hospital. Computation time is less
Infrastructure for Secure Smart City	[79]	Long-term short-term memory (LSTM), Software-Defined Networking (SDN), BlockChain.	Improved efficiency, taking into account privacy, centralization, connexion latency networking, scalability	The complexity of the system increases

(Continued)

Table 5.1 Highlights of some of the most well-known AI and IoT techniques. (*Continued*)

Main goal	References	Methods and device used	Results	Pros/cons
Blockchain-enabled Signature Matching	[80]	Block-Chain. CIDS, MSN.	Effective, time-saving rate of 28.68%	Less GPU computational time
Computing IoT Networks Allowed for Smart Cities	[81]	New IoT Algorithms for selecting a gateway (NIGS), controlling topology based on Hungary (HTC), allocating resources based on vacation (VRA), and allocating dynamic resources (DRA).	Usage of computing capital by 4x, use of production resources by 12x	No adverse effect on the latency constraints of the applications
Power optimization of smart city wireless sensor networks	[82–85]	Dynamic Stochastic Optimization Technique (DSOT), Hierarchical Computation Strategic Making (HCSM), Bluetooth Low Energy (BLE) [84] and Traffic Adaptive Control (TAC) [85].	Better results obtained	Lower environmental effect
Boost productivity by putting inequalities through a standard system

(Continued)

Table 5.1 Highlights of some of the most well-known AI and IoT techniques. (*Continued*)

Main goal	References	Methods and device used	Results	Pros/cons
FL-based emergency vehicle routing	[86]	Open Source Routing Machine (OSRM).	CPU utilization = 38%, Avg. database access time = 2 ms.	It can be integrated with healthcare-recommender systems
Integrated Fire Detection System using IoT and Image Processing	[87]	UAV, Thing Speak cloud application and Image processing.	In same cloud: Average Response Time (ms) = 26.56 with load of 512 Kbps = 40.28, Mean and Standard Deviation = 96.	The system proposed is simpler
Energy-balanced Clustering Protocol for Smart Cities	[88]	Improved-Adaptive Ranking based Energy-efficient Opportunistic Routing protocol (I-AREOR).	Performance of the system is increased by 6.4%.	The algorithm proposed is simple to implement.
Intrusion Detection System	[89, 90]	Deep feature extraction and selection (D-FES), MATLAB R2018B, AWID dataset, WEKA 3.8.3, R studio, and MLP classifier.	Increase performance compares to [90]. Processing time = 73.52 sec.	Simplex algorithm.
Meritocratic trust-based group formation	[90]	MultiAgent Systems (MASs), social capital, Friendship, and Group Formation (FGF) algorithm.	Better results obtained.	Algorithm complexity has increased.

(Continued)

Table 5.1 Highlights of some of the most well-known AI and IoT techniques. (*Continued*)

Main goal	References	Methods and device used	Results	Pros/cons
Built a single IoT and smartphone-based smart city system	[91]	Unified smart city architecture (USCA), Arduino Pro mini, Bluetooth Module, ESP-8266.	Developed a unified framework for IoT and smartphone-based applications for the smart city.	Not considered the Big data
Device authentication protocol	[92]	Blockchain-based IoT Device to Device Authentication Protocol for Smart City Applications using 5G (BIDAPSCA5G), blockchain-based revocation phase and registration and Random Oracle Model (RoM).	Total execution time = 41 ms, Storage cost of secret values in smart card (bits) = 1312 and Communication cost (in bits) = 1984.	Protocol authentication performs depending on system position. Location-based computer authentication. IoT System revocation of blockchain.
Typhoon early warning demo system	[93]	Fast R-CNN, convolution neural networks - GoogLeNet, Resnet 50, and vgg16.	Precision = 90.2% Recall = 80.6 & Average error (lat/long) = 0.1301	Simpler system
Ad-hoc automotive data transfer networks	[94]	VANET MobiSim-1.1	Avg. packet loss probability reduced, Throughput increase,	The algorithm proposed is simple

(*Continued*)

Table 5.1 Highlights of some of the most well-known AI and IoT techniques. (*Continued*)

Main goal	References	Methods and device used	Results	Pros/cons
Scalable cognitive smart city network architecture	[65]	CIoT-based smart city network (CIoT-Net), cognitive internet of things (CIoT), and cognitive computing.	CIoT-Net architecture resolves complexity and scalability.	Separate configuration criteria for complex and dynamic smart-city systems are decreased
Routing scheme for advanced metering infrastructure (AMI)	[95]	Contiki OS, Cooja simulator, a routing protocol for low power and lossy network (RPL).	Simulation time = 6 min. Packet delivery rate for inter-packet-interval performance is better than conventional RPL and OF-EC [95]	The algorithm is fast and simple.
Complex communication architecture based on soft computing.	[96]	Soft computing.	Performance increased	Higher communication efficiency and transmission speed.

(Continued)

Table 5.1 Highlights of some of the most well-known AI and IoT techniques. (*Continued*)

Main goal	References	Methods and device used	Results	Pros/cons
Health/accessibility monitoring services	[97]	Dumpster–Shafer theory (DST); health/accessibility monitoring service (HAMS)	Mean data trustworthiness in more than 70%	The complexity of the algorithm increases
Management of events in the IoT environment	[98]	IoT Block SIEM. Security Information and Event Management (SIEM) systems.	simpler and centralized management of the IoT ecosystem	The system will run overtime slower
Edge Computing and Cloud Computing	[99]	Max-Min Ant Method (MMAS), ETF, MCP, DLS, ISH, and HLFET.	MMAS was the strongest solution, ETF and MCP marginally poor, and ISH and HLFET were the poorest results	N/A
Architecture for centralized energy efficiency for the IoT paradigm and ML technique	[100]	Washing machine, Dishwasher, Freezer, Heat pump, and Refrigerator	Precision: WM = 0.453 Di = 0.42 Fr = 0.834 Re = 0.882	N/A
IoT-based visual contact components	[101]	Graffiti art scheme	Better results obtained	Does not have people's graffiti color and scale needs

(*Continued*)

Table 5.1 Highlights of some of the most well-known AI and IoT techniques. (*Continued*)

Main goal	References	Methods and device used	Results	Pros/cons
To boost MEC IoT, distributed AI, Ultra-reliable and Low-latency Communications (URLLC)	[102, 103]	Multiaccess edge computing (MEC), MEC-enabled IoT, Cloud-Native, Mobility Management.	Lower and stable latency, Consistent bandwidth performance of 5 Mbps	Does not endorse network slicing across heterogeneous network slices through edge clouds.
Mobile-Agent Collaborative Knowledge Tangle-based method (MADIT) as an IOTA (Tangle)-based solution	[104]	Exchange in broad P2P networks allows two-level distributed knowledge.	Average Transaction Per Second (TPS) = 5.422 tx/s with Minimum Weight Magnitudes (MWM) = 9	**Pros**- IOTA Tangle can be used to address the offline power issue. **Cons**- the expense of managing and installing dedicated servers to protect Pow location and create a static agent itinerary clustering the network.

(Continued)

Table 5.1 Highlights of some of the most well-known AI and IoT techniques. (*Continued*)

Main goal	References	Methods and device used	Results	Pros/cons
Fog Computing-based Security (FOCUS)	[105]	Virtual Private Network (VPN) hybrid fog-cloud model.	Balance the trade-off between answer time and network expense.	Limited computational capacity low response time.
AI4SAFE-IoT: stable architecture driven by AI and IoT	[106, 107]	Fog computing, edge tier, three-layer architecture with AI-based protection modules, the part operates as a base architecture cloud gateway.	IoT service management score (Approximately) : [106] AI4SAFE = 83 and [107] IIoTEED = 64.	The complexity of the system increased.
Computer-based dew cloud music crowdsourcing platform	[108]	Internet of Music Things, Fog Computing, Cloud computing, and Sound sensor.	The average data transmission time of the Proposed framework is 11.35% lesser than the conventional cloud. Computing paradigm. The average energy dissipation Proposed framework is 23.56% lesser than the conventional cloud Computing paradigm.	Less data transmission and service latency.

(Continued)

Table 5.1 Highlights of some of the most well-known AI and IoT techniques. (*Continued*)

Main goal	References	Methods and device used	Results	Pros/cons
Design of intelligent equipment by cognitive IoT (CIoT)	[109]	Industrial robot	Better results obtained.	N/A
ML-based model for tracking student's condition	[71]	Support Vector Machine (SVM), Multilayer Perceptron (MLP), Decision Tree (DT), Random Forest (RF)	SVM performed better than, DT, RF, and MLP with 93.2% F-score, 99.1% accuracy, 97.2% precision and 99.5% recall	Improve emergency services response time, and Bandwidth of the system is less.
Data storage security	[110–112]	Double secret key encryption, Hadoop, hash computing, Attribute-based encryption scheme [111], and Seven alliance chain-based encryption [112].	Operation time (read, write, open, close, encrypt) of [111] is 5-7% less as compared to is [112] for the 100-500MB file.	[111] reduces the hidden danger of Hadoop. Just one node's read-write output was weighed. Reading file takes more time than expected.

(*Continued*)

Table 5.1 Highlights of some of the most well-known AI and IoT techniques. (*Continued*)

Main goal	References	Methods and device used	Results	Pros/cons
Group Signcryption scheme based on IoT	[113–116]	Short Group Signcryption (SGSC) [113], SGBPP [114], SGSBV [115] and ECPB [116]	Time consumption: SGBPP = 16.2 ms, SGSBV = 27 ms, ECPB = 17.4 ms and SGSC = 15 ms and SGSC is fastest.	Supports assembly and batch verification. Eliminate the computation delay problem.
Intelligent radiation monitoring systems by information collection scheme	[117–119]	Dijkstra algorithm and WSN	[117] The proposed scheme is 65% more efficient than [118] and [119] scheme, and it provides more rounds of "First Device Depletion" up to 2200.	TDMA may be used for channel control in control applications. The probability of data loss depends on the scaling and parameters of the design.

1. Customer self-service: computational capabilities can be made available on demand without the need for any human interaction between the buyer and service provider.
2. Flexibility: Computing resources can be delivered and released on demand, allowing them to scale up and down in response to demand. Hence, the purchaser has the discernment of limitless and consistently excellent computer capabilities.
3. Measured benefit: The consumption of resources can be tracked and documented in accordance with the type of benefit provided.

AI means the capacity of machines to conduct the actions of a human being. This is a mixture of deep learning and machine learning. AI is a kind of know-how capable of enhancing the current cloud infrastructure and strengthening the latest cloud computing technologies. Businesses are adopting these technological advances to do better on the market. Both the cloud and the mobile are in operation as the future of technology. Today, everybody is involved in studying how Artificial Intelligence will improve cloud computing as AI develops the cloud. The use of cloud computing by businesses has affected the appearance of artificial intelligence.

The influence of Artificial Intelligence on next-generation cloud computing modules has introduced enormous improvements, including the introduction of disruptive technology such as smartphones or IoT (Internet of Things). IoT and mobile resources have originated from the perspective of emerging cloud infrastructure technologies due to the current cloud potential. Applications operating on AI are incompatible with mobile and IoT and involve thorough run-time optimization with experienced backend providers. If AI, data, and machine learning are combined, both AI and humans will analyze a vast volume of data to obtain valuable knowledge. Consequently, a high amount of data can be handled effectively within a limited period.

5.4.1   Application Areas of Cloud Computing

Technology fields of Cloud Computing are diverse. Based on the latest technology solutions available, the most described technology segments where Cloud Computing and Artificial Intelligence are giving impressive results are shown in Figure 5.8.

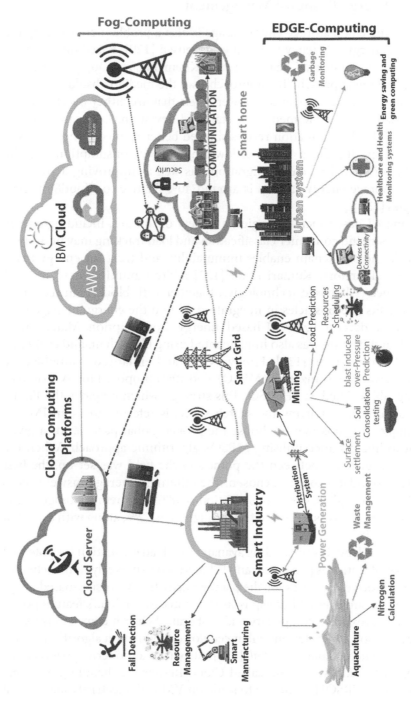

Figure 5.8 Application areas of cloud computing.

5.4.2   Energy/Resource Management

Optimizing cloud storage energy usage is also a problem considering the range of energy-efficiency techniques proposed [129]. Based on the existing charging strategy, Chaabouni and Khemakhem [130] proposed an energy-saving approach. The approach uses the median absolute variance formula to measure upper and lower levels that are either overloaded or underloaded using the median or standard deviation. Compared to current models, the simulation results showed better results of the proposed solution, specifically in terms of lowering energy consumption and the number of virtual machine migrations, as well as improving active host times. Average energy savings is around 40% relative to CloudSim technologies [131].

Using AI-based methodologies, a variety of utilities, including energy load assessment, consumer classification and load tracking may be accomplished. The blockchain enables immutability and trust for energy management. Therefore, Kumari *et al.* [132] address multiple new artificial intelligence (AI)-based technologies, together with blockchain technology's benefits and obstacles in integrating AI into the energy management system. A decentralized AI-based Energy Consumption Management (ECM) architecture was also implemented using blockchain and evaluated using the case study [133]. Firefly hybrid and enhanced multiobjective particle swarm optimization (MPSO) algorithm proposed for W load balancing, abbreviated as FIMPSO. This strategy, which employs the Firefly (FF) algorithm to narrow the search space, is referred to as an IMPSO technique. It is possible to choose the proper global particle for a given point-to-line distance utilising MPSO's algorithmic approach. When the minimum distance between the point and the field was set up, the best particle candidates could be chosen. The minimum average answer time is 13.58 ms; the highest CPU consumption is 98%, the memory usage rate is 93%, the durability is 67%, and the throughput is 72%, along with a created period of 148.

In the work by Reshmi and Saravanan [134] load estimation for potential resource allocation is presented, and IFPA is used to make dynamic scheduling and allocate resources for the planned activities. Gaussian-based adaptive least mean square filter gap is used to forecast the load's feature points used to approximate complexity and cost scale. When it comes to resource allocation, soft computation (enhanced flower pollination algorithm) is frequently applied. Malarvizhi *et al.* [135] introduces a modern hypervisor for Complex Cloud Computing called Cloud Resource Scheduling Maximal Hypervisor (CRSOH). Climate to settle on VM with electricity and factual limitations. Proposed algorithm for the most resource usage with the help of VMs. Proper utilization of sources finishes in electricity production. Karthiban and Raj [136] proposed an equal renewable distribution of capital, it is suggested to include an effective resource distribution system for consumers within the context of a deep reinforcement learning model. The Net. Conventional Q-learning paradigm struggles to solve the dimensional issue as state space grows exponentially. Power consumption is one of the primary concerns of cloud providers. Vakilinia *et al.* [137] suggested that the energy usage of DC may be optimally minimized with the cooperation of optimization preparation and calculation techniques. An estimate module has been implemented in the model for the forecast of potential machine loads, and two planners are then called for the preparation of planned and unpredicted loads. The programmer intends to use the column generation (CG) methodology to tackle the issue of optimization of integer linear/quadratic programming (ILP/IQP).

5.4.3   Edge Computing

Edge computing (EC) is an approach to processing vast amounts of data created by devices linked to the Internet via the Internet of Things (IoT) [138]. Due to a number of challenging issues, such as computational difficulties and increased delay in cloud computing, edge computing has surpassed the traditional way in IoT-based industrial applications by effectively and evenly distributing resources, such as electricity and battery life. Edge computing has a limited amount of energy, computing, and communication capacity, so it is important for several edge nodes to split the work of a task so that it can be done as quickly as possible. Zhang *et al.* [139] suggest a task allocation approach focused on measuring task specifications and time delay in the edge computing setting. For this, the proxy server obtains the relevant data to determine the current position of the edge nodes. Task-based edge node selection is then set up to pick the edge nodes that need to be chosen to reach a certain goal, uses the Bloom filter to keep bad nodes from getting into the edge nodes that have been set as the target. The proposed algorithm optimizes the task of distribution to satisfy the task specifications and obtain a minimal delay in the edge computing setting. Cloud computing and edge computing alone cannot account for an exponential scale and complexity of technology demand. To build a useful device that minimizes both the use of resources and server-side feedback for urban implementation, Baucas and Spachos [140] proposed optimization methods.

To dodge information compression processing, which may devour higher vitality rates [141], an edge computing-based approach was shown.

The data compression is considered basic preparation to decrease transmitted information within the IoT environment. There are certain IoT applications where this strategy works and others where it does not. Li *et al.* [142] came up with a way to improve the reliability and availability of edge-cloud computing by using the grey Markov chain. A method that focuses on the Fast Non-Dominant Genetic Sorting Algorithm. Additionally, this article discusses a delay-adaptive replica synchronisation approach. A replica recovery technique based on load balancing enabled data replica synchronisation and recovery in an edge cloud environment. Jararweh [143] proposed architecture that indicates advanced computing technology enhances service efficiency by 22.6% in contrast with the existing infrastructure platform to handle energy cloud services effectively and simplify them while at the same time improving stability, protection, and safety. The proposed architecture utilizes the latest growth of edge computing and 5G technologies in computing capacities. Also, latency is decreased by 69.1%. The suggested architecture includes the opportunity to identify threats by utilizing the edge layer as an extra layer for the protection against energy cloud assaults. However, this protection method incurs an average of 10.9% overhead, and 9.6% added wait per order for operation.

Wireless channel connectivity is insecure and unsafe to avoid future threats, such as replay, switch, etc., to build a protected session on cloud-based mobile edge computing—transparent, protected anonymous authentication schemes (S-SAAS) proposed by Deebak *et al.* [144]. As the Internet of Things, cloud computing, big data, and mobile technologies combine to form group-based communication systems, it is critical that the authentication process be enhanced to mitigate security risks and vulnerabilities. The proposed heterogeneity-aware elastic provisioning approach in the cloud-assisted edge computing setting is an elastic supply approach. It considers tenanted costs and overhead costs to accommodate customer requirement diversity and minimize response time; the multi-target optimization issue of replication placement is proposed in the absence of the file [145]. Miao *et al.* [146] present a new intelligent statistic-Downloaded MEC architecture in conjunction with Artificial Intelligence (AI) technologies. The calculation algorithm focused on task prediction is suggested for the data size of smartphone users' computational challenges and the output of edge computing nodes. The LSTM algorithm-based calculation task prediction listed a mobile device strategy based on task prediction and task migration for edge cloud scheduling.

The quick advancement of computer vision technologies has rendered automated surface control a hot topic. The evolving convolutional neural networks (CNN) automatically extracted functions and achieved good results in many cases. However, CNN image recognition approaches are more suited for flat-surface texture inspections. In geometrically structured goods, it is challenging to identify little defects reliably. A smart surface control device with faster R-CNN algorithms in the computer-based cloud processing setting is proposed by Wang *et al.* [147] to solve those problems. Mutations on the server to resolve this [148] is a combination of the middleware solution and the WebSocket-free communication protocol that has resulted in the better design. The RAMWS reduces network operating time by up to seven times compared to the direct-cloud approach, allowing for the resolution of the Time-out problem and the achievement of reliable web service utilisation.

Privacy security and continuous development are demanding ML models to resolve these concerns, Qu *et al.* [149] suggested a model ML training architecture to accomplish intelligent edge computing in a modern cloud-based cooperative way consisting of two phases. The federated pre-training period is the reasonable period between cloud and edge server influenced by federal teaching and a federated learning phase. Amarasinghe *et al.* [150] had introduced the ECSNeT++ toolkit for the operation of DSP applications in edge and cloud environments s. ECSNeT++ simulation and processing of DSP applications in edge cloud environments designed on top of OMNeT++/INET They demonstrate that ECSNeT++ can be modeled to render a specific implementation utilizing different configurations of two real DSP applications. To keep data caching costs to a minimum and maximize service latency reduction, Xia *et al.* [151] proposed a methodology based on the edge data caching (EDC) problem as a restricted optimization problem. The authors show that this EDC problem is NP-complete and show how to solve it using integer programming.

To optimize the data management access architecture, Wang and Zhang [152] suggested HDFS for optimizing the cloud data based on the access storage algorithm and IoT data access management architecture issues, which completely take into account the data access storage processing factors in IoT read and write file speed, as well as the usage of memory compared to the conventional hash algorithm. Xu *et al.* [153] had proposed ARVMEC, Adaptive IoT Virtual Machine Recommendation in Edge-Cloud world, which will often offer users the right VM recommendation in line with their own budget or time restrictions. ARVMEC uses a tree-based ensemble learning algorithm to estimate the output of the workload for all VM forms. In a more versatile and general mode, it will describe consumer intentions. While considering the server allocation issue for the edge computing system [154], a method to reduce the average response time for all mobile devices/users. There were two ways to put edge clouds in place: flat deployment, where all edge clouds are near base stations, and hierarchical deployment, where edge clouds can be near other parts of the system as well as base stations.

5.4.4   Distributed Edge Computing and Edge-of-Things (EoT)

Applications requiring data analysis from distributed networked data sources usually entail computing conducted centrally in a datacentre or cloud system, with some limited preprocessing likely conducted at data sources. Cooke and Fahmy [155] proposed a logic paradigm for distributed edge and network computing, with support for heterogeneous systems and alternate software and application accelerator implementations. By considers the cost of computing for computer-intensive software, it embraces a range of hardware architectures and considers a heterogeneous network. Edge-of-Things (EoT) is a modern emerging programming paradigm powered by IoT). It allows data collection, storage, and application to be transferred from the cloud to neighboring Edge devices/systems. Including tablets, routers, and IoT paradigm base stations, Almogren [156] proposed a methodology strategy for the swift and precise identification of disruptive behaviors within the EoT network to understand the maximum potential of IoT. They propose a deep faith network (DFN) focused on an innovative intrusion detection strategy.

5.4.5   Fog Computing in Cloud Computing

Fog computing is a new way to cut down on the load on the cloud and the core network. It does this by moving resource-heavy tasks like computing, networking, storage, and analytics closer to end-users (EUs). A fog computing system could be smart enough to use public data and computing resources for time-critical Internet of Things (IoT) applications. LA et al. [157], using two case studies, came up with a way to cut down on energy consumption and fog latency by using device and human-driven information. The first one makes use of machine learning to detect user patterns and to schedule sensor systems in an adaptive low-latency Medium Access Control (MAC) layer between them. In the second case study on task unloading, where the algorithm for the EU Intelligent Device selects its unloading decision in the presence of multiple fog nodes nearby, it minimizes its own energy and latency goals. In Abbasi et al. [158], two approaches focused on the LCS (XCS) learning classifier schemes, namely XCS and BCM-XCS, was introduced. Balancing the resource usage at the edge of the network and reducing delays in transmission workloads.

The results of our experiments demonstrate the supremacy of BCM-XCS over the simple XCS-based system. The existing approaches shall allocate the workloads in such a way as to postpone their delivery, and the gap in contact between cloud and fog nodes is decreased. In Amin *et al.* [159], the data flow model layout for cloud and fog computing was presented. Then authors develop an authentication protocol with the correct key configuration for the server, fog, and person by simulating the proposed procedure using the Scyther simulator.

Because fog nodes are still authorised and are part of a network that uses valid identities, cryptographic-based measures can help prevent external threats from occurring. However, these strategies are not effective. Al-khafajiy *et al.* [160] had suggested fog COMputIng Trust manageMENT (COMITMENT) methodology that uses the quality of operation and quality of security experience metrics from previous direct and indirect fog node experiences to determine and maintain the degree of trust between nodes within the fog computing environment. Das *et al.* [161] suggested the fog devices provide geographical data about their current location and conduct geospatial queries using nearby tools in a fog computing system, called Spatio-FogThe fog system can solve geospatial queries on its own or with help from cloud servers or fog devices in another country, depending on where the geospatial query is coming from. In Forcan and Maksimović [162], two collaboration frameworks are chosen and designed with the key objective of fostering real-time tracking and data processing in SG. Cloud-based methods are suggested and evaluated as contact device templates for real-time SG monitoring. Posting large volumes of Cloud data usually faces a severe challenge due to latency, locality, and network congestion. Again to minimize energy usage, Forcan and Maksimović [162] developed an energy-aware approach utilizing Dynamic Voltage and Frequency Scaling (DVFS). A combination of Invasive Weed Optimization and Culture (IWO-CA) evolutionary algorithm creates relevant job sequences. It guarantees that the proposed algorithm would boost any of the existing energy usage algorithms.

To resolve the restriction of migration in FCbCC, Hosseinioun *et al.* [163] proposed a model MobFogSim that enables the modeling of system versatility and fog computing service migration. MobFogSim is tested by comparing simulation results to data from a testbed where fog services are provided as containers. As a large number of production lines will exist in a single facility, one of the key challenges is how these data are interpreted in real-time to solve the emerging Hybrid Deep-Learning Architecture based on Fog (FC-HDLF) that detect suspected faulty goods [164]. The machine will manage too massive volumes of data by unloading the load from the central servers to the fog nodes. The suggested technique offers substantial benefits. First, the Convolutional Neural Network (CNN) paradigm is tailored to the fog computing environment, enhancing its computational efficiency. The other is that a control model is developed that can concurrently show the shape and magnitude of the defect. A decision-making process for multi-agents shall be developed to ensure production process design for optimizing production processes.

The Infrastructure of Health Stuff (IoHT) has been a rigorous feature of the IoT and Cloud Computing. The Internet of Health and Technology (IoHT) allows for the sharing and analysis of health data in order to track patients' health status in order to meet the growing demand for energy and latency regulated health services. Mukherjee and Ghosh [165] proposed indoor and outdoor nebula-based Internet of Health Items. In the suggested method, the weighted majority game theory is used to pick fog devices in indoor and outdoor environments. The current fog computing framework decreases the average latency, average jitter, and energy usage by roughly 15%, 20%, and 15%, respectively, relative to the current cloud-only healthcare system. Tao et al. [166] suggested a fog computation system to identify assembly processes, which brings processing resources near the data source to obtain real-time identification. For data collection, the operator's operation is filmed from various angles using visual cameras. In order to understand the process, instead of simply creating and teaching a deep learning model from scratch that requires a large amount of data, transfer learning is used to transfer learning knowledge to our application. Peralta et al. [167] presented a stable and interactive infrastructure that minimizes the time spent by the end node or user to retrieve the necessary data. An optimized storage algorithm that specifies the amount of information that should be processed or retrieved from each node reduces the total period of retrieval of the data. It also suggests two ways to resolve these problems to ensure that fog computing remains a secure alternative for IoT-related applications. Baucas and Spachos [168] developed an Internet of Things-based sensing system that uses an urban sound classification model. A network layout by active low and high power states and resource reallocation, Sarabia-Jácome et al. [169] proposed an advanced, high-performance, fog-cloud computing architecture-based "smart framework" for quickly detecting falls using DL technology on low-resource devices (fog nodes). The portable tri-axial accelerometer was used to capture patient tracking results. To facilitate remote deployment and maintenance of DL models, they propose a smart-IoT-Gateway framework in fog. To maximize resources and compare efficiency and inference time, two DL models (LSTM/GRU) were used for virtualization.

5.4.6   Soft Computing and Others

Using artificial intelligence (AI), soft computing techniques are gaining market adoption to ensure efficient energy usage, secure and successful comparative velocity monitoring, decreased impact on host power grid networks, and expanded motor drive networks while preventing magnetic saturation and current conditions. Random search algorithms such as particle swarm optimization (PSO) and genetic algorithm (GA), which are used in modern soft computing to increase certain target functions, are also becoming more popular in dynamic online configuration, self-regulation, and controller customization [170]. SMART attributes, which are used to self-monitor, analyse, and report (SMART), are used to explore the relationship between the hard drive parameter and loss. It also examines the predictive ability of five machine learning models, including naive Bayes and artificial neural networks (ANN), to create a cloud infrastructure failure prediction module. For allowing cloud customer to evaluate available service offerings based on QoS requirements, Kumar *et al.* [171] proposed a new system called Optimal Service availability and cloud computing service rating (CCS-OSSR). The CCS-OSSR uses a multi-criteria hybrid decision-making approach. The worst process is used to rate and assign priority to the QoS requirements and order choice technologies, equivalent to the perfect solution method, to reach the final cloud services rate.

Beheshti and Safi-Esfahani [172] presented a BFPF-Cloud architecture that contains many features for the prediction of Byzantine failures to be applied to algorithms based on support vector machine (SVM). Along with the constructive approach, the reactive policy is implemented to cope with Byzantine deficiencies. The primary priority is to ensure stability in addition to the availability of the device. Compared with BFT-Cloud, average re-filling and execution times decreased by 69.91%, repeat requests were reduced by 69.78% on average, while average performance was increased by 69.90%. Applying soft computing models to solve real-life problems has yielded many significant benefits, particularly in mining. Nguyen and Bui [173] proposed a new blast-induced air overpressure (AOP) soft computing paradigm. The genetic algorithm (GA) and the boosted smoothing spline (BSTSM) were investigated and integrated, resulting in GA-BSTSM. For this reason, a total of 121 explosions were recorded at the CocSau coal mine in Vietnam. The essential input variables for AOP prediction were explosive force (W) and distance (R).

Table 5.2 shows a brief description of the mentioned AI and Cloud Computing popular approaches.

Table 5.2 A brief description of the mentioned AI and Cloud Computing popular approaches.

Main goal	Reference	Methods and device used	Results	Pros/cons
The intelligent air-quality monitoring system	[174]	Cloud and Edge Computing architecture, Ganglia Monitoring System, Open Stack. Micro-services, Kubernetes by Google, Dockers, and Ubuntu-OS.	Maximum utilization is 13s Boot pods; the CPU and memory have not been substantially changed; when booting, the Capsule and CPU resources are consumed at Rate = 7629.24 kb/s.	The system is complex, and as well as it is not cost-effective.
Manage and optimize cloud applications	[143]	Using EdgeCloudSim and Energy Cloud Implementation.	Application performance is 22.6% better than cloud infrastructure, and latency is 69.1% better.	Provides capabilities to identify threats utilizing edge layer.
Heterogeneity-Aware Elastic Provisioning Strategy/System [HAEPS]	[145]	Cloud Assisted Edge Computing System(CAECS).	The cost of HAEPS can averagely achieve up to 19.23%.	Reduce response time.

(*Continued*)

Table 5.2 A brief description of the mentioned AI and Cloud Computing popular approaches. (*Continued*)

Main goal	Reference	Methods and device used	Results	Pros/cons
Seamless stable cloud authentication	[144]	Seamless Secure Anonymous Authentication Scheme (S-SAAS), Elliptic-curve cryptograph, and One-way hash function.	Achieve less computation cost.	Congestion, routing control overhead, and service link rate have all increased.
Task Estimation and Device Offloading	[146]	Mobile-Edge Cloud Computing (MEC) architecture, Task Migration Algorithm, and LSTM Architecture.	Reduce the cumulative delay of the process as the data sum of the computation Increase in subtask number and subtask level.	The algorithm proposed is simpler.
The smart surface inspection system	[147]	Faster R-CNN + ResNet101 and Nvidia GeForce GTX TITAN X.	Precision = 0.81 and Recall = 0.72.	High detection accuracy.
The real-time sound classification system	[140]	Sound classifier with Urban Sound 8K Dataset.	Avg. latency (ms) = 0.6, Avg. Power Consumption (mW) = 1852.00 and Avg. runtime (s) = 57.77.	Configuration lag improved dramatically as end devices improved.

(*Continued*)

Table 5.2 A brief description of the mentioned AI and Cloud Computing popular approaches. (*Continued*)

Main goal	Reference	Methods and device used	Results	Pros/cons
Reliable web service consumption	[148]	Reliable Approach using Middleware and Web Sockets (RAMWS) and Web Socket open connection communication protocol.	Time-out problem that makes cloud service unstable is solved.	Boosts customer satisfaction while reducing network utilisation by up to seven times more than the direct-cloud option.
Privacy-preserving Model Training Architecture	[149]	Cloud-Edge Cooperative Federated Pre-Training And Edge device Model Segmentation Training.	Accuracy = 91.88% within 10 epochs.	Speed of accuracy improvement.
Simulator for asynchronous streaming	[150]	ECSNeT++, OMNeT++/ INET and Raspberry Pi 3.	Simulation and implementation of asynchronous stream systems.	Model actual implementation with proper calibration.
Graph-based Data Caching Optimization	[151]	N P-completeness of Edge Data Caching (EDC), AEDC, IPEDC, and Integer Programming.	Minimize caching costs and optimize service latency reduction.	The proposed algorithm computational time is more.

(*Continued*)

Table 5.2 A brief description of the mentioned AI and Cloud Computing popular approaches. (*Continued*)

Main goal	Reference	Methods and device used	Results	Pros/cons
Data storage algorithm in the distributed system	[116]	HDFS.	Experiment times = 200, Maximum data processing efficiency = 93% but proposed practically it can reach 89%.	Improves file upload and transfer performance, computer processing performance, and tolerance to faults.
Virtual Machines Recommendation	[153]	ARVMEC: Adaptive Recommendation of Virtual Machines for IoT in Edge-Cloud Environment. Tree-based ensemble learning algorithm.	Percentage error on Choosing VM = 7.3%.	Better predictions with 15% and improvement in accuracy.
Hierarchical System Deployment	[154]	A Largest Weighted Reduction Time First and (LWRTF) algorithm.	The proposed methodology leads to 6% less overall average response time.	Minimize cumulative estimated reaction time.
Adaptive fault-tolerant model	[170]	Self-Monitoring Analysis and Reporting Technology (SMART) and Artificial Neural Network (ANN).	Accuracy = 95.55%, Relative absolute error = 65.32%, Root relative squared error = 85.88%, Precision = 95% and Recall = 95.6%.	A collapsed state can be estimated based on the values of certain SMART attributes.

(*Continued*)

Table 5.2 A brief description of the mentioned AI and Cloud Computing popular approaches. (*Continued*)

Main goal	Reference	Methods and device used	Results	Pros/cons
Coordinating and controlling cloud, fog, and edge capital	[175]	Fuzzy-based Systems for Resource Management (FSRM), FSRM1 and FSRM2, Vehicular Ad hoc Networks (VANETs), and Software-Defined Networking (SDN).	Only a few real-time details may be edged depending on their number.	The maintenance of network infrastructure increases the viability of networks.
Firefly and multi-objective particle hybridization Optimizing	[133]	Firefly and Improved Multi-Objective Particle Swarm Optimization (FIMPSO) technique and selecting the global best (GBESt) particle with a small distance of the point to a line.	Average Response Time = 13.58ms, CPU Utilization = 98%, Memory Utilization = 93%, Reliability = 67% and Throughput = 72%.	The algorithm presented combines the advantages of both FF and Algorithms from IMPSO.
Distributed In-Network And Near-Edge Computing Model	[155]	Heterogeneous Network, SimPy library, FIFO (priority given to the oldest data packets).	Latency = 0.87s, Throughput = 133 frames/s, Cost = 9000 and Energy = 1.56.	The model-simulator gap is equivalent to 6%.

(*Continued*)

Table 5.2 A brief description of the mentioned AI and Cloud Computing popular approaches. (*Continued*)

Main goal	Reference	Methods and device used	Results	Pros/cons
Task-based delivery of assignments and delays	[139]	Task-Based Edge Node Selection Algorithm (TENS), Bloom filter, and Filter malicious node.	Reduce time, bandwidth usage, energy consumption.	Too many algorithms.
Intrusion detection	[156]	Deep Belief Network (DBN), ANN and SVM	Maximum Accuracy = 85.76%.	The accuracy of the system is still less but better than its peers.
Minimize Latency in Hybrid Fog-Cloud Computing	[176]	Genetic Algorithm (GA) and Round-Trip Time (RTT).	Overall latency from 21.9% up to 46.6%.	Simpler algorithm.
Resource Management And Workload Allocation	[158]	XCS learning classifier systems (LCS) and BCM-XCS.	Reduce processing delays by 42%.	Reduce the response time, and methods can also be used to recharge renewable batteries.

(*Continued*)

Table 5.2 A brief description of the mentioned AI and Cloud Computing popular approaches. (*Continued*)

Main goal	Reference	Methods and device used	Results	Pros/cons
Secure communication protocol	[159]	CFSec and Scyther.	Computation time is less as Point Multiplication=0.063 s, Point addition/subtraction = 0.009 s and Symmetric Key Encryption 0.0008s.	Simplex system.
Fog Computing Trust Management Approach	[160]	COMputIng Trust manageMENT (COMITMENT), Random Walks Offloading (RWO), and Nearest Fog Offloading (NFO).	Service response time = 15s.	The algorithm proposed is simple.
Geospatial Question Response Process	[161]	Spatio-Fog.	The average system response time is less than 25s, and the user's power consumption is 0.577W.	30%–60% less power usage of the consumer computer and less latency.
Smart Grid monitoring	[177]	A MATLAB/Simulink, IEEE test grid topology.	Number of variables = 1 with File size [kB] = 2.	Less resource requirement.

(*Continued*)

Table 5.2 A brief description of the mentioned AI and Cloud Computing popular approaches. (*Continued*)

Main goal	Reference	Methods and device used	Results	Pros/cons
Energy-aware tasks scheduling	[163]	Dynamic Voltage and Frequency Scaling (DVFS), Invasive Weed Optimization, and Culture (IWO-CA), HEFT-B, and HEFT-T.	Numbers of processors = 12 and task = 400.	Task offloading is not considered.
Simulation of mobility and migration	[178]	MobFogSim, iFogSim, and Luxembourg SUMO Traffic system (LuST).	Simulation of mobility.	The simulator will use a user-defined migration strategy.
Inspection System For Smart Manufacturing	[164]	Fog Computing based Hybrid Deep-Learning Framework (FC-HDLF) and CNN.	The device can manage extremely large volumes of data by way of Discharging the load to the fog nodes from the central servers.	Reduce the core operation burden.
Reduce time to download the data stored in a fog/cloud architecture	[164]	NC-network-Coding.	Total computational time = 5.087 s.	Communication delay is less.

(*Continued*)

Table 5.2 A brief description of the mentioned AI and Cloud Computing popular approaches. (*Continued*)

Main goal	Reference	Methods and device used	Results	Pros/cons
Delay-sensitive fog network for IoT	[167]	Game Theory, FogIoHT, and QualNet.	Energy Consumption = 34% and Time Delay = 18%.	Portable l as compared to the RSU.
Assembly operation recognition with FOG	[166]	Human-Cantered Intelligent Manufacturing and CNN.	Accuracy = 94.7%, Precision = 92.8 %, Recall = 92.1% and F1 Score = 92.1%.	Computational time is still undesirable.
Framework for urban sound sensing	[168]	Urban Sound Classification Model.	Latency = 45% more than IoT-FOG with 300ms, Average Runtime = 16.42 s and Avg Power Consumption (P_{avg}) = 1.8W.	Less power consumption.
AAL fall detection system	[169]	Ambient Assisted Living (AAL), DL technics deployment, Tri-Axial Accelerometer Smart-IoT-Gateway, and LSTM/GRU.	Efficiency = 98.75%, Total inference time = 0.866, Sensitivity = 97.60% and Specificity = 97.44%.	Response time is high.

(Continued)

Table 5.2 A brief description of the mentioned AI and Cloud Computing popular approaches. (*Continued*)

Main goal	Reference	Methods and device used	Results	Pros/cons
Green computing resource allocation in CC	[136]	Modified Deep Reinforcement Learning (M-DRL) algorithm, Q-learning, the rule-based resource manager, and CloudSim.	Waiting time = 140s, Precision = 94.2 %.	The overall efficiency of the model is not good, but the proposed algorithm is simpler.
Resource Scheduling for CC	[135]	Cloud Resource Scheduling Optimal Hypervisor (CRSOH).	Skewness is 4.63% less than MRAA UBRA, and efficiency is more or less similar to UBRA.	Conservation of energy and scalable model.
Service Selection and Ranking of CC	[171]	BWM-TOPSIS and Optimal Service Selection and Ranking (OSSR).	Time complexity has reduced.	Not able to accommodate periodic and simultaneous changes.
Byzantine Failure Prediction and maintain reliability	[172]	BFPF-Cloud and support vector machine (SVM).	Execution Time = 69.91%, Repeated Requests = 69.78% and Throughput Is = 69.90%.	The complexity of the system increases.

(*Continued*)

Table 5.2 A brief description of the mentioned AI and Cloud Computing popular approaches. (*Continued*)

Main goal	Reference	Methods and device used	Results	Pros/cons
Load prediction using (DoG–ALMS)	[134]	Gaussian-adaptive least mean square (GALMS) filter, soft computing, and difference of Gaussian-based adaptive least mean square algorithm (DoG–ALMS).	Accuracy = 92%, Time consumption = 432 ms and Resource utilization = 82.15%.	Computation time is less compare to ARIMA [146].
Medical Decision Support Model and the healthcare system	[179]	VIKOR (Višekriterijumsko KOmpromisno Rangiranje), MCDM, TOPSIS (The Technique for Order of Preference by Similarity to Ideal Solution) and WBAN.	Enhance The Accuracy Prediction, Reduce Execution Time By 9.8%, and High Sensitivity.	Better accuracy of diagnosis With mysterious data.
Predicting blast-induced air overpressure	[173]	Genetic algorithm boosted smoothing spline (GA-BSTSM). CART (classification and regression tree), KNN (k-nearest neighbors), BRR (Bayesian ridge regression), and SVR (support vector regression).	Root Mean Squared Error (RMSE) = 1.726, Coefficient of determination (R^2) = 0.971 and Variance = 97.069.	Complex algorithm.

(*Continued*)

Table 5.2 A brief description of the mentioned AI and Cloud Computing popular approaches. (*Continued*)

Main goal	Reference	Methods and device used	Results	Pros/cons
Prediction of soils consolidation coefficient	[180]	ANN-BBO, Network-based Fuzzy Inference System (ANFIS), SVM and Monte Carlo simulation.	Mean Absolute Error (MAE) = 0.108), R^2 =0.965 and RMSE = 0.222.	Better prediction.
Prediction of surface settlement	[181]	Extreme Gradient Boosting (XGBoost), ANN, SVM, and MARS (Multivariate Adaptive Regression Spline).	RMSE = 0.31 , R^2 = 0.71 and Bias = 1.11.	The performance of the system is good.

5.5   Conclusion

As new technologies continuously drive the workplace and business's digital transformation, we need to understand how it occurs. Some age-defining technologies have taken the lead in transforming workplace and business, such as big data, artificial intelligence (AI), IoT, and cloud computing. Cloud computing helps leverage big data analytics via cloud server data connectivity everywhere. To benefit from IoT data, an organization needs cloud storage. On the other hand, AI plays a significant role in the embedded computing world, allowing devices to perform certain user-driven functions. Using machines, linked computers, machinery, and data analysis together offers great opportunities to improve process automation. These technologies, tuned to work in modern manufacturing environments, help increase unmatched quality and company efficiency. These technologies appear to hold hope for developers, tech wizards, and company IT specialists in data-driven automation. Integrating these innovations will clear fresh grounds for tech developments in the years ahead.

References

1. Ghosh, A., Chakraborty, D., Law, A., Artificial intelligence in internet of things. *CAAI Trans. Intell. Technol.*, 3, 208–218, 2018, https://doi.org/10.1049/trit.2018.1008.
2. Yampolskiy, R.V. and Spellchecker, M.S., Artificial intelligence safety and cybersecurity: A timeline of AI failures, 2016.
3. Adams, T., AI-powered social bots. 1, arXiv, 2017, doi:10.48550/ARXIV.1706.05143.
4. Dilek, S., Çakır, H., Aydın, M., Applications of artificial intelligence techniques to combating cyber crimes: A review, 2015, https://doi.org/10.5121/ijaia.2015.6102.
5. Brundage, M., Avin, S., Clark, J. *et al.*, The malicious use of artificial intelligence: Forecasting, prevention, and mitigation, 2018, https://doi.org/10.17863/CAM.22520.
6. Al-Jarrah, O.Y., Yoo, P.D., Muhaidat, S. *et al.*, Efficient machine learning for big data: A review. *Big Data Res.*, 2, 87–93, 2015.
7. Chandrakar, R., Raja, R., Miri, R., Animal detection based on deep convolutional neural networks with genetic segmentation. *Multimed. Tools Appl.*, 2021, https://doi.org/10.1007/s11042-021-11290-4.
8. Tsai, C.W., Lai, C.F., Chiang, M.C., Yang, L.T., Data mining for internet of things: A survey. *IEEE Commun. Surv. Tutor.*, 16, 77–97, 2014, https://doi.org/10.1109/SURV.2013.103013.00206.

9. Chen, F., Deng, P., Wan, J. *et al.*, Data mining for the internet of things: Literature review and challenges. *Int. J. Distrib. Sens. Netw.*, 2015.

10. Raja, R., Kumar, S., Choudhary, S., Dalmia, H., An effective contour detection based image retrieval using multi-fusion method and neural network. *Wirel. Pers. Commun.*, DOI: 10.21203/rs.3.rs-458104/v1.

11. Adi, E., Anwar, A., Baig, Z., Zeadally, S., Machine learning and data analytics for the IoT. *Neural Comput. Appl.*, 132, 20, 1–29, 2020, https://doi.org/10.1007/s00521-020-04874-y.

12. Jain, D.K., Shamsolmoali, P., Sehdev, P., Extended deep neural network for facial emotion recognition. *Patt. Recognit. Lett.*, 120, 69–74, 2019, https://doi.org/10.1016/j.patrec.2019.01.008.

13. Witten, I.H., Frank, E., Hall, M.A., Pal, C.J., *Data mining: Practical machine learning tools and techniques*, Elsevier Inc., 2016.

14. Ge, Z., Song, Z., Ding, S.X., Huang, B., Data mining and analytics in the process industry: The role of machine learning. *IEEE Access*, 5, 20590–20616, 2017, https://doi.org/10.1109/ACCESS.2017.2756872.

15. Kumar, S., Raja, R., Gandham, A., Tracking an object using traditional MS (Mean Shift) and CBWH MS (Mean Shift) algorithm with kalman filter, in: *Applications of machine learning. Algorithms for intelligent systems*, P. Johri, J. Verma, S. Paul (Eds.), Springer, Singapore, 2020, https://doi.org/10.1007/978-981-15-3357-0_4.

16. Jin, X., Wah, B.W., Cheng, X., Wang, Y., Significance and challenges of big data research. *Big Data Res.*, 2, 59–64, 2015, https://doi.org/10.1016/j.bdr.2015.01.006.

17. Bikakis, N., Papastefanatos, G., Papaemmanouil, O., Big data exploration, visualization and analytics. *Big Data Res.*, 18, 100123, 2019.

18. Park, J.S. and Park, J.H., Future trends of iot, 5G mobile networks, and AI: Challenges, opportunities, and solutions. *J. Inf. Proces. Syst.*, 16, 743–749, 2020, https://doi.org/10.3745/JIPS.03.0146.

19. Sicari, S., Rizzardi, A., Coen-Porisini, A., 5G in the internet of things era: An overview on security and privacy challenges. *Comput. Netw.*, 179, 107345, 2020, https://doi.org/10.1016/j.comnet.2020.107345.

20. Zheng, C., Yuan, J., Zhu, L. *et al.*, From digital to sustainable: A scientometric review of smart city literature between 1990 and 2019. *J. Clean. Prod.*, 258, 120689, 2020.

21. Crespo-perez, G. and Ojeda-castro, A., Convergence of cloud computing internet of things and machine learning the future of decision support systems. *Int. J. Sci. Technol. Res.*, 06, 131–136, 2017.

22. Kassab, W. and Darabkh, K.A., A–Z survey of internet of things: Architectures, protocols, applications, recent advances, future directions and recommendations. *J. Netw. Comput. Appl.*, 163, 2020, https://doi.org/10.1016/j.jnca.2020.102663.

23. Techradar, Rise of the Internet of Things (IoT) |Techradar, in: *Web source*, 2019, https://www.techradar.com/news/rise-of-the-internet-of-things-iot.

24. Times, E., Intelligent IoT: Bringing the power of AI to the internet of things, in: *ELE Times*, 2020, https://www.eletimes.com/intelligent-iot-bringing-the-power-of-ai-to-the-internet-of-things.

25. Said, O., Al-Makhadmeh, Z., Tolba, A., EMS: An energy management scheme for green IoT environments. *IEEE Access*, 8, 44983–44998, 2020, https://doi.org/10.1109/ACCESS.2020.2976641.

26. Sinha, T.S., Patra, R.K., Raja, R., A Comprehensive analysis of human gait for abnormal foot recognition using neuro-genetic approach. *Int. J. Tomograph. Stat. (IJTS)*, 16, W11, 56–73, http://ceser.res.in/ceserp/index.php/ijts.

27. Shen, J., Wang, A., Wang, C. *et al.*, An efficient centroid-based routing protocol for energy management in WSN-assisted IoT. *IEEE Access*, 5, 18469–18479, 2017, https://doi.org/10.1109/ACCESS.2017.2749606.

28. Yaghmaee, M.H. and Hejazi, H., Design and implementation of an internet of things based smart energy metering, in: *2018 6th IEEE International Conference on Smart Energy Grid Engineering, SEGE 2018*, Institute of Electrical and Electronics Engineers Inc., pp. 191–194, 2018.

29. Ku, T.Y., Park, W.K., Choi, H., IoT energy management platform for microgrid, in: *2017 IEEE 7th International Conference on Power and Energy Systems, ICPES 2017*, Institute of Electrical and Electronics Engineers Inc., pp. 106–110, 2017.

30. Choi, C.S., Jeong, J.D., Lee, I.W., Park, W.K., Lora based renewable energy monitoring system with open IoT platform, in: *International Conference on Electronics, Information and Communication, ICEIC 2018*, Institute of Electrical and Electronics Engineers Inc., pp. 1–2, 2018.

31. Pan, J., Jain, R., Paul, S. *et al.*, An internet of things framework for smart energy in buildings: Designs, prototype, and experiments. *IEEE Internet Things J.*, 2, 527–537, 2015, https://doi.org/10.1109/JIOT.2015.2413397.

32. Ejaz, W., Naeem, M., Shahid, A. *et al.*, Efficient energy management for the internet of things in smart cities. *IEEE Commun. Mag.*, 55, 84–91, 2017, https://doi.org/10.1109/MCOM.2017.1600218CM.

33. Anzanpour, A., Rashid, H., Rahmani, A.M. *et al.*, Energy-efficient and reliable wearable internet-of-things through fog-assisted dynamic goal management, in: *Procedia Computer Science*, Elsevier B.V, pp. 493–500, 2019.

34. Chandrakar, R., Raja, R., Miri, R., Tandan, S.R., Ramya Laxmi, K., Detection and identification of animals in wild life sancturies using convolutional neural network. *Int. J. Recent Technol. Eng. (IJRTE)*, 8, 5, 30 January 2020.

35. Zhang, D., Zhou, Z., Mumtaz, S. *et al.*, One integrated energy efficiency proposal for 5G IoT communications. *IEEE Internet Things J.*, 3, 1346–1354, 2016, https://doi.org/10.1109/JIOT.2016.2599852.

36. Sahu, A.K., Sharma, S., Tanveer, M., Raja, R., Internet of things attack detection using hybrid deep learning model. *Comput. Commun.*, 176, 146–154, 2021, https://doi.org/10.1016/j.comcom.2021.05.024.

37. Zhang, S., Wang, Y., Zhou, W., Towards secure 5G networks: A survey. *Comput. Netw.*, 162, 2019, https://doi.org/10.1016/j.comnet.2019.106871.

38. Akyildiz, I.F., Wang, P., Lin, S.C., SoftAir: A software defined networking architecture for 5G wireless systems. *Comput. Networks*, 85, 1–18, 2015, https://doi.org/10.1016/j.comnet.2015.05.007.

39. Rohit Kumar, K. and Raja, R., Broadcasting the transaction system by using blockchain technology. *Des. Eng.*, 2115 –21, June 2021, http://thedesignengineering .com/ index.php/DE/article/view/1912.

40. Chettri, L. and Bera, R., A comprehensive survey on Internet of Things (IoT) Toward 5G wireless systems. *IEEE Internet Things J.*, 7, 16–32, 2020.

41. He, K., Wang, Z., Li, D. *et al.*, Ultra-reliable MU-MIMO detector based on deep learning for 5G/B5G-enabled IoT. *Phys. Commun.*, 43, 101181, 2020, https://doi.org/10.1016/j.phycom.2020.101181.

42. Bockelmann, C., Pratas, N., Nikopour, H. *et al.*, Massive machine-type communications in 5G: Physical and MAC-layer solutions. *IEEE Commun. Mag.*, 54, 59–65, 2016, https://doi.org/10.1109/MCOM.2016.7565189.

43. Tarek, D., Benslimane, A., Darwish, M., Kotb, A.M., A new strategy for packets scheduling in cognitive radio internet of things. *Comput. Netw.*, 178, 2020, https://doi.org/10.1016/j.comnet.2020.107292.

44. Schulz, P., Matthe, M., Klessig, H. *et al.*, Latency critical IoT applications in 5G: Perspective on the design of radio interface and network architecture. *IEEE Commun. Mag.*, 55, 70–78, 2017.

45. Borgia, E., The internet of things vision: Key features, applications and open issues. *Comput. Commun.*, 54, 1–31, 2014.

46. Palattella, M.R., Dohler, M., Grieco, A. *et al.*, Internet of Things in the 5G Era: Enablers, architecture, and business models. *IEEE J. Select. Areas Commun.*, 34, 510–527, 2016, https://doi.org/10.1109/JSAC.2016.2525418.

47. Al-Turjman, F. and Alturjman, S., 5G/IoT-enabled UAVs for multimedia delivery in industry-oriented applications. *Multimed. Tools Appl.*, 79, 8627–8648, 2020, https://doi.org/10.1007/s11042-018-6288-7.

48. Cheng, J., Chen, W., Tao, F., Lin, C.L., Industrial IoT in 5G environment towards smart manufacturing. *J. Ind. Inf. Integr.*, 10, 10–19, 2018, https://doi.org/10.1016/j.jii.2018.04.001.

49. Sharma, M., Joshi, S., Kannan, D., Govindan, K., Singh, R., Purohit, H.C., Internet of Things (IoT) adoption barriers of smart cities' waste management: An Indian context. *J. Clean. Prod.*, 270, 122047, 2020.

50. Schinianakis, D., Alternative security options in the 5G and IoT era. *IEEE Circuits Syst. Mag.*, 17, 6–28, 2017, https://doi.org/10.1109/MCAS.2017.2757080.

51. Khalfi, B., Hamdaoui, B., Guizani, M., Extracting and exploiting inherent sparsity for efficient IoT support in 5G: Challenges and potential solutions. *IEEE Wirel. Commun.*, 24, 68–73, 2017, https://doi.org/10.1109/MWC.2017.1700067.

52. Chen, X., Liu, S., Lu, J. *et al.*, Smart channel sounder for 5G IoT: From wireless big data to active communication. *IEEE Access*, 4, 8888–8899, 2016, https://doi.org/10.1109/ACCESS.2016.2628820.

53. Xu, L., Collier, R., O'Hare, G.M.P., A survey of clustering techniques in WSNs and consideration of the challenges of applying such to 5G IoT scenarios. *IEEE Internet Things J.*, 4, 1229–1249, 2017, https://doi.org/10.1109/JIOT.2017.2726014.

54. Chien, W.C., Huang, S.Y., Lai, C.F., Chao, H.C., Resource management in 5g mobile networks: Survey and challenges. *J. Inf. Process. Syst.*, 16, 896–914, 2020, https://doi.org/10.3745/JIPS.03.0143.

55. Radoglou Grammatikis, P.I., Sarigiannidis, P.G., Moscholios, I.D., Securing the internet of things: Challenges, threats and solutions. *Internet Things*, 5, 41–70, 2019, https://doi.org/10.1016/j.iot.2018.11.003.

56. Huang, Y., Guan, X., Chen, H. *et al.*, Risk assessment of private information inference for motion sensor embedded IoT devices. *IEEE Trans. Emerg. Topics Comput. Intell.*, 4, 265–275, 2020, https://doi.org/10.1109/TETCI.2019.2902866.

57. Tiwari, L., Raja, R., Awasthi, V., Miri, R., Sinha, G.R., Alkinani, M.H., Polat, K., Detection of lung nodule and cancer using novel mask-3 FCM and TWEDLNN algorithms. *Measurement*, 172, 108882, 2021, https://doi.org/10.1016/j.measurement.2020.108882.

58. Casola, V., De Benedictis, A., Rak, M., Villano, U., Toward the automation of threat modeling and risk assessment in IoT systems. *Internet Things*, 7, 100056, 2019, https://doi.org/10.1016/j.iot.2019.100056.

59. Albataineh, A. and Alsmadi, I., IoT and the risk of internet exposure: Risk assessment using shodan queries, in: *20th IEEE International Symposium on A World of Wireless, Mobile and Multimedia Networks, WoWMoM 2019*, Institute of Electrical and Electronics Engineers Inc, 2019.

60. George, G. and Thampi, S.M., Vulnerability-based risk assessment and mitigation strategies for edge devices in the internet of things. *Pervasive Mob. Comput.*, 59, 101068, 2019, https://doi.org/10.1016/j.pmcj.2019.101068.

61. Kandasamy, K., Srinivas, S., Achuthan, K., Rangan, V.P., IoT cyber risk: A holistic analysis of cyber risk assessment frameworks, risk vectors, and risk ranking process. *Eurasip J. Inf. Secur.*, 2020, 8, 2020, https://doi.org/10.1186/s13635-020-00111-0.

62. Liao, B., Ali, Y., Nazir, S. *et al.*, Security analysis of IoT devices by using mobile computing: A systematic literature review. *IEEE Access*, 8, 120331–120350, 2020.

63. Solutions, R., Smart City, IoT and AI, in: *Web source*, 2020, https://riberasolutions.com/smart-city-iot-and-ai/.

64. Raja, R., Kumar, S., Rashid, M., Color object detection based image retrieval using ROI segmentation with multi-feature method. *Wirel. Pers. Commun.*, 1–24, 2020, https://doi.org/10.1 007/s11277-019-07021-6.

65. Park, J.H., Salim, M.M., Jo, J.H. *et al.*, CIoT-net: a scalable cognitive IoT based smart city network architecture. *Hum.-centric Comput. Inf. Sci.*, 9, 29, 2019, https://doi.org/10.1186/s13673-019-0190-9.

66. Guo, K., Lu, Y., Gao, H., Cao, R., Artificial intelligence-based semantic inter-net of things in a user-centric smart city. *Sensors*, 18, 1341, 2018, https://doi.org/10.3390/s18051341.

67. Qolomany, B., Mohammed, I., Al-Fuqaha, A., Guizani, M., Qadir, J., Trust-based cloud machine learning model selection for industrial IoT and smart city services, in: *IEEE Internet of Things Journal*, vol. 8, no. 4, pp. 2943–2958, 15 Feb.15, 2021, doi: 10.1109/JIOT.2020.3022323.

68. Lenka, R.K., Rath, A.K., Tan, Z., Sharma, S., Puthal, D., Simha, N.V.R., Tripathi, S.S., Prasad, M., Building Scalable Cyber-physical-social network-ing infrastructure using IoT and low power sensors, 6, 1, 30162–30173. Print, Online Digital object Identifier: 10.1109/ACCESS.2018.2842760.

69. Design, E.C., How IoT is transforming the healthcare industry, in: *Web source*, 2020, https://www.embedded-computing.com/guest-blogs/how-iot-is-transforming-the-healthcare-industry.

70. Fouad, H., Hassanein, A.S., Soliman, A.M., Al-Feel, H., Analyzing patient health information based on IoT sensor with AI for improving patient assis-tance in the future direction. *Meas.: J. Int. Meas. Confed.*, 159, 107757, 2020, https://doi.org/10.1016/j.measurement.2020.107757.

71. Souri, A., Ghafour, M.Y., Ahmed, A.M. *et al.*, A new machine learning-based healthcare monitoring model for student's condition diagnosis in internet of things environment. *Soft Comput.*, 1–11, 2020, https://doi.org/10.1007/s00500-020-05003-6.

72. Yan, P., Choudhury, S., Al-Turjman, F., Al-Oqily, I., An energy-efficient topology control algorithm for optimizing the lifetime of wireless ad-hoc IoT networks in 5G and B5G. *Comput. Commun.*, 159, 83–96, 2020, https://doi.org/10.1016/j.comcom.2020.05.010.

73. Haider, S.A., Adil, M.N., Zhao, M.J., Optimization of secure wireless communications for IoT networks in the presence of eavesdroppers. *Comput. Commun.*, 154, 119–128, 2020, https://doi.org/10.1016/j. comcom. 2020.02.027.

74. Saddoud, A., Doghri, W., Charfi, E., Fourati, L.C., 5G radio resource man-agement approach for multi-traffic IoT communications. *Comput. Netw.*, 166, 106936, 2020, https://doi.org/10.1016/j.comnet.2019.106936.

75. Awoyemi, B.S., Alfa, A.S., Maharaj, B.T.J., Resource optimisation in 5G and internet-of-things networking. *Wirel. Pers. Commun.*, 111, 2671–2702, 2020.

76. Sheikh, J.A., Akhter, S., Parah, S.A., Bhat, G.M., Blind digital speech water-marking using filter bank multicarrier modulation for 5G and IoT driven networks. *Int. J. Speech Technol.*, 21, 715–722, 2018, https://doi.org/10.1007/s10772-018-9541-6.

77. Gowtham, P., Arunachalam, V.P., Vijayakumar, V.A., Karthik, S., An effi-cient monitoring of real time traffic clearance for an emergency service vehicle using IoT. *Int. J. Parallel Program.*, 48, 786–812, 2020, https://doi.org/10.1007/s10766-018-0603-9.

78. Raja, R., Sinha, T.S., Dubey, R.P., Recognition of human-face from side-view using progressive switching pattern and soft-computing technique. *Assoc. Adv. Model. Simul. Tech. Enterp. Adv. B*, 58, 1, 14–34, 2015.

79. Singh, S.K., Jeong, Y.S., Park, J.H., A deep learning-based IoT-oriented infrastructure for secure smart city. *Sustain. Cities Soc*, 60, 102252, 2020, https://doi.org/10.1016/j.scs.2020.102252.

80. Meng, W., Li, W., Tug, S., Tan, J., Towards blockchain-enabled single character frequency-based exclusive signature matching in IoT-assisted smart cities. *J. Parallel Distrib. Comput.*, 144, 268–277, 2020, https://doi.org/10.1016/j.jpdc.2020.05.013.

81. Srinivasa Desikan, K.E., Kotagi, V.J., Siva Ram Murthy, C., Topology control in fog computing enabled IoT networks for smart cities. *Comput. Netw.*, 176, 107270, 2020, https://doi.org/10.1016/j.comnet.2020.107270.

82. Meenaakshi Sundhari, R.P. and Jaikumar, K., IoT assisted hierarchical computation strategic making (HCSM) and dynamic stochastic optimization technique (DSOT) for energy optimization in wireless sensor networks for smart city monitoring. *Comput. Commun.*, 150, 226–234, 2020, https://doi.org/10.1016/j.comcom.2019.11.032.

83. Habibzadeh, H., Qin, Z., Soyata, T., Kantarci, B., Large-scale distributed dedicated- and non-dedicated smart city sensing systems. *IEEE Sens. J.*, 17, 7649–7658, 2017, https://doi.org/10.1109/JSEN.2017.2725638.

84. Nair, K., Kulkarni, J., Warde, M. *et al.*, Optimizing power consumption in iot based wireless sensor networks using bluetooth low energy, in: *Proceedings of the 2015 International Conference on Green Computing and Internet of Things, ICGCIoT 2015*, Institute of Electrical and Electronics Engineers Inc., pp. 589–593, 2016.

85. Memos, V.A., Psannis, K.E., Ishibashi, Y. *et al.*, An efficient algorithm for media-based surveillance system (EAMSuS) in IoT smart city framework. *Fut. Gener. Comput. Syst.*, 83, 619–628, 2018, https://doi.org/10.1016/j.future.2017.04.039.

86. Rout, R.R., Vemireddy, S., Raul, S.K., Somayajulu, D.V.L.N., Fuzzy logic-based emergency vehicle routing: An IoT system development for smart city applications. *Comput. Electr. Eng.*, 88, 106839, 2020, https://doi.org/10.1016/j.compeleceng.2020.106839.

87. Swapna, N., An improved network-based spam detection framework for review in online social media. *Int. J. Sci. Res. Eng. Manage. (IJSREM)*, 03, 09, Sep 2019.

88. Chithaluru, P., Al-Turjman, F., Kumar, M., Stephan, T., I-AREOR: An energy-balanced clustering protocol for implementing green IoT in smart cities. *Sustain. Cities Soc*, 61, 102254, 2020, https://doi.org/10.1016/j.scs.2020.102254.

89. Rahman, M.A., Asyhari, A.T., Leong, L.S. *et al.*, Scalable machine learning-based intrusion detection system for IoT-enabled smart cities. *Sustain. Cities Soc.*, 61, 102324, 2020, https://doi.org/10.1016/j.scs.2020.102324.

90. Aminanto, M.E., Choi, R., Tanuwidjaja, H.C. *et al.*, Deep abstraction and weighted feature selection for Wi-Fi impersonation detection. *IEEE Trans. Inf. Forensics Secur.*, 13, 621–636, 2017, https://doi.org/10.1109/TIFS.2017.2762828.

91. Dutta, J., Roy, S., Chowdhury, C., Unified framework for IoT and smartphone based different smart city related applications. *Microsyst. Technol.*, 25, 83–96, 2019, https://doi.org/10.1007/s00542-018-3936-9.

92. Vivekanandan M, V.N.S. and SR, U., BIDAPSCA5G: Blockchain based internet of things (IoT) device to device authentication protocol for smart city applications using 5G technology. *Peer-to-Peer Netw. Appl.*, 1–17, 2020, https://doi.org/10.1007/s12083-020-00963-w.

93. Wang, E.K., Wang, F., Kumari, S. *et al.*, Intelligent monitor for typhoon in IoT system of smart city. *J. Supercomput.*, 77, 3, 1–20, 2020, https://doi.org/10.1007/s11227-020-03381-0.

94. Saleem, M.A., Shijie, Z., Sharif, A., Data Transmission using IoT in vehicular ad-hoc networks in smart city congestion. *Mobil. Netw. Appl.*, 24, 248–258, 2019, https://doi.org/10.1007/s11036-018-1205-x.

95. Lamaazi, H. and Benamar, N., RPL enhancement using a new objective function based on combined metrics, in: *13th International Wireless Communications and Mobile Computing Conference, IWCMC 2017*, Institute of Electrical and Electronics Engineers Inc., pp. 1459–1464, 2017.

96. Li, D., Cai, Z., Deng, L., Yao, X., IoT complex communication architecture for smart cities based on soft computing models. *Soft Comput.*, 23, 2799–2812, 2019, https://doi.org/10.1007/s00500-019-03827-5.

97. Shayesteh, B., Hakami, V., Akbari, A., A trust management scheme for IoTenabled environmental health/accessibility monitoring services. *Int. J. Inf. Secur.*, 19, 1, 93–110, 2020.

98. Miloslavskaya, N. and Tolstoy, A., IoT Block SIEM for information security incident management in the internet of things ecosystem. *Clust. Comput.*, 23, 1911–1925, 2020, https://doi.org/10.1007/s10586-020-03110-5.

99. Boveiri, H.R., Khayami, R., Elhoseny, M., Gunasekaran, M., An efficient swarm-intelligence approach for task scheduling in cloud-based internet of things applications. *J. Ambient Intell. Human. Comput.*, 10, 3469–3479. 1q -1, 2019.

100. Tomazzoli, C., Scannapieco, S., Cristani, M., Internet of things and artificial intelligence enable energy efficiency. *J. Ambient Intell. Human. Comput.*, 1–22, 2020, https://doi.org/10.1007/s12652-020-02151-3.

101. Wu, H. and Li, G., Visual communication design elements of internet of things based on cloud computing applied in graffiti art schema. *Soft Comput.*, 24, 8077–8086, 2020, https://doi.org/10.1007/s00500-019-04171-4.

102. Zhu, R., Liu, L., Song, H., Ma, M., Multi-access edge computing enabled internet of things: Advances and novel applications. *Neural Comput. Appl.*, 32, 15313–15316, 2020.

103. Raja, R., Sinha, T.S., Dubey, R.P., Orientation calculation of human face using symbolic techniques and ANFIS. *Int. J. Eng. Fut. Technol.*, 7, 7, 37–50, 2016.

104. Alsboui, T., Qin, Y., Hill, R., Al-Aqrabi, H., Enabling distributed intelligence for the internet of things with IOTA and mobile agents. *Comput.*, 102, 1345–1363, 2020, https://doi.org/10.1007/s00607-020-00806-9.

105. Maharaja, R., Iyer, P., Ye, Z., A hybrid fog-cloud approach for securing the internet of things. *Clust. Comput.*, 23, 451–459, 2020, https://doi.org/10.1007/s10586-019-02935-z.

106. HaddadPajouh, H., Khayami, R., Dehghantanha, A. *et al.*, AI4SAFE-IoT: an AI-powered secure architecture for edge layer of internet of things. *Neural Comput. Appl.*, 32, 16119–16133, 2020, https://doi.org/10.1007/s00521-020-04772-3.

107. Pinto, S., Gomes, T., Pereira, J. *et al.*, IIoTEED: An enhanced, trusted execution environment for industrial IoT edge devices. *IEEE Internet Comput.*, 21, 40–47, 2017, https://doi.org/10.1109/MIC.2017.17.

108. Roy, S., Sarkar, D., De, D., Dew music: Crowdsourcing-based internet of music things in dew computing paradigm. *J. Ambient Intell. Human. Comput.*, 1, 3, 2020, https://doi.org/10.1007/s12652-020-02309-z.

109. Wan, J., Li, J., Hua, Q. *et al.*, Intelligent equipment design assisted by cognitive internet of things and industrial big data. *Neural Comput. Appl.*, 32, 4463–4472, 2020, https://doi.org/10.1007/s00521-018-3725-5.

110. Duan, Y., Li, J., Srivastava, G., Yeh, J.H., Data storage security for the internet of things. *J. Supercompu.*, 76, 8529–8547, 2020, https://doi.org/10.1007/s11227-020-03148-7.

111. Khan, R. and Raja, R., Introducing L1-sparse representation classification for facial expression. *Imperial J. Interdiscipl. Res. (IJIR)*, 115–122, 2016.

112. Qiao, R., Zhu, S., Wang, Q., Qin, J., Optimization of dynamic data traceability mechanism in internet of things based on consortium blockchain. *Int. J. Distrib. Sens. Netw.*, 14, 155014771881907, 2018, https://doi.org/10.1177/1550147718819072.

113. Alamer, A., An efficient group signcryption scheme supporting batch verification for securing transmitted data in the internet of things. *J. Ambient Intell. Human. Comput.*, 1–18, 2020, https://doi.org/10.1007/s12652-020-02076-x.

114. Zhang, L., Li, C., Li, Y. *et al.*, Group signature based privacy protection algorithm for mobile ad hoc network, in: *IEEE International Conference on Information and Automation, ICIA 2017*, Institute of Electrical and Electronics Engineers Inc., pp. 947–952, 2017.

115. Feng, W., Yan, Z., Xie, H., Anonymous authentication on trust in pervasive social networking based on group signature. *IEEE Access*, 5, 6236–6246, 2017, https://doi.org/10.1109/ACCESS.2017.2679980.

116. Wang, Y., Zhong, H., Xu, Y. *et al.*, ECPB: Efficient conditional privacy-preserving authentication scheme supporting batch verification for vanets

yimin. *Int. J. Netw. Secur.*, 18, 374–382, 2016, https://doi.org/10.1002/sec.1710.

117. Gaber, M.I., Khalaf, A.A.M., Mahmoud, I.I., El_Tokhy M.S. Development of information collection scheme in internet of things environment for intelligent radiation monitoring systems. *Telecommun. Syst.*, 1–16, 2020, https://doi.org/10.1007/s11235-020-00697-3.

118. John, A., Rajput, A., Vinoth Babu, K., Energy saving cluster head selection in wireless sensor networks for internet of things applications, in: *Proceedings of the 2017 IEEE International Conference on Communication and Signal Processing, ICCSP 2017*, Institute of Electrical and Electronics Engineers Inc., pp. 34–38, 2018.

119. Qiu, T., Qiao, R., Han, M. *et al.*, A Lifetime-enhanced data collecting scheme for the internet of things. *IEEE Commun. Mag.*, 55, 132–137, 2017, https://doi.org/10.1109/MCOM.2017.1700033.

120. Velte, T., Velte, A., Elsenpeter, R., *Cloud computing, a practical approach*, 1st, McGraw-Hill, Inc., USA, 2009.

121. Satyanarayanan, M., A brief history of cloud offload. *GetMobil.: Mobi. Comput. Commun.*, 18, 19–23, 2015, https://doi.org/10.1145/2721914.2721921.

122. Raj, A.P., Raja, R., Akella, S., A new framework for trustworthiness of cloud services. *Int. J. Res.*, 04, 1, December 2017. e-ISSN: 2348-6848, p-ISSN: 2348-795X.

123. Li, P., Li, J., Huang, Z. *et al.*, Privacy-preserving outsourced classification in cloud computing. *Clust. Comput.*, 21, 277–286, 2018, https://doi.org/10.1007/s10586-017-0849-9.

124. Kumar, P.R., Raj, P.H., Jelciana, P., Exploring data security issues and solutions in cloud computing, in: *Procedia Computer Science*, Elsevier B.V, pp. 691–697, 2018.

125. Varghese, B. and Buyya, R., Next generation cloud computing: New trends and research directions. *Fut. Gener. Comput. Syst.*, 79, 849–861, 2018, https://doi.org/10.1016/j.future.2017.09.020.

126. Subramanian, N. and Jeyaraj, A., Recent security challenges in cloud computing. *Comput. Electr. Eng.*, 71, 28–42, 2018, https://doi.org/10.1016/j.compeleceng.2018.06.006.

127. Yang, C., Huang, Q., Li, Z. *et al.*, Big Data and cloud computing: innovation opportunities and challenges. *Int. J. Digit. Earth*, 10, 13–53, 2017, https://doi.org/10.1080/17538947.2016.1239771.

128. De Donno, M., Tange, K., Dragoni, N., Foundations and evolution of modern computing paradigms: Cloud, IoT, edge, and fog. *IEEE Access*, 7, 150936–150948, 2019, https://doi.org/10.1109/ACCESS.2019.2947652.

129. Lee, Y.C. and Zomaya, A.Y., Energy efficient utilization of resources in cloud computing systems. *J. Supercomput.*, 60, 268–280, 2012, https://doi.org/10.1007/s11227-010-0421-3.

130. Chaabouni, T. and Khemakhem, M., Energy management strategy in cloud computing: A perspective study. *J. Supercomput.*, 74, 6569–6597, 2018, https://doi.org/10.1007/s11227-017-2154-z.

131. Chowdhury, M.R., Mahmud, M.R., Rahman, R.M., Implementation and performance analysis of various VM placement strategies in cloud sim. *J. Cloud Comput.*, 4, 1–21, 2015, https://doi.org/10.1186/s13677-015-0045-5.

132. Kumari, A., Gupta, R., Tanwar, S., Kumar, N., Blockchain and AI amalgamation for energy cloud management: Challenges, solutions, and future directions. *J. Parallel Distrib. Comput.*, 143, 148–166, 2020, https://doi.org/10.1016/j.jpdc.2020.05.004.

133. Devaraj, A.F.S., Elhoseny, M., Dhanasekaran, S. *et al.*, Hybridization of firefly and improved multi-objective particle swarm optimization algorithm for energy efficient load balancing in cloud computing environments. *J. Parallel Distrib. Comput.*, 142, 36–45, 2020, https://doi.org/10.1016/j.jpdc.2020.03.022.

134. Reshmi, R. and Saravanan, D.S., Load prediction using (DoG–ALMS) for resource allocation based on IFP soft computing approach in cloud computing. *Soft Comput.*, 24, 15307–15315, 2020, https://doi.org/10.1007/s00500-020-04864-1.

135. Malarvizhi, N., Priyatharsini, G.S., Koteeswaran, S., Cloud resource scheduling optimal hypervisor (CRSOH) for dynamic cloud computing environment. *Wirel. Pers. Commun.*, 115, 1, 1–16, 2020, https://doi.org/10.1007/s11277-020-07553-2.

136. Karthiban, K. and Raj, J.S., An efficient green computing fair resource allocation in cloud computing using modified deep reinforcement learning algorithm. *Soft Comput.*, 24, 14933–14942, 2020, https://doi.org/10.1007/s00500-020-04846-3.

137. Vakilinia, S., Heidarpour, B., Cheriet, M., Energy efficient resource allocation in cloud computing environments. *IEEE Access*, 4, 8544–8557, 2016, https://doi.org/10.1109/ACCESS.2016.2633558.

138. Sittón-Candanedo, I., Edge computing: A review of application scenarios. *Adv. Intell. Syst. Comput.*, 1004, 197–200, 2020.

139. Zhang, P.Y., Zhang, A.Q., Xu, G., Optimized task distribution based on task requirements and time delay in edge computing environments. *Eng. Appl. Artif. Intell.*, 94, 103774, 2020, https://doi.org/10.1016/j.engappai.2020.103774.

140. Baucas, M.J. and Spachos, P., Using cloud and fog computing for large scale IoT-based urban sound classification. *Simul. Model. Pract. Theory*, 101, 102013, 2020, https://doi.org/10.1016/j.simpat.2019.102013.

141. Azar, J., Makhoul, A., Barhamgi, M., Couturier, R., An energy efficient IoT data compression approach for edge machine learning. *Fut. Gener. Comput. Syst.*, 96, 168–175, 2019, https://doi.org/10.1016/j.future.2019.02.005.

142. Li, C., Song, M., Zhang, M., Luo, Y., Effective replica management for improving reliability and availability in edge-cloud computing environment.

J. Parallel Distrib. Comput., 143, 107–128, 2020, https://doi.org/10.1016/ j.jpdc.2020.04.012.

143. Jararweh, Y., Enabling efficient and secure energy cloud using edge computing and 5G. *J. Parallel Distrib. Comput.*, 145, 42–49, 2020, https://doi. org/10.1016/j.jpdc.2020.06.014.

144. Deebak, B.D., Al-Turjman, F., Mostarda, L., Seamless secure anonymous authentication for cloud-based mobile edge computing. *Comput. Electr. Eng.*, 87, 106782, 2020, https://doi.org/10.1016/j.compeleceng.2020.106782.

145. Li, C., Bai, J., Ge, Y., Luo, Y., Heterogeneity-aware elastic provisioning in cloud-assisted edge computing systems. *Fut. Gener. Comput. Syst.*, 112, 1106–1121, 2020, https://doi.org/10.1016/j.future.2020.06.022.

146. Miao, Y., Wu, G., Li, M. *et al.*, Intelligent task prediction and computation offloading based on mobile-edge cloud computing. *Fut. Gener. Comput. Syst.*, 102, 925–931, 2020, https://doi.org/10.1016/j.future.2019.09.035.

147. Wang, Y., Liu, M., Zheng, P. *et al.*, A smart surface inspection system using faster R-CNN in cloud-edge computing environment. *Adv. Eng. Inform.*, 43, 101037, 2020, https://doi.org/10.1016/j.aei.2020.101037.

148. Abdelfattah, A.S., Abdelkader, T., EI-Horbaty, E.S.M., RAMWS: Reliable approach using middleware and WebSockets in mobile cloud computing. *Ain Shams Eng. J.*, 2020, https://doi.org/10.1016/j.asej.2020.04.002.

149. Qu, X., Hu, Q., Wang, S., Privacy-preserving model training architecture for intelligent edge computing. *Comput. Commun.*, 162, 94–101, 2020, https:// doi.org/10.1016/j.comcom.2020.07.045.

150. Amarasinghe, G., de Assunção, M.D., Harwood, A., Karunasekera, S., ECSNeT++: A simulator for distributed stream processing on edge and cloud environments. *Fut. Gener. Comput. Syst.*, 111, 401–418, 2020, https:// doi.org/10.1016/j.future.2019.11.014.

151. Xia, X., Chen, F., He, Q. *et al.*, Graph-based data caching optimization for edge computing. *Fut. Gener. Comput. Syst.*, 113, 228–239, 2020, https://doi. org/10.1016/j.future.2020.07.016.

152. Wang, M. and Zhang, Q., Optimized data storage algorithm of IoT based on cloud computing in distributed system. *Comput. Commun.*, 157, 124–131, 2020, https://doi.org/10.1016/j.comcom.2020.04.023.

153. Xu, Y., Li, J., Lu, Z. *et al.*, ARVMEC: Adaptive recommendation of virtual machines for IoT in edge–cloud environment. *J. Parallel Distrib. Comput.*, 141, 23–34, 2020, https://doi.org/10.1016/j.jpdc.2020.03.006.

154. Wang, E., Li, D., Dong, B. *et al.*, Flat and hierarchical system deployment for edge computing systems. *Fut. Gener. Comput. Syst.*, 105, 308–317, 2020, https://doi.org/10.1016/j.future.2019.12.004.

155. Cooke, R.A. and Fahmy, S.A., A model for distributed in-network and near-edge computing with heterogeneous hardware. *Fut. Gener. Comput. Syst.*, 105, 395–409, 2020, https://doi.org/10.1016/j.future.2019.11.040.

156. Almogren, A.S., Intrusion detection in edge-of-things computing. *J. Parallel Distrib. Comput.*, 137, 259–265, 2020, https://doi.org/10.1016/j.jpdc.2019.12.008.

157. La, Q.D., Ngo, M.V., Dinh, T.Q. *et al.*, Enabling intelligence in fog computing to achieve energy and latency reduction. *Digit. Commun. Netw.*, 5, 3–9, 2019.

158. Abbasi, M., Yaghoobikia, M., Rafiee, M. *et al.*, Efficient resource management and workload allocation in fog–cloud computing paradigm in IoT using learning classifier systems. *Comput. Commun.*, 153, 217–228, 2020, https://doi.org/10.1016/j.comcom.2020.02.017.

159. Amin, R., Kunal, S., Saha, A. *et al.*, CFSec: Password based secure communication protocol in cloud-fog environment. *J. Parallel Distrib.Computing*, 140, 52–62, 2020, https://doi.org/10.1016/j.jpdc.2020.02.005.

160. Al-khafajiy, M., Baker, T., Asim, M. *et al.*, Comitmment: A fog computing trust management approach. *J. Parallel Distrib. Comput.*, 137, 1–16, 2020, https://doi.org/10.1016/j.jpdc.2019.10.006.

161. Das, J., Mukherjee, A., Ghosh, S.K., Buyya, R., Spatio-fog: A green and timeliness-oriented fog computing model for geospatial query resolution. *Simul. Model. Pract. Theory*, 100, 102043, 2020, https://doi.org/10.1016/j.simpat.2019.102043.

162. Forcan, M. and Maksimović, M., Cloud-fog-based approach for smart grid monitoring. *Simul. Model. Pract. Theory*, 101, 101988, 2020, https://doi.org/10.1016/J.SIMPAT.2019.101988.

163. Hosseinioun, P., Kheirabadi, M., Kamel Tabbakh, S.R., Ghaemi, R., A new energy-aware tasks scheduling approach in fog computing using hybrid meta-heuristic algorithm. *J. Parallel Distrib. Comput.*, 143, 88–96, 2020, https://doi.org/10.1016/j.jpdc.2020.04.008.

164. Lin, S.Y., Du, Y., Ko, P.C. *et al.*, Fog computing based hybrid deep learning framework in effective inspection system for smart manufacturing. *Comput. Commun.*, 160, 636–642, 2020, https://doi.org/10.1016/j.comcom.2020.05.044.

165. Mukherjee, A., De, D., Ghosh, S.K., FogIoHT: A weighted majority game theory based energy-efficient delay-sensitive fog network for internet of health things. *Internet Things*, 11, 100181, 2020, https://doi.org/10.1016/j.iot.2020.100181.

166. Tao, W., Al-Amin, M., Chen, H. *et al.*, Real-time assembly operation recognition with fog computing and transfer learning for human-centered intelligent manufacturing. *Procedia Manufacturing*, vol. 48, pp. 926–931, 2020, https://doi.org/10.1016/j.promfg.2020.05.131.

167. Peralta, G., Garrido, P., Bilbao, J. *et al.*, Fog to cloud and network coded based architecture: Minimizing data download time for smart mobility. *Simul. Model. Pract. Theory*, 101, 102034, 2020, https://doi.org/10.1016/j.simpat.2019.102034.

168. Baucas, M.J. and Spachos, P., A scalable IoT-fog framework for urban sound sensing. *Comput. Commun.*, 153, 302–310, 2020, https://doi.org/10.1016/j.comcom.2020.02.012.

169. Sarabia-Jácome, D., Usach, R., Palau, C.E., Esteve, M., Highly-efficient fog-based deep learning AAL fall detection system. *Internet Things*, 11, 100185, 2020, https://doi.org/10.1016/j.iot.2020.100185.

170. Ragmani, A., Elomri, A., Abghour, N. *et al.*, Adaptive fault-tolerant model for improving cloud computing performance using artificial neural network, in: *Procedia Computer Science*, Elsevier B.V, pp. 929–934, 2020.

171. Kumar, R.R., Kumari, B., Kumar, C., CCS-OSSR: A framework based on hybrid MCDM for optimal service selection and ranking of cloud computing services. *Cluster Comput.*, 1–17, 2020, https://doi.org/10.1007/s10586-020-03166-3.

172. Beheshti, M.K. and Safi-Esfahani, F., BFPF-cloud: Applying SVM for byzantine failure prediction to increase availability and failure tolerance in cloud computing. *SN Comput. Sci.*, 1, 276, 2020, https://doi.org/10.1007/s42979-020-00299-5.

173. Nguyen, H. and Bui, X.N., Soft computing models for predicting blast-induced air over-pressure: A novel artificial intelligence approach. *Appl. Soft Comput. J.*, 92, 106292, 2020, https://doi.org/10.1016/j.asoc.2020.106292.

174. Kristiani, E., Yang, C.T., Huang, C.Y. *et al.*, The implementation of a cloud-edge computing architecture using open stack and kubernetes for air quality monitoring application. *Mobil. Netw. Appl.*, 26, 1070–1092, https://doi.org/10.1007/s11036-020-01620-5.

175. Qafzezi, E., Bylykbashi, K., Ikeda, M. *et al.*, Coordination and management of cloud, fog and edge resources in SDN-VANETs using fuzzy logic: A comparison study for two fuzzy-based systems. *Internet Things*, 11, 100169, 2020, https://doi.org/10.1016/j.iot.2020.100169.

176. Aburukba, R.O., AliKarrar, M., Landolsi, T., El-Fakih, K., Scheduling internet of things requests to minimize latency in hybrid fog–cloud computing. *Fut. Gener. Comput. Syst.*, 111, 539–551, 2020, https://doi.org/10.1016/j.future.2019.09.039.

177. Forcan, M. and Maksimović, M., Cloud-fog-based approach for smart grid monitoring. *Simul. Model. Pract.Theory*, 101, 101988, 2020, https://doi.org/10.1016/j.simpat.2019.101988.

178. Puliafito, C., Gonçalves, D.M., Lopes, M.M. *et al.*, Mob fog sim: Simulation of mobility and migration for fog computing. *Simul. Model. Pract. Theory*, 101, 102062, 2020, https://doi.org/10.1016/j.simpat.2019.102062.

179. Abdel-Basset, M., Manogaran, G., Gamal, A., Chang, V., A novel intelligent medical decision support model based on soft computing and IoT. *IEEE Internet Things J.*, 7, 4160–4170, 2020, https://doi.org/10.1109/JIOT.2019.2931647.

180. Nguyen, M.D., Pham, B.T., Ho, L.S. *et al.*, Soft-computing techniques for prediction of soils consolidation coefficient. *Catena*, 195, 104802, 2020, https://doi.org/10.1016/j.catena.2020.104802.
181. Zhang, W.G., Li, H.R., Wu, C.Z. *et al.*, Soft computing approach for prediction of surface settlement induced by earth pressure balance shield tunneling, in: *Underground Space*, 2020, https://doi.org/10.1016/j.undsp.2019.12.003.

6

Analysis of Internet of Things Acceptance Dimensions in Hospitals

Subhodeep Mukherjee[1]*, Manish Mohan Baral[1], Venkataiah Chittipaka[2] and Sharad Chandra Srivastava[3]

[1]Department of Operations, GITAM School of Business, GITAM (Deemed to be University), Visakhapatnam, Andhra Pradesh, India
[2](School of Management) at Indira Gandhi National Open University, Delhi, India
[3]Department of Industrial and Production Engineering, Guru Ghashidas Vishwavidyalaya (A Central University), Bilaspur, Chhatisgarh, India

Abstract

The Internet of Things (IoT) refers to a network of devices interconnected that can collect and transfer data without human intervention. IoT in healthcare helps healthcare professionals better interact and record data more straightforwardly. This research aims to study the adoption factors of IoT in healthcare organizations. Previous research showed that innovative technology adoption is done using the technological-organization-environmental (TOE) framework. After identifying the factors, we developed a questionnaire for a survey-based study in the hospitals of India. We used exploratory factor analysis and the structural equation modeling approach for data analysis.

Keywords: Internet of Things, technological-organizational-environmental, healthcare, hypothesis, hospitals

*Corresponding author: subhodeepmukherjee92@gmail.com

Md Rashid Mahmood, Rohit Raja, Harpreet Kaur, Sandeep Kumar and Kapil Kumar Nagwanshi (eds.) *Ambient Intelligence and Internet of Things: Convergent Technologies*, (189–214) © 2023 Scrivener Publishing LLC

6.1   Introduction

The Internet of Things (IoT) is a technology that empowers the combination and correspondence of things or articles, for example, RFID labels, sensors, diodes. IoT gadgets are portrayed as digital gadgets with the capacity to detect, impart, and measure information in any specific circumstance. The IoT should have creative answers for changing mechanical frameworks' actions and jobs. These gadgets are utilized for different current industry purposes, including observing, following, information assortment, and examination. A few primer IoT executions have effectively been presented in numerous areas, like emergency clinics, public administrations, and the auto business. By 2025, IoT medical care applications' expense is relied upon to associate with one trillion dollars. IoT is an overall gathering for dividing data among versatile well-being (mHealth) gadgets and different universal advancements in the medical care space. IoT permits information from various gadgets, including phones, implantable devices, wearable gadgets, and encompassing helped living arrangements. Because of its IP-based network capacities, the IoT idea fills in as a connecting design for mHealth innovation.

Embracing I.C.T. frameworks in medical care is analyzed in past research [1]. These investigations take a gander at how RFID, electronic clinical records, electronic patient records (EPR), clinical data frameworks, telemedicine, tablets, electromagnetic medical care frameworks, and other RFID frameworks are utilized in the medical services industry [2]. They use innovation acknowledgement models and hypotheses found in writing on the subject. Even though these investigations lead to the selection, none examines IoT executions in medical care. Likewise, the more significant part of them does not order choice factors regarding various clients' points of view.

This research studies the adoption of IoT in healthcare organizations. For this, we selected technology-organization-environmental (TOE) framework. This framework has been used in many previous studies of technology adoption [3–15]. Three contexts, technological, organizational, and environmental are had different variables. The variables for technological context (TC) are performance expectancy (PE), technology maturity (TMA), perceived compatibility (PC). The variables for environmental context (EC) are regulatory policy (RP), competitive pressure (CP), legal uncertainty (LU), external data (ED). One dependent variable is Internet of Things (IoTH) in healthcare, four indicators IoTH1, IoTH2, IoTH3, and IoTH4.

6.2   Literature Review

6.2.1   Overview of Internet of Things

Kevin Ashton coined the word "IoT" in the feeling of supply chain management in 1999. IoT is a worldwide organization and administration framework with variable thickness and network and self-designing capacities dependent on the norm and interoperable conventions and arrangements. It comprises heterogeneous things with characters, physical and virtual ascribes and is flawlessly and safely fused into the Internet. In light of the expanded accessibility of cell phones, remote sensor and actuator organizations, and radio-recurrence ID (RFID) advancements, the IoT, as characterized above, has as of late drawn nearer to being a reality. Moreover, IoT technology has three essential characteristics that are summarized as follows [16, 17]:

(1) Ordinary objects are instrumented: Ordinary things, such as cups, chairs, screws, food, and car tyres, can be uniquely defined using information perception technologies such as RFID, wireless sensor networks, and other methods [18].

(2) Autonomic terminals are interconnected: This means that multinetwork fusion technologies are used to connect the instrumented physical objects [19].

As a result, the IoT is a sophisticated, all-encompassing interdisciplinary technology that spans computer science, communications, microelectronics, and sensor technology.

6.2.2   Internet of Things in Healthcare

Remote monitoring in the healthcare sector is now partially attributable to IoT (IoT)-enabled devices, which can keep patients safe and secure while inspiring physicians to provide superior treatment as interactions with doctors have become more straightforward and practical, increased patient involvement and satisfaction. Furthermore, remote monitoring of a patient's well-being shortens hospital stays and avoids readmissions. IoT has a significant effect on lowering healthcare costs and improving patient quality.

IoT is undeniably changing the healthcare industry by redefining the space of devices and human involvement in delivering healthcare solutions. Patients, families, doctors, hospitals, and insurance providers all profit from IoT applications in healthcare.

IoT for Patients: These gadgets can be modified to help you remember calorie tallying, workout arrangements, pulse changes, and substantially more. IoT has wholly changed people, especially older patients, by permitting them to screen their ailments continuously. This significantly affects single individuals and their families. An admonition framework conveys messages to relatives and concerned well-being experts if their regular exercises are disturbed or changed.

IoT for Hospitals: Clinical staff organizations can likewise be constantly investigated [20]. Disease transmission is a critical worry for medical clinic patients. IoT-empowered cleanliness observing frameworks aid the anticipation of contamination in patients. IoT gadgets likewise help resource the board, for example, drug store stock following and ecological checking, like testing fridge temperatures and controlling stickiness and temperature [21].

IoT for Health Insurance Companies: With IoT-associated gadgets, well-being backup plans have different freedoms. Protection suppliers may utilize information gathered by well-being global positioning frameworks for guaranteeing and claims preparation. They will want to identify misrepresentation guarantees and arrange to endorse possibilities using this data. Supporting, estimating, claiming the board, and hazard assessment measures, IoT gadgets lucidity among safety net providers and customers. Clients would have a great understanding of the basic idea behind any choice taken and measure results coming about because of IoT-caught information-driven choices taking all things together activity measures [22].

If insurers provide incentives, customers can be compensated for using and sharing health data created by IoT devices. Customers will be compensated by using IoT devices to monitor their everyday activities and adherence to care plans and preventative health measures. This will assist insurers in dramatically reducing claims. Insurance firms will verify claims using data obtained by IoT devices [23].

Traditional acceptance models, according to the author, lack characteristics. This is a function that only healthcare technology has. Furthermore, the author claims that the well-developed UTAUT ignores individual emotion in deciding to follow IoT despite its emphasis on cognition [24]. A semi-structured interview with home healthcare patients and healthcare practitioners was conducted, and the results were analyzed using Kvale's procedure [2]. Also, 185 participants from eastern US home healthcare organizations were reunited for survey questionnaires. Compared to other studies, this one used an interview to define a novel new construct responding to IoT adoption [25]. The quantitative study's empirical support for that context was verified [26]. They also demonstrated how healthcare organizations could attract home-based patients and increase patients' engagement with technology. Although this study has many advantages for community and future studies, it has one inevitable drawback [27].

Furthermore, even though the research aimed to examine the IoT from both patients' and medical professionals' viewpoints, the analysis only looked at patients' perspectives, which is a frustrating flaw. UTAUT was used in the analysis to determine the study's goal. A total of 101 people took part in this report. The findings were then evaluated using variable modeling. The web-based intervention was discovered using both quantitative and qualitative methods. One hundred sixty-eight patients with CHD from primary care facilities in North London, United Kingdom, were observed. They came from a range of socioeconomic and ethnic backgrounds.

6.2.3   Research Hypothesis

The TOE structure can be used to define characteristics of novel ideas that influence their implementation when it is implemented. Although the technology acceptance model and the unified technology acceptance theory [1]. Tornatzky and Fleischer were the first to suggest the T.O.E. system. According to Oliveira and Martins, a sound theoretical base can be a valuable analytical method when the three contexts' determinants are adapted to the technology under consideration [28].

6.2.3.1   Technological Context (TC)

6.2.3.1.1   Performance Expectancy (PE)
It refers to the degree to which technological advancement is deemed superior to existing technology [29].

H1: PE influences the adoption of IoTH.

6.2.3.1.2　Technology Maturity (TMA)

This indicates how ready a technical architecture is to be introduced within a corporation [30].

　　H2: TMA influences the adoption of IoTH.

6.2.3.1.3　Perceived Compatibility (PC)

This framework describes how well an emerging technology complies with the current IT infrastructure's technological standards and specifications.

　　H3: PC influences the adoption of IoTH.

6.2.3.2　*Organizational Context (OC)*

6.2.3.2.1　Firm Size (FS)

This is a necessary prerequisite for technological adoption, which is also operationalized as the number of employees [5].

　　H4: FS influences the adoption of IoTH.

6.2.3.2.2　Organizational Slack (OS)

This refers to an organization's uncommitted capital and is one of the most often discussed variables in an organization's context [31].

　　H5: OS influences the adoption of IoTH.

6.2.3.2.3　Attitude Toward Change (ATC)

This measures a company's willingness and its ability to respond to technological change and its transform business. Employees' innate desire for the status quo and resistance to change is understandable [32].

　　H6: ATC influences the adoption of IoTH.

6.2.3.2.4　Perceived Technical Capability (PTC)

This can be described as managing technological resources to obtain a competitive market advantage [34]. Firms with good specialized skills are more likely and easier to leverage emerging technology's nuances, giving them a competitive edge [34].

　　H7: PTC influences the adoption of IoTH.

6.2.3.2.5   Security Concerns (SC)

This occurs when businesses are unsure if their properties are vulnerable to attacks in the digital world [35]. Companies face a daunting challenge in assessing vulnerabilities, enforcing controls effectively, keeping the residual risk to a minimum, and conducting frequent reevaluation and monitoring.

H8: PTC influences the adoption of IoTH.

6.2.3.3   Environmental Concerns (EC)

6.2.3.3.1   Regulatory Policy (RP)

Regulation is required to create a legal framework; however, ensuring compliance may be difficult [36].

H9: RP influences the adoption of IoTH.

6.2.3.3.2   Competitive Pressure (CP)

This provides an opportunity for a business to incorporate new technology within the industry [37].

H10: CP influences the adoption of IoTH.

6.2.3.3.3   Legal Uncertainty (LU)

This is present where there is no or just a hazily defined rule [38].

H11: LU influences the adoption of IoTH.

6.2.3.3.4   External Data (ED)

The organizations share the data with the service providers [39].

H12: CP influences the adoption of IoTH.

6.3   Research Methodology

This study uses a questionnaire-based study. A questionnaire was developed to get primary hospital data [40, 41]. The questionnaire mentioned the research objective, and the questionnaire was divided into two parts [42, 43]. Part one consisted of the respondents' demographic details [44, 45]. Part two consisted of the questions related to the study. The questionnaire was sent to the employees working in the hospitals. The questionnaire was sent to 461 targeted respondents, but only 308 returned the filled and used questionnaire for further analysis. After collecting the data biasness of the collected data was checked using single factor Harman test. The value for this construct came to be 21.436% for the TC, 32.792% for the OC, and 41.847% for the EC. All the values were below 50% as shown by Podsakoff [46].

6.3.1   Demographics of the Respondents

Table 6.1 below shows the demographics of the respondents. The gender of the respondents is as follows male respondents are 63 percent, followed by 37 percent of female respondents. Respondent's current position is as follows doctor's percentage is 42 percent, followed by the nursing staff of 37 percent, followed by medical officers of 21 percent.

6.4   Data Analysis

6.4.1   Reliability and Validity

6.4.1.1   Cronbach's Alpha

Cronbach's alpha is a measure of internal consistency, or how closely related a group of items is. It is regarded as a scale reliability metric [47]. Table 6.2 shows the values of Cronbach's alpha.

Table 6.1 Demographics of the respondents.

Sl. no.	Characteristics	Percentage
A	Gender	
1	Male	63
2	Female	37
B	Respondents Current Position	
1	Doctors	42
2	Nursing Staff	37
3	Medical Officers	21

Table 6.2 Parameters of factor analysis, Cronbach alpha, CR, and AVE.

Context	Latent variable	Indicators	Cronbach's alpha	Composite reliability	Rotated component matrix	K.M.O. value	Average variance extracted
TC	PE	PE1	0.747	0.748	0.844	0.703	0.815
		PE2			0.784		
		PE			0.816		
	TMA	TMA1	0.728	0.737	0.823		0.801
		TMA2			0.867		
		TMA3			0.713		
	PC	PC1	0.752	0.752	0.734		0.818
		PC2			0.874		
		PC3			0.845		

(Continued)

Table 6.2 Parameters of factor analysis, Cronbach alpha, CR, and AVE. (*Continued*)

Context	Latent variable	Indicators	Cronbach's alpha	Composite reliability	Rotated component matrix	K.M.O. value	Average variance extracted
OC	OS	OS1	0.849	0.889	0.791	0.859	0.889
		OS2			0.845		
		OS3			0.865		
		OS4			0.763		
	SC	SC1	0.862	0.894	0.835		0.894
		SC2			0.839		
		SC3			0.849		
		SC4			0.768		
	FS	FS1	0.832	0.887	0.838		0.887
		FS2			0.768		
		FS3			0.782		
		FS4			0.863		

(*Continued*)

Table 6.2 Parameters of factor analysis, Cronbach alpha, CR, and AVE. (*Continued*)

Context	Latent variable	Indicators	Cronbach's alpha	Composite reliability	Rotated component matrix	K.M.O. value	Average variance extracted
	PTC	PTC1	0.844	0.905	0.854		0.905
		PTC2			0.955		
		PTC3			0.803		
	ATC	ATC1	0.730	0.849	0.848		0.849
		ATC2			0.879		
		ATC3			0.687		
EC	RP	RP1	0.887	0.913	0.885	0.883	0.913
		RP2			0.821		
		RP3			0.816		
		RP4			0.877		

(*Continued*)

Table 6.2 Parameters of factor analysis, Cronbach alpha, CR, and AVE. (*Continued*)

Context	Latent variable	Indicators	Cronbach's alpha	Composite reliability	Rotated component matrix	K.M.O. value	Average variance extracted
	LU	LU1	0.871	0.905	0.825		0.905
		LU2			0.886		
		LU3			0.895		
		LU4			0.742		
	CP	CP1	0.875	0.889	0.889		0.889
		CP2			0.901		
		CP3			0.874		
		CP4			0.639		
	ED	ED1	0.78	0.869	0.866		0.869
		ED2			0.891		
		ED3			0.725		

6.4.1.2   Composite Reliability

Composite reliability measures internal consistency in scale items, much like Cronbach's alpha [48]. It can be considered equal to the total amount of actual score variance relative to the full-scale score variance. Table 6.2 shows the value of composite reliability.

6.4.2   Exploratory Factor Analysis (EFA)

EFA is a statistical method for determining the underlying structure of a large set of variables. EFA is a factor analysis technique with the overarching goal of identifying the underlying relationships between measured variables. Table 6.2 shows the values of EFA parameters.

6.4.3   Confirmatory Factor Analysis Results

Figures 6.1, 6.2, 6.3 represent the CFA model of the TC, OC, EC constructs. Table 6.3 shows the values of model fit measures for the CFA.

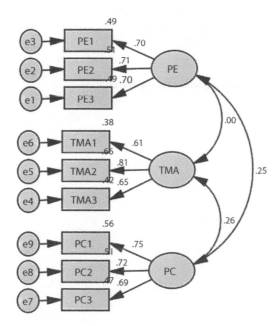

Figure 6.1 CFA for the latent variables for the TC context.

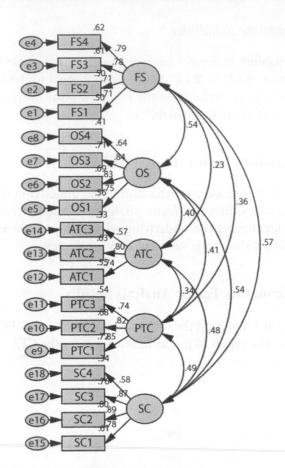

Figure 6.2 CFA for the latent variables for the OC context.

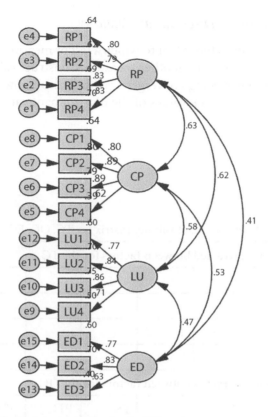

Figure 6.3 CFA for the latent variables for the EC context.

Table 6.3 Model fit measures for the CFA for the TC, OC, and EC context.

Goodness-of-fit indices	Default model for TC	Default model for OC	Default model for EC	Benchmark
$\chi 2/df$ (CMIN/DF)	4.548	2.025	2.624	Lower Limit:1.0; Upper Limit 2.0/3.0 or 5.0
GFI	0.927	0.918	0.913	>=0.90
CFI	0.884	0.952	0.95	>=0.90
IFI	0.886	0.952	0.95	>=0.90
TLI	0.826	0.941	0.937	>=0.90
PCFI	0.589	0.778	0.76	>=0.50
PNFI	0.572	0.743	0.738	>=0.50

6.4.3.1   Divergent or Discriminant Validity

Discriminant validity is the extent to which a test or measure deviates from (i.e., does not correlate with) another measure. Construct validity is one of two aspects, the other being convergent validity, also known as divergent validity. Table 6.4 shows the values of the discriminant validity matrix for the TC, OC, EC.

Table 6.4 Discriminant validity matrix for TC, OC, EC.

Variance extracted between factors for the TC				
	PC	PE	TMA	
PC	1			
PE	0.666	1		
TMA	0.655	0.653	1	
Variance extracted between factors for the OC				
	OS	SC	FS	PTC	ATC
OS	1				
SC	0.671	1			
FS	0.663	0.669	1		
PTC	0.712	0.717	0.709	1	
ATC	0.657	0.662	0.654	0.702	1
Variance extracted between factors for the EC				
	RP	LU	CP	ED	
RP	1				
LU	0.711	1			
CP	0.702	0.691	1		
ED	0.703	0.693	0.683	1	

6.4.4   Structural Equation Modeling

Three variables in the TC context. Performance expectancy (PE) has three indicators PE1, PE2, and PE3; technology maturity (TMA) has three indicators TMA1, TMA2, and TMA3; perceived compatibility (PC) have three indicators PC1, PC2, and PC3. One dependent variable is Internet of Things (IoTH) in healthcare, four indicators IoTH1, IoTH2, IoTH3, and IoTH4. The CMIN/Df is 2.944, RMSEA is 0.080, CFI is 0.909, TLI is 0.879, GFI is 0.920, AGFI is 0.876, NFI is 0.870, and IFI is 0.910. Figure 6.4 shows the structural model for TC. Figure 6.5 shows the structural model for OC. Figure 6.6 shows the structural model for EC.

Firm size (FS) has four indicators FS1, FS2, FS3, and FS4; organizational slack (OS) has four indicators OS1, OS2, OS3, and OS4; attitude toward change (ATC) has three indicators ATC1, ATC2, and ATC3; perceived technical capability (PTC) has three indicators PTC1, PTC2, and PTC3; security concerns (SC) has four indicators SC1, SC2, SC3, and SC4. The CMIN/Df is 2.272, RMSEA is 0.064, CFI is 0.929, TLI is 0.915, GFI is 0.888, AGFI is 0.854, NFI is 0.881, and IFI is 0.930.

Regulatory policy (RP) has four indicators RP1, RP2, RP3, and RP4; competitive pressure (CP) has four indicators CP1, CP2, CP3, and CP4; legal uncertainty (LU) has four indicators LU1, LU2, LU3, and LU4. External data (ED) has three indicators ED1, ED2, and ED3. The CMIN/Df 2.564, RMSEA is 0.071, CFI is 0.934, TLI is 0.921, GFI is 0.890, AGFI is 0.852, NFI is 0.898, and IFI is 0.935.

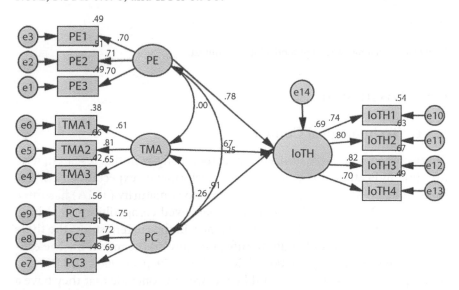

Figure 6.4 Final measurement model for TC context.

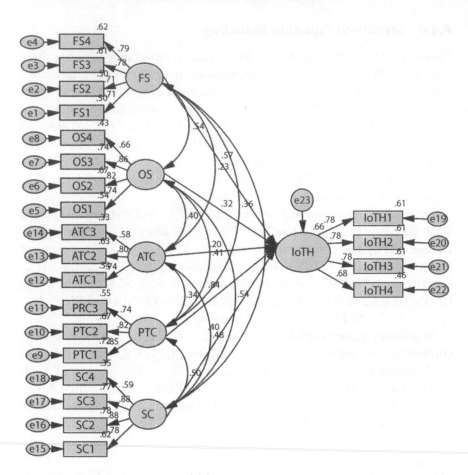

Figure 6.5 Final measurement model for OC context.

6.5 Discussion

6.5.1 Technological Context

Three components were utilized for further analysis in this research, having nine indicators. The component is performance expectancy (PE) has three indicators PE1, PE2, and PE3; technology maturity (TMA) has three indicators TMA1, TMA2, and TMA3; perceived compatibility (PC) have three indicators PC1, PC2, and PC3. Hence, in the current study, the three latent variables also contribute significantly toward the model fit. The estimate of PE ($\beta = 0.789$, $p = 0.000$), TMA ($\beta = 0.679$, $p = 0.000$), and PC ($\beta = 0.912$, $p = 0.000$) are positive, and hence, we can conclude that they have a

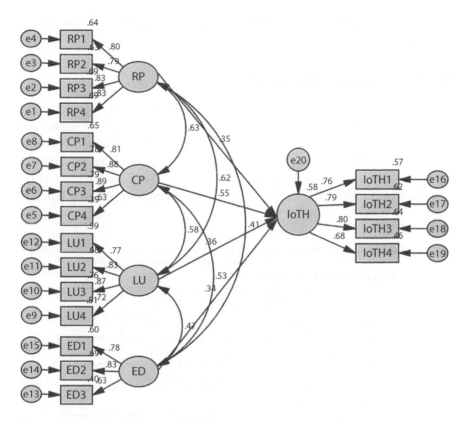

Figure 6.6 Final measurement model for EC context.

significantly positive impact on IoTH. The study is supported by previous studies in different sectors [20, 21, 26, 27, 49].

6.5.2   Organizational Context

Five components were utilized for further analysis in this research, having 18 indicators. The component firm size (FS) has four indicators FS1, FS2, FS3, and FS4; organizational slack (OS) has four indicators OS1, OS2, OS3, and OS4; attitude toward change (ATC) has three indicators ATC1, ATC2, and ATC3; perceived technical capability (PTC) has three indicators PTC1, PTC2, and PTC3; security concerns (SC) has four indicators SC1, SC2, SC3, and SC4. The estimate of FS ($\beta = .577$, p = 0.000), OS ($\beta = .318$, p = 0.000), ATC ($\beta = .201$, p = 0.000), PTC ($\beta = .841$, p = 0.000), and SC ($\beta = .397$, p = 0.000) are positive, and hence, we can conclude that they have significantly positive impact on IoTH. The study is supported by previous studies in different sectors [1, 24, 32].

6.5.3   Environmental Context

Four components were utilized for further analysis in this research, having 15 indicators. The latent variables along with its indicators are regulatory policy (RP) has four indicators RP1, RP2, RP3, and RP4; competitive pressure (CP) has four indicators CP1, CP2, CP3, and CP4; legal uncertainty (LU) has four indicators LU1, LU2, LU3, and LU4. External data (ED) has three indicators ED1, ED2, and ED3. The estimate of RP (β = 0.0.352,

Table 6.5 Path analysis results for TC, OC, and EC.

Path analysis result for TC				
	Estimate	SE.	CR.	P
IoTH<---PE	0.789	0.082	9.622	***
IoTH<---TMA	0.679	0.075	9.053	***
IoTH<---PC	0.912	0.104	8.769	***
Path analysis result for OC				
	Estimate	SE.	CR.	P
IoTH<---FS	0.577	0.084	6.869	***
IoTH<---OS	0.318	0.063	5.047	***
IoTH<---ATC	0.201	0.054	3.722	***
IoTH<---PTC	0.841	0.044	19.11	***
IoTH<---SC	0.397	0.052	7.634	***
Path analysis result for EC				
	Estimate	SE.	CR.	P
IoTH<---RP	0.352	0.075	4.693	***
IoTH<---CP	0.552	0.097	5.69	***
IoTH<---LU	0.363	0.089	4.078	***
IoTH<---ED	0.34	0.072	4.722	***

p = 0.000); CP (β = 0.552, p = 0.000); LU (β = .363, p = 0.000), and ED (β = 0.340, p = 0.000) are positive, and hence, we can conclude that they have significantly positive impact on IoTH. The study is being supported by previous studies in different sectors [7, 49–54]. Table 6.5 shows the path analysis results.

6.6 Conclusion

The impact of IoT in India's healthcare sector is the main aim of this study. A structured literature review is being conducted to identify the factors influencing IoT adoption in India's healthcare firms. TOE framework was adopted for the study, which comprises three contexts, TC, OC, EC. After collecting the data, its biasness was checked, and the data was not biased. All the proposed hypotheses could not be rejected. The developed model showed a good fit and satisfied all the parameters.

References

1. Ahmadi, H., Nilashi, M., Ibrahim, O., Organizational decision to adopt hospital information system: An empirical investigation in the case of Malaysian public hospitals. *Int. J. Med. Inf.*, 84, 3, 166–188, 2015, https://doi.org/10.1016/j.ijmedinf.2014.12.004.

2. Matalka, M.S., Visich, J.K., Li, S., Reviewing the drivers and challenges in RFID implementation in the pharmaceutical supply chain. *Int. J. Electron. Bus.*, 7, 5, 473, 2009, https://doi.org/10.1504/ijeb.2009.028152.

3. Abed, S.S., Social commerce adoption using TOE framework: An empirical investigation of Saudi Arabian SMEs. *Int. J. Inf. Manage.*, 53, 102118, 2020, https://doi.org/10.1016/j.ijinfomgt.2020.102118.

4. Alsetoohy, O., Ayoun, B., Arous, S., Megahed, F., Nabil, G., Intelligent agent technology: What affects its adoption in hotel food supply chain management? *J. Hosp. Tour. Technol.*, 10, 3, 317–341, 2019, https://doi.org/10.1108/JHTT-01-2018-0005.

5. Clohessy, T., Acton, T., Rogers, N., Blockchain adoption: Technological, organisational and environmental considerations, in: *Business Transformation through Blockchain*, pp. 47–76, 2019, https://doi.org/10.1007/978-3-319-98911-2_2.

6. Cruz-Jesus, F., Pinheiro, A., Oliveira, T., Understanding CRM adoption stages: Empirical analysis building on the TOE framework. *Comput. Ind.*, 109, 1–13, 2019, https://doi.org/10.1016/j.compind.2019.03.007.

7. Ergado, A.A., Desta, A., Mehta, H., Determining the barriers contributing to ICT implementation by using technology-organization-environment

framework in Ethiopian higher educational institutions. *Educ. Inf. Technol.*, 3, 3115–33, 2021 May 26.

8. Haryanto, B., Gandhi, A., Giri Sucahyo, Y., The determinant factors in utilizing electronic signature using the TAM and TOE framework. *2020 5th International Conference on Informatics and Computing, ICIC 2020*, 2020, November 3, https://doi.org/10.1109/ICIC50835.2020.9288623.

9. Hiran, K.K. and Henten, A., An integrated TOE-DoI framework for cloud computing adoption in higher education: The case of Sub-Saharan Africa, Ethiopia. *Adv. Intell. Syst. Comput.*, *1053*, 1281–1290, 2020, https://doi.org/10.1007/978-981-15-0751-9_117.

10. Ngah, A.H., Zainuddin, Y., Thurasamy, R., Applying the TOE framework in the halal warehouse adoption study. *J. Islam. Account. Bus. Res.*, 8, 2, 161–181, 2017, https://doi.org/10.1108/JIABR-04-2014-0014.

11. Pateli, A., Mylonas, N., Spyrou, A., Organizational adoption of social media in the hospitality industry: An integrated approach based on DIT and TOE frameworks. *Sustainability*, *12*, 17, 7132, 2020, https://doi.org/10.3390/su12177132.

12. Senyo, P.K., Effah, J., Addae, E., Preliminary insight into cloud computing adoption in a developing country. *J. Enterp. Inf. Manage.*, *29*, 4, 505–524, 2016, https://doi.org/10.1108/JEIM-09-2014-0094.

13. Skafi, M., Yunis, M.M., Zekri, A., Factors influencing SMEs' adoption of cloud computing services in Lebanon: An empirical analysis using TOE and contextual theory. *IEEE Access*, 8, 79169–79181, 2020, https://doi.org/10.1109/ACCESS.2020.2987331.

14. Tashkandi, A.A. and Al-Jabri, I., Cloud computing adoption by Higher Education Institutions in Saudi Arabia: Analysis based on TOE. *2015 International Conference on Cloud Computing, ICCC 2015*, pp. 1–8, 2015, https://doi.org/10.1109/CLOUDCOMP.2015.7149634.

15. Sahu, A.K., Sharma, S., Tanveer, M., Raja, R., Internet of Things attack detection using hybrid Deep Learning Model. *Comput. Commun.*, 176, 146–154, 2021, https://doi.org/10.1016/j.comcom.2021.05.024.

16. Lou, P., Liu, Q., Zhou, Z., Wang, H., Agile supply chain management over the Internet of Things. *2011 International Conference on Management and Service Science*, pp. 1–4, 2011, https://doi.org/10.1109/ICMSS.2011.5998314.

17. Ma, H.-D., Internet of Things: Objectives and scientific challenges. *Springer*, *26*, 6, 919–924, 2011, https://doi.org/10.1007/s11390-011-1189-5.

18. Schmitt, G., Mladenow, A., Strauss, C., Schaffhauser-Linzatti, M., Smart contracts and Internet of things: A qualitative content analysis using the technology-organization-environment framework to identify key-determinants. *Proc. Comput. Sci.*, 160, 189–96, 2019 Jan 1.

19. Yan, J., Xin, S., Liu, Q., Xu, W., Yang, L., Fan, L., Chen, B., Wang, Q., Intelligent supply chain integration and management based on cloud of things. *Int. J. Distr. Sens. Netw.*, 10, 3, 624839, 2014 Mar 16.

20. Tu, M., An exploratory study of Internet of Things (IoT) adoption intention in logistics and supply chain management a mixed research approach. *Int. J. Logist. Manage.*, *29*, 1, 131–151, 2018, https://doi.org/10.1108/IJLM-11-2016-0274.
21. Nausheen, F. and Begum, S.H., Healthcare IoT: Benefits, vulnerabilities and solutions. *Proceedings of the 2nd International Conference on Inventive Systems and Control, ICISC 2018*, pp. 517–522, 2018, https://doi.org/10.1109/ICISC.2018.8399126.
22. Rathee, G., Sharma, A., Saini, H., Kumar, R., Iqbal, R., A hybrid framework for multimedia data processing in IoT-healthcare using blockchain technology. *Multimed. Tools Appl.*, *79*, 9711–9733, 2020, https://doi.org/10.1007/s11042-019-07835-3.
23. Bhatt, Y. and Bhatt, C., Internet of things in healthcare, in: *Internet of things and big data technologies for next generation HealthCare*, pp. 13–33, Springer, Cham, 2017.
24. El Zouka, H.A. and Hosni, M.M., Secure IoT communications for smart healthcare monitoring system. *Int. Things*, 13, 100036, 2021 Mar 1.
25. Reyes, P.M., Li, S., Visich, J.K., Determinants of RFID adoption stage and perceived benefits. *Eur. J. Oper. Res.*, *254*, 3, 801–812, 2016, https://doi.org/10.1016/j.ejor.2016.03.051.
26. Dachyar, M., Nadhira, A., Dachyar, M., Selection factor analysis for Internet of Things (IoT) implementation using DEMATEL based ANP and COPRAS method at the hospital Intensive Care Unit (ICU) hospital improvement process view project selection factor analysis for Internet of Things (IoT) implementation using DEMATEL based ANP and COPRAS method at the hospital Intensive Care Unit (ICU). *Int. J. Adv. Sci. Technol.*, *29*, 7s, 3614–3622, 2020, https://www.researchgate.net/publication/341965681.
27. Oliveira, T. and Fraga Martins, M., Literature review of information technology adoption models at firm level. *Electron. J. Inf. Syst. Eval.*, *14*, 110, 2011, https://repository.ju.edu.et/handle/123456789/4563.
28. Zhu, K., Dong, S., Xu, S.X., Kraemer, K.L., Innovation diffusion in global contexts: Determinants of post-adoption digital transformation of European companies. *Eur. J. Inf. Syst.*, *15*, 6, 601–616, 2006, https://doi.org/10.1057/palgrave.ejis.3000650.
29. Dey, A., Vijayaraman, B.S., Choi, J.H., RFID in US hospitals: An exploratory investigation of technology adoption. *Manage. Res. Rev.*, *39*, 4, 399–424, 2016, https://doi.org/10.1108/MRR-09-2014-0222.
30. Gangwar, H., Date, H., Raoot, A.D., Review on IT adoption: Insights from recent technologies. *J. Enterp. Inf. Manage.*, *27*, 4, 488–502, 2014, https://doi.org/10.1108/JEIM-08-2012-0047.
31. Ichsan, M., Dachyar, M., Farizal, Readiness for implementing industry 4.0 in food and beverage manufacturer in Indonesia. *IOP Conf. Ser.: Mater. Sci. Eng.*, *598*, 1, 0–7, 2019, https://doi.org/10.1088/1757-899X/598/1/012129.

32. Baker, C.G., Ranken, M.D., Kill, R.C., Food industries manual. Springer Science & Business Media, 2012 Dec 6.

33. Ayoobkhan, A. and Asirvatham, D., Adoption of cloud computing services in healthcare sectors: Special attention to private hospitals in Colombo District, Sri Lanka. *Curr. J. Appl. Sci. Technol.*, 23, 2, 1–10, 2017, https://doi.org/10.9734/cjast/2017/34597.

34. Lin, D., Lee, C.K.M., Lin, K., Research on effect factors evaluation of Internet of Things (IoT) adoption in Chinese agricultural supply chain. *IEEE International Conference on Industrial Engineering and Engineering Management, 2016-Decem*, pp. 612–615, 2016, https://doi.org/10.1109/IEEM.2016.7797948.

35. Wulandari, A., Suryawardani, B., Marcelino, D., Social media technology adoption for improving MSMEs performance in bandung: A Technology-Organization-Environment (TOE) framework. *2020 8th International Conference on Cyber and IT Service Management, CITSM 2020*, 2020, October 23, https://doi.org/10.1109/CITSM50537.2020.9268803.

36. Yadav, S., Garg, D., Luthra, S., Development of IoT based data-driven agriculture supply chain performance measurement framework. *J. Enterp. Inf. Manage.*, 34, 1, 292–327, 2020, https://doi.org/10.1108/JEIM-11-2019-0369/FULL/PDF

37. Lambok Siregar, K. and Asvial, M., Analysis of IoT implementation using the dematel method and TOES framework. *MECnIT 2020 - International Conference on Mechanical, Electronics, Computer, and Industrial Technology*, pp. 19–23, 2020, https://doi.org/10.1109/MECnIT48290.2020.9166602.

38. Fosso Wamba, S., Gunasekaran, A., Bhattacharya, M., Dubey, R., Production planning & control the management of operations determinants of RFID adoption intention by SMEs: An empirical investigation. *Taylor Francis*, 27, 12, 979–990, 2016, https://doi.org/10.1080/09537287.2016.1167981.

39. Baral, M.M., Singh, R.K., Kazançoğlu, Y., Analysis of factors impacting survivability of sustainable supply chain during COVID-19 pandemic: An empirical study in the context of SMEs. *Int. J. Log. Manage.*, 2021 Oct 13.

40. Baral, M.M. and Verma, A., Cloud computing adoption for healthcare: An empirical study using SEM approach. *FIIB Bus. Rev.*, 10, 3, 255–75, 2021 Sep.

41. Mukherjee, S., Baral, M.M., Chittipaka, V., Srivastava, S.C., Pal, S.K., Discussing the impact of industry 4.0 in agriculture supply chain, in: *Lecture Notes in Mechanical Engineering*, pp. 301–307, 2021, https://doi.org/10.1007/978-981-16-3033-0_28.

42. Mukherjee, S. and Chittipaka, V., Analysing the adoption of intelligent agent technology in food supply chain management: An empirical evidence. *FIIB Bus. Rev.*, 23197145211059243, 2021 Nov.

43. Mukherjee, S., Chittipaka, V., Baral, MM., Developing a model to highlight the relation of digital trust with privacy and security for the blockchain technology, in: *Blockchain Technology and Applications for Digital Marketing*, pp. 110–125, IGI Global, 2021.

44. Pal, S.K., Baral, M.M., Mukherjee, S., Venkataiah, C., Jana, B., Analyzing the impact of supply chain innovation as a mediator for healthcare firms' performance. *Mater. Today: Proc.*, 2021, https://doi.org/10.1016/j.matpr.2021.10.173.

45. Podsakoff, N.P., Common method biases in behavioral research: A critical review of the literature and recommended remedies. *J. Appl. Psychol.*, *885*, 879, 10–1037, 2003.

46. Peter, J.P., Olson, J., Ray, M.L., Ryan, M.J., Sawyer, A.G., Silk, A.J., Measurement abstracts. *J. Mark. Res.*, *19*, 1, 152–155, 1982, https://doi.org/10.1177/002224378201900115.

47. Chan, F., Lee, G.K., Lee, E.J., Kubota, C., Allen, C.A., Structural equation modeling in rehabilitation counseling research. *Rehabil. Couns. Bull.*, *51*, 1, 44–57, 2007, https://doi.org/10.1177/00343552070510010701.

48. Laurenza, E., Quintano, M., Schiavone, F., Vrontis, D., The effect of digital technologies adoption in healthcare industry: A case based analysis. *Bus. Process Manage. J.*, *24*, 5, 1124–1144, 2018, https://doi.org/10.1108/BPMJ-04-2017-0084.

49. Amini, M. and Bakri, A., Cloud computing adoption by SMEs in the Malaysia: A multi-perspective framework based on DOI theory and TOE framework. *J. Inf. Technol. Inf. Syst. Res. (JITISR)*, *9*, 2, 121–135, 2015.

50. Gökalp, E., Gökalp, MO., Çoban, S., Blockchain-based supply chain management: understanding the determinants of adoption in the context of organizations. *Inf. Syst. Manage.*, 39, 2, 100–21, 2022 Apr 3.

51. Kamble, S., Gunasekaran, A., Arha, H., Understanding the blockchain technology adoption in supply chains-Indian context. *Int. J. Prod. Res.*, *57*, 7, 2009–2033, 2019, https://doi.org/10.1080/00207543.2018.1518610.

52. Umam, B., Darmawan, A.K., Anwari, A., Santosa, I., Walid, M., Hidayanto, A.N., Mobile-based smart regency adoption with TOE framework: An empirical inquiry from Madura Island Districts. *ICICoS 2020 - Proceeding: 4th International Conference on Informatics and Computational Sciences*, 2020, November 10, https://doi.org/10.1109/ICICoS51170.2020.9299025.

53. Wu, K., Zhao, Y., Zhu, Q., Tan, X., Zheng, H., A meta-analysis of the impact of trust on technology acceptance model: Investigation of moderating influence of subject and context type. *Int. J. Inf. Manage.*, *31*, 6, 572–581, 2011, https://doi.org/10.1016/J.IJINFOMGT.2011.03.004.

54. Yang, Z., Sun, J., Zhang, Y., Wang, Y., Understanding SaaS adoption from the perspective of organizational users: A tripod readiness model. *Comput. Hum. Behav.*, *45*, 254–264, 2015, https://doi.org/10.1016/J.CHB.2014.12.022.

7

Role of IoT in Sustainable Healthcare Systems

Amrita Rai[1]*, Ritesh Pratap Singh[2] and Neha Jain[3]

[1]*Department of Electronics & Communication Engineering., G. L. Bajaj Institute of Technology and Management, Greater Noida,UP, India*
[2]*School of Electrical and Computer Engineering, Haramaya Institute of Technology, Haramaya University, Dire Dawa, Ethiopia*
[3]*Department of Electronics & Communication Engineering, Shobhit Institute of Engineering and Technology, (Deemed-to-be-University), Modipuram, Meerut, UP, India*

Abstract

Globally, the healthcare sector has recognized the worth of information and communication technologies (ICTs) based on smart sensors and IoT within the delivery of healthcare. However, the recently developed in ICTs were restricted to managerial and monetary applications and played only a little role in direct look after patients. But, within the past years, there have been noteworthy changes regarding the implementation of ICT within the way medical care systems is delivered. The main approach of this chapter is to discuss the benefits, advantages, and application of different ICTs in the healthcare system. One of the ICTs tools is IoT, which is being integrated into too many healthcare applications and services at an adequate pace. Although the Internet on Things has many applications in the medical science area, several healthcare organizations across the world are still uncertain to fully deploying it in their operations as IoT is still in the scaling stage and is not completely uniform. The present headway and advancement in the field of the Internet of Things (IoT) are giving an extraordinary potential over the span of the imaginative time of human administrations. The vision of the therapeutic administrations is expansively preferred, as it impels the significance of life and quality of individuals, including a couple of prosperity rules. The perpetual augmentation of the multifaceted IoT

**Corresponding author*: amritaskrai@gmail.com

Md Rashid Mahmood, Rohit Raja, Harpreet Kaur, Sandeep Kumar and Kapil Kumar Nagwanshi (eds.)
Ambient Intelligence and Internet of Things: Convergent Technologies, (215–242) © 2023 Scrivener Publishing LLC

contraptions in prosperity is exhaustively attempted by troubles, for instance, driving the IoT terminal center points used for prosperity watching, consistent data dealing with and splendid decision and even the board. Therefore, in this chapter, the detailed overview of the recent issues in the healthcare sector lineup with smart sensors and IoT technologies. Additionally, this chapter discusses some pros and cons of IoT technology in medical science, specific utilization, and advancement of healthcare systems with IoT and some application of IoT in the complete healthcare system.

Keywords: IoT technology, healthcare systems, wearable devices, E-health, pulse rate sensor

7.1   Introduction

Today, innovative advances should be joined by their applications and execution in human-possessed conditions, where general well-being and energy efficiency assume a significant part of an environment for the benefit of people and the planet. By allocating a singular identification to every object within the network, IoT permits its users to measure smart, safe lives [1]. In healthcare systems, IoT is especially used to increase fast access to information related to patients and doctors. IoT is often defined as an interrelated network that links an outsized number of devices to at least one another for purposes of creating large-scale information accessible to all or many [2]. Since the most recent multidecade, IoT has been a challenging area of application for real-time environmental studies and simulation. Quick changes in data and correspondence innovations have helped to the more extensive use of the Internet of Things (IoT) in regions like clever vehicle frameworks, savvy urban areas, insightful medical care, shrewd homes, keen lattice, industry robotization, brilliant cultivating and numerous others [3]. Among them, medical care has consistently been a hot interest among different examination networks and is a quickly developing region with the progression of innovation. Overseeing medical problems is turning into a genuine factor in the medical care framework, as deficient medical services administrations are accessible to satisfy the expanding needs of the maturing populace with constant sicknesses. Thus, the world medical services framework needs the change from center-driven climate to customized data unified climate. In present-day medical care framework, doctors and patients can be united with the utilization of IoT advances for robotized and proficient checking of everyday exercises of all age bunch individuals and to give "one-stop" administration to individuals at distant areas by network design that gives consistent observing of body signals dependent on sensors [4].

The revolution in the information and communication technologies (ICTs) like the Internet of Things (IoT) is remodeling and reforming the healthcare system scientifically, economically and publicly [5]. The developing and quickly growing IoT-based Smart Healthcare System (SHCS) is seen as an ecological resolution to decrease the problem on the existing healthcare system due to accumulative diseases and inadequate medical infrastructure. IoT technology–based design SHCS plays a dynamic role in providing healthcare services in pastoral and remote areas where the essential medical facilities and adequate healthcare system are not available [6]. Nowadays, medical device market needs various things to add the value of devices and data. It requires real-time analytics for improving decisions and transforming health information exchanges to take fast actions. These devices are also portable for both sides of communication and monitoring [7]. As a result, while implementing any mobile healthcare device, some key features are taken into account for facilitating the portability among medical devices and monitoring systems required by hospitals. Some of the key features are standardization, availability of structure, expertise of resources, regulatory and compliances issues, data life cycle management and cyber security management (Interoperable devices, 2019) [8]. They are looking forward to such devices because they are transportable, stress-free to use, compact in size and lightweight. A classic example of a complete healthcare system (CHS) with smart sensors that commonly uses a smart microcontroller and various smart sensors for sensing and monitoring various diseases and sending information through electronic media to a doctor's mobile phone or any family member, which will be responsible for emergency assistance [9]. The key purpose of such systems is based on smart sensors, which is carried by persons anywhere, and it can continue monitoring the health of the person in real time and generating an alarm for any abnormal health condition. The complete healthcare system (CHS) is very useful for elderly people for monitoring the heart rate, blood pressure, and body temperature and caring in a hospital or at home. All the information can be handled by different smart sensors and microcontroller-based systems [10].

7.2   Basic Structure of IoT Implementation in the Healthcare Field

The IoT has comprehensive uses and applications within the field of medical aid also as healthcare. Its would-be to supply ascend to several healthcare facilities and applications like faraway or distant healthcare monitoring, tracking of patient and doctor data, enhanced medicine usage and records, medical equipment records, emergency call care, health situation recording, etc. The IoT features a sort of application arena, which incorporates health situations. The fashionable healthcare devices are becoming stylish and reformatted by an advance IoT technology involvement in this field [11]. The IoT is probably going to empower a variety of health system solutions. Within the environment of medical care, medical facility and application cannot be differentiated accurately, and both are mutually dependent. To overcome all drawbacks in healthcare systems, both IoT-based services and IoT-related applications need to take faster consideration. This chapter is going to discuss numerous medical applications utilizing IoT platforms, combined with approximately new advanced technologies in healthcare systems. Currently, many encouraging and supporting IoT-based technologies are working for reasonable healthcare solutions, and thus it is important to place some light on those technologies. In this respect, the subsequent investigation emphasizes on some essential technologies, which have the potential to update IoT-enabled healthcare services [12].

Complete medical care framework gets an opportunity to augment the usage of technological innovations, which can work together with the cloud climate by incorporating distributed computing and IoT. Applications, which utilize IoT innovations, are accessible at any time instant if working together with the cloud network-based storage system. The converging of CC with IoT is displayed in Figure 7.1. Cloud gives a stage to portable and remote clients to utilize all the demanded data and applications for IoT connections with the network, and it will help in different applications and administrations of medical services framework [13].

IoT is giving numerous advantages in the field of healthcare systems and medical equipment. The first and foremost utilization of IoT in this field begins during the pandemic COVID-19, when doctors are not physically available in the hospital for COVID patients, then the patient can contact to doctor through some IoT specific application and book their appointments using their mobile phone. IoT can help the healthcare system in all the perspectives, like patients and their family to keep their all records and monitor their own health condition, the doctors and Physicians for contact with the patient and their family members, Hospitals and Insurance companies [14].

IoT helps Patients—gadgets as wearables like Smartwatch, other wellness equipment, and other distantly connected gadgets like circulatory strain and heartbeat observing sleeves, glucometer (for sugar control) and

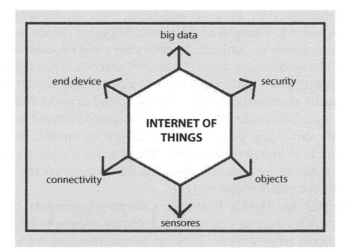

Figure 7.1 Entities of IoT used for various purposes in the healthcare system.

so on give patients access to modified consideration. This type of wearable or compact gadget is used by the patient to regulate to nudge carbohydrate level, plans, practice check, circulatory strain assortments and substantially. Internet of Things has changed individuals, especially more seasoned patients, by enabling reliable after of clinical issues. This altogether influences people living solitary and their relatives. On any disrupting impact or changes in standard activities of an independent, prepared instrument passes on messages to family members and concerned prosperity providers [15].

Internet of Things utilized by specialists—by using wearables and additional house monitoring equipment embedded with the Internet of Things, specialists can observe patients' prosperity even more effectively. They can observe patients' state to treatment plans or any prerequisite without a doubt fire medical thought. IoT enables clinical benefits facilities to be more cautious and connect with patients actively. Data assembled from IoT devices can help specialists with recognize the best treatment for patients and show up at the standard outcomes [16].

IoT helpful in Hospitals—apart from observing patients' prosperity, there are various areas where IoT devices are extraordinarily important in hospitals. IoT devices equipped with sensors are used for the following areas of medical hardware, such as nebulizers, wheelchairs, oxygen siphons, and other monitoring gear. Plan of clinical staff at different regions can similarly be analyzed constant [17].

Aside from observing patients' well-being, there are numerous differ-ent regions where IoT gadgets are extremely helpful in clinics. IoT gadgets labeled with sensors are utilized for following constant areas of clinical hardware, like wheelchairs, defibrillators, nebulizers, oxygen siphons, and other observing gear. The arrangement of clinical staff in various areas can likewise be examined continuously. The spread of pollutions is a huge concern for patients in clinical centers. IoT-engaged neatness monitoring devices help in holding patients back from getting tainted. IoT devices furthermore help in asset the leaders, like pharmacy stock control, and natural monitoring, for instance, observing the temperature of cooler, and tenacity and temperature control [18].

IoT helpful for Health Insurance Companies—insurers may offer impulses to their customers for using and sharing prosperity data made by IoT-empowered astute devices. They can remunerate customers for using IoT devices to observe their ordinary activities and adherence to treatment plans and reasonable prosperity measures. This will help back up plans with diminishing cases altogether [19].

There are different opportunities for insurers with IoT-enabled smart devices. Organizations can utilize data obtained through well-being moni-toring devices for their ensuring and claims exercises. This data will enable them to recognize extortion ensures and perceive opportunities for sup-port. IoT devices get uncomplicated among backup strategy and customers the embracing, assessing, claims managing, and hazard examination meas-ures. In the light of IoT-obtained data-driven decisions in all action means, customers will have agreeable detectable quality into primary thought behind every decision made and cycle results [20].

The essential thought of utilizing the IoT where patients hospitalized whose physiological state ought to be checked the persistently regard-less presence of specialists or others in the clinic. With the assistance of well-being, sensors are used to gather sweeping physiological information and usages entries and the cloud to research and store the information and a short period later forward the confined data distantly to parental bits of knowledge on the side of additional assessment and review as showed up. In another period of distant medical services, how is the IoT empowering new types of clinical therapy, comprehension and care?

- The goal of 5G is beginning to make the veritable pivotal ability of splendid development and the trap of things a reality.
- Also, with the persistent COVID-19 putting new demands on clinical consideration and making the prerequisite for

courses of action that can uphold giving thought remotely, away from a clinical care association, this could not have come at a prevalent time.

- The use of smart development in clinical care has been developing reliably throughout past years, putting fantastic devices such as sharp asthma screens, insulin pens, related inhalers, and more in the ownership of normal buyers and allowing them to more promptly administer and address their own prosperity needs—similarly, as to quickly will help if something ends up being awful. Wearable devices like biosensors and splendid watches can allow clinical care specialists to remotely screen nonstop conditions and gather data, allowing discernment and treatment that was ahead of time only possible in an institutional setting to happen any place [21].

7.3   Different Technologies of IoT for the Healthcare Systems

The development of the IoT for the healthcare systems requires complete knowledge of the communication system, sensors and their network design and a thorough knowledge of a client-server model. The technological advancement of any of these areas can enhance the ability of the system [22]. Hence, the development of an IoT-based healthcare system requires an integration of the many states of art technologies. The technological classifications of an IoT-based healthcare system are mainly divided into three categories and are shown in Figure 7.2.

(a) On the basis of the node identification.
(b) On the basis of the communication methods.
(c) Depending upon the location of the object.

Let us see the abovementioned Figure 7.3, which presents the overview of the involvements of IoT architecture and Robotics to elucidate the feasibility of the latest healthcare system. The figure shows the counterpart of the cloud side environment located at the edge side of the subject for monitoring. The perceivable devices and their associative equipment for real-time patient monitoring at the edge side, such as sensor/transducer, actuators and hardware, are known to the cloud through a gateway,

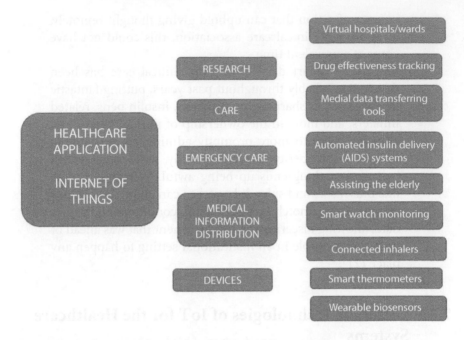

Figure 7.2 Application and examples of IoT in healthcare systems.

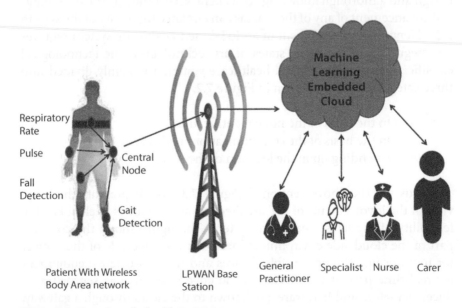

Figure 7.3 Overview of a healthcare system.

which is mainly responsible for the establishment of the connections between the cloud service and the things to coordinate between the devices and the associated things used for monitoring the health parameters.

7.3.1   On the Basis of the Node Identification

The IoT system for healthcare (IoT) is designed to access the patient's information remotely from the authorized sensor or node. However, in practice, the numbers of sensors or nodes are unlimited in any healthcare network, which requires an assignment of unique identification (UIC) code for the recognition of each sensor or node available over the network. Moreover, the overall healthcare system utilizes various resources, which cover the entire medical world. The involvement of every resource in the medical sciences, e.g., hospitals, doctors, nurses, all electrical equipment or devices used in the medical world, requires an assignment of a digital unique identification number [23] for the authorization and recognition of every entity over the IoT network. In the literature, many methods for assigning the identification codes have been proposed [24].

7.3.2   On the Basis of the Communication Method

The communication system is the backbone of an IoT system. The smallest entity in an overall system requires some means to communicate among the devices. The technological aspect of any communication method depends upon the coverage area for propagating any information. On the basis of the coverage area, communication technology can be broadly classified as short-range communication and long-range communication [25].

(i) Short-range communication:
In an IoT network, continuous patient monitoring is performed by some kind of wearable device. These devices are usually worn over the body to acquire physiological data and are usually known as wearable sensors. There are various types of wearable sensors available for the measurement of the various crucial parameters of a human body, like body temperature, respiratory rate, blood pressure, blood glucose level, etc. These wearable sensors are used to collect the patient's data and forward it to the center node by using a short-range communication method, e.g., bluetooth. Bluetooth is a standardized protocol communicating at a short distance (ranges less than 100 m) via a 2.4-GHz wireless link. It is a secured protocol and perfect for short-range communication, which is a very low-cost device and requires very little operating power. However, when the IoT

demands a long-distance transmission of information, this technique fails to meet the requirements. On the other hand, Zig bee is a similar technique for better communication compared to Bluetooth. This technique offers an uninterrupted connection among other devices as it works over the meshed network topology and consists of end nodes, routers and a processing center in the network [26–29].

(ii) Long-range communication:
The data forwarded by the wearable sensor to the central node is useless until some processing is not performed over it. Hence, the received data has to be forwarded to the database. This data can be accessed by the experts by performing the proper authorization to seek their advice. This data transmission is possible through a suitable long-range communication device working over a cellular network or a Wi-Fi device. These devices have high transmission and processing power and are suitable for long-distance communication with an acceptable time delay. These devices are capable of transmitting all kinds of multimedia files. However, the level of security, robustness, low latency and error correction are the primary consideration while selecting a suitable communication standard. Moreover, Satellite communication is also an effective method of communication and also offers high data transfer rates with highly stable, secured ways of communication for the geographically separated remote areas, where other communication methods are unavailable. Nowadays, thousands of satellites are continuously orbiting around the earth, which can be a medium for communication for such areas. However, this method is quite a power-hungry compared to the all available source of communication [30, 31].

7.3.3   Depending on the Location of the Object

The development of an entire healthcare network system based on IoT may raise an issue of identification of any particular object, which plays an important role in the system like a doctor, nurse, medical devices, equipment, patients, and everything, which is a part of this system. Hence, a method of identification of any object based on its location for his availability to take action in emergencies is very important. This is only possible by connecting that object with a Global Positioning System (GPS), which make use of satellite for tracking purpose and directly connects the object with the system. The object can be easily tracked through GPS if a direct line of sight is available with the four different satellites [32].

7.4   Applications and Examples of IoT in the Healthcare Systems

The IoT is a system that physically integrates the devices to intelligently route the information in the appropriate direction for communication and knowledge sharing. This system has applicability in every area, which can be connected with the Internet, or the devices can be developed to interface any particular device with the network. In the earlier days, the devices in the healthcare system did not have any connections with the network—for example, an ECG machine, scanning devices, sensing instruments, etc. However, the limitations in the olden days have been wiped out completely with the invention of IoT, and its applications in the healthcare system has unlimited benefits. The applications of IoT in the healthcare system have been discussed further in detail [33, 34].

7.4.1   IoT-Based Healthcare System to Encounter COVID-19 Pandemic Situations

COVID-19 has given a heavy economic shock to every nation in the world. This forced the governments to change their policies toward the people of their nation. On March 23, 2020, the entire world was put into a lockdown state. All the social activities were paused, which forced the entire world to adopt such a technique that could provide a drift to all the necessary activities which could not be put on hold completely. These social limitations refuelled the entire system to adopt IoT and their application to a greater extent, especially in the area of healthcare. Moreover, in the days to come when this pandemic comes to an end, the world will return to normal routine life, the adoption of IoT in every field is expected to be accelerated in a broader range [35].

Coronavirus is a medical services emergency, and consequently, the quick effect on medical services is more self-evident. An examination from Juniper Research found that the increment in the revenues in the entire IoT business over the world is expected to be boosted to $66 billion in 2020, which remained $55 billion in 2019, mostly because of its speed up selection in medical care area [4]. The most popular devices, which are speeding up the adoption of IoT in the medical services area, are discussed in a further section [36, 37].

7.4.2 Wearable Devices

The popularity of wearable's like smart bands, finger rings and smartwatches remained for many years. However, COVID-19 has set off an enormous expansion in their interest. Wearables can assume indispensable parts in battling against COVID-19 and other future pandemics [39]. For instance, the information from wearable gadgets can be utilized to set an alert for the wearer when any changes in the measured value match with those related to COVID-19 or different infections [38]. The wearable gadgets can likewise be utilized for broadcasting well-being information, ensuring the user to main the social distance [39], and the user can feel stress-free [8] by following a person's comprehension and disposition progressively, consequently empowering customized mediations [40]. These and other comparative applications are boosting the interest in wearable. Philips has also developed disposable patches for early detection of COVID-19 symptoms in the patients [41] and also developed disposable biosensors for the early detection of any deterioration in the normal parameters like respiratory rate, heart rate, activity level and so forth to identify the COVID-19 patient. The different types of wearable devices available in the market are used for different applications are shown in Figure 7.4.

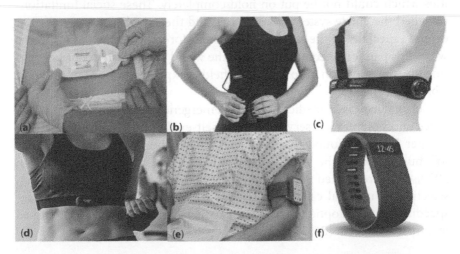

Figure 7.4 (a) Heart monitoring band. (b) Complete fitness belt. (c) Hand movement trackers band for cervical patient. (d) Sweat and interstitial monitoring biosensor based band. (e) Enable tracking and fitness band. (f) Smart watch for health monitoring.

7.4.3   IoT-Enabled Patient Monitoring Devices From Remote Locations

The most crucial fundamental parameters for monitoring and measurement in any human being are body temperature, breathing rate, pulse rate, blood pressure, and oxygen content in the blood. The conventional methods of measurement of these parameters require a physical visit to the nearest hospital or pathology. With the advent of IoT in healthcare, these parameters of any patient can be monitored by the health worker from any remote location.

Figure 7.5 shows the way of adopting IoT for measuring the aforementioned crucial parameters. The methods of measurement of these parameters using IoT have been discussed further in detail [33–40].

7.4.3.1   Pulse Rate Sensor

The diagnosis of the sound health of any human being, pulse rate is the common vital sign, as it is the best mechanism for tactile arterial palpation of the cardiac functions. This simple physical test can be easily performed to determine any kind of medical emergencies like pulmonary lung embolism, heart attack or vasovagal syncope etc. This process of arterial palpation is possible in a certain area over a human body where a pulse can be

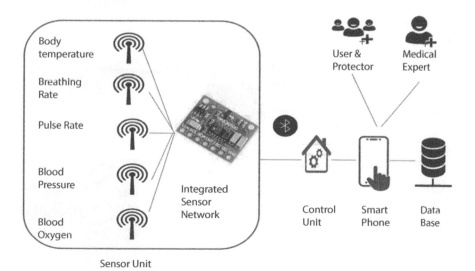

Figure 7.5 Structure diagram of the system.

identified, such as the neck, wrist, groin, beside the knee, fingertip, earlobe, etc., by placing a pulse sensor [42].

Various kinds of wearables have been developed for continuous monitoring, which is suitable for patients, as well as for tracking fitness. These wearables are better for the chest, but the sensor bands developed for the

(a)

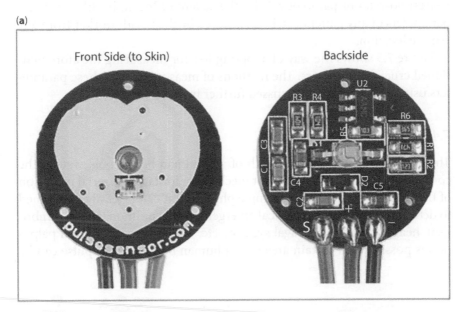

(b)

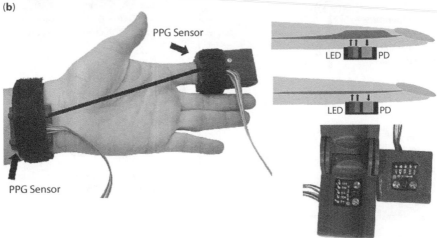

Figure 7.6 (a) Front and backside view of a pulse rate sensor. (b) PPG-based pulse measurement.

wrist are more comfortable as it can be worn for a longer period of time [11, 40–42]. However, better results are obtained from the fingertip and the earlobes. The readings from the fingertip provide higher accuracy compared to the other region chosen for the pulse rate measurement. The sensor developed for the pulse rate measurement from the fingertip is shown in Figure 7.6 (a).

This sensor works on the principle of photoplethysmography (PPG). This is a simple optical technique to detect the blood volume changes in the peripheral circulation. This sensor consists of an LED that transmits the light into the artery. This incident light is partially absorbed into the bloodstream, and the remaining portion is reflected back. The LED is positioned in such a way that the incident light is reflected back to an angle where a photodiode is located, as shown in Figure 7.6 (b). The intensity of reflected light waves depends on the volumetric change in the blood flow. The variation in the light intensity can be recorded and can further calibrate to determine the pulse rate.

However, various other research and studies have been performed, and the commercially developed devices available in the market use other methods of analysis like pressure, ultrasonic waves, radio frequencies (RF). The commercially developed pulse rate sensors by several manufacturers available in the Market do not recommend their devices to be used for medical purposes. These devices include Tom Spark Cardio, H7 by Polar, HRM-Tri by Garmin, and FitBit Pure Pulse [43–45].

7.4.3.2   Respiratory Rate Sensors

The respiration system is one of the most important functions in the human body. The estimation of the respiratory rate is another vital sign for determining the human health condition. The regular monitoring of respiration rate can be an easy aid to pre-determine serious health issues like asthma attack, tuberculosis, apnea, lung disease, hyperventilation, etc. The importance of determining the respiration rate is seeking the interest of researchers to develop a device for accurate real-time measurement. Many kinds of literature found in the past have been working over the different mechanisms for the measurement of respiration rate.

The most general type of nasal sensor was developed using the mister described by Angelov *et al.*, [16]. This sensor was working based on the method of sensing the exhaled air through the nose. In general, the exhaled air from the human lungs is warmer than the ambient temperature. The thermistor is a type of resistive transducer which has an inverse relationship between resistance and temperature. Hence, many times a human exhaled air during respiration can be easily detected, and its count can be figured out as a respiration rate. This method provides good accuracy. However, these types of sensors have some limitations, like a person working in some high temperature zones would make it difficult for the sensor to distinguish between the exhaled air and the surrounding air temperature.

Another method of respiration rate measurement is derived by analyzing the electrocardiogram (ECG). This method is used to detect apnea or to determine the pattern of a human breathing rate and is also known as EDR. The ECG-derived breathing rate measurement is very accurate but has a limitation of the noncontinuous wearability because the ECG electrodes are uncomfortable and irritate the wearer if worn for a prolonged time duration. Moreover, these electrodes, which are used for ECG measurement, are not reusable, and hence, it has to be replaced every time.

The more appropriate method for breathing rate measurement is based on pressure sensor. In this mechanism, the two capacitive plates of equal dimensions are set in such a way, one laying on the chest and another on the back. During breathing, the plates move far during inhalation which increases the distance between the plates and afterward reduces the gap during the process of exhalation, taking into account computation of respiratory rate as shown in Figure 7.7. This method showed a 95% trust in respiratory rate estimations when contrasted with a nasal sensor. This method is genuinely precise and definitely more suitable than the nasal sensor.

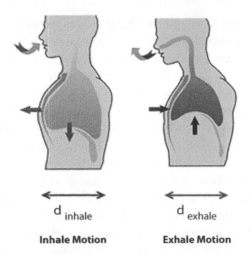

d_{inhale} d_{exhale}

Inhale Motion   **Exhale Motion**

Figure 7.7 Breathing process cycle in a human being.

7.4.3.3   Body Temperature Sensors

Another important parameter of the human being is the body temperature (BT), which clearly indicates the sound body health. The variation in the BT can be the cause of any malfunctioning inside the human body. The BT can be used to detect heatstroke, fever, etc. The continuous monitoring of BT can be carried out by some designated wearables designed for a high degree of accuracy and measurement. Many researchers worked in this area of developing such sensors, which can be easily worn and the closest contact of the sensor with the human body provides the more accurate result. Most of the research carried out in this area indicates that the temperature sensor is responsible for the measurement of BT.

A thermistor is the most common temperature sensor, which is suitable in this specified range of BT with an acceptable level of error. However, some researchers have also used sensor with positive temperature coefficient like RTD or thermocouple. Thermistor has a negative temperature coefficient and most rottenly used sensor. The output of this sensor can be calibrated in the form of temperature and can be forwarded to the concerned health worker or specialist through HIoT system for proper monitoring and better advice, as shown in Figure 7.8.

Moreover, the degree of accurate measurement of BT in such systems depends on the distance between the sensor and the human body. So, the motive of the designer is to embed the sensor into the processed fabric in such a way that the sensor comes physically in direct contact with the human body [20]. In the studies of Susarla *et al.*, and Rohit *et al.*, the authors proposed a method of developing a flexible polymer embedded

Figure 7.8 IoT-based BT measurement.

with a printed sensor and pasted with a small amount of adhesive over it, such that the sensor can be attached directly to the human skin.

7.4.3.4   Blood Pressure Sensing

Blood pressure measurement is not among the basic signs for measurement. However, it is a crucial indicator, which tells about the healthy heart condition of any human being. The measurement of blood pressure can be in the range of hypertension or hypotension. Both conditions indicate an abnormality in heart health and is the major cause of premature death in the world. Hypertension is a condition of inducing a heavy force on the arteries walls, which may cause serious issues if left untreated. In today's world, the life of a human being has become highly stressed and full of workload, which causes most of people to face the condition of hypertension. This condition of hypertension for a prolonged period of time could have an adverse effect on the heart health and may lead to cardiovascular malfunctioning issues, brain hemorrhage, etc. According to the latest data published by who indicates that around 1.13 billion people are suffering from the problem of hypertension all over the world. In such a scenario, it is advisable to monitor the BP using IoT wearable sensors continuously. This sensor may help an individual to protect himself from getting a sudden emergency trauma and also can get immediate assistance from the specialist.

The development of such sensors for continuous monitoring and noninvasive measurement of BP remained a big challenge for researchers in the field of IoT. However, many significant works have been proposed in the literature for the accurate measurement of BP by measuring the transit time between the pulse at heart and any other location in the human body like radial artery or earlobe, etc. Pulse transmit time has an inverse relation with the systolic blood pressure induced by the human heart. This pressure can be calculated by using ECG electrodes, which can be placed on the chest and the photoplethysmograph sensor (PPG) at the ear, wrist, or any other location. This measurement can be carried on by placing the electrodes at different locations. Shanmugasundaram and Sankarikaarguzhali [22] measured the BP by putting the electrodes at the ear and wrist, whereas another researcher [23] used the different locations for the measurement. The picture of an IoT-based BP measurement system is shown in Figure 7.9.

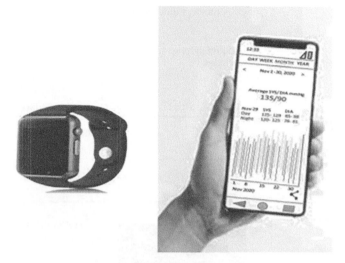

Figure 7.9 IoT-based BP measurement system.

7.4.3.5   Pulse Oximetry Sensors

Blood oxygen is another nonvital parameter to be measured by the health worker. A pulse oximeter (POx) is a device that is used to measure the level of oxygen or the saturation level of oxygen in the red blood cells. It is a noninvasive and painless test that works on the principle of optical reflection and absorbance of light from any particle. This test is performed to determine the respiratory disorder or to diagnose the condition of low oxygen levels in a different parts of body tissues.

This Pox test is performed to determine the oxygen level in the blood by estimating the photoplethysmography (PPG) signal. Plethysmogram is used to detect the volumetric flow of blood in the microvascular bed of tissue. This PPG is obtained optically by putting two LEDs in such a way that one LED acts as an Infrared transmitter. The rays emitted from the infrared transmitter falls on the skin, and usually, some portion of the light is absorbed by the hemoglobin present in the blood, and the rest is reflected back in such an angle, where a photodiode is situated, which receives that portion of reflected rays. The difference between the incident light and the reflected rays can be calibrated on the scale to measure the level of oxygen. The arrangement of transmitter and receptor is shown in Figure 7.10. This arrangement can be made in two ways. The first arrangement works on the principle of reflection of light. The second arrangement can be made such

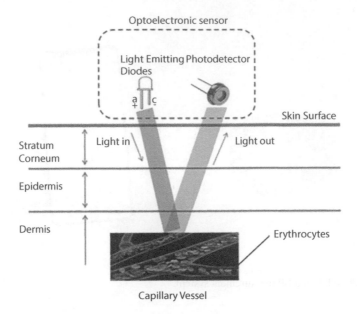

Figure 7.10 Blood oxygen measurement.

that the transmitter and receiver can be placed in the opposite side of the finger at an angle of 180 degrees, and the light is made to fall on the finger. The portion of light falling on the finger can be absorbed; depending upon the level of oxygen in the blood and the remaining light will be passed on to the receiver. These two methods of oxygen level measurements are categorized as the absorbance and the reflectance modes of PPG method, respectively. This complete system can be connected with the internet to forward the measured data to the health worker or specialists to continuously monitor or to seek the advice as and when required.

7.5   Companies Associated With IoT and Healthcare Sector Worldwide

"The global The Healthcare IT Market is projected to grow at a CAGR of 13.8% from 2019 to 2027 to reach $511.06 billion by 2027" says, Meticulous Research.

The following companies provide the Market of healthcare solution using IoT overall world are Medtronic (Ireland), Cisco Systems (US), IBM Corporation (US), GE Healthcare (US), Resideo Technologies (US),

AgaMatrix (US), ARMIS (US), Bosch (GERMANY), Capsule Technologies (US), Comarch SA (Poland), HQSoftware (Estonia), Huawei (China), etc.

Medical services IoT arrangements guarantee to modernize and smooth out medical services and to associate various partners in the E-healthcare marketplace. Comprehensively characterized, health IT alludes to equipment and programming, together with electronic data frameworks, used to make, store, send, get and break down health-related data and information. Few of the IT-supported healthcare companies are listed here.

I. Cerner Corporation (US) Founded in 1979 and settled at North Kansas City, Missouri, US; It is engaged with construction and giving smart arrangements & administrations to the medical services industry. The organization gives advances that associate individuals and frameworks by the extensive scope of administrations through 27,000 supplier offices all over the world to help the clinical, monetary, and functional necessities of associations of each dimension. Through a solid organization of the network and present firms and wholesalers, the organization are extended its topographical occurrence all over the world.

II. McKesson Corporation (US): Established in 1833 and settled at SAN FRANCISCO, California, US; it is occupied with medical care production network the executive's arrangements, retail drug store, local area oncology and strength care, and medical care data innovation. The McKesson Distribution Solutions circulates marked, and nonexclusive drugs and other medical service-related items and give the practice the executives, innovation, clinical help, and business answers for local area-based oncology and another claim to fame rehearses, while the McKesson Technology Solutions gives clinical, monetary, and inventory network the board answers for medical care associations. Its topographical occurrence in all over the world.

III. International Business Machine Corporation (US): IBM Established in 1911 & settled in New York, US; IT enables pioneers, supporters, and forces to be reckoned with in addressing the global greatest well-being challenges. This organization gives Mediclinical IT arrangements complete by auxiliary IBM Watson Health. The organization has the situation essence in different districts like of the Middle East World.

IV. GE Healthcare (US): GE Healthcare was established in 1994 and settled at Chicago, Illinois, US. This company is an extension of auxiliary of General Electric (GE), works as medical care area supporting IT answers for improve patient consideration & functional effectiveness related to medical care suppliers. This organization offers for the situation administrations, and items to different clinical foundations, healthcare clinics, investigation establishments, drug, biotechnology organizations, and natural life science research focuses throughout the world. The organization gives healthcare IT arrangements under the medical care digital professional fragment.

V. Allscripts Healthcare Solutions (US): This Company was Established in 1896 and settled at Chicago, Illinois, US. The said company conveys data innovation arrangements and administrations to help medical care associations in accomplishing ideal clinical, monetary, and functional outcomes. It is the key distributor in countries, like US, Canada, Australia, United Kingdom, etc.

VI. Koninklijke Philips N.V. (Netherlands): Koninklijke Philips N.V. Established in 1891 and settled at Amsterdam, The Netherlands; Koninklijke Philips N.V. works as a healthcare innovation organization around the world. The Company has five business portions, to be specific Individual Healthcare, Illumination, Investigative and Handling, Related Care and Health Informatics, and Health Tech Other. Within excess of 50 divisions and a solid organization of networking, the organization has its quality all over the world in the field of medical science.

VII. Cognizant Technology Solutions Corporation (US) Established in 1994 and head center at Teaneck, New Jersey, US. It is to be responsible for ICT services together with digital technology involvement in medical science, consulting of a physician, and operation services related to the healthcare sector. The company is responsible for medical care ICT solutions over and done with its healthcare business subdivision. It has a very high network of distribution and a large number of subsidiaries, with the help of that the company has its market in overall world including North America, Europe, Asia-Pacific, Latin America, and Middle East & Africa.

VIII. Athenahealth, Inc. (US) It started in 1997, and the main office is situated in Massachusetts, US. It is an ICT-based medical care supplier that associates with hospital and ambulatory healthcare suppliers. Athenahealth, Inc. work with their two business sections, first one segment is business services and the second one is implementation distribution and others. The company deals with network-enabled health records, expenses succession, patient commitment, patient care management, and people condition services through a IoT and cloud-based platforms. It has a very high network of distribution and a large number of subsidiaries, with the help of that the Company has its Market in overall world including the Middle East.

IX. UnitedHealth Group Incorporated (US) Originated in 1977 and its head office was established in Minnesota, US. This group is associated with healthcare products and providing services in the field of health insurance. It is also arranged for data and medical records, intelligent and improved technology, and medical proficiency to encounter the reasonable response of the healthcare system. This company has intentionally associated occupational stands, such as healthiness benefits under UnitedHealthcare and health services working under Optum.

X. Infor Inc. (US) Established in 2009 and main office at New York, U.S. This company is involved in developing IoT-based software for health organizations, marketing strategy software for medical equipment, distributing areas based on geographical needs, and examining innovativeness software applications that will be helping organizations to accomplish businesses. This corporation controls over three subdivisions, that is License of medical equipment and hospitals, maintenance of the records, and consulting. The said company has market over many contrary of the world.

7.6 Conclusion and Future Enhancement in the Healthcare System With IoT

In today's world, doctors can treat more patients and can also advise their patients remotely from any location due to the presence of IoT in healthcare. In the days to come, this technological advancement can boom this industry with the infusion of artificial intelligence and machine learning where a doctor can operate any patient or can perform complex surgeries remotely from any location in the world. This technological advancement can be used to train new interns from anywhere in the world. They can view live demos where experts are performing surgeries.

The fusion of IoT with artificial intelligence and data analysis can provide the best possible solution in operating any complex surgery or the most appropriate treatment to be offered to any patient. The data analysis in the IoT-based healthcare system requires the overall system to be connected with the internet. This requires all the important information is to be uploaded over the server to carry on the big data analysis for obtaining the most accurate solution to any problem.

However, IoT-based healthcare system requires a high level of security to protect the important patient's information stored in the server. It also requires the high speed servers, high bandwidth and data rate, to connect all the equipment's and machinery in real-time.

References

1. Espinosa, V., Lopez, A., Mata Mata, J.L., Estevez, F., M.E., Application of IoT in healthcare: Keys to implementation of the sustainable development goals. *Sensors*, 21, 2330, 2021, https://doi.org/10.3390/s21072330.

2. Rekha, H.S., Nayak, J., Sekhar, G.T.C., Pelusi, D., Impact of IoT in healthcare: Improvements and challenges, in: *The Digitalization Conundrum in India. India Studies in Business and Economics*, K. Das, B.S.P. Mishra, M. Das (Eds.), Springer, Singapore, 2020, https://doi.org/10.1007/978-981-15-6907-4_5.

3. Turcua, C.E. and Turcua, C.O., Internet of Things as key enabler for sustainable healthcare delivery. *Proc. – Soc. Behav. Sci.*, 73, 251–256, 2013.

4. Sahu, M.L., Atulkar, M., Ahirwal, M.K., IOT-based smart healthcare system: A review on constituent technologies. *J. Circuits, Syst. Comput. Online Ready*, 45, 473–485, 2021, https://doi.org/10.1142/S0218126621300087.

5. https://www.i-scoop.eu/internet-of-things-guide/internet-things-healthcare/.

6. Rai, A., Sharma, D., Rai, S., Singh, A., Singh, K.K., IoT-aided robotics development and applications with AI, in: *Emergence of Cyber-Physical System and IoT in Smart Automation and Robotics. Advances in Science, Technology & Innovation (IEREK Interdisciplinary Series for Sustainable Development)*, K.K. Singh, A. Nayyar, S. Tanwar, M. Abouhawwash (Eds.), Springer, Cham, 2021, https://doi.org/10.1007/978-3-030-66222-6_1.

7. Nazir, S., Ali, Y., Ullah, N., García-Magariño, I., Internet of Things for healthcare using effects of mobile computing: A systematic literature review. *Wireless Commun. Mobile Comput.*, 2019, Article ID 5931315, 20 pages, 2019, https://doi.org/10.1155/2019/5931315.

8. Sahu, A.K., Sharma, S., Tanveer, M., Raja, R., Internet of Things attack detection using hybrid Deep Learning Model. *Comput. Commun.*, 176, 146–154, 2021.

9. Rusia, K., Rai, S., Rai, A., Kumar Karatangi, S.V., Artificial intelligence and robotics: Impact & open issues of automation in workplace. *2021 International Conference on Advanced Computing and Innovative Technologies in Engineering (ICACITE)*, pp. 54–59, 2021.

10. Pradhan, B., Bhattacharyya, S., Pal, K., IoT-based applications in healthcare devices. *J. Healthcare Eng.*, 2021, Article ID 6632599, 18 pages, 2021, https://doi.org/10.1155/2021/6632599.

11. Rakshit, P., Nath, I., Pal, S., Application of IoT in healthcare, in: *Principles of Internet of Things (IoT) Ecosystem: Insight Paradigm. Intelligent Systems Reference Library*, S.L. Peng, S. Pal, L. Huang, (Eds.), vol. 174, Springer, Cham., 2020. https://doi.org/10.1007/978-3-030-33596-0_10

12. Rai, A., Sehgal, A., Singal, T.L., Agrawal, R., Spectrum sensing and allocation schemes for cognitive radio, in: *Machine Learning and Cognitive Computing for Mobile Communications and Wireless Networks*, 2020, https://doi.org/10.1002/9781119640554.ch5.

13. https://www.finoit.com/blog/the-role-of-iot-in-healthcare-space/.

14. Dauwed, M. and Meri, A., IOT service utilisation in healthcare, in: *Internet of Things (IoT) for Automated and Smart Applications*, p. 4, 2020, http://dx.doi.org/10.5772/intechopen.86014.

15. Naresh, V.S., Pericherla, S.S., Murty, P.S.R., Reddi, S., Internet of Things in healthcare : Architecture, applications, challenges, and solutions. *Int. J. Comput. Syst. Sci. Eng., Comput. Syst. Sci. Eng.*, 6, 411–421, 2020.

16. Angelov, G.V., Nikolakov, D.P., Ruskova, I.N., Gieva, E.E., Spasova, M.L., Healthcare sensing and monitoring, in: *Enhanced Living Environments. Lecture Notes in Computer Science*, vol. 11369, I. Ganchev, N. Garcia, C. Dobre, C. Mavromoustakis, R. Goleva (Eds.), Springer, Cham, 2019.

17. Romare, C., Hass, U., Skär, L., Healthcare professionals' views of smart glasses in intensive care: A qualitative study. *Intensive Crit. Care Nurs.*, 45, 66–71, April 2018.

18. Susarla, M., Akhil, C., Reddy, A., Hema, D.D., Heartbeat detection and monitoring using IOT. *J. Netw. Commun. Emerg. Technol.*, 8, 5, 18–20, 2018.

19. Raja, R., Kumar, S., Rashid, Md, Color object detection based image retrieval using ROI segmentation with multi-feature method. *Wirel. Pers. Commun. Springer J.*, 1–24, 1 May 2020, Print ISSN0929-6212 online ISSN1572-834.

20. Thai, T.T., Yang, Y., De Jean, G.R., Tentzeris, M.M., Nanotechnology enables wireless gas sensing. *IEEE Microwave Mag.*, 12, 84–95, 2011, 2017.

21. Yuehong, Y., The internet of things in healthcare: An overview. *J. Ind. Inf. Integr.*, 1, 3–13, 2016.

22. Shanmugasundaram, G. and Sankarikaarguzhali, G., An investigation on IoT healthcare analytics. *Int. J. Inf. Eng. Electron. Bus.*, 9, 2, 11, 2017.

23. Lee, J.-Y. and Scholtz, R.A., Ranging in a dense multipath environment using an UWB radio link. *IEEE J. Sel. Areas Commun.*, 20, 1677–1683, 2002.

24. Lenka, R.K., Rath, A.K., Tan, Z., Sharma, S., Puthal, D., Simha, N.V.R., Building scalable cyber-physical-social networking infrastructure using IoT and low power sensors. *IEEE Access*, 6, 1, 30162–30173, 2018.

25. Sawyer, J., Wearable Internet of Medical Things Sensor Devices, artificial intelligence-driven smart healthcare services, and personalized clinical care in COVID-19 telemedicine. *Am. J. Med. Res.*, 7, 71–77, 2020.

26. Seshadri, D.R., Davies, E.V., Harlow, E.R., Hsu, J.J., Knighton, S.C., Walker, T.A., Voos, J.E., Drummond, C.K., Wearable sensors for COVID-19: A call to action to harness our digital infrastructure for remote patient monitoring and virtual assessments. *Front. Digit. Health*, 2, 8, 2020.

27. Waheed, A. and Shafi, J., Successful role of smart technology to combat COVID-19, in: *Proceedings of the 2020 Fourth International Conference on I-SMAC (IoT in Social, Mobile, Analytics and Cloud) (I-SMAC)*, Palladam, India, 7–9 October 2020, pp. 772–777.

28. League, K., Boonnag, C., Sudhawiyangkul, T., Leelaarporn, P., Gulistan, A., Chen, W., Mukhopadhyay, S.C., Wilaiprasitporn, T., Piyayotai, S., Potential applications of mobile and wearable devices for psychological support during the COVID-19 pandemic: A review. *IEEE Sens. J.*, 21, 7162–7178, 2020.

29. Sahakian, B., Vatansever, D., Wang, S., COVID-19 and promising solutions to combat symptoms of stress, anxiety and depression. *Neuropsychopharmacology*, 46, 217–218, 2021.

30. Ženko, J., Kos, M., Kramberger, I., Pulse rate variability and blood oxidation content identification using miniature wearable wrist device. *2016 International Conference on Systems, Signals and Image Processing (IWSSIP)*, pp. 1–4, 2016.

31. Milici, S., Lorenzo, J., Lazaro, A., Villarino, R., Girbau, D., Wireless breathing sensor based on wearable modulated frequency selective surface. *IEEE Sens. J.*, 17, 99, 1, 2016.

32. Varon, C., Caicedo, A., Testelmans, D., Buyse, B., Huffel, S.V., A novel algorithm for the automatic detection of sleep apnea from single-lead ECG. *IEEE Trans. Biomed. Eng.*, 62, 9, 2269–2278, 2015.

33. Min, S.D., Yun, Y., Shin, H., Simplified structural textile respiration sensor based on capacitive pressure sensing method. *IEEE Sens. J.*, 14, 9, 3245–3251, 2014.

34. Nakamura, T., Yokota, T., Terakawa, Y., Reeder, J., Voit, W., Someya, T., Sekino, M., Development of flexible and wide-range polymer-based temperature sensor for human bodies. *2016 IEEE-EMBS International Conference on Biomedical and Health Informatics (BHI)*, pp. 485–488, 2016.

35. Eshkeiti, A., Joyce, M., Narakathu, B.B., Emamian, S., Avuthu, S.G.R., Joyce, M., Atashbar, M.Z., A novel self-supported printed flexible strain sensor for monitoring body movement and temperature. *IEEE Sensors 2014 Proceedings*, pp. 1615–1618, 2014.

36. Aqueveque, P., Gutierrez, C., Saavedra, F., Pino, E.J., Morales, A., Wiechmann, E., Monitoring physiological variables of mining workers at high altitude. *IEEE Trans. Ind. Appl.*, 99, 1, 2017.

37. Narczyk, P., Siwiec, K., Pleskacz, W.A., Precision human body temperature measurement based on thermistor sensor. *2016 IEEE 19th International Symposium on Design and Diagnostics of Electronic Circuits & Systems (DDECS)*, pp. 1–5, 2016.

38. Zhang, B. and Lo, Wireless wearable photoplethysmography sensors for continuous blood pressure monitoring. *2016 IEEE Wireless Health (WH)*, pp. 1–8, 2016.

39. Wannenburg, J. and Malekian, R., Body sensor network for mobile health monitoring, a diagnosis and anticipating system. *IEEE Sens. J.*, 15, 12, 6839–6852, 2015.

40. Hui-Wen Chuah, S., Rauschnabel, P.A., Krey, N., Nguyen, B., Thurasamy, Wearable technologies: The role of usefulness and visibility in smartwatch adoption. *Comput. Hum. Behav.*, 65, 276–284, 2016, www.elsevier.com/locate/comphumbe.

41. Thone, J., Radiom, S., Turgis, D., Carta, R., Gielen, G., Puers, R., Design of a 2 Mbps FSK near-field transmitter for wireless capsule endoscopy. *Sens. Actuators A: Phys.*, 156, 1, 43–48, 2009.

42. Sidheeque, A., Kumar, A., Balamurugan, R., Deepak K, C., Sathish, K., Heartbeat sensing and heart attack detection using Internet of Things: IoT. *Int. J. Eng. Sci.1 Comput.*, 7, 4, 6662–6666, 2017.

43. *The future of the public's health in the 21st century*, The National Academy Press, Institute of Medicine (US) Committee on Assuring the Health of the Public in the 21st Century, Washington (DC): National Academies Press (US), 2002.

44. Thai, T.T., Yang, Y., DeJean, G.R., Tentzeris, M.M., Nanotechnology enables wireless gas sensing. *IEEE Microwave Mag.*, 12, 84–95, 2011.

45. Valdastri, P., Menciassi, A., Arena, A., Caccamo, C., Dario, P., An implantable telemetry platform system for in vivo monitoring of physiological parameters. *IEEE Trans. Inf. Technol. Biomed.*, 8, 3, 271–278, 2004.

8

Fog Computing Paradigm for Internet of Things Applications

Upendra Verma* and Diwakar Bhardwaj

Dept. of Computer Engineering & Application, GLA University,
Mathura, UP, India

Abstract

The traditional cloud model is unable to meet the expectations of the Internet of Things (IoT) because it lacks the necessary capabilities. Some IoT applications, such as smart transportation and healthcare, necessitate characteristics, such as responsiveness, geographical distribution, latency, and location awareness, which are lacking in cloud-based Internet of Things systems. The fog computing paradigm is linked with the Internet of Things (IoT) in order to enable these characteristics, resulting in the creation of the Fog-IoT paradigm model. Through the use of "fog computing," it is possible to move computer power closer to the network edge, where it may be used more efficiently. With an emphasis on Internet of Things applications, this chapter investigates fog-assisted IoT applications and summarizes current fog computing research with a focus on IoT applications. Finally, challenges related to fog computing are highlighted in order to evoke new research opportunities within the framework of the Fog-IoT paradigm model.

Keywords: Fog-IoT paradigm model, IoT applications, Cloud-IoT model, IoT challenges

8.1 Introduction

IoT refers to the use of Internet-connected devices to create a more intelligent environment through the generation and transmission of vast amounts of data over the Internet for analysis and decision-making

---

*Corresponding author: upendra4567@gmail.com

Md Rashid Mahmood, Rohit Raja, Harpreet Kaur, Sandeep Kumar and Kapil Kumar Nagwanshi (eds.)
Ambient Intelligence and Internet of Things: Convergent Technologies, (243–272) © 2023 Scrivener Publishing LLC

purposes. Healthcare [1], transportation [2], home automation [3], energy management [4], and all other systems that affect human life are addressed through these decisions and analyses. However, the ITU-T definition is the most frequently accepted definition of IoT, which defines it as "global infrastructure for the information society," enabling improved services by integrating (physical and virtual) things with already available and emerging compatible ICTs [5]. Several major phrases jump out in the description, such as global infrastructure, physical and virtual items, communication technologies, the information society, and interoperability. Kevin Ashton coined the phrase "Internet of Things" [6]. According to Cisco [7, 8], by 2021, there will be 3.5 networked gadgets for every person on the planet. The Internet of Things is depicted in Figure 8.1 in an abstract manner.

Figure 8.2 depicts the Internet of Things' exponential growth. In IoT, interoperability is a major stumbling block to exponential growth. Interoperability refers to a system's capacity to communicate with other components regardless of their technical standards [9]. There can be different perspectives on interoperability, such as device, network, syntactic, and platform interoperability [10]. Interoperability in IoT is the key factor and crucial issue for assuring the connection between devices [11]. Interoperability issue arises in IoT because there is no common identification scheme for IoT [12]. Different IoT architectures are one of the

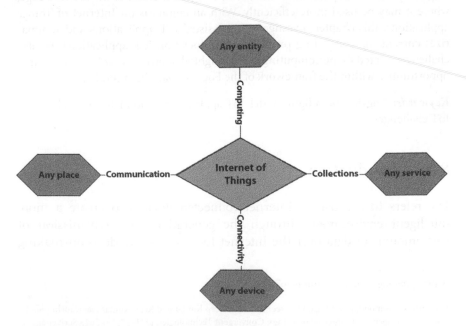

Figure 8.1 Abstract view of IoT.

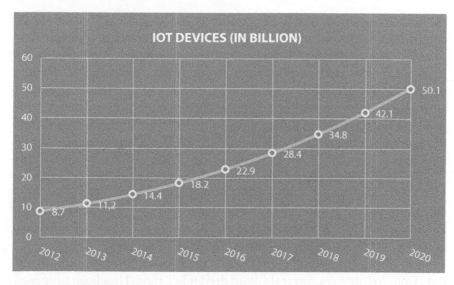

Figure 8.2 Growth of IoT.

consequences for interoperability. There is no universal accepted architecture of IoT defined till now [13]. Figure 8.3 depicts the basic, fundamental, and generic Internet of Things architecture, there are three layers in this system: the application layer, the perception layer and the network layer [14]. IoT architecture supports communication and transmission of data between IoT devices.

Traditional communication protocols such as IPV4 are not feasible in the IoT due to its resource-constrained nature and because address space

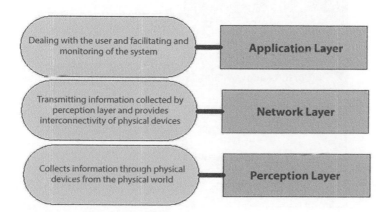

Figure 8.3 Generic architecture of IoT.

cannot accommodate the huge number of IoT devices [15]. As a result, communication protocols should be light and support the resource constraints of IoT devices. There are various communication challenges involved in IoT [16], such as identification and addressing of devices, mobility of devices, protocols with lower memory requirements, protocols with low power communication, high-speed communication, etc. An IoT protocol stack is used to link devices to the Internet in the IoT, as shown in Figure 8.4, and IoT protocols are optimized for constrained devices and networks.

Several communication protocols have been defined for IoT such as CoAP [17], IPV6 over low power WAN (6LowPAN) [18], DTLS [19], Time synchronized mesh protocol (TSMP) [20], MQTT [21], LWM2M [22], ZigBee [23], NFC [24], XMPP [25] etc. In comparison to traditional IoT architecture, cloud-driven IoT offers a number of benefits.

Most of the time, cloud computing is the best way to store and process data from IoT devices. Several Cloud driven IoT model has been proposed in the literature [26–30]. In particular, cloud computing is the centralized data center to provide storage, network management and computation for IoT devices. Now computing environment is shifted from centralized computing to distributed computing to fulfil the requirements of emerging IoT applications. The new requirements and challenges faced by Internet of things are latency constraints, resource constrained devices, security

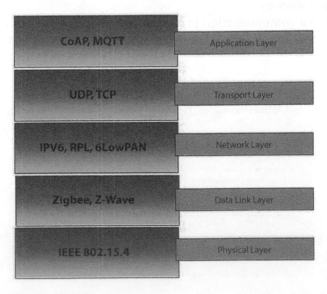

Figure 8.4 IoT protocol stack.

challenges [31]. The present cloud-IoT model is unable to meeting with new challenges and difficult to address requirements of IoT application. To overcome the challenges, Cisco has been introduced a fog computing paradigm [32]. Fog and cloud computing are interdependent and mutually beneficial. Fog computing provides networking, storage and computation services nearer to the IoT devices [33]. Taking the idea of cloud and fog computing into account, a number of new computing paradigms have been developed, such as mobile cloud computing (MCC), edge computing, and so on. According to Mahmud *et al.* [34], there are a lot of different ways to do computing, but fog computing is thought to be the best way to use the Internet of Things. In this way, we go into great detail about the essence of fog computing for the internet of things.

It is organized as follows throughout the remainder of the chapter: Section 8.2 examines the difficulties associated with the Cloud-IoT computing model. Section 8.3 reviews the concept of fog computing and their architecture followed by how fog computing address new challenges of IoT. Section 8.4 discusses the related work in context of fog computing. Section 8.5 addresses the various challenges in fog computing paradigm. Section 8.6 describes the fog assisted IoT applications. Section 8.7 concludes the chapter.

8.2   Challenges

Cloud computing has a lot of potential. Distributed computing and virtualization [35] are the foundations of cloud computing. Using the cloud deployment architecture, you can store and access data on a distant server. There are four types of cloud deployment models that can be used: private, public, hybrid, and community cloud. There are many smart and intelligent applications that can be made with the aid of the Internet of Things-Cloud Computing paradigm. These applications include smart homes [37, 38], smart cities, smart healthcare [39], smart transportation [40] and so on. IoT: In this paradigm, cloud computing acts as a front end for IoT service offerings [41]. This hybrid design has a lot of big problems when it comes to time-sensitive IoT applications. It costs more to communicate with IoT devices that are far away from the cloud server [36]. Network congestion, data processing, and the time it takes to send and receive data all depend on how far away they are. The Cloud-IoT model can't meet the needs of IoT applications [42]. In Figure 8.5, you can see the present cloud computing model.

The current cloud computing model's most serious flaws are network bandwidth and response time (latency). The response time for cloud-based

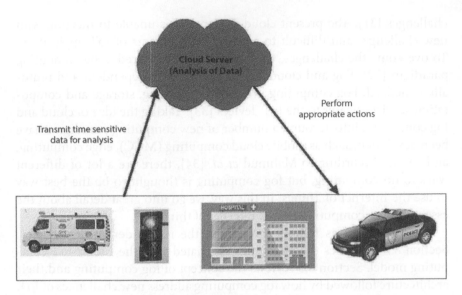

Figure 8.5 Current cloud computing model.

IoT application is computed as follows: time required to send data from IoT device to Cloud ($T_{sending}$: Device to Cloud) + time required to perform computation and analysis over data ($T_{computation/analysis}$: Cloud server) + time required to send data from cloud to IoT device ($T_{sending}$: cloud to device), where T is the time. As a result, the geographical distance between the device, and the cloud is a hurdle for the current cloud model. When reaction action reaches the device under the cloud-IoT model, incidents may have already occurred. This is the crucial challenge of present cloud-IoT model. A number of approaches to addressing and solving the difficulty of cloud computing can be taken advantage of by utilizing the fog computing paradigm.

8.3   Fog Computing: The Emerging Era of Computing Paradigm

8.3.1   Definition of Fog Computing

CISCO made the first proposal for fog computing in January 2014. The OpenFog consortium claims, "fog computing is the technology that distributes services and resources of computing, control, networking and storage anywhere along the continuum from cloud of thing" [43]. Another common fog computing definition is "Fog computing is proposed to enable computing directly at the edge of the network, which can deliver new applications and services especially for the future of Internet" [44].

8.3.2   Fog Computing Characteristic

The major characteristic of fog computing is to process IoT data locally rather than globally. Fog computing brings the storage and processing load at the proximity of edge. Fog computing has following features and characteristics:

- Low latency: There are certain IoT applications, which require faster response time and lower latency e.g. smart traffic light, video surveillances, healthcare system. fog computing provides computation services at edge of the network and make decisions based on the local data. Fog nodes placed nearer to the IoT devices, which provide higher response time services as compared to cloud.
- Mobility support: Generally, two types of devices are the part of IoT system—static and mobile devices. Mobile devices are required in most of the IoT application and fog nodes are nearer to the devices, which enable communication between devices and cloud in context of mobility support.
- Interoperability: Fog computing can be integrated and work with other technologies, c.g., cloud computing, software defined network, 5G, IoT.
- Geographical distribution: Fog computing is a distributed technology in contrast to centralized cloud computing. Fog nodes are distributed over the network and can be placed anywhere (generally deployed at edge of the network).
- Heterogeneity: Many standard bodies and organizations provide different platforms and specifications for IoT applications that need to be deployed according to their specification and platform. The fog computing has the ability to work with different specification and platform.
- Support for scalability: Internet of things is the very large, open, and scalable network. As per statistics in every second, 127 new devices are connected to internet [45]. Scalability is the major indicator in distributed computing and fog supports distributed computing environment which can work with large scale of IoT devices.

- Interaction with cloud computing: Cloud-fog-IoT is a fog computing architecture where fog node is placed between IoT devices and cloud servers. In the architecture, fog is responsible to process high-prioritized data and low-prioritized data sends to the cloud servers for further processing.
- Real-time interface and interaction: In fog computing, fog nodes are placed proximity to IoT devices. So, fog provides real time analysis of data as compared to cloud computing.

8.3.3   Comparison Between Cloud and Fog Computing Paradigm

The difference between fog and cloud computing is depicted in Table 8.1.

8.3.4   When to Use Fog Computing

Fog computing cannot be used for every IoT application rather than it can be used for specific IoT application and in some certain situations like

Table 8.1 Cloud v/s fog computing.

Parameters	Fog computing	Cloud computing
Conservation of bandwidth	Less	More
Responsiveness	High	Low
Operating expenses	High	Low
Geodistribution	Decentralized	Centralized
Location of service	Nearer to device	Far from device
Location awareness	Yes	No
Architecture	Distributed	Centralized
Response time	Seconds or milliseconds	Several minutes
Resource optimization	Global	Local
Mobility management	Hard	Easy

- If IoT devices require faster response time for applications, such as traffic light management and smart healthcare system;
- If data needs to be analyzed in a matter of a few seconds;
- If millions of devices are generating data across a large geographic area;
- If data is gathered at the edge, i.e., shopping floors and vehicles.

8.3.5   Fog Computing Architecture for Internet of Things

Bonomi *et al.* [46] proposed the first fog computing architecture. A distributed architecture between the sensor network and the core network has been defined by the authors. Fog computing offers a wide range of features, including mobility, interoperability, wireless connectivity, real-time data processing, and cloud interconnection. Until now, no globally accepted fog computing architecture has been defined. Several architectures have been proposed in the literature based on the type of service and application requirements [47–55]. Three-layer architecture, as depicted in Figure 8.6, is the most basic and generic architecture.

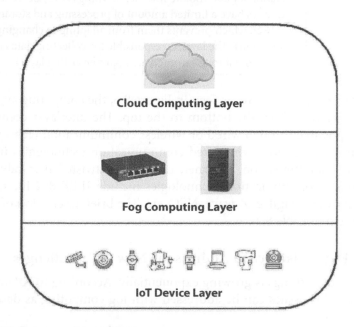

Figure 8.6 Fog computing architecture.

Table 8.2 Description of layers in fog computing architecture.

Layers	Description
Cloud Layer (Tier 3)	In fog computing, this is the topmost layer. From a global perspective, the cloud layer conducts computer, networking, and storage functions. The fog layer receives data from data centres and servers, which is then processed on a worldwide scale. The fog layer provides latency-sensitive services to devices, and the cloud layer defines administration and policies.
Fog Layer (Tier-2)	Switches, gateways, and routers make up the middle and core layers of the fog node infrastructure. Any network device that can perform computation, networking, and storage from a local perspective can be considered a fog device. In general, fog nodes can be installed at the edge of the network (the network of devices) and within one or two hops of the devices they are intended to connect. Data is sent to the cloud server on a regular basis by fog nodes, which have local knowledge of devices. With or without the cloud layer, this layer provides a wide range of services to the device layer.
Device Layer (Tier 1)	This is the most fundamental layer, and it includes both stationary and mobile Internet of Things (IoT) devices. The devices have a limited amount of processing and storage power, which prevents them from adapting to changing situations. The layer is responsible for collecting data and reporting it to the immediate upper layer (fog layer).

In a layered architecture, as seen in Figure 8.6, the computing and storage capacity rises from the bottom to the top. The interlayer communication is possible through wired or wireless communication technologies or combination of both. The wired communication technologies include fiberoptic communication, ethernet, coaxial and twisted pair cable, etc. The wireless communication technologies include IEEE 802.11, satellite communication, ZigBee, Z-wave, NFC, etc. The brief description of layers is illustrated in Table 8.2.

8.3.6 Fog Assistance to Address the New IoT Challenges

The Internet of things is growing exponentially. According to Atlam *et al.* [56], many IoT issues can be addressed with fog computing as described in Figure 8.7.

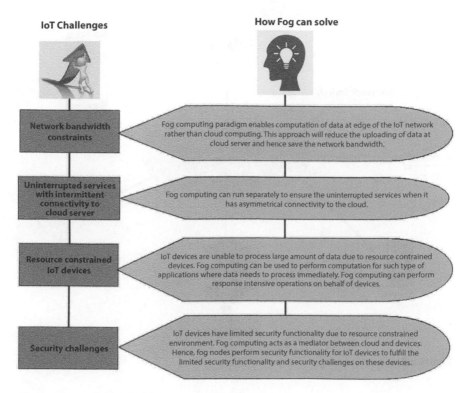

Figure 8.7 Fog helps to address new IoT challenges.

8.3.7 Devices Play a Role of Fog Computing Node

An important question is how to decide whether a given device is a fog node or not. Device capability is the criterion used to categorize normal devices and fog devices, and this criterion is useful for deciding whether a device can work as a fog node or not. Fog computing device can be any network device with the capability of computation, networking, and storage, such as servers, switches, routers, mobile phone, vehicles, traffic light, base station, etc., as shown in Figure 8.8. These devices can be deployed over the field at any place and collect data from IoT devise. The one important point is noted here fog devices must be deployed at edge of the IoT network with network connections either in the form of wired or wireless connection.

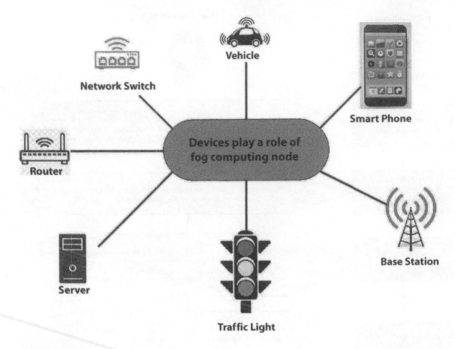

Figure 8.8 Fog nodes.

8.4 Related Work

Fog computing extends cloud-based facilities nearer to IoT devices. Fog computing is critical for resource-constrained networks, such as WSNs and IoT. This section reviews the available research on the Fog-IoT integration model. A brief summary of research articles has been emphasized in Table 8.3.

8.5 Fog Computing Challenges

Based on the literature survey, we may address key challenges in fog computing. Fog commuting has various advantages for IoT applications that require immediate processing of high-priority data. In addition to the advantages, integrating fog commuters with the IoT may provide certain challenges. The first challenge is resource management in fog computing [76]. The first challenge stated how to efficiently and effectively manage fog computing resources. Resource allocation between fog computing nodes

Table 8.3 Related research works.

Network model entities	Layer	Devices used as fog nodes	Application domain	Summary of contribution
Gateway-based fog node, micro server, wireless sensor and actuator network (as in [57])	Three	Gateway	IoT applications	WSAN's fog computing architecture was proposed, and the scalability concerns were discussed.
Cloud, Fog and Mobile phone (as in [58])	Three	Smart phone	Virtual and Smart Learning	Proposed fog- and big stream-based educational framework towards a better understanding of students educational behavior.
IoT devices, fog nodes and cloud platform (as in [59])	Three	General fog node	IoT applications	Provided a state of art study and literature of fog-based applications to identity privacy and security issues.
Cloud platform, fog node and various devices (as in [60])	Three	General fog node	Data assignment to each fog node	Fog computing was proposed as a distributed resource sharing management technique for pre-processing data streams from cloud platform-based apps.

(Continued)

Table 8.3 Related research works. (*Continued*)

Network model entities	Layer	Devices used as fog nodes	Application domain	Summary of contribution
User and base stations (as in [61])	Two	Base station	Medical cyber physical system	Proposed fog computing-based mobile cyber physical system in order to tackle cost efficiency and resource management problem.
Operator & manufacturer in adaptive operations platform (as in [62])	Two	Network devices	Industrial IoT applications	Proposed a fog computing paradigm to improve the operational efficiency and deal with the resource management.
End users, public cloud, health fog, user, smart home, and hospital (as in [63])	Three	Window-based machine	Healthcare	Provided health fog framework for processing health related information and to ensure data privacy and security.
Users, smart devices (mobile devices) and cloud of sensors (as in [64])	Three	Network devices	Mobile network applications	Provided an approach in order to enable seamless access between smart devices and sensors using CoAP application protocol.

(*Continued*)

Table 8.3 Related research works. (*Continued*)

Network model entities	Layer	Devices used as fog nodes	Application domain	Summary of contribution
Users, vehicles, and cloud platform (as in [65])	Three	Network devices	Vehicular network	Proposed a fog computing paradigm to offer consumer centric IoT services and discovery of services of connected vehicles.
Clients, storage, and communication servers (as in [66])	Three	Cellular base station	IoT applications	Proposed approach of task scheduling, resource management.
Device, fog, and cloud (as in [67])	Three	Network devices	IoT applications	Provided fog computing architecture and fog assisted applications and reviewed various solutions to address privacy and security in fog computing.
Thing, fog, and cloud (as in [68])	Three	Network devices	IoT applications	Provided a fog-based framework to understand and evaluate delay minimizing policy for IoT application.

(*Continued*)

Table 8.3 Related research works. (*Continued*)

Network model entities	Layer	Devices used as fog nodes	Application domain	Summary of contribution
Mobile devices, cloud-based storage devices (as in [69])	Three	Network devices	Mobile network	Proposed strength of fog computing for mobile application offloading and storage expansion
Vehicles, RSU, traffic light, and trusted authority (as in [70])	Three	Traffic light	Vehicular Network	Proposed a fog-based secure traffic light control scheme and the scheme is based on computational hash collision puzzle.
Terminals, stations, and cloud platform (as in [71])	Three	Base station & Access point	Radio access network	Proposed a fog computing-based radio access network for the fifth generation wireless communication system (5G) in order to reduce the heavy burden on centralized unit.
Hybrid IoT devices, fog node and trusted authority (as in [72])	Three	Router	IoT applications	A privacy-preserving data aggregation approach for fog-enabled Internet of Things was proposed.

(*Continued*)

Table 8.3 Related research works. (*Continued*)

Network model entities	Layer	Devices used as fog nodes	Application domain	Summary of contribution
Devices, edge devices and cloud (as in [73])	Five	Network devices	IoT applications	Proposed a reference fog-based architecture, which process requests in the local fog without need of cloud.
Vehicle, devices and cloud (as in [74])	Three	Network devices	IoT applications	Proposed a concept of mobile fog computing paradigm that allows applications to store and compute data locally without need of cloud
Sensor, vehicle, base station, and RSU (as in [75])	Three	Vehicles	Vehicular Network	Presented a fog computing architecture where vehicles play a role of fog node and infrastructure for computation and communication

and between fog nodes and IoT nodes is the critical issue and challenge [77]. The allocation of resources depends on the fog computing infrastructure and architecture. There are various fog computing architectures, such as fog architectures based on the nervous system [78], fog computing network architecture [79], integrated fog cloud IoT architecture [80], and hierarchical fog computing architecture, and the architectures depend on the necessity of applications. Another possible challenge is how to efficiently

Table 8.4 Description of cryptographic attacks.

Cryptographic attacks	Attack descriptions
Fog node forgery	In this attack, adversaries act as a fog node to the genuine user.
Activity tracking attack	Activity can be monitored by attacker and used against to fog node
Eavesdropping attack	In this attack, cryptanalyst tries to find weak network connection between IoT device and fog server.
Cloning attack	Attacker can create clone of the fog server and performs attack.
Impersonation attack	Intruder assumes the identity of legitimate server (fog node).
Replay attack	Adversary captures the data from device and forward it to the fog node.
Stolen device attack	In this attack, adversaries performs attack based on the credentials on stolen fog node or device.
Fog capture attack	Adversary captures fog node and manipulate their functionalities.
Desynchronization attack	In this attack, attackers block the communication between device and fog node.
Data manipulation attack	In this attack, attacker does not delete data instead of deleting attackers modify actual data and sends to the targeted server.
By passing attack	In this attack, attacker captures packets from device and responds to fog node as genuine device.
Changing distance attack	In this attack, attacker changes the original route with false route that misleads the distance between device and fog server. This is possible through wormhole node.
Brute force attack	Adversary uses a cryptanalysis method (trial-error method) to get into the system.
Anonymity attack	Adversary hides the real identity and performs attack among the fog nodes or between device and fog node.
Denial of service attack (DoS)	DoS attack is quite common in fog computing network. In this attack, unauthorized entity (adversaries) sends bogus request messages to fog node to shut down the operations temporarily.

manage fog computing nodes to provide requested services. There are different IoT devices deployed over the network, and each device requests different services from fog nodes. As a result, it is difficult for fog nodes to provide requested services in order to meet the requirements of IoT applications. Fog computing is integrated with IoT, which opens another possible challenge of security and privacy. Traditional networking components are used to design fog computing, and this type of design is highly vulnerable to different cryptographic attacks. Cloud computing is vulnerable because of its centralized computing paradigm and the existing cloud computing security countermeasures are incompatible with fog computing due to heterogeneity, dynamic mobility, and geographical distribution. So, fog computing inherits various security risks from cloud computing, and many cryptographic attacks have been launched to disrupt the privacy and security of fog computing. The description of attacks in the context of the layered fog computing architecture is illustrated in Table 8.4.

One of the most difficult problems in fog computing is interoperability. In the context of fog computing, there are different categories of interoperability issues, e.g. syntactic and semantic interoperability, programmatic and methodological interoperability, organizational interoperability, and technical interoperability. Fog computing is integrated not only with IoT but also with 5G, SDN, wired networks, telecommunication networks and other enterprises. To work with fog computing, a universal and standard fog computing framework must have been developed to distribute services and resources. Fog consortium shown in Figure 8.9 helps to address the

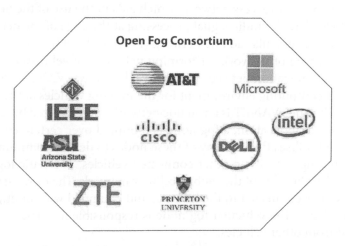

Figure 8.9 Open fog consortium.

interoperability challenge and provide a robust new platform for product development.

Global high-tech and academic organizations have formed the Open Fog Consortium to advance and standardize fog computing across numerous fields. The vital goal of the open fog consortium is to create an open reference architecture for fog computing. The open fog reference architecture framework helps to create standards to enable interoperability in artificial intelligence (AI), 5G, IoT and other network-intensive applications. The key pillars of reference architecture are autonomy, agility, hierarchy, scalability, programmability, and security.

8.6   Fog Supported IoT Applications

(i) Fog assisted patient health monitoring [81]

Fog computing can play a vital role in healthcare monitoring system. Fog computing can be used to detect sudden cardiac attack for cardiac patients. Fog device sends warning signals to hospital once they detect sudden events happening. It is possible to remotely monitor patient health using the concept of fog computing. Fog server is able to handle and monitor trigger-based event at edge of the network, which is happening suddenly in healthcare system environment.

(ii) Fog radio access network (F-RAN) [74]

F-RAN is a promising computing paradigm for the fifth generation (5G) of mobile telecommunication networks. FRAN inhibits this feature effectively. The combination of a radio access network and fog computing results in a fog radio access network, which aids in the use of the network's edge. FRAN provides radio signal processing at the edge of the network.

(iii) Fog-based vehicular ad hoc network (F-VANET) [82]

VANET is a type of network for forming networks of vehicles and establishing communication between vehicles on highways. VANET requires a distributed computing environment for the moving vehicles at the edge of the network. An F-VANET is an ad hoc network characterized by fog computing. In this application, a fog node is mounted over certain connected vehicles and utilises the mobility of these nodes to deliver communication and computing capacity to other connected vehicles. The static fog nodes are located at the edge of the mobile cellular network. The moving vehicular fog node is connected to the internet and equipped with multiple network interfaces. The vehicular fog node is responsible for processing data collected from other vehicles.

(iv) Smart road traffic light management and surveillances [73]

Smart traffic light management and surveillance are essential parts of a smart and intelligent transportation system. Traffic lights can act as fog nodes to ensure road traffic management and surveillance of the city. One possible application of fog computing can be used to detect the presence of pedestrians crossing over a road. This can be achieved by deploying sensors on the road and changing traffic lights to make them more convenient for pedestrians. The rapid response feature of fog computing can be used to avoid collisions between vehicles. In a traffic light management system, a traffic light may act as a fog node and also communicate with neighboring traffic lights and nearby vehicles. Traffic lights (fog nodes) may use a traffic schedule algorithm to change the light sequence, as well as detect the flashing light of an ambulance to open lanes for faster driving.

(v) Fog-based energy management [83]

Energy management is required to govern power consumption and power generation for IoT applications. In cloud-IoT model, the scalability and latency is the crucial issue in context of energy management. Fog computing-based energy management (F-EM) is the solution for efficiently management of consumption of energy. Smart grid application is integrated with fog computing for efficient management foe energy. For offering uninterpretable services to end users, smart grid applications require a high response time and low latency. Therefore, fog computing is used between smart metre and cloud server for efficient use of energy consumption.

(vi) Fog-based crowd sensing [84]

Mobile crowd sensing (MCS) is an emerging area and new trend, particularly in the development of human life. MCS differs from wireless sensor networks (WSN), which require focus on the collection of user data from mobile phones. In 2020, the number of mobile users is predicted to reach 4.78 billion [85]. MCS is a technology that uses smart mobile phones to collect information from smart microsensors and analyze it. It collects information from the environment and people around them. This refined information after analysis can be used to perform several operations, such as service-related operations to provide services to end users in an effective way, operations related to dynamic evaluation of network architecture, operations related to statistical analysis of groups of people, forecasting policy of the government, operations related to revealing secret information of group activity, etc. In MCS, mobile devices play an important role for data collection and service interaction, and it is user-centric. MCS has various services, including City Sense [86]. MCS can be integrated with IoT, IoV, IoS, and M2M communication. Fog computing can be integrated with MCS and is called "fog-based crowd sensing," where computation is performed at the edge of the network. The possible challenge of fog-based crowd sensing is privacy and security issues.

(vii) Fog-based industry automation [87]

IIoT, also called Industry 4.0, is the emerging area for the automation of industry and is growing rapidly. Accenture estimated that by 2030, IIoT could be 14.2 trillion US dollars' worth [88]. IIoT is useful to automate the system and improve the performance of asset, business process, and entire machinery. The major benefits of IIoT include increased productivity, improved operational efficiency, and enhanced customer experience. In fog-based industry automation, a new layer fog layer is introduced between process control system and machine control system. The fog-based industry automation can be used in various applications, such as cyber physical system (CPS), Industry 4.0, augmented reality (AR) for virtual training, etc.

(viii) Fog-based malware defence [89]

Several cryptographic attacks have been launched to expose the security of IoT. The biggest challenge for the IoT is security and privacy. IoT is an open environment with less human intervention and is vulnerable to various attacks. Fog computing is supposed to be more secure as compared to cloud computing due to transient analysis and local storage of data. Fog computing–based malware defences are used to protect applications from IoT malware, e.g., Mirai. Fog computing-based anti-malware

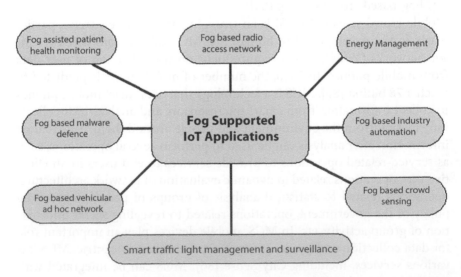

Figure 8.10 Fog-supported IoT application.

for IoT systems (e.g., Antibiotic 1.0 and 2.0) has been designed and developed for insecure IoT systems and malware [90]. Figure 8.10 shows the fog-supported IoT applications.

8.7   Summary and Conclusion

In this chapter, fog computing was examined for several applications, particularly in the field of IoT. The IoT has become an important aspect of people's lives in recent years. IoT devices are becoming increasingly interconnected with the open environment. Computation and storage constraints are two of the most significant IoT challenges. The cloud paradigm has various challenges, such as high latency, high bandwidth latency, and network traffic, which are addressed by combining IoT and cloud. To resolve these issues, fog computing has been introduced. Fog computing is a high-potential computing architecture for IoT applications, but it is still in its infancy due to a number of limitations and challenges. This chapter reviewed various challenges of the IoT and Cloud-IoT models to identify the necessity of fog computing in resource-constrained IoT networks. We demonstrated various fog-assisted IoT applications and fog computing architectures. Based on the literature, we addressed some significant challenges and issues in fog computing. Positively, the work described here will be valuable in addressing future research directions for response-intensive IoT applications.

References

1. Wu, T., Wu, F., Redoute, J.M., Yuce, M.R., An autonomous wireless body area network implementation towards IoT connected healthcare applications. *IEEE Access*, 5, 11413–11422, 2017.
2. He, W., Yan, G., Da Xu, L., Developing vehicular data cloud services in the IoT environment. *IEEE Trans. Ind. Inform.*, 10, 2, 1587–1595, 2014.
3. Froiz-Míguez, I., Fernández-Caramés, T.M., Fraga-Lamas, P., Castedo, L., Design, implementation and practical valuation of an IoT home automation system for fog computing applications based on MQTT and ZigBee-WiFi sensor nodes. *Sensors*, 18, 8, 2660, 2018.
4. Liu, Y., Ang, C., Jiang, L., Xie, S., Zhang, Y., Intelligent edge computing for IoT-based energy management in smart cities. *IEEE Netw.*, 33, 2, 111–117, 2019.
5. Wortmann, F. and Flüchter, K., Internet of things. *Bus. Inf. Syst. Eng.*, 57, 3, 221–224, 2015.

6. Govinda, K. and Saravanaguru, R.A.K., Review on IoT technologies. *Int. J. Appl. Eng. Res.*, 11, 4, 2848–2853, 2016.

7. Shanmuganathan, H. and Mahendran, A., Current trend of IoT market and its security threats, in: *International Conference on Innovative Computing, Intelligent Communication and Smart Electrical Systems (ICSES)*, vol. 2021, pp. 1–9, IEEE, 2021.

8. Attaran, M., The impact of 5G on the evolution of intelligent automation and industry digitization, in: *Journal of Ambient Intelligence and Humanized Computing*, vol. 2021, pp. 1–17, 2021.

9. Growth in the internet of things, 26th April 2021. http://www.ncta.com.

10. Noura, M., Atiquzzaman, M., Gaedke, M., Interoperability in internet of things: Taxonomies and open challenges. *Mobil. Netw. Appl.*, 24, 3, 796–809, 2019.

11. Abdelouahid, R.A., Oqaidi, M., Marzak, A., Towards to a new IoT interoperability architecture, in: *IEEE International Conference on Technology Management, Operations and Decisions (ICTMOD)*, IEEE, pp. 148–154, 2018.

12. Aftab, H., Gilani, K., Lee, J., Nkenyereye, L., Jeong, S., Song, J., Analysis of identifiers on IoT platforms. *Digit. Commun. Netw.*, 6, 3, 333–340, 2019.

13. Yun, M. and Yuxin, B., Research on the architecture and key technology of internet of things (IoT) applied on smart grid, in: *International Conference on Advances in Energy Engineering*, IEEE, pp. 69–72, 2010.

14. Tewari, A. and Gupta, B.B., Security, privacy and trust of different layers in internet-of-things (IoTs) framework. *Fut. Gener. Comput. Syst.*, 108, 909–920, 2020.

15. Sobin, C.C., A survey on architecture, protocols and challenges in IoT. *Wirel. Pers. Commun.*, 112, 3, 1383–1429, 2020.

16. Zeng, D., Guo, S., Cheng, Z., The web of things: A survey. *JCM*, 6, 6, 424–438, 2011.

17. Järvinen, I., Daniel, L., Kojo, M., Experimental evaluation of alternative congestion control algorithms for Constrained Application Protocol (CoAP), in: *2nd World Forum on Internet of Things (WF-IoT)*. vol. 2015, pp. 453–458, IEEE, 2015.

18. Shelby, Z. and Bormann, C., *6LoWPAN: The wireless embedded internet*, vol. 43, John Wiley & Sons, United Kingdom, 2011.

19. Banerjee, U., Juvekar, C., Fuller, S. H., Chandrakasan, A. P., eeDTLS: Energy-efficient datagram transport layer security for the Internet of Things, in: *GLOBECOM, Global Communications Conference*, vol. 2017, pp. 1–6, IEEE, 2017.

20. Pister, K. and Doherty, L., TSMP: Time synchronized mesh protocol. *IASTED Distrib. Sens. Netw.*, 391, 398, 61, 2008.

21. Hunkeler, U., Truong, H.L., Stanford-Clark, A., MQTT-S—A publish/subscribe protocol for wireless sensor networks, in: *3rd International*

Conference on Communication Systems Software and Middleware and Workshops (COMSWARE'08), IEEE, pp. 791–798, 2008.

22. Alliance, O.M., *Lightweight machine to machine technical specification*, vol. 1, Open Mobile Alliance, California, United States, 2017.

23. Alliance, Z., Zigbee alliance, in: *WPAN industry group*, The industry group responsible for the ZigBee standard and certification, 508 Second Street, Suite 206 Davis, California, 2010. http://www. zigbee.org/.

24. Coskun, V., Ozdenizci, B., Ok, K., A survey on near field communication (NFC) technology. *Wirel. Pers. Commun.*, 71, 3, 2259–2294, 2013.

25. Saint-Andre, P., XMPP: Lessons learned from ten years of XML messaging, in: *IEEE Communications Magazine*, vol. 47, no. 40, pp. 92–96, IEEE, 2009.

26. Wazid, M., Das, A.K., Hussain, R., Succi, G., Rodrigues, J.J., Authentication in cloud-driven IoT-based big data environment: Survey and outlook. *J. Syst. Arch.*, 97, 185–196, 2019.

27. Liao, Y.P. and Wang, S.S., A secure dynamic ID based remote user authentication scheme for multi-server environment. *Comput. Standards Interfaces*, 31, 1, 24–29, 2009.

28. Zhou, L., Li, X., Yeh, K.H., Su, C., Chiu, W., Lightweight IoT-based authentication scheme in cloud computing circumstance. *Fut. Gener. Comput. Syst.*, 91, 244–251, 2019.

29. Firouzi, F. and Farahani, B., Architecting IoT cloud, in: *Intelligent internet of things*, pp. 173–241, Springer, Springer Nature Switzerland, 2020.

30. Zhang, Y., Wang, H., Xie, Y., An intelligent hybrid model for power flow optimization in the cloud-IoT electrical distribution network. *Clust. Comput.*, 22, 6, 13109–13118, 2019.

31. Chiang, M. and Zhang, T., Fog and IoT: An overview of research opportunities. *IEEE Internet Things J.*, 3, 6, 854–864, 2016.

32. Verma, U. and Bhardwaj, D., Security challenges for fog computing enabled internet of things from authentication perspective. *Int. J. Comput. Intell. IoT*, 2, 1, 382–387, 2019.

33. Vaquero, L.M. and Rodero-Merino, L., Finding your way in the fog: Towards a comprehensive definition of fog computing. *ACM SIGCOMM Comput. Commun. Rev.*, 44, 5, 27–32, 2014.

34. Mahmud, R., Kotagiri, R., Buyya, R., Fog computing: A taxonomy, survey and future directions, in: *Internet of everything*, pp. 103–130, Springer, Singapore, 2018.

35. Cloud, H., The nist definition of cloud computing, in: *National Institute of Science and Technology, Special Publication*, vol. 800, no. 2011, pp. 145, 2011.

36. Dillon, T., Wu, C., Chang, E., Cloud computing: Issues and challenges, in: *24th IEEE international conference on advanced information networking and applications*, pp. 27–33, 2010.

37. Soliman, M., Abiodun, T., Hamouda, T., Zhou, J., Lung, C.H., Smart home: Integrating internet of things with web services and cloud computing, in:

IEEE 5th international conference on cloud computing technology and science, vol. 2, pp. 317–320, 2013.

38. Jaiswal, K., Sobhanayak, S., Turuk, A.K., Bibhudatta, S.L., Mohanta, B.K., Jena, D., An IoT-cloud based smart healthcare monitoring system using container based virtual environment in edge device, in: *International Conference on Emerging Trends and Innovations In Engineering And Technological Research (ICETIETR)*, IEEE, pp. 1–7, 2018.

39. Petrolo, R., Loscri, V., Mitton, N., Towards a smart city based on cloud of things, a survey on the smart city vision and paradigms. *Trans. Emerg. Telecommun. Technol.*, 28, 1, e2931, 2017.

40. Saarika, P.S., Sandhya, K., Sudha, T., Smart transportation system using IoT, in: *International Conference On Smart Technologies For Smart Nation (SmartTechCon)*, IEEE, pp. 1104–1107, 2017.

41. Rao, B.P., Saluia, P., Sharma, N., Mittal, A., Sharma, S.V., Cloud computing for internet of things & sensing based applications, in: *Sixth International Conference on Sensing Technology (ICST)*, IEEE, pp. 374–380, 2012.

42. Ali, B., Pasha, M. A., ul Islam, S., Song, H., Buyya, R., A volunteer-supported fog computing environment for delay-sensitive iot applications, in: *IEEE Internet of Things Journal*, vol. 8, no. 5, pp. 3822–3830, 2020.

43. Sabireen, H. and Neelanarayanan, V., A review on fog computing: Architecture, fog with IoT, algorithms and research challenges. in: *ICT Express*, vol. 7, no. 2, pp. 162–176, Elsevier, 2021.

44. Yi, S., Li, C., Li, Q., A survey of fog computing: Concepts, applications and issues, in: *Proceedings of the workshop on mobile big data*, pp. 37–42, 2015.

45. Al-Fuqaha, A., Guizani, M., Mohammadi, M., Aledhari, M., Ayyash, Internet of things: A survey on enabling technologies, protocols, and applications, in: *IEEE communications surveys & tutorials*, vol. 17, no. 4, pp. 2347–2376, IEEE, 2015.

46. Bonomi, F., Milito, R., Zhu, J., Addepalli, S., Fog computing and its role in the internet of things, in: *Proceedings of the first edition of the MCC workshop on Mobile cloud computing*, pp. 13–16, 2012.

47. Atlam, H.F., Walters, R.J., Wills, G.B., Fog computing and the internet of things: a review. *Big Data Cogn. Comput.*, 2, 2, 10, 2018.

48. Kunal, S., Saha, A., Amin, R., An overview of cloud-fog computing: Architectures, applications with security challenges. *Secur. Privacy*, 2, 4, e72, 2019.

49. Cha, H.J., Yang, H.K., Song, Y.J., A study on the design of fog computing architecture using sensor networks. *Sensors*, 18, 11, 3633, 2018.

50. Byers, C.C., Architectural imperatives for fog computing: Use cases, requirements, and architectural techniques for fog-enabled IoT networks. *IEEE Commun. Mag.*, 55, 8, 14–20, 2017.

51. Naha, R.K., Garg, S., Chan, A., Fog computing architecture: Survey and challenges, 2018. arXiv preprint arXiv:1811.09047.

52. Luan, T.H., Gao, L., Li, Z., Xiang, Y., Wei, G., Sun, L., Fog computing: Focusing on mobile users at the edge, 2015. arXiv preprint arXiv:1502.01815.

53. Giang, N.K., Blackstock, M., Lea, R., Leung, V.C., Developing IoT appli-cations in the fog: A distributed dataflow approach, in: *5th International Conference on the Internet of Things (IoT)*, IEEE, pp. 155–162, 2015.
54. OCAW Group, *Openfog architecture overview*, White Paper, California, United States, February 2016.
55. Nadeem, M.A. and Saeed, M.A., Fog computing: An emerging paradigm, in: *2016 Sixth International Conference on Innovative Computing Technology (INTECH)*, IEEE, pp. 83–86, 2016.
56. Hu, P., Dhelim, S., Ning, H., Qiu, T., Survey on fog computing: Architecture, key technologies, applications and open issues. *J. Netw. Comput. Appl.*, 98, 27–42, 2017.
57. Lee, W., Nam, K., Roh, H.G., Kim, S.H., A gateway based fog computing architecture for wireless sensors and actuator networks. *18th International Conference on Advanced Communication Technology (ICACT)*, IEEE, pp. 210–213, 2016.
58. Pecori, R., A virtual learning architecture enhanced by fog computing and big data streams. *Fut. Internet*, 10, 14, 4, 2018.
59. Khan, S., Parkinson, S., Qin, Y., Fog computing security: A review of current applications and security solutions. *J. Cloud Comput.*, 6, 1, 19, 2017.
60. Yin, B., Shen, W., Cheng, Y., Cai, L.X., Li, Q., Distributed resource sharing in fog-assisted big data streaming, in: *2017 IEEE international conference on communications (ICC)*, IEEE, pp. 1–6, 2017.
61. Gu, L., Zeng, D., Guo, S., Barnawi, A., Xiang, Y., Cost efficient resource man-agement in fog computing supported medical cyber-physical system. *IEEE Trans. Emerg. Topics Comput.*, 5, 1, 108–119, 2015.
62. Gazis, V., Leonardi, A., Mathioudakis, K., Sasloglou, K., Kikiras, P., Sudhaakar, R., Components of fog computing in an industrial internet of things context, in: *12th Annual IEEE International Conference on Sensing, Communication, and Networking-Workshops (SECON Workshops)*, pp. 1–6, IEEE, 2015.
63. Ahmad, M., Amin, M.B., Hussain, S., Kang, B.H., Cheong, T., Lee, S., Health fog: A novel framework for health and wellness applications. *J. Supercomput.*, 72, 10, 3677–3695, 2016.
64. Shi, H., Chen, N., Deters, R., Combining mobile and fog computing: Using CoAP to link mobile device clouds with fog computing, in: *IEEE International conference on data science and data intensive systems IEEE*, pp. 564–571, 2015.
65. Datta, S.K., Bonnet, C., Haerri, J., Fog computing architecture to enable con-sumer centric internet of things services, in: *International symposium on con-sumer electronics (ISCE)*, IEEE, pp. 1–2, 2015.
66. Lin, M., Zhang, L., Wierman, A., Tan, J., Joint optimization of overlapping phases in MapReduce, in: *Performance Evaluation*, vol. 70, no. 10, pp. 720–735, Elsevier, 2013.
67. Ni, J., Zhang, K., Lin, X., Shen, X.S., Securing fog computing for internet of things applications: Challenges and solutions. *IEEE Commun. Surv. Tutor.*, 20, 1, 601–628, 2017.

68. Yousefpour, A., Ishigaki, G., Jue, J.P., Fog computing: Towards minimizing delay in the internet of things, in: *IEEE international conference on edge computing (EDGE)*, IEEE, pp. 17–24, 2017.

69. Hassan, M.A., Xiao, M., Wei, Q., Chen, S., Help your mobile applications with fog computing, in: *12th Annual IEEE International Conference on Sensing, Communication, and Networking-Workshops (SECON Workshops)*, IEEE, pp. 1–6, 2015.

70. Liu, J., Li, J., Zhang, L., Dai, F., Zhang, Y., Meng, X., Shen, J., Secure intelligent traffic light control using fog computing. *Fut. Gener. Comput. Syst.*, 78, 817–824, 2018.

71. Peng, M., Yan, S., Zhang, K., Wang, C., Fog-computing-based radio access networks: Issues and challenges. *IEEE Netw.*, 30, 4, 46–53, 2016.

72. Lu, R., Heung, K., Lashkari, A.H., Ghorbani, A.A., A lightweight privacy-preserving data aggregation scheme for fog computing-enhanced IoT. *IEEE Access*, 5, 3302–3312, 2017.

73. Dastjerdi, A.V., Gupta, H., Calheiros, R.N., Ghosh, S.K., Buyya, R., Fog computing: Principles, architectures, and applications, in: *Internet of things*, pp. 61–75, Morgan Kaufmann, Burlington, Massachusetts, 2016.

74. Hong, K., Lillethun, D., Ramachandran, U., Ottenwälder, B., Koldehofe, B., Mobile fog: A programming model for large-scale applications on the internet of things, in: *Proceedings of the second ACM SIGCOMM workshop on Mobile cloud computing*, pp. 15–20, 2013.

75. Xiao, Y. and Zhu, C., Vehicular fog computing: Vision and challenges, in: *IEEE International conference on pervasive computing and communications workshops (PerCom Workshops)*, IEEE, pp. 6–9, 2017.

76. Ghobaei-Arani, M., Souri, A., Rahmanian, A.A., Resource management approaches in fog computing: a comprehensive review. *J. Grid Comput.*, 18, 1, 1–42, 2019.

77. Singh, K. and Tomar, D.S., Architecture, enabling technologies, security and privacy, and applications of internet of things: A survey, in: *2nd International Conference on I-SMAC (IoT in Social, Mobile, Analytics and Cloud) (I-SMAC))*, IEEE, pp. 642–646, 2018.

78. Sun, Y. and Zhang, N., A resource-sharing model based on a repeated game in fog computing. *Saudi J. Biol. Sci.*, 24, 3, 687–694, 2017.

79. Intharawijitr, K., Iida, K., Koga, H., Analysis of fog model considering computing and communication latency in 5G cellular networks, in: *IEEE International Conference on Pervasive Computing and Communication Workshops (PerCom Workshops)*, IEEE, pp. 1–4, 2016.

80. Munir, A., Kansakar, P., Khan, S.U., IFCIoT: Integrated fog cloud IoT: A novel architectural paradigm for the future internet of things. *IEEE Consum. Electron. Mag.*, 6, 3, 74–82, 2017.

81. Verma, P. and Sood, S.K., Fog assisted-IoT enabled patient health monitoring in smart homes. *IEEE Internet Things J.*, 5, 3, 1789–1796, 2018.

82. Kai, K., Cong, W., Tao, L., Fog computing for vehicular ad-hoc networks: Paradigms, scenarios, and issues. *J. China Univ. Posts Telecommun.*, 23, 2, 56–96, 2016.

83. Al Faruque, M.A. and Vatanparvar, K., Energy management-as-a-service over fog computing platform. *IEEE Internet Things J.*, 3, 2, 161–169, 2015.

84. Sun, G., Sun, S., Sun, J., Yu, H., Du, X., Guizani, M., Security and privacy preservation in fog-based crowd sensing on the internet of vehicles. *J. Netw. Comput. Appl.*, 134, 89–99, 2019.

85. Park, S. S. and Park, B., Advertising on mobile apps versus the mobile web: Which delivers better advertisement recognition and willingness to buy?, in: *Journal of Advertising Research*, vol. 60, no. 4, pp. 381–393, 2020.

86. Ganti, R. K., Ye, F., Lei H., Mobile crowdsensing: Current state and future challenges. *IEEE Commun. Mag.*, 49, 11, 32–39, 2011.

87. Matt, C., Fog computing. *Bus. Inf. Syst. Eng.*, 60, 4, 351–355, 2018.

88. http://www.accenture.com (Accessed online on 10th May 2021)

89. Rantapelkonen, J. and Salminen, M., The fog of cyber defence, in: *Julkaisusarja 2*, vol. 10, Artikkelikokoelma n: o, Helsinki Finland, 2013.

90. De Donno, M., Felipe, J.M.D., Dragoni, N., ANTIBIOTIC 2.0: A fog-based anti-malware for internet of things, in: *IEEE European Symposium on Security and Privacy Workshops (EuroS&PW)*, pp. 11–20, IEEE, 2019.

9

Application of Internet of Things in Marketing Management

Arshi Naim*, Anandhavalli Muniasamy and Hamed Alqahtani

College of Computer Science, Department of Information Systems, King Khalid University, Abha, KSA

Abstract

Internet of Things (IoT) has already reached its threshold of success in all the disciplines, and marketing management (MMgnt) has also been applying it in many of its areas for optimum growth, development, and safe working. This chapter is a case-based qualitative analysis that explains how IoT contributed to three fields MMgnt which are customer relationship management (CRM), building advanced business process models (BPM) and product life cycle (PLC). This is a descriptive study, and for the purpose of analysis, many instances from the real retail firms' are compared before and after the application of IoT and presented the distinguished achievement of classification of IoT. This study proposes five IoT plans for measuring the effectiveness of IoT for the abovementioned three sections of MMgnt that depend on the collection and sharing of data from external and internal environments. The results show that IoT plays an important role in the general marketing framework and specifically in three major areas of MMgnt for growth and development.

Keywords: Internet of Things, marketing management, customer relationship management, business process management, product life cycle

9.1 Introduction

This era is termed as digital era, and the Internet of Things (IoT) has helped in developing new and innovative products that can know, sense and share

---

**Corresponding author*: arshi@kku.edu.sa

Md Rashid Mahmood, Rohit Raja, Harpreet Kaur, Sandeep Kumar and Kapil Kumar Nagwanshi (eds.)
Ambient Intelligence and Internet of Things: Convergent Technologies, (273–300) © 2023 Scrivener Publishing LLC

data as well as information to all the users, such as companies, suppliers, and consumers [4]. There are many retail products' examples, such as Sunsilk shampoo, Reebok sneakers, or even beverages, such as Pepsico or fruit juices like Tropicana; all these products have extended the basic functionalities of regular goods by offering the facility to assemble and allocate data on the network [1, 2]. This new category of data collecting and sharing products are called IoT-ready products or simply IoT products (IP) [1, 2].

Such IoT can be understood as an interim stage in the growth of smart products (SP), which are able to examine and, carefully, "interpret" usage data in a goal-oriented way. SP can make decisions that would require human learning and critical thinking. For example, DSS or machine learning methods can analyze the stage of SP and use the data to evaluate customer behavior, preferences, and complaints too that may contribute in the process of new product development considering the achievement of customer satisfaction that is reliant on the product category and functional principle and decisions. These features are made by an SP that can be used to provide users and the company with recommendations or ratings and reviews for further research and development. Figure 9.1 shows the growth stage from traditional products (TP) to (IoT) to (SP) where TP has only basic functionalities, IotP includes the function of autonomous data collection and product analysis through virtual interfaces, and finally, SP encompasses data analysis, Artificial applications, machine learning DSS applications for decision-making processes [1–6].

There are many products in the current IoT environment marketed as SP, but as a researcher, we clearly comprehend that it is just a transition phase and developing SP involves many features and applications, such as IoT with CRM and BPM. IoT has not left any field without its relevance in the process of growth, such as in the medical sector, education, automobile, retailing, traffic control automation, smart cities and home automation, etc. In a few manufacturing units, the present stage of growth is already moving toward SP at a fast pace, such as cooking in the smart kitchen, self-driving cars in the automobile industry, etc., but we can still, IoT constitutes a relatively new phenomenon for many sectors. This paper discusses the positive impact of IoT for various MMgnt, such as CRM, PLC, and BPM. We have proposed five research ideas and analyzed the impact of IoT qualitatively, and referred to a few real examples of firms

Figure 9.1 Transformation from TP to SP [2].

showing success with the application of IoT. This paper is divided into five sub-topics; the first topic will cover the historical aspects of the concepts used in this paper in the literature review, the second topic gives a brief outline on the research methodology applied in this paper; thirdly, all five research proposals are discussed for IoT for three MMgnt concepts; CRM, PLC and BPM. The fourth topic gives the results, and the fifth topic illustrates the final outline as a conclusion.

9.2   Literature Review

This part explains the concept of the applications of IoT techniques in MMgnt. In past years the IoT has focused on essential areas in MMgnt and explained the benefits of communication over the net where people worldwide can get connected from all places and without any restriction on time. IoT is an open and comprehensive network of intelligent objects that have the capacity to auto-organize, share information, data and resources, reacting and acting in the face of situations and changes in the environment [3].

Figure 9.2 shows the general IoT system that comprises three inclusive, such as sensors, network connectivity, and data storage applications.

Global communication is possible with IoT that bridged the contacts at various levels. These levels include human interaction with another human

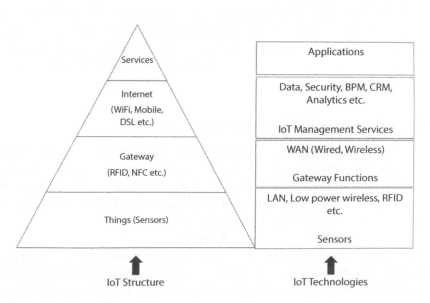

Figure 9.2 IoT system [3, 4, 12].

Table 9.1 IoT System applications in enterprise [20].

Event processing for analyzing data in real-time.
Build applications using IoT services, development kits, software tools and services, which support the platform to a range of applications and use-cases.
Driving innovation, enables new revenue streams, and improves operational efficiencies.
Security and identity management service to manage data security and identity of devices/apps.
User Interface (UI) services for visualization, operational and analytical data through mobile/desktop.
Analytics services that offers analysis based on past data, real-time and predictive analytics.
Integration services to act on machine-to-machine (Mch2Mch) data and events.

and devices [12]. The IoT services help the enterprise for many benefits, which are given in Table 9.1 [20].

In the drastic development at the global level by the application of IoT, Mch2Mch interaction has increased its scope and benefits too. IoT services can collect requested data from different sources and transfer it to other devices and systems automatically. As a result, routine and simple problems are solved. Not only this business-related solutions and recommendations are also possible [20].

9.2.1   Customer Relationship Management

Customer Relationship Management (CRM) [1, 9, 10] refers to all strategies, techniques, tools, and technologies used by enterprises for developing, retaining and tracking customers. It is a comprehensive strategy and process of acquiring, retaining, and clubbing with selective customers to create superior value for the company and the customer.

The scope of CRM is shown in Figure 9.3.

There are many CRM software available in the market which is helping in communication between consumers and firms. The main applications of this software are to confirm the effective working of the devices, offer effective communication and provide error-free services. Therefore the CRM

Figure 9.3 Scope of CRM [10].

software helps in profit maximization for the firms and achieving good relations with the consumers. CRM software involves the integration of marketing, sales, customer service, and the supply-chain functions of the organization to achieve greater efficiencies and effectiveness in delivering customer value [9].

CRM benefits for any firm [9, 10, 13]:

- Enhance communication at internal and external organizational levels.
- Keep track of customer journey map.
- Helps in resolving customer cases.
- Improves sales force efficiency.
- Improves customer relationships leading to customer loyalty.

9.2.2   Product Life Cycle (PLC)

PLC is the historical study of (sales of) the product [1]. PLC covers the product life cycle shown in Figure 9.4.

- When the product was introduced (Introduction Phase)
- When The Product Was Getting Rapid Acceptance (Growth Phase)
- When The Product Was On The Peak Of Its Position (Between Growth and Maturity Phase)

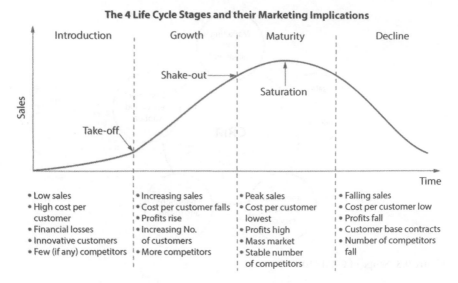

Figure 9.4 PLC phases in terms of time and revenue with their descriptions [18].

- When The Product Started Falling From The Peak (Maturity Phase)
- When The Product disappeared (Decline Phase)

The life of the product can be determined by its capacity to meet the market's expectations. It lasts or exists as long as it satisfies its users [18, 19].

9.2.3   Business Process Management (BPM)

Business process management (BPM) is a discipline involving any combination of modelling, automation, execution, control, measurement,

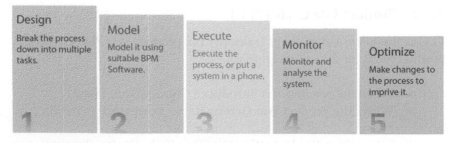

Figure 9.5 Business process management (BPM) with five steps [7, 11].

and optimization of business activity flows, in support of enterprise goals, spanning systems, employees, customers, and partners within and beyond the enterprise boundaries [11] which is shown above in the Figure 9.5.

9.2.4   Ambient Intelligence (AmI)

Ambient intelligence (AmI) supports the environments integrated with sensors and intelligent systems. AmI needs to be driven by humanistic concerns, "not technologically determined once" and should be "controllable by ordinary people." It is able to deliver personalized services automatically in anticipation of the needs of the inhabitants and visitors [4, 12].

The "ambient" side of the system includes sensors, processors, communications, and adaptive software. The smartphone, wearables, and IoT markets will continue to drive miniaturization and cost reduction [12] [21]. The "intelligence" side of the system will determine the success or failure of an AMI deployment. I am applicable to most of the IoT applications as well.

Factors that will influence the adoption of AmI are given below [12] in the Figure 9.6:

1. Usability: the interaction with Ambient Intelligence should be unobtrusive, not involving a steep learning curve. Many companies, influenced by Apple's design philosophy, have

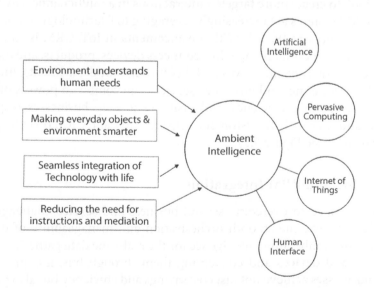

Figure 9.6 Ambient intelligence [12].

adopted user-friendly design principles in their products. There is no need for a manual to participate in AmI environments. It should just work as the user walk into its environment.

2. Technical feasibility: AmI needs to work reliably within the constraints of state-of-the-art technologies. Factors, like accuracy, capacity, and fail-safe measures for all the hardware and software components, need to be taken into consideration.

3. Trust and confidence: Besides, AmI needs to gain the confidence and trust of users before it will be widely adopted. IoT infrastructure that delivers AmI services will be like the energy infrastructure. The inherent nature of AmI is the capability to uniquely identify and track people. We need to explicitly define privacy policies in public and private spaces to gain users' trust.

4. Social and economic impacts: AmI should be able to enhance the social interactions of all the participants within the environment.

9.2.5　IoT and CRM Integration

CRM will be at the heart of digital initiatives in the coming years as enterprises look to create more targeted interactions in a multichannel environment. CRM systems are increasingly leveraging IoT technology to improve front-end processes [9, 10]. With advancements in IoT, CRM is all set to change the business landscape. IoT connects devices, products, and equipment to the Internet and drives insights throughout departments, including sales, marketing, and customer service. The combined powers of IoT and CRM enhance efficiency and visibility to help businesses respond quickly and effectively to customers. Impact of IoT and CRM on enterprise performance (see Figure 9.7).

9.2.6　IoT and BPM Integration

Businesses need to overcome several business and service challenges to be able to realize the smooth orchestration and manageability of disparate systems. Embedding intelligence for the real-time data gathering from gateways and devices and consuming them through business processes helps businesses achieve not just cost savings and efficiency but also generate more revenue patterns [14–16].

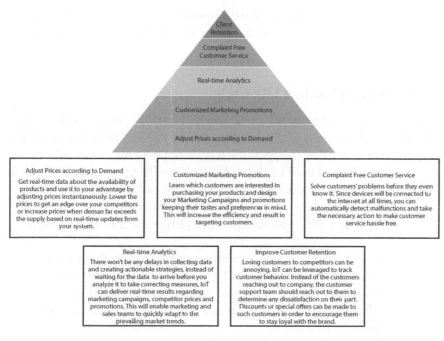

Figure 9.7 Benefits of IoT and CRM on firms functionality with their description [13].

Table 9.2 Benefits of IoT in BPM.

Event processing for analyzing data in real-time.
Build applications using IoT services, development kits, software tools and services, which support the platform to a range of applications and use-cases.
Driving innovation, enables new revenue streams, and improves operational efficiencies.
Security and identity management service to manage data security and identity of devices/apps.
User Interface (UI) services for visualization, operational and analytical data through mobile/desktop.
Analytics services that offers analysis based on past data, real-time and predictive analytics.
Integration services to act on machine-to-machine (Mch2Mch) data and events.

The IoT is changing the way we live our lives and that all businesses need to adapt to. The benefits of adopting IoT in business are explained in Table 9.2 [20].

9.2.7   IoT and Product Life Cycle

In PLM software, the customer feedback about the product only comes after the purchase, so it is almost impossible to collect real-time feedback as the customer is using the product. It does not help much once the product has been sold and used by the end customer. Therefore, this feedback is not as actionable as product developers would like [18]. This is where IoT can be applied for the improvement of the PLC process.

IoT can enhance PLM software because [19] of the following reasons:

    i.   It uses intelligent devices and sensors that are both interconnected and connected to the Internet. They can collect important information and relay it to interested parties. These gadgets can be embedded in any product, from vehicles to clothing.

    ii.   It can inform product developers and manufacturers in real-time how a certain product is performing out in the world. This can be valuable to engineers and designers thinking about the next iteration of the product.

    iii.   Companies can spot problems with the products on the field and fix them before they escalate and the product breaks down. Such a preventive measure will help customers avoid unnecessary downtimes and increase their bottom line.

    iv.   Companies can use both IoT and AI to predict future problems with a product and address them before they create inconvenience for the customer.

However, companies will become more customer-centric, and the manufacturers will have mountains of data on how customers are using their products so that they can build new products in line with the customer's behaviors and usage patterns [21].

9.2.8   IoT in MMgnt

The modern smartphone technology facilitates discussions on the potential impact of the IoT on industries, markets, companies, products, services,

Table 9.3 Benefits of IoT for PA and RA for MMgnt [5].

PA relies on the autonomous collection of usage data from the customer's environment that provides companies with insights into the actual product usage.
RA offers options for remotely operating the IoT product, changing the parameters or adjustment of product attributes, activating and deactivating product functions, and controlling data flowing inbound to the IoT product.

and consumers due to the advancement of IoT. The existing economic literature investigating IoT and smart products primarily focus on research questions in new business models [29], supply chain management [28], the fields of management [21–26], transportation [27], market competition [2], smart home, and ambient assisted living [35], the organizational structure of companies [31], consumers' attitudes toward autonomously acting products [30], production planning and control [32], privacy and secrecy [33], wearable devices [34].

From the perspective of marketing management, IoT products are of particular interest due to two functionalities, namely "product analytics" (PA) and "remote access" (RA); the description is given in Table 9.3.

Product analytics and remote access open up a wide range of new opportunities for marketing management.

9.2.9   Impacts of AmI on Marketing Paradigms

The AmI vision expects that ICT will increasingly become part of peoples' activities, social interaction, and functionality that enhance people's lives. AmI concepts establish a collaborative working environment where virtualized entities will communicate with each other. These entities can be humans, artificial agents, web/grid services, and able to interact with each other in an AmI environment to leverage the full potentiality of network-centric environments for productivity gains, boosting innovation, and creativity improvement [36].

The implementation of AmI concepts to support the PLM business paradigm will drastically change PLM systems [37]. Different processes from different chains will be integrated into one virtual environment. The components of this environment will be entities, which can be humans, IT systems (as ERP), intelligent software or mechanical agents [1, 5, 6, 39]. These entities will communicate on a peer-to-peer way and build up product-oriented dynamic networks [38]. These networks are dynamic

Table 9.4 Benefits of AmI in MMgnt [40].

- Focus on product information and creation of product-oriented environment for all steps of product lifecycle.
- Enabling information sharing, easier access and management of that the product- and customer-related data.
- Product information updates performed in real time and in intelligent ways.
- Enabling products to carry and process information, which influences their destiny.

because on different steps of the product lifecycle, different entities participate in the product-oriented network [18, 40].

The implementation of the ambient intelligent concept and integration it into the PLM business paradigm will lead the ambient intelligent product life-cycle management (AmI PLM) [42, 43]. Table 9.4 shows the main benefits of AmI environment in marketing [1, 5, 6, 41].

9.3   Research Methodology

This paper is the study showing the application of IoT and its realization in MMgnt under three areas; CRM, BPM, and PLC, where many research questions are answered showing the relationship between IoT and MMgnt concepts and how well they have been implemented by various firms in a real scenario. We developed some proposals and recommendations for MMgnt ideas with an application of IoT. This is a qualitative analysis and various firms are studied for the application of IoT and its classification in above mentioned MMgnt sectors. Real examples will justify the usefulness of IoT, and comparative analysis will prove the success of IoT.

For the purpose of the study, five proposals are given to show the impact of IoT in different fields of MMgnt. Table 9.5 presents the framework of proposals on which the research paper will confer its analysis and results.

9.4   Discussion

The academic literature on IoT-related topics can be traced back to early publications on ubiquitous computing that correspond to the idea of information technologies penetrating "the fabric of everyday life until they are

Table 9.5 Research proposals with their descriptions.

Description of five research proposals
First Proposal: Customers can easily be communicated for product specification and awareness can be created through IoT, in technical terms said as creating touch lines via IoT, additionally data collection can be transformed to data handling leading to resolving CRM issues along with developing multiple interactive platforms and media between Customers and firms.
Second Proposal: IoT helps developing customized pricing strategies focusing on individual customers that can result in greater return on investment and in developing smart Products for building CRM.
Third Proposal: IoT products will create new kinds of customer switching costs. Customer switching costs have been a popular research subject in various studies on customer retention, competition, enterprise profitability, and others. Switching costs can be interpreted as "onetime costs that customers associate with the process of switching from one provider to another". With IoT products, new indicators of company's performance can become available for CRM models. Most empirical studies on CRM consider company's performance in one way or the other.
Fourth Proposal: IoT products may come without product generations. Generation substitution models tend to emphasize repeat purchases, arguing that technological aging outweighs the durability of products. Especially technology-rich and innovation-driven products, such as personal computers and smartphones, are predominantly replaced because they are technologically outdated although still fully functional. PLC models need to consider gradual adoption of IoT products. Existing PLC models usually focus on the initial purchase of a product, that is, the adoption process only and subsequent repeat purchases as the pivotal reference values.
Fifth Proposal: The Internet of Things facilitates the application of Internet-based business models with physical products. Traditional products are commonly marketed with a transaction-dependent revenue model. IoT products facilitate joint value creation with third parties. As part of the business model concept the network model represents a management tool for checking and controlling the value distribution in a joint value creation setting.

Table 9.6 Development of sectors with IoT applications [4].

Internet of things
Sensor technologies
Wireless communication
Layered architectures of digital technology
Energy consumption
Harvesting
Strategic management
Transportation
Supply chain management (SCM)
Market competition and new business models
Customer relationship management (CRM)
Privacy and security applications
Wearable devices

indistinguishable from it." IoT development has affected many areas, and some of these areas are shown as examples in Table 9.6.

There are many examples and one example that can be witnessed extensively in the application of smartphones. This device is the real example of the growing application and usefulness of IoT in communication and information technology. Another example is the automation of traffic management with the help of IoT applications. Homes are also not left behind with the successful implementation of IoT; smart homes are protected, secured, and prevented from accidents with the help of IoT. It has a potential impact on industries, markets, companies, products, services, and consumers, and if we refer to MMgnt; IoT has introduced more and better functionalities in the products, which are not only beneficial to the customers but also to the company's owners for data analysis. Therefore, IoT in M. Mgnt for product development is also called product analytics (PAs) that allows remote access and virtual use. These examples evidently show the positive impact of IoT in MMgnt under three areas namely, CRM, PLC, and BPM. We discuss five research propositions in the fields of CRM, PLC, and BPM [9, 15, 18].

CRM has developed into market-based learning. Comparing learning connections have been recognized as the key achievement factor in CRM that improves an organization's capacity to increase selling potentially, diminish costs, give informal promotions, and eventually increment exchanging expenses. This field of exploration initially rose up out of the relationship of strategic management and high-profile executives, but in the current situation, it manages the mix of client-related connections and the utilization of frameworks that gather and dissect information across the organization. CRM frameworks hence target connecting and making both organization worth and client esteem along with the value chain. An achievement in the improvement of CRM was the worldview change from item direction to client direction. Early work on CRM hence expounded satisfying client needs rather than "just" selling items. Advances in the CRM field then, at that point, incorporated structure connections. In such a manner, hypothesis advancement concerned structure client connections, vital organizations, coalitions, and organizations, new standards from exchanges to connections, and administration connections [7–10]. Stream of work on CRM underscored the pertinence of business sectors and the managed market direction and market concentration.

A decade ago, many prestigious journals in marketing research witnessed a drastic growth in CRM by the application of IoT that explained the concept of dual creation of value. This concept under CRM elaborates the cocreation of value rests on creating and sharing economic rents for the firms and the users. The two ways communications have increased between all users in the process of marketing are with the help of the Internet and precisely with the help of social media and emails. Some of the good examples of social media platforms are Facebook, Twitter, online discussion forums, Instagram, Youtube, WhatsApp, etc. These platforms have immensely affected the sale and product's awareness for all the firms which are using E-commerce or IoT based CRM solutions. One of the current topical needs in CRM is to understand the client's experience and his ventures. For example, while considering the services and information, the firms are required to know and comprehend the customer involvement in the process. To meet this need, IoT has played a major role, and even today, the importance of IoT is aggravating because it has aided in increasing return on investment (ROI) or to the limit of reaching breakeven in less time. Apart from benefits in sales, IoT has also affected the overall psychological behavior and understanding of the customers. IoT helped evaluate the positive and negative customer influences and reactions for the products, particularly SP. These events of the association are generally alluded to as client touchpoints (TPs) [10].

9.4.1   Research Proposition 1

When multiple channels are involved, we spell them as touchlines (TL); IoT helps customers to use this TL for various TPs; therefore, customers may interact with a firm through a multitude of TP in multiple TL. We have defined the purchase behavior throughout the life of a customer as a customer's journey (CJ), where the set of TPs are experienced by the customers for a firm and its different products. The emergence of the Internet and the www with all its applications increased a company's set of options to interact with customers that indicating an explosion in potential customer TP regarding the availability of web-based and mobile applications. Current developments suggest that the IoT will push this development process even further and turn customer TP into customer TL. IoT regularly collects product data, its usage, and dissemination to the company in addition to enhancing the interaction with customers at different TP. PAs offer the option for the firms to check the CJ in real situations and provide connection, management and control remotely. IoT works in coordination with Pas for one customer's needs and preferences.

The CJ starts with a TP at the purchase stage for all products. In this theoretical situation can be illustrated to explain the scenario. For instance, many products may fail in the post-purchase stage due to the serious rejection and dissatisfaction for the benefits of products resulting in developing the negative behavior that will count for negative retrospective behavior (see Figure 9.8). This example if it is substituted during TP when Internet or IoT did not have any importance of application, the number of customer TPs will be negligible or even least, simply because the firms are unable to

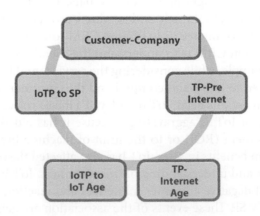

Figure 9.8 Changes in medium of communication [2].

receive authentic information and reasons for the failure and cannot even control negative word of mouth and therefore the product may decline and the customer may not use in future [2, 7, 8]. This will result not in product failure but also affect the firms' image for future products. Some examples during the web era where IoT has great existence and presence TP can be increased easily because firms are able to do research and collect data on reasons and information on customers' preferences, disliking or complaints and eventually work on the improvement on the issues to achieve customer's satisfaction. A firm may have to bear a temporary loss or interruption in product's development, but in the long run, the product will not decline, and the firm will be able to get ROI and develop good CRM. This can happen with the help of IoT that can give the firm true and authentic information on product usage. This resulted in regular development of virtual customers' TL. Besides, PAs also contribute positively in this by allowing the firms to find or even forecast the reasons for product's failure, sometimes this process can be successful before the knowledge of a customer, and therefore firms can solve the issues with the help of IoT remotely or virtually.

There are many firms that have taken advantage of IoT, but automobile firms are the pioneers in this; they used customer's TL and repaired the issues with the help of IoT. Smartphones are also good examples of using IoT for achieving CRM. Nokia and Samsung are regularly exchanging data with their customers and solving detected software problems remotely [8]. In the current scenario, all smartphone firms are following the same customer's TLs and offering services remotely for the solutions and updates too.

IoTPs are affected by the customer's TL because MMgnt assumes that the category of CRM is present in all sectors. Also, CRM permits IoTP to enhance two ways of communication between customers and companies.

Earlier, the CRM was more focused on the collection of data, but IoT made a change over from collection to analysis and handling. IoT is facilitated in building the CRM of the firms by analyzing the data of customers and providing them with what they expect from the products' services, and also firms show annual growth and increase in firms' performances and IoT has also increased TP for CRM like now firms can use video conferencing or another virtual platform for communications. In the current scenario, many such tools have come, such as online sales chat, social media interface, or even webinars on applications, such as Zoom or other private networks, that have enhanced CRM functionalities. These interactions have helped in developing SP as per the preferences of customers' choices. Although in the earlier times, CRM concepts just aimed for data collection for the users of the firms' product through the survey but other analysis was not the pa rather limitation in CRM. As explained earlier, with the growth of the Internet age, the IoT also started to function for several fields, and MMgnt field is the most important one among all. IoT has given many benefits, and one integral use is in the production and collection of customer data in the post-purchase stage because this provides important information for further research and development in production concerning positive and negative feedback directly through the users remotely. Besides, IoT usually has more functionalities and benefits for the customers, such as product usage, resale value, price comparison, etc. Based on their need and capacity to pay, customers can choose their products, and all this could happen with the inclusion of IoT in CRM. Applications of IoT also lead to the emergence of "big marketing data", shifting the challenge for CRM systems from data collection to efficient data analysis or, more precisely, to "marketing analytics" (MktgA) [7–10]. Monitoring and managing the CJ in real-time requires PAs to handle a huge and often complex array of data with high accuracy and least delay. Analytical processes that include manual human interactions are likely to be inappropriate for real-time Pas. Strategic customer behavior for CRM theory will have more relevance to IoT in the coming time [13].

9.4.2   Research Proposition 2

IoTP facilitates the application of price discrimination strategies (PDS). The implementation of one-to-one pricing strategies (o2oPS) allows companies to maximize prices with respect to the price an individual customer is ready to pay. PDS are commonly used and found their way into online shops and online marketplaces. During 2000 many retail firms condemned the idea of PDS and suggested the net neutrality and equality should be the aim of online retail marketing and all customers should pay the same price for the same unit of products but the vision changed with more application on IoT, and the same firms introduced dynamic pricing strategies based on the frequency of purchase, being the active user, using a particular web service, affiliation to online membership, online payment methods, etc. The companies that are using PDS extensively are Noon. Sa, Amazon.com, eBay, Alibaba, etc. Most of these online retail and online auction firms criticize the concept of PDS [22]. IoT currently follows PDS that is based on all the reasons mentioned above, and a few more are presented in the below-given Figure 9.9.

While there are several reasons and advantages for PDS, there are many concerns also for applying o2oPS for IoT because PDS confers the idea of

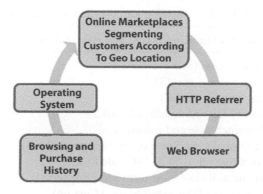

Figure 9.9 Criteria for IoTP for PDS [22].

inequality among customers, which may lead to customer turnover for the firms' products and services due to this reason. This may continue for CJ and customers may choose to opt-out. However, the growth of the Internet has enhanced the concept of personalization. Therefore, PDS works the best in this situation, and customers also do not feel inequality and unimportant for the firms. Customers are usually choosing differentiated products, and IoT has made it easier by providing remote access, but at the same time, customers find difficulty in making price comparisons for other customers because of personalization as well as customization. Firms now have a complete edge on PDS from customers, and customers also do not deny accepting the prices asked for. The most common examples are in the online purchase of software and other programs, where software firms ask for PDS based on the individual requirements and version they are willing to buy. PAs help firms to collect data for the functionalities of their products and customers too, which can aid in deciding on a range of dynamic pricing strategies.

9.4.3   Research Proposition 3

Generally, the cost is associated as an expenditure made by the firms in the process of production, managing supply chain, CRM and many more MMgnt functions, but switching costs (SCo) are associated and understood in terms of customers' expenditure as considered as one-time purchase [13]. Customers make SCo in the process of searching for the best available deal for them and the value of money; therefore, they compare and decide on changing or switching from one firm to another. It has been seen that most of the time, customers do SCo for

Table 9.7 IoT favoring SCo for costs and risk [12, 13].

IoT facilitate in SCo for cost and risk analysis
1. Search Costs (SC)
2. Transaction Costs (TC)
3. Learning Costs (LC)
4. Loyalty Discounts/offers (LDo)
5. Customer style and culture (CSC)
6. Emotional Cost/Sense of belongingness (ECB)
7. Cognitive Effort/Skills/Attitude Risks
8. Financial Risks (Short term and Long term)
9. Social Risks (Demographic and Custom)
10. Psychological Risk (Esteem and Self Awareness)

durable or high-value products. IoT has facilitated customers in the effective decision-making process for SCO also (see Table 9.7). Other applications, such as machine learning, data analytics, can be used for SCo. IoT aids customers in CSO and firms too for measuring customer retention, competition, enterprise profitability, satisfaction, and other essential aspects of MMgnt. There are various reasons for customers to SCo and IoT offers comprehension for this analysis. Customers can have the following knowledge of different types of costs and risks through IoT applications that contribute to SCO, and IoT helps in comparing the following costs and risks from one firm to another [13].

When IoT facilitates for customers, it is helpful for firms also as IoT can achieve mass sale and profit too by creating awareness through digital technologies for personalization and customization, and customers will acquire positive behavior and trust for SCo. IoT provides data for R and D for firms and CRM and also helps customers to know their previous purchases, complaints and satisfaction too. For example, there are many IoT that help customers to know their success in using particular services like services pertaining to health, security, education or even recreation. Online fitness and health clubs provide customers to understand their health benefits, track their progress, the requirements needed to reach a particular milestone, etc. In the education sector, for example, online learning helps users to learn remotely and can be easily accessed and eventually receive a credential for their education. Such sectors are also a part of IoT [12, 13].

Every product, TP or SP has a life cycle commonly known as the product life cycle (PLC). PLC has stages and phases from introduction to

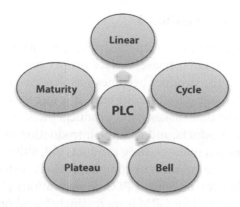

Figure 9.10 Shapes of PLC in IoT environment [18].

decline, but the product may have a different duration for each phase depending on various factors, but mostly, PLC has bell shape showing the movement of the product from one stage to another (refer Figure 9.10). PLC has stages, such as introduction, growth, maturity, and decline [18, 19]. Apart from bell shape, there are other shapes also associated with PLC, and TP or SP may have either of these shapes for the phases too; some of these shapes are shown below.

If we check the historical perspectives, PLC mostly concentrated on verification of functionalities of MMgnt and methods of product's introduction; these two criteria help in evaluating the shapes of PLC also. Some marketing researchers have elaborated other criteria, factors also for the shape and length of the PLC. Below given, Table 9.8 shows the list of these factors and criteria.

In this chapter, we have tried to focus on changes introduced by IoT for the phases, shapes and length of the PLC. Also, we discussed how TP products had shorter PLC in comparison to SP.

Table 9.8 Factors affecting the shape and length of PLC [8, 19].

Sales of Products
Changes in market and customers' needs
Changes in micro and macro economics
Level of Competition for the product category
Technological changes or advancements
Existing products and threats from new entrants

9.4.4   Research Proposition 4

As discussed above, PLC has various stages, but with the implication of IoT, it may not have regular phases or lack proper generation of products. This is not because the product becomes obsolete or not usable for customers or any other complications; instead, it is due to the role of technological advancement that makes good products ineffective. IoT or SP are technology-driven products, and with the introduction of any new version of updated features can make existing products old, although performance wise, the products have no issues or complaints from customers. This is the main reason for IoT for undefined PLC or generations [18]. The primary purpose of IoT generated for CRM is increasingly based on software that is less prone to technological aging and because PAs and remote access allow the company to continuously monitor and update the software of IoT. The more software accounts for a product's basic utility, the less relevant repurchases based on hardware upgrades become. For example, some online assistants, such as Siri or Alexa, have overcome the issues of product's generations and have automatic updates in their applications and hardware too. They are excellent examples of IoT having greater PLC. We can conclude that IoTP focuses on utilization and has wider options of scalability for their hardware and software; PLC will have a longer generation and more linear shape. IoT will also have repurchase behavior, and customers will, in general, feel value for their money and also be willing to adopt new IoT.

9.4.5   Research Proposition 5

The IoT assists the application of Internet-based business processes (IBM) with the TP and is commonly marketed with a transaction-dependent revenue mode (TDRM). In previous times or during the pre-Internet age, these BPMs were facilitating the firms and customers positively because the purpose of BPM was more restricted to movement of products and maintain SPM and logistics, but with the introduction of Internet and IoT, new BPM came into the significance and started to execute many functions successfully in a virtual environment. Life in the cloud is an excellent example of IoT for BPM. Also, examples of Alphabet (Google), Amazon, Instagram, Snapchat, Linkedin, WhatsApp are other examples of IoT in BPM. IoT has given rise to many BPM; some of them are listed below in Table 9.9.

IBM is the most cost-effective BPM because of the least OPC, having hardware and software scalability and performing analysis remotely for

Table 9.9 Types of Internet-based model BPM [16].

Internet-Based Business Models (IBBM)
Software-As-A-Service (Saas)
Product-As-A-Service (Paas)
In-Product Purchases (IPP)
The Network Business Model (NBM)

data for MMgnt. There are other BPM for IoT, such as IBM, SaaS, PaaS, IPP, and NBM. In the Internet era, companies can create value for customers through information drawn from other customers by the application of the above-mentioned IoTP for BPM. These models can be used from service industries to durable goods, such as for vehicles, such as the use of location tracking technologies for security and other purposes [14, 17]. Often, we mention such SP as smart cars, Chevrolet and General Motors have been using IoT by applying IBM. Another good example is an online purchase for retail products, where NBM works for BPM using recommendation methods to define purchase behavior and decisions. Currently, all E-Commerce in retail use this method for effective BPM and achieve CRM. Also, IBM facilitates customers to make SCo comparisons and decide on the best option and best value for their money. For firms, this IoTP help in knowing customer demand, their profile and the trend of the economic cycle. Also, with IoT, firms can know the various products' usage, the right customer, the right method of accessing data and making the availability of the products or services to the end-users. The feasibility does not restrict to a single firm. IBM helps in providing learning and decision making strategies for different related firms and know-how customers related to joining benefits from products [14–17].

9.5   Results

The Internet has made fundamental changes in all the functions of MMgnt, and with the IoT online environment has expanded to a greater extent. All major branches of MMgnt got affected, and CRM, PLC and BPM also received a complete changeover for customers and firms. The notion of joining the TP to IoT, growth of new product mix for collecting, analyzing the data remotely and automatically that eventually aids CRM. PAs are done by the IoT for product usage and its value for the customers and sharing this information with other customers, firms and their competitors. This process constitutes enhancing the PLC and solving SP related issues more efficiently, and achieving CRM more easily. With IoT products, customers are constantly checked by many sensors and TP, giving rise to the TL. Also, IoT challenges the traditional CRM systems and introduces a change from only data collection to data analysis remotely. IoT has also witnessed the increase of strategic relevance for CRM. IoT has also facilitated the application of PDS and SCo and developed new performance indicators for CRM.

PLC is adopting IoT at a slower pace because IoTP usually does not have a product's age. The IoT facilitates the application of IBM with SP, as well as joint value creation for competitors.

The growth of the IoT era gave a new direction to MMgnt where customers use more IoTP or an SP. The CJ from the viewpoint of a single firm may therefore evolve to a CJ in an environment operated by a network of many related firms. IoTPs are likely to affect theories and concepts from other marketing fields in similar ways, such as for marketing mix and brand management, and the practical aspect of IoT can be seen in CRM and increase in strategic customer behavior. Further, the impact of SP is immense and significant on given MMgnt, such as CRM, PLC, and BPM, by connecting the SP in the process of decision making for purchase behavior and product's usage. Finally, IoT has not only affected the B2C but also in the B2B or C2C categories of MMgnt.

9.6   Conclusions

Customer relationship management: IoT gives bright nature to existing products, and customers are facilitated in having multiple channels for completing purchase behavior, building customer relationships with the firms, and developing strategies to enhance awareness and brand loyalty. IoT can develop a price discrimination policy focusing on individual customers, achieving profit maximization.

Product Life Cycle Management: Smart products developed by IoT products will have steep growth and longer maturity, and before the decline stage IoT contribute to new product development to retain its PLC.

Business Process Model Development: The IoT facilitates the application of Internet-based business models with physical products. IoT products facilitate joint value creation, developing automatic options for business environments.

References

1. Thoma, M., Meyer, S., Sperner, K., Meissner, S., Braun, T., On IoT-services: Survey, classification and enterprise integration, in: *2012 IEEE International Conference on Green Computing and Communications*, pp. 257–260, IEEE, Besancon, France France, 2012, November.
2. Porter, M.E. and Heppelmann, J.E., How smart, connected products are transforming competition. *Harv. Bus. Rev.*, 92, 64–88, 2014.
3. Khan, M.A. and Salah, K., IoT security: Review, blockchain solutions, and open challenges. *Future Gener. Comput. Syst.*, 82, 395–411, 2018.
4. Lee, I. and Lee, K., The Internet of Things (IoT): Applications, investments, and challenges for enterprises. *Bus. Horiz.*, 58, 4, 431–440, 2015.
5. Nguyen, B. and Simkin, L., The Internet of Things (IoT) and marketing: The state of play, future trends and the implications for marketing, . *J. Marketing Manage.*, 33, 1–2, 1–6, 2017.
6. Decker, R. and Stummer, C., Marketing management for consumer products in the era of the Internet of Things. *Adv. Internet Things*, 7, 3, 47–70, 2017.
7. Simões, D., Filipe, S., Barbosa, B., An overview on IoT and its impact on marketing, in: *Smart Marketing with the Internet of Things*, pp. 1–20, 2019.
8. Kotabe, M.M. and Helsen, K., *Global marketing management*, John Wiley & Sons, 2020.
9. Rizvi, M., *Implications of Internet of Things (IoT) for CRM*, 2017.
10. Yerpude, S. and Singhal, T.K., Internet of Things based customer relationship management–a research perspective. *Int. J. Eng. Technol.*, 7, 2.7, 444–450, 2018.
11. Junior, M.R.F.B., Batista, C.L., Marques, M.E., Pessoa, C.R.M., Business models applicable to IoT, in: *Handbook of Research on Business Models in Modern Competitive Scenarios*, pp. 21–42, IGI Global, 2019.
12. Hashem, D.T.N., The reality of Internet of Things (IoT) in creating a data-driven marketing opportunity: Mediating role of Customer Relationship Management (CRM). *J. Theor. Appl. Inf. Technol.*, 99, 2, 2021.
13. Ghazaleh, M.A. and Zabadi, A.M., Promoting a revamped CRM through Internet of Things and big data: An AHP-based evaluation. *Int. J. Organ. Anal.*, 28, 1, 66–91, 2020.
14. Janiesch, C., Koschmider, A., Mecella, M., Weber, B., Burattin, A., Di Ciccio, C., Zhang, L., The Internet-of-Things meets business process management: Mutual benefits and challenges. arXiv preprint arXiv:1709.03628, 2017.
15. Chiu, H.H. and Wang, M.S., A study of IoT-aware business process modeling. *Int. J. Model. Optim.*, 3, 3, 238, 2013.
16. Suri, K., Gaaloul, W., Cuccuru, A., Gerard, S., Semantic framework for Internet of Things-aware business process development, in: *2017 IEEE 26th International Conference on Enabling Technologies: Infrastructure for Collaborative Enterprises (WETICE)*, pp. 214–219, IEEE, Poznan, Poland, 2017, June.

17. Janiesch, C., Koschmider, A., Mecella, M., Weber, B., Burattin, A., Di Ciccio, C., Zhang, L., The Internet of Things meets business process management: A manifesto. *IEEE Syst. Man Cybern. Mag.*, 6, 4, 34–44, 2020.

18. Kumar, S., Choudhary, S., Dalmia, H., An effective contour detection based image retrieval using multi-fusion method and neural network. Submitted to *Wirel. Pers. Commun.*, Preprint (Version 2) available at Res. *Square*, 1–38, 2021.

19. Xin, Y. and Ojanen, V., The impact of digitalization on product lifecycle management: How to deal with it?, in: *2017 IEEE International Conference on Industrial Engineering and Engineering Management (IEEM)*, pp. 1098–1102, IEEE, Singapore, 2017, December.

20. Mendling, J. and Simon, C., Business process design by view integration, in: *International Conference on Business Process Management*, 2006, September, Springer, Berlin, Heidelberg, pp. 55–64.

21. Allmendinger, G. and Lombreglia, R., Four strategies for the age of smart services. *Harv. Bus. Rev.*, 83, 131–134, 2005.

22. Dhebar, A., Information technology and product policy: "smart" products. *Eur. Manage. J.*, 14, 477–485, 1996.

23. Korling, M., Smart products: Why adding a digital side to a toothbrush could make a lot of sense. *Ericsson Bus. Rev.*, 18, 26–31, 2012.

24. Kowatsch, T., Maass, W., Filler, A., Janzen, S., Knowledge-based bundling of smart products on a mobile recommendation agent. *Proceedings of the 7th International Conference on Mobile Business (ICMB 08)*, Barcelona, 7-8 July 2008, pp. 181–190, 2008.

25. Mayer, P., *Economic aspects of smart products*, White Paper, Institute of Technology Management, University of St. Gallen, St. Gallen, 2010.

26. Resatsch, F., *Ubiquitous computing: Developing and evaluating near field communication applications*, Springer, Wiesbaden, 2010.

27. Meyer, G.G., Buijs, P., Szirbik, N.B., Wortmann, J.C., Intelligent products for enhancing the utilization of tracking technology in transportation. *Int. J. Oper. Prod. Manage.*, 34, 422–446, 2014.

28. Zhou, L., Chong, A.Y.L., Ngai, E.W.T., Supply chain management in the era of the Internet of Things. *Int. J. Prod. Econ.*, 195, 1–3, 2015.

29. Glova, J., Sabol, T., Vajda, V., Business models for the Internet of Things environment. *Proc. Econ. Financ.*, 15, 1122–1129, 2014.

30. Rijsdijk, S.A. and Hultink, E.J., How today's consumers perceive tomorrow's smart products. *J. Prod. Innov. Manage.*, 26, 24–42, 2009.

31. Porter, M.E. and Heppelmann, J.E., How smart, connected products are transforming companies. *Harv. Bus. Rev.*, 93, 1–37, 2015.

32. Meyer, G.G., Wortmann, J.C., Szirbik, N.B., Production monitoring and control with intelligent products. *Int. J. Prod. Res.*, 49, 1303–1317, 2011.

33. Weinberg, B.D., Milne, G.R., Andonova, Y.G., Hajjat, F.M., Internet of Things: Convenience vs. privacy and secrecy. *Bus. Horiz.*, 58, 615–624, 2015.

34. Robson, K., Pitt, L.F., Kietzmann, J., APC forum: Extending business values through wearables. *MIS Q. Executive*, 15, 167–177, 2016.
35. Rocker, C., Intelligent environments as a promising solution for addressing current demographic changes. *Int. J. Innov. Manage. Technol.*, 4, 76–79, 2013, https://doi.org/10.1509/jmkg.2005.69.4.155.
36. Riva, G., Vatalaro, F., Davide, F., Alcañiz, M., *Ambient intelligence. The evolution of technology, comm. and cognition towards the future of human-computer interaction*, 1–320, IOS Press, Amsterdam, Netherlands, 2005.
37. Heinze, T.S., Amme, W., Moser, S., Static analysis and process model transformation for an advanced business process to petri net mapping. *Softw.: Pract. Exp.*, 48, 1, 161–195, 2018.
38. Weske, M., *Business process management architectures*, pp. 305–343, Springer Berlin Heidelberg, 2007.
39. Buttle, F. and Maklan, S., *Customer relationship management: Concepts and technologies*, Routledge, 2019.
40. Sahu, A.K., Sharma, S., Tanveer, M., Internet of Things attack detection using hybrid deep learning model. *Comput. Commun.*, 176, 146–154, 2021, https://doi.org/10.1016/j.comcom.2021.05.024.
41. Marolt, M., Zimmermann, H.D., Žnidaršič, A., Pucihar, A., Exploring social customer relationship management adoption in micro, small and medium-sized enterprises. *J. Theor. Appl. Electron. Comer. Res.*, 15, 2, 38–58, 2020.
42. Chatterjee, S., Chaudhuri, R., Vrontis, D., Thrassou, A., Ghosh, S.K., Chaudhuri, S., Social customer relationship management factors and business benefits. *Int. J. Organ. Anal.*, 2020.
43. Naim, A., Khan, M.F., Hussain, M.R., Khan, N., "Virtual doctor" management technique in the diagnosis of ENT diseases. *JOE*, 15, 9, 88, 2019.

10

Healthcare Internet of Things: A New Revolution

Manpreet Kaur[1]*, M. Sugadev[2], Harpreet Kaur[1], Md Rashid Mahmood[1] and Vikas Maheshwari[1]

[1]Department of ECE, Guru Nanak Institutions Technical Campus, Hyderabad, India
[2]Department of ECE, Sathyabama Institute of Science and Technology, Chennai, India

Abstract

In today's era, when technology is growing rapidly, the Internet of Things (IoT) is a technology having massive applications, which are employed in various domains. Similarly, the Healthcare Internet of Things (IoT) applies IoT to the healthcare industry. The IoT is indeed a networked platform comprising connectable devices that can acquire, transfer, and store data without human or computer intervention. The IoT promises a plethora of benefits for refining and improving healthcare delivery, including the potential to diagnose, examine, and cure the patient. It reduces the need for human intervention while also allowing for the early diagnosis of health hazards. It is becoming equally important to consider how existing, as well as upcoming, IoT technologies might help healthcare systems provide therapeutic benefits. The goal of this chapter is to provide an understanding of recent IoT in healthcare and to illustrate how the Internet of Things devices are boosting healthcare delivery and how IoT technology may revolutionize and disrupt global healthcare in the coming decade. Healthcare IoT capabilities are additionally investigated in order to theorize how IoT might assist us in moving away from our existing different levels of health systems towards a more integrated, progressive, and continuous approach. Patient care may be ensured on time, and with on-time assistance, treatment expenses can be decreased, and therapies can be made more effective by employing IoT in healthcare practitioners. From smartwatches to cancer care, smartwatches are used to monitor one's health and wellbeing. Finally, this chapter will look into potential concerns with IoT, such as impediments to market

*Corresponding author: manu.jaildarni@gmail.com

Md Rashid Mahmood, Rohit Raja, Harpreet Kaur, Sandeep Kumar and Kapil Kumar Nagwanshi (eds.) *Ambient Intelligence and Internet of Things: Convergent Technologies*, (301–338) © 2023 Scrivener Publishing LLC

acceptability from healthcare providers and consumers, interoperability, security and privacy, remuneration and standardization, information storage, and control and ownership. Policy support, cybersecurity-focused guidelines, rigorous strategic planning, and open policies will be critical enablers of IoT in contemporary healthcare within healthcare organizations. IoT has a lot of potential for enhancing the efficiency of the healthcare system and societal well-being.

Keywords: Internet of Things (IoT), Healthcare Internet of Things (HIoT), ECG, EEG, EMG, IoT cloud, Adverse Drug Reaction (ADR), cognitive computing

10.1   Introduction

Medical imaging merged with IoT technology for healthcare applications [1]. The healthcare sector may enhance treatment quality while decreasing costs thanks to IoT technology's automation and resource optimization in healthcare applications. The IoT in medical imaging allows for real-time identification and remedial actions, as well as easy auto-analysis of imaging apparatus characteristics [2, 3]. Because digitization has affected many aspects of medical technology, the IoT in healthcare imaging will minimize patient and physician waiting times and irritation [4]. As a result, the chapter gives a brief overview of IoT-dependent healthcare systems based on medical imaging techniques as well as their relevance in medical imaging.

The Internet of Things (IoT) has breathed fresh life into telemedicine. This enables the doctor and the patient to communicate about the patient's condition even if they are physically apart [5, 6]. Medical picture segmentation is necessary for telemedicine for medical image analysis, storage, and preservation. As a result, several approaches for quick and accurate medical picture segmentation have been investigated [7, 8]. To do segmentation in multiple organs, a medical picture must have an accurate assessment of the region [9, 10]. On the other hand, the removal of an area within a small territory is caused by insufficient information to define the region. In this chapter, we looked at ways of rebuilding a segmented zone in a constrained area to obtain better segmentation results. Here, a linear equation is used to create an anticipated slice segmentation and present an improved approach for tiny areas based on the projected segmentation [11]. The lung area was divided from chest CT scans to test the suggested method's performance. According to studies, the accuracy of volume data segmentation improved with 0.003 and 0.094 efficiencies, with a validated standard deviation improvement [59].

In the last decade, there has been a lot of research into healthcare technology and service advancements in recent decades. To be more specific,

IoT technology has demonstrated its ability to connect a myriad of health sensors, healthcare devices, and specialists to provide high-quality medical care from a distance [12]. Healthcare costs have fallen, patient care and safety have improved, medical care has become more accessible, and the industry's operational efficiency has increased. In addition, the new study provided a rapid array of possible applications for healthcare Internet of Things (IoT)-hinged technologies [13]. From the perspectives of healthcare services and applications as well as supporting technology, this study documents the growth in usage of the H-IoT for solving several healthcare concerns. Furthermore, potential IoT system issues and concerns are being investigated [13]. To summarise, the current research gives a complete supply of data on the numerous applications related to Healthcare-IoT, intending to enable future academics interested in working in the subject to have a better understanding of the problem [14].

10.2   Healthcare IoT Architecture (IoT)

The IoT framework for patient monitoring makes it easier to integrate cloud-based IoT benefits into the medical industry. It comprises ways of sending patient data to a healthcare network from a range of sensors and medical equipment [15, 16]. The topology of a healthcare IoT is the organization of multiple elements of an IoT healthcare structure that are logically integrated into a medical environment. The publisher, broker, and subscriber are the three main components of a basic healthcare IoT system [17]. The publisher represents linked sensing devices and other medical components and equipment as a network that may independently or concurrently capture essential patient data [18]. EMG, blood pressure, ECG, oxygen saturation, heart rate, EEG, and temperature, as well as other measures such as temperature, heart rate, ECG, EEG, EMG, and blood pressure, may be employed. A publisher can transmit this data to a broker in a continuous stream across a network [19, 20]. The broker is in charge of processing and storing the collected data in the cloud [21]. Finally, the user continuously monitors the patient's data by accessing it on a tablet, smartphone, computer, or other device. The publisher can analyze the collected data and provide feedback if there is any physiological irregularity or decline in the health of the patient. In the IoT, which integrates separate components into a hybrid grid, each element in the healthcare network's IoT network and cloud has a specific purpose [22, 23]. It is challenging to build a standard foundation for IoT because the topology is entirely dependent on healthcare requirements and applications.

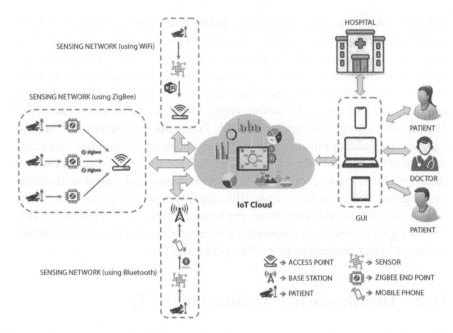

Figure 10.1 Architecture of healthcare IoT.

Figure 10.1 represents the architecture of IoT using different wireless connectivities, making it feasible for patients and doctors to connect within or outside hospitals. The architecture varies depending upon the requirements and services. Some structural alterations have been made in the past for an IoT system. While developing a new healthcare system based on IoT for real-time monitoring of patients, it is critical to make a list of all related tasks relevant to the planned health application [24, 25]. How effectively the IoT system satisfies the demands of healthcare professionals determines its success. The structures must conform to medical norms and phases in the diagnosis procedure because each ailment necessitates a complex chain of health services [26].

10.3   Healthcare IoT Technologies

Several technologies deployed to obtain a HIoT system are critical due to the usage of specialized technologies as they can improve an IoT system's capabilities [27]. As a result, several cutting-edge technologies are being utilized to connect various healthcare applications to an IoT system. These technologies are categorized as identification technologies, communication

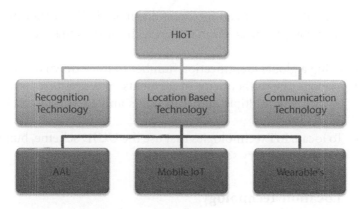

Figure 10.2 Different healthcare IoT technologies.

technologies, and location technologies [28]. Figure 10.2 shows the hierarchy of various IoT technologies.

10.3.1   Technology for Identification

The visibility of the patient's information away from allowed nodes (sensors) that may be located in remote places is a practical challenge in the design of a HIoT network [29, 30]. It may be achieved by accurately recognizing the healthcare network's nodes and sensors. The practice of providing a unique identity (UID) to everyone allowed in such a way that it can be easily recognized and information can be transferred without ambiguity is known as identification [31]. Each resource connected to the healthcare system has a digital UID associated with it (doctors, medical equipment, nurses, hospitals, caregivers, and so forth). In the digitized environment, this offers resource identification and resource connection. In the literature, several identifying techniques have been discussed [32]. A universally unique identification (UUID) and a globally developed unique identity (GDUID) have been produced by the Open Software Foundation (OSF) (GUID). Without centralized coordination, it is possible to use UUID. A UUID is an element of the distributed computing environment (DCE). In a health system, actuators and sensor nodes are identified and dealt with separately—that aids in the proper functioning of the system. However, because of the rapid growth of IoT-based technologies, a component's unique identity may change during the IoT system's life cycle. To maintain the quality of the healthcare equipment/system, the device should have a mechanism to update this data [33–35]. It is the result of a configuration change affecting the operation of tracking the system component(s), which has the potential to result in an incorrect diagnosis [63]. Furthermore, IoT in healthcare prompts the creation of new technologies that can

a) Using a global identification number to track down objects,
b) Manage the authenticity of elements in a secure manner by utilizing multiple authentications and encryption techniques, and
c) To locate IoT technologies that use the UUID scheme, build a global directory search.

10.3.2   Location Technology

In healthcare networks, geographical locating technologies or real-time location systems (RTLS) are used to track and identify an object's location [36–38]. It also keeps track of the primary treatment depending on the allocation and distribution of available resources. GPS (Global Positioning System) is the most extensively used technology. Satellites are used for tracking purposes. Also, it keeps a record of a primary therapy depending on the distribution of available resources. It may be used in IoT to locate an ambulance, patients, a healthcare professional, and carers, among other things [37]. However, GPS is confined to exterior applications because of the possibility of adjacent facilities interfering with transmission between the object and the satellite. In these circumstances, the LPS (local positioning system) connection may be beneficial. Tracking an object by detecting the moving object's radio signal and transmitting it to a series of pre-positioned receivers can be done by using LPS. LPS may be used with a number of short-range communication networks. RFID, Wi-Fi, and Zigbee are a few examples [38]. On the other hand, because of its greater temporal resolution, ultra-wideband (UWB) radio is preferred. This allows the recipient to precisely determine the arrival time. For tracking, a UWB-based approach that depends on the arrival time difference (TDOA) was developed. While developing a localization system based on UWB, several measurement criteria, as an example, comparative as well as differential arrival times, length of round-trip flights, etc. GPS and other high-bandwidth communication technologies could be used to build smart healthcare networks for the next generation of medical devices [39–43].

10.3.2.1   Mobile-Based IoT

The Internet of Things has increased in prominence as information and communication technology has improved (IoT). In new healthcare systems, doctors and patients collaborate using Internet-of-Things technology to monitor senior adults' daily activities intelligently and automatically [62]. Body sensors (wearables) and mobile devices are progressively being used to track personal health and wellness. Wearable sensor technology is among the most important IoT breakthroughs in health monitoring equipment. Furthermore, the combination of healthcare and IoT has resulted in the development of smart platforms such as intelligent healthcare monitoring systems and mobile healthcare (m-Healthcare) [44–46]. Data mining methods are applied in order to understand an IoT-based smart m-healthcare system that can detect human activity everywhere. In this chapter, we provide a consumer-based data mining approach for offline human behaviour categorization and leverage IoT technology to build an exact and robust human activity recognition framework. For the aim of human activity recognition, the proposed model uses a dataset that comprises 12 physical activities. Ten individuals with various profiles had their body motions and vital signs recorded. According to the findings, the proposed system exceeds the competition with 99.89% accuracy and is exceptionally effective, durable, and dependable in offering m-Healthcare services across a variety of activities. When it comes to patient health data and other physiological parameters, the mobile IoT or m-IoT) is used to track them using mobile computers, sensors, communication technologies, and cloud computing. It is used as a communication link between local area networks and mobile networks (such as 4G and 5G) in order to deliver a secure Internet-based healthcare service [47]. Because of the increasing usage of mobile devices, healthcare professionals can now access patient data more quickly, identify problems more quickly, and treat patients more quickly than ever before. In the field of healthcare, a number of research papers have been published on the application of mobile computing. Using the Internet of Things (IoT), Istepanian developed a gadget that could monitor glucose levels in diabetic patients, assisting in the treatment of hypoglycemia. Other researchers developed a mobile gateway-based Internet of Things system called "AMBRO" that included various sensors for fall detection and heart rate management. It could also make use of an integrated GPS module to locate the patients [48]. It has been stated that an Internet of Things-based real-time monitoring system may detect abnormal cardiac activity and alert the patient when the heart rate surpasses 60 to 100 beats per minute. The privacy of the user and their data is crucial in an IoT system that uses mobile devices. Physical and technical protection, network security, audit reports, and technical policies are just a few of the solutions that have been proposed to address the aforementioned problems and concerns [49]. Mobile IoT refers to low-power wide-area (LPWA) IoT networks that operate in licenced spectrum, are 3GPP-compliant, secure, and managed by the network operator. The low-cost wide-area (LPWA) network is specifically developed for low-cost Internet of Things applications that require low data rates and long battery lifetimes, as well as those that routinely operate in remote and difficult-to-reach locations. In order to provide coverage to billions of additional devices, existing cellular networks have been upgraded, making the Internet of Things (IoT) connections a reality [50].

Mobile Internet of Things technologies are, by their very nature, more secure than other solutions. There are several reasons for this, including the fact that mobile IoT networks use separate frequency bands to minimize interference, SIM cards contain highly secure integrated circuits, as well as the fact that mobile carriers are augmenting these natural abilities by implementing additional security measures [51].

A GSMA cellular IoT Intervention aims to speed up the commercialization of low-power, broad-range services using existing bandwidth (licenced).

10.3.2.2   Wearable Devices

Wearable technology has a wide range of advantages, from greater productivity to increased transparency. Our everyday lives are developing because of these benefits, allowing us to enjoy the splendours of modern advances. To demonstrate how pragmatic wearable gadgets, consider the following examples of how the world around us is changing due to this intelligent technology [52].

Wearable technology is currently a developing field, as shown by Intel's recent $5,000 "make it wearable" challenge. This competition will honor innovators and architects who create or develop wearable apps that have the potential to take personal computing in new directions [53]. Wearable technology is already at the core of nearly every discussion about IoT technology and the plethora of new possibilities that pervasive connectivity may bring.

Many of these arguments end up with many unanswerable questions. Although reasonable, given that wearable technologies are already in their early stages of development research, numerous issues must be resolved before a genuine "rollout" of these gadgets may appear. As an example, "Are wearable gadgets merely accessories for a smartphone, or will they play a more vital function as part of the Internet of Things?" is indeed a prominent issue these days for many individuals. Should this also not apply to wearable gadgets if we are transitioning to a more general intelligence deployment in almost everything we interact with? To understand this issue better, let us look at some of the more important jobs that we may expect wearable devices to accomplish, in addition to certain usage instances that show how enormously networked gadgets could provide new features [55–57]. Biometric capabilities can be used to improve the security of such badges, for example, fingerprint activation, which allows a locked door to be opened only by the badge owner. Badges may potentially be able to detect the surroundings that may be necessary for a time of need to confirm that everyone has been able to get out of the building safely. A worn bracelet provides a more specific location, which becomes less inclined to be abandoned in a garment leaned behind a chair [58].

Wearable gadgets used for wellness and heath give biometric measures, for example, heartbeat, concentrations of sweat, and more advanced metrics, such as oxygen levels in the bloodstream, which are becoming more commonly available. Thanks to technological advancements [60, 61], alcohol levels and other equivalent measurements may one day be measured using a wearable device. The ability to store, track, and identify biometric data over time, as well as evaluate the results, is a promising prospect. Body temperature monitoring, for example, might alert you to the onset of the cold or flu.

Figure 10.3 shows a smartwatch example of wearables that can be used for measuring heart rate, stress levels etc. Similarly, Figure 10.4 represents the usage of wearables for health monitoring. Some of the complementary functions of wearable devices are increasingly prevalent, yet they may provide information that might aid environmental management. Wearable technologies may detect whether one is wearing their jacket inside the car or only in the rear (potentially by embedding a couple of stress or anxiety measurement devices threaded into the garment's fabric) [64]. These may aid in maintaining a pleasant temperature in the vehicle. If the wristband detects sweat, it can be used as a piece of data for changing humidity and temperature.

Is it an efficient method to offer the above-discussed features if all of the situations above use a smartphone as the primary control? Is it better if IoT devices could communicate with one another directly [65]? It is not

Figure 10.3 Smart watch.

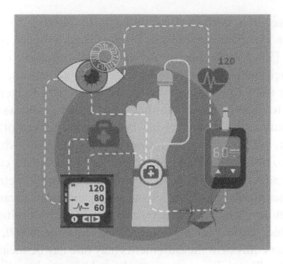

Figure 10.4 Wearables for health monitoring [91, 92].

necessary to approve each operation your wearable gadget requests with your phone. A more suitable structure would be for your smartphone to configure the operating modes and the amount of privacy you wish to impose. The devices are intended to interact using the "strategy" that one has chosen for communication [66–68].

Consider the following example: Assume you have got your smartwatch on, and it is collecting biometric data to alert you to an approaching illness (maybe because you were just on an aeroplane). Assume you have flown in for a job interview and are currently driving to your first meeting [68–70]. Would you like the professional holding your interview to have access to your biometric data? Almost not without a doubt, one can use their smartphone to hide their biometric data in real-time from the interviewer (as well as any prior reading) [71]. If you are going to your doctor for a yearly check-up rather than a job interview, you will want to make your biometrics accessible to them.

Wearable gadgets will be able to connect to devices in the house automatically. When watching TV from a specific chair, you may have a favourite lightning level. You might switch on the television, and the associated LED lights on your wearable technology might be able to assist you in adjusting the illumination level in the room [72–75]. In an intelligent home, automatically filtering light through windows that create glare on the television could be conceivable. Even the LCD TV screen illumination could be changed, and all configurations could be tuned to save energy while providing the best possible viewing experience. Once the general plan is defined using a smartphone interface, each of these exchanges might be automated and carried out instantly between devices [76–79].

Would this technology also be applied to wearables? Can your worn gadgets, for instance, connect with the devices of others in a crowded environment? Do you want to know whether the individual on the train next to you has a high fever? [80] You have a strong desire to know, yet the ill person may refuse to tell you. If you both go to the same doctor, though, that information can be exchanged, maybe with the use of a smartphone or tablet filter. For years to come, privacy concerns will remain a worry, yet there will be occasions when broad biometric sharing is beneficial or at least fascinating [81–85].

For example, a concert with a large audience on the main stage. Would one consent to the DJ monitoring their heart rate (coupled with everyone else's heart rates in the room) to assist him in selecting music (or even to evaluate the impact of music selection on the audience) if you were there [86–88]? That restricted biometric sharing may help and perhaps be "needed" to gain access to the venue. Our wearable gadgets may potentially be utilized as a part of a new concert experience to get everyone dancing "in sync." An accelerometer might be placed in your wearable gadget, allowing you to synchronize your movements on the concert floor with one another. The DJ plays music but also suggests "dance moves" to accompany it. LEDs may also be used as visual signals in your concert wearables to show you what to perform (or not do). It has the potential to be the ultimate Dance Dance Revolution event.

Low power [87] will be a recurring theme in these ubiquitous designs. Energy harvesting will be one method of obtaining reduced power use. Energy harvesting by dancing and moving will be simple in the previous example. However, in the majority of cases, solutions based on batteries will be the preferred approach. You would assume that the battery is a major stumbling hurdle, but the rapid change in trends means that the battery will most likely not be the limiting element in wearables [89]. Wearable gadgets will most likely become obsolete before they resolve battery issues (Figure 10.5)! For longer-lasting wearable gadgets, battery technology will develop to provide more power in a smaller size and make charging more convenient, perhaps from a small range. The armbands, watches, or other wearable gadgets are easily rechargeable, allowing them to perform longer-term, higher-power functions.

Extremely clever and low-power MCUs will be necessary for these sorts of ubiquitous interactions. High-end IoT applications will need a lot of processing and interface capabilities (including wireless choices) as well as advanced security features like a secure boot. These advanced applications

Figure 10.5 TV control using wearables [93].

might take advantage of some of the most modern technologies, such as Figure 10.6 Intel Quark X1000 (CPUs), to simplify development by using much of the existing software base [90]. Enabling a number of connecting approaches enables data aggregation and bridging from a variety of sources, lowering the "peripheral" power consumption of the wearable device network. Basic sensor connections, security, and low-speed wireless communication would be all that is required of lower-end programmes, all while running on a cheap battery. Microcontrollers such as the Silicon Laboratories EFM®32 Zero Gecko would run for a long period of time while consuming very little power, making them perfect for biometric frequency detection, processing, and storing in wearable applications. Even though these sensor-based gadgets may demand certain periodic computational power, most system power will be saved by reducing wireless data transmission delays [89].

Figure 10.6 Intel Quark X1000 SoC.

Whatever route wearable devices take in the next few years, it appears that they will need to become increasingly connected to the IoT to deliver the wide variety of functions we have all come to anticipate [68].

a. Glucose monitors: Diabetes affects one in every eleven individuals worldwide. Furthermore, 46% of diabetics go undiagnosed. Several systems for monitoring glucose levels and delivering insulin to the body are available on the market. Continuous glucose monitoring monitors and automated insulin administration devices are examples of diabetic wearables.
b. People with irregular heartbeats (arrhythmia) and excessively fast heartbeats (tachycardia) can use implanted defibrillators and wearables. Patients at risk of abrupt cardiac arrest can use wearable defibrillators like the ZollLifeVest 4000 to stop cardiac arrhythmias that can be life-threatening. The gadget constantly monitors the cardiac rhythm of the patient and, if a life-threatening rhythm is found, the device alerts the patient. Shock therapy can be used to restore the patient's heart rate to normal.
c. Concussion protection: the brain is protected against sports injuries and concussions by a neck-worn wearable gadget. The brain's movement inside the skull is what causes concussions. Rapid motions in the brain can cause structural anomalies as well as protracted harm that inhibits brain activity. By constricting the jugular vein in the neck, the Q-Collar harnesses the body's physiology to stabilize the brain inside the skull. This pressure raises the blood volume within the skull, which helps to prevent concussions by reducing brain movement.
d. Sensors for electromyography (EMG) in stroke patients: Electromyography (EMG) sensors monitor muscular contractions and assist in the rehabilitation of prosthesis and stroke patients. EMG sensors, in particular, assist in self-monitoring and muscle strengthening by sensing the activity related to muscle contractions. These sensors can assess nerve and muscle activity in injured tissues and are non-invasive and wireless.
e. Asthma detection: In the traditional scenario, most asthmatics will be unaware of their condition and experience an attack until it has progressed to a later stage. It is both inconvenient and dangerous. Individuals can act against the assault if they have medicine on hand, but weariness will have crept upon them and sapped their vitality.
f. Movement disorders: People with movement disorders and Parkinson's disease can use the Apple Watch to track and measure their tremors and dyskinetic symptoms. The Apple Watch software keeps track of the intensity of symptoms and helps users schedule their activities around them. The Apple Watch Health app may be used to assess a patient's response to the medicine and follow the course of a condition.

g. Coagulation monitoring: For certain individuals, blood coagulation is regularly monitored to ensure that it remains within normal limits. If they have a longer duration of blood coagulation than usual, they are more likely to have a stroke or haemorrhage.

h. Depression is tracked using an app. Compared to other physiological diseases, depression is a rather abstract condition. However, technological advancements in the Internet Age have made it more detectable and preventive.

i. Medical smart contact lenses are an ambitious effort in the Internet of Things (IoT) environment, given that there has not been much progress in this medical sector.

j. Due to forgetfulness, a portion of patients with hypertension, diabetes, psychosis, and other illnesses do not take their prescriptions as recommended. Noncompliance with prescribed medications leads to more hospital readmissions and clinical consequences. Wearable smart necklaces may tell if a medication has been swallowed by measuring the skin movement of the neck as the individual swallows. With a total precision rate of 90%, Bayesian networks assist incorrectly in categorizing the swallowing of pharmaceutical capsules, drinking water, speaking, and saliva swallows. These wearable necklaces are capable of accurately evaluating drug adherence and assisting patients with forgetfulness.

10.3.2.3 Ambient-Assisted Living (AAL)

It refers to technical methods to help the elderly and others with specific needs with their daily routines. AAL's primary goal is to preserve and enhance the autonomy of those individuals, thus enhancing their safety in their everyday lives and in their homes. The demand for such apps arises from the shifting demography of developed countries, where life expectancy is rising, but birth rates are falling. To keep healthcare expenditures within normal bounds, inventive and cost-effective solutions are necessary in these circumstances. Commodities, services, and concepts that assist the elderly in enhancing their standard of living, wellbeing, and safety are included in AAL applications. Individuals (through enhancing their protection and wellbeing), the economy (by improving the productivity of scarce resources), and society are all beneficiaries of AAL (better living conditions). In AAL applications, older people's needs include safety and security, peace of mind, freedom, health, mobility, and social connection. The number of conceivable applications in these fields is vast. As a result, AAL environments are separated into three categories: hardware (sensors, wireless networks), software (collecting data, information security, and IT administration), and services (application-based processes, biosignal processing, and community services) [46].

Ambient-assisted living (AAL) is indeed an artificial intelligence subtype that aids the elderly by combining it with the IoT. The most important goal of AAL is to assist older people in remaining independent and safe in their own homes. In the event of a medical emergency, AAL allows for monitoring these patients in real-time and ensuring that they receive human-like treatment. This has been made possible by big data analytics, machine learning (ML), artificially intelligent technologies, and their use in the healthcare industry. Researchers focused on three key areas of AAL: ambient identification, activity recognition, and critical monitoring. However, activity recognition drew the greatest attention since it deals with identifying possible dangers or emergency health problems that might harm senior citizens' well-being. The use of IoT in AAL has been shown in a lot of research. Shahamabadi suggested a system for delivering healthcare to the elderly. For AAL, flexible architecture for automation, security, and communication was created. The communication protocols employed during development were 6LoWPAN (IPv6-based low-power wireless personal area networks), NFC, and RFID. To connect the patient with the healthcare practitioners, the device uses a closed-loop communication service. The aforementioned AAL systems were structured using IoT, which was then utilized to create a more sophisticated protocol that could be used to develop complicated systems. (kits, smart objects, and devices). An emergency detector for older people was recently created to aid in the monitoring of chronic diseases and other health-based emergencies that might occur. In addition, during an emergency, the system notifies caretakers. With the assistance of robots, HIoT systems can now analyze interior air quality. These gadgets keep track of the air quality in the patient's environment and alert caregivers if it falls below a set level. Cloud computing and IoT were combined through an IoT-based gateway to provide an open, secure, and scalable AAL platform. The gateway assisted in the resolution of various security, data storage, and interoperability issues in the IoT system.

10.3.3 Communicative Systems

Communication techniques enable various parts of a HIoT network to interact with others. There are two types of communication systems: short-range and mid-range. Small-range mass communication links items together within a limited set or in a BAN (body area network), but moderate communication technologies enable communication over long distances, such as a BAN's base station and central node [46].

10.3.3.1   Radiofrequency Identification

Radiofrequency identification (RFID) can communicate across a small distance of 10 cm to 200 m. A microchip and an antenna make up the tag. It is used on the Internet of Things to identify a specific device or item (healthcare equipment). By engaging with the object via radio waves, the reading device sends and receives data from it. Data utilized in the tag in the case of IoT is already in electronic-product-code (EPC) form. Using RFID, healthcare professionals can quickly monitor and locate medical equipment. RFIDs have the advantage of not requiring any additional sources of power. Moreover, it is a relatively secure standard that might pose compatibility issues when used with a cell phone. Figure 10.7 represents an IoT network using communicative technology RFID to transfer data.

10.3.3.2   Bluetooth

Bluetooth is a ultra-high frequency (UHF) radio-based short-range wireless communication technology that is known as Bluetooth. Wireless communication between two or more medical equipment is possible with this technology. Bluetooth's frequency range is 2.4 GHz. It can send and receive data up to a range of 100 metres. Bluetooth ensures data security by encrypting and authenticating data. Below given Figure 10.8 represents HIoT architecture where data transfer is done using Bluetooth. Bluetooth's main advantages are its low cost and power efficiency. This ensures that the connected devices are less prone to interference during data transfer. When it comes to long-distance communication in healthcare; however, this technology falls short [35].

Figure 10.7 IoT-Communication using RFID.

Figure 10.8   IoT communication using bluetooth.

10.3.3.3   Zigbee

Zigbee is one of the most popularly accepted standards for connecting and sharing data between medical equipment. Bluetooth and Zigbee are comparable in terms of the frequency range. Figure 10.9 depicts how communication is done using ZigBee Network. Furthermore, compared to Bluetooth devices, it has a more excellent range of connectivity. The mesh network topology is used in this wireless network. The system consists of a processing center, routers, and end nodes. The processing center handles data analysis and aggregation. Even if one or two devices fail, the mesh network guarantees that the rest of the devices will remain connected. Zigbee's benefits include low energy consumption, rapid data rate, and a hugely increasing network.

10.3.3.4   Near Field Communication

A *near field communication* (NFC) is formed by electromagnetic induction between antenna arrays that are close to each other. This technology is comparable to RFID, which transmits data by electromagnetic induction. There are two types of operation for NFC devices: passive and active. Only one device generates radiofrequency (RF) in passive mode, while the other serves as a receiver. In inactive way, both gadgets can emit radio waves simultaneously and carry data transmission without the need for pairing. NFC's major advantages are its ease of use and a reliable network

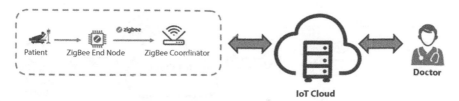

Figure 10.9   IoT-Communication using ZigBee.

for communicating wirelessly. However, it is limited to a limited range of communication [85].

10.3.3.5   Wireless Fidelity (Wi-Fi)

It refers to wireless local area network (WLAN), which complies with the 802.11 IEEE standard. Figure 10.10 represents data transfer using Wi-Fi communicative technology in IoT. When compared to Bluetooth, wireless fidelity has a greater communication range of 70 feet. Wi-Fi gives you the feasibility of rapid setup and allows you to quickly and easily set up a network. On the contrary, it is primarily used in medical facilities. Because of its simple compatibility with cellphones, as well as its capacity to provide robust security and control, Wi-widespread Fi is widely used. Unfortunately, it uses a lot more energy due to the fact that the network is not always reliable.

10.3.3.6   Satellite Communication

It is more efficient and helpful in inaccessible (remote) and far-separate geographic places (including hills, oceans, glaciers, mountains, rural areas, etc.) where other kinds of communication are difficult to reach. Satellites gather the signals from the ground, amplify them, and send them back to Earth. Satellite communication technology offers technical stability, data transfer at a high rate, interoperability, and immediate access to the Internet. However, as compared to other communication methods, satellite transmission has relatively high power consumption [42].

The above-given figures represent how HIoT network communicates using satellite communication technology. Figure 10.11a shows direct satellite communication, whereas Figure 10.11b illustrates IoT network communicating using satellite, but the data transfer is done via a gateway.

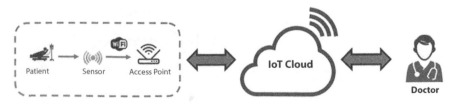

Figure 10.10 IoT-Communication using Wi-Fi.

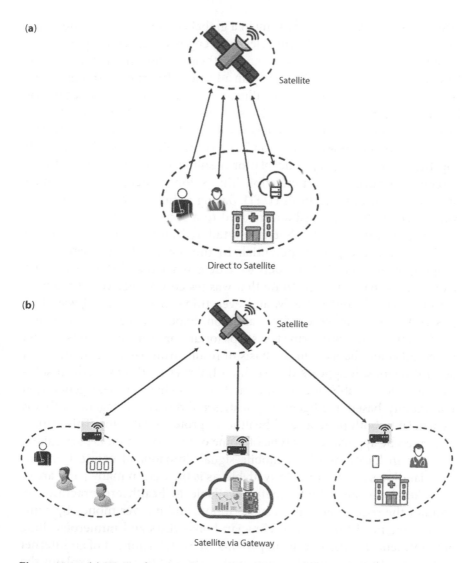

Figure 10.11 (a) HIoT—direct satellite communication. (b) HIoT—satellite via gateway communication.

10.4   Community-Based Healthcare Services

As a result, healthcare cannot be viewed as independent from this paradigm as a result of the widespread adoption of Internet of Things (IoT) technologies. We hope to pioneer new techniques to build global communication between the Internet of Things (IoT) and the medical field by doing this research. Implementing in a global context is a huge undertaking for everyone involved (from electrical engineers to data engineers). It is changing the way we think about healthcare, from the smallest sensor to vast volumes of data collected by an advanced Internet of Things point-of-care biofluid analyzer, a LoRa/Bluetooth-enabled electronic reader for biomedical strip-based diagnostics systems; and everything in between. Test simulations (technology trials without patient participants) are carried out with a disposable test "key" and companion Android app, which together provide a diagnostic platform suited for distant point-of-care screening for urinary tract infection. This is done to demonstrate the possibility of long-range analysis (UTI). Seeing as how every UTI test result was successfully diagnosed and relayed to a secure cloud server located at a distance, the LoRaWAN-enabled tailored monitor operating at 868 MHz showed exceptional potential. In the tests, radiation path losses ranging from 119 to 141 decibels were detected across distances ranging from 1.10 to 6.0 km. Everything that was tested was received at the base station correctly and robustly, and everything that was tested was then passed to the secure server for evaluation. Experts visually examine and confirm the accuracy of urine test strips for urinary tract infections (UTIs) based on color change. On the basis of results from testing conducted in several regions, it appears that such an Internet of Things medical solution is a dependable and simple method of delivering next-generation community-based intelligent diagnostics and disease management that is beneficial to both patients and healthcare professionals [46]. This critical phase can be applied to any type of home or location, but it is particularly valuable in locations where mobile signals, broadband connections, or even landlines are not readily available, as is the case in many rural areas. It makes long-range biotelemetry available to healthcare practitioners without the requirement for a subscription, and it saves money by eliminating the need for frequent clinician home visits and numerous clinic appointments for chronically ill patients. The establishment of an Internet of Medical Things network is now underway, and this paper explains the practical problems that must be overcome in order for such networks to be deployed in the near future.

In the field of community-based healthcare monitoring, the concept refers to the establishment of a healthcare network that encompasses a local community, such as an individual private clinic, a small residential area, a hotel, and so on, in order to monitor the health conditions of the people who live in that area. In the field of community-based healthcare monitoring, the concept refers to the establishment of a healthcare network that encompasses a local community, such as an individual private clinic a small residential area; the term "community-based network" refers to a collection of networks that are concatenated and can collaborate to provide a collaborative service to members of a community. Healthcare monitoring in rural areas has been made possible through the establishment of an Internet of Things (IoT)-based cooperative medical network (CMN). It was decided to use a number of authentication and authorization procedures in order to build a secure connection between the networks [55]. In another study, the researchers proposed a community medical network, which they called a "virtual hospital," which was generally considered to be a good idea. This helped in the provision of medical care to people in need who were located in remote places. It has been suggested that a resident health network be established in the city. It is proposed in this work to use a four-layer structural architecture for sharing health information, which includes patient medical data, to facilitate the exchange of information. Health clinics can utilize this information to provide appropriate medical recommendations to those in the local region who are in need of care.

10.5   Cognitive Computation

The process of providing computers with the ability to solve complex issues on their own is known as "cognitive computing." In the same way that individuals profit from experience, cognitive systems benefit greatly from learning effective strategies to solve problems. When a traditional system fails to perform a task, cognitive computing sees an opportunity to make it smarter [34]. According to experts, cognitive computing and the IoT are becoming increasingly intertwined, with cognitive systems' artificial intelligence capabilities providing an unparalleled combination of IoT speed and scale. The Internet of Things delivers the data volumes needed to boost the value and return on investment of cognitive analytics systems.

It can be conceived of as a digital model that simulates human thought processes. It consists of self-learning algorithms that use natural language processing, data mining, and vision to replicate the human brain's functioning and pattern recognition [78]. Cognitive computing systems employ machine learning algorithms and deep learning neural networks.

Intelligent systems are constantly learning and accumulating knowledge as a result of the data that is continuously sent into them. As a result, the system learns to explicitly express how they look for patterns as a result of this approach, and their data processing activities improve. As a result, they are more capable of assessing and evaluating new difficulties, as well as implementing alternate solutions [79].

By utilizing their brains, AI cognitive computing allows you to mimic the cognitive functions that every human performs. IoT use cases enable devices to communicate with customers by using internet service technology. The primary aim of cognitive computing is to gain practical applications by putting human thoughts into a programmatic model.

We have collected a few key advantages of cognitive computing that directly impact real life: If we consider the healthcare industry, then the cognitive computing system helps collect data through medical journals and personal patient history. It provides better data analysis, which can improve patient care levels [56]. Cognitive computing provides a better level of space for customer interactions because it possesses massive potential.

AI has such a wide range of abilities that it enables a machine for decision-making processing and data analysis. Today, artificial intelligence is available on thousands of application platforms. On the other hand, cognitive computing is a type of AI technology used by International Business Machines (IBM). Computers are not cognitive. AI covers a set of techniques.

People who are working in any business sector are always asked a question. There is a significant difference between cognitive computing and AI [46].

Cognitive computing also explains how computer sciences are productive in our personal lives, healthcare, etc.

In computer language, artificial intelligence is a very distant goal of computing. But we are coming closer with the new cognitive computing model to a point where we will be entirely dependent on it in the coming time.

AI is being used to support a wide range of human-centered solutions, including healthcare and autonomous mobility. Next-generation technology and cognitive computing enable personalized human-machine interaction and applications that emulate people's behavior. Innovative city applications, on the other hand, such as intelligent transit, healthcare, firefighting, and retail, create vast amounts of data. The challenge of how to effectively manage the massive amount of data produced is always present [39, 40]. Several recent studies have looked into the use of cognitive computing to analyze huge volumes of data. However, these studies have failed to address fundamental difficulties in a smart city context, such as data scalability and adaptability. Millions of sensors are used for data collection, which is further cross-implemented across a wide range of cognitive computing systems to maintain real-time reactions. We examine the cognitive Internet of Things (IoT) and present a CIoT-based smart city network (CIoT-Net) architecture that demonstrates how data from smart city applications may be analyzed using cognitive computing while simultaneously addressing challenges of flexibility and scalability. To achieve the proposed architecture, we leverage a variety of technologies, including artificial intelligence (AI) and big data analysis. Finally, we look at the research problems and opportunities that may arise as a result of putting the suggested design in place.

10.6   Adverse Drug Reaction

Drug adherence and adverse drug reactions (ADR) are the most critical challenges in the global healthcare industry when it comes to patient safety. ADR affects 6.7% of patients in hospitals around the world, with a death incidence of 0.32% of all patients. This rate is significantly higher in AAL settings, where 15% of patients have clinically relevant reactions as a result of patient noncompliance with prescription schedule and dosage. As people get older, these occurrences become more common, resulting in toxicity and posing a risk of drug interactions and side effects [88]. The consequences of inappropriate drug use can be reduced if drug therapy is managed on a regular basis. The IoT is being used to identify drugs and monitor medicine. The Internet of Things is used to detect harmful allergies, pharmaceutical excipient side effects, pregnancy concerns, and liver/renal abnormalities, as well as test drugs to reach therapeutic goals. The IoT design supports a wide range of near-field communication, IoT sensing technologies, radio frequency identification, including barcodes, and a new IrDA-based solution developed in collaboration with the World Health Organization for low-income countries because the aforementioned issues are global. Personal gadgets like PDAs, PCs, and cellphones, as well as Movital, an Internet-of-things personalized health gadget, employ these technologies.

One of the essential uses of information and communication technology (ICT) is to provide effective and appropriate healthcare. The IoT is a relatively new breakthrough in information and communication technology that allows global networking and control of devices, users, data, and sensors [24, 46]. A drug-related research system based on the Internet of Things (IoT) is based on the Internet of Things (IoT), which makes use of smartphones and the Internet for ubiquitous access, 6LoWPAN technology for ubiquitous data collection from patients, sensors, and hospitals, and RFID/NFC for worldwide identification and authentication. A range of applications for these technologies is possible in healthcare, including enhancing service quality, minimizing errors, and even detecting abnormalities in health using vital signs [33]. This paper describes how the Internet of Things (IoT) is being used in a pharmaceutical system to screen for adverse drug reactions (ADRs), negative effects of pharmaceutical excipients, allergies, problems, and contraindications related to liver and kidney abnormalities, as well as harmful side effects during pregnancy or nursing. Because of this, the system takes a more thorough approach to aiding clinicians with clinical choices and medication prescribing than it previously did. A wide range of gadgets, including smartphones, personal digital assistants (PDAs), and personal computers (PCs), have near-field communication (NFC) and barcode recognition technology included. In order to establish whether a drug is appropriate for a patient's medical history, the drug identification number is compared to the pharmaceutical intelligent information system [34].

Geriatric patients with a variety of comorbidities are more likely to experience an adverse medication reaction while in the hospital (ADR). The study's goal was to compare the rate of adverse pharmaceutical reactions predicted by a computerized pharmacological database to the actual rate in a group of geriatric individuals identified through direct observation [44].

In hospitals across the world, the rate of the grave and fatal susceptible drug reactions (ADR) and excipients used in pharmaceuticals has a wide range of effects. According to certain research, ADRs develop at a rate of around 6.5% in hospitals across the world. The consequences of these incidents include an 80% rate of ADR occurrences necessitating patient admission, a cost of $847 million dollars obtained on an average bed stay of eight days, and a 0.15% overall fatality rate [45]. The majority of these effects are avoidable. As a consequence, this research suggests a medication checker enabled by the Internet of Things, as well as an information system to identify adverse drug reactions and allergic interactions. Specifically, utilizing ordinary gadgets, including personal digital assistants, mobile phones, and computers, the patient's terminal recognizes the medicines via barcode or near field communication (NFC). This data is compared to the EHR to see if a drug or product is compatible with a patient's allergy profile. A pharmacist uses a pharmaceutical intelligent information system. A first estimate based on intelligent phones and a genuine patient with NSAID intolerance is often used to test the approach. Some active components (AI) are intolerable to this patient, such as ibuprofen [52]. As a consequence, when a patient checks out a drug that contains one of the not tolerated AI, the system tells the patient via a user-friendly interface that his allergy profile and EHR are out of sync.

10.7   Blockchain

Internet-connected devices can send information to private blockchain networks that create tamper-proof records of shared transactions. Without the need for centralized management and administration, IBM Blockchain lets you exchange and access IoT data with your business partners [46]. Every transaction is reviewed carefully to avoid conflicts and develop trust among all authorized network users. Blockchain and the Internet of Things are both often mentioned as important digital transformation technologies. But what about a combination of both? At the end of 2019, especially in the US, Gartner called blockchain adoption in combination with IoT adoption a "DX sweet spot." And that has not changed. An overview of blockchain and IoT in combination [50].

The Internet of Things, which makes use of sensors, as well as other edge devices and infrastructure, is revolutionizing the way enterprises conduct their business operations. Due to the fact that data protection must be guaranteed at all levels of the Internet of Things ecosystem, this is a major cause of concern for organizations. As the number of devices connected to the Internet continues to grow year after year, maintaining data security is becoming increasingly difficult. It is possible that Internet of Things devices will prove to be beneficial in the fight against cybersecurity issues.

Incorporating blockchain technology with the Internet of Things enables the establishment of distributed ledger systems, which may be used to facilitate the exchange of information between machines. A shared ledger that includes all nodes is maintained in a shared ledger, which is then saved in a database, evaluated by several sources, and eventually recorded in a shared ledger [45]. One advantage of combining the Internet of Things with blockchain technology is the capacity of a smart device to operate independently of a central authority, which could be helpful in certain scenarios. Using the Internet of Things and blockchain technology together has several advantages [46]. The system can also keep track of how various gadgets interact with one another.

The decentralized aspect of blockchain is an architectural advantage. However, the deployment of the Internet of Things may be hampered as a result of this decentralized nature of blockchain. It is common to practice in the Internet of Things to adopt a client-server design or a hub-and-spoke architecture, which has a centralized authority. It is possible, however, that setting up IoT sensors to manage their own processing and data storage will be difficult due to the fact that they rely on centralized computation and storage resources. Building a decentralized Internet of Things platform would aid in assuring compatibility with a blockchain network, which is currently under development.

A wide range of applications, spanning from autos to industrial to financial to agricultural to banking, have included blockchain technology in conjunction with the Internet of Things (IoT). It has been utilized in connection with supply chains, logistics, smart homes, and a groundbreaking technique referred to as "smart contracts," to name a few applications [78]. When specific criteria are met, smart contracts can be used to automate contract execution in the Internet of Things (IoT) ecosystems. Smart contracts leverage blockchain technology to automate contract execution in IoT ecosystems. This is the only way in which an intelligent gadget can function because it does not require the support of a centralized authority to do so.

Businesses may manage data on edge devices in an Internet of Things system with the help of this blockchain application, which reduces the need for device maintenance and data transfer costs for the system. The ledger does not require the maintenance of a central data repository, and the ledger is not vulnerable to cyberattacks, hence eliminating the risks associated with data management [77]. In addition, it reduces processing time by doing away with the necessity for an Internet of Things gateway or any other form of the intermediary device between data sources and users.

Blockchain technology delivers extremely high levels of security since it makes use of decentralized, distributed ledgers to authenticate and validate encrypted device-generated data. As part of a distributed ledger, data computation and storage are dispersed among millions of workstations in a distributed computing environment [76]. In contrast to previous years, the loss of a device, a server, or a network has had little impact on the Internet of Things ecosystem as a whole in this decade. In order for a blockchain network to be robust, it must be on the verge of becoming fault-tolerant, which means that the network must continue to function even if certain nodes are brought offline.

Many Internet of Things ecosystems is accessible targets for cybercriminals as a result of inadequate access controls and client/server designs that are common in the industry. Over the past few years, there has been an increase in the frequency of distributed denial of service (DDoS) attacks. DDoS attacks are designed to cause disruptions in normal connections to connected devices by flooding the target or surrounding infrastructure with a torrent of internet data [45]. The botnets Mirai and Hajime, which are connected to the Internet of Things, make it simple to launch distributed denial of service attacks. The distributed security architecture of a blockchain can be deployed in order to protect IoT devices and networks from botnet-driven distributed denial of service (DDoS) attacks [75]. It is proposed that each device in a network be protected on an individual basis using a blockchain-based peer-to-peer network, similar to the one used by Bitcoin.

Despite the fact that blockchain technology for the Internet of Things (IoT) is still in its infancy, a number of significant information technology businesses have begun to investigate its potential. Consider the IBM Blockchain Platform, which allows enterprises to connect blockchain with cognitive IoT, a set of technologies that bring together the Internet of Things and cognitive computing [46].

Due to technological issues and operational constraints, the deployment of blockchain technology in the Internet of Things (IoT) is still constrained. Inefficiently maintaining a large centralized ledger on edge nodes is due to the fact that smart devices at the edge are not yet capable of storing massive amounts of data or processing equal amounts of computational power [32]. These are some of the difficulties that IoT networks may encounter when they transition to blockchain-based systems.

The concept is still in its early stages, but it is predicted to have a considerable impact within the next few years, despite the fact that it is still relatively new. In order to encourage the implementation of Internet of Things blockchain technology, it is necessary to develop standard security regulations and laws [26]. Through the introduction of new data openness and peer-to-peer communication protocols, blockchain technology has the potential to increase the level of security available on the Internet.

10.8 Child Health Information

Healthcare IoT research trends highlight the technology's potential to improve service quality. It aids in the provision of preventive care and the promotion of automation in order to minimize the human error risk [22]. Because the mortality rates of maternity and child patients remain high in Indonesia, mother and child healthcare remain a top priority for the government. This article lays out a conceptual architecture for the Internet of Things (IoT) applications that will aid in the delivery of mother-and-child healthcare. We considered government norms and standards as a starting point for determining the needs. Following that, the design's networks (topology, architecture, and platform), services and applications, security, and technology were defined. In this multi-platform system design, medical data is collected using portable medical devices with several sensors and sent to the server [35].

The SNOO bassinet from Happiest Baby offers a slew of features designed to keep babies sleeping safer and longer, including white noise and "womb-like rocking," a cry sensor that changes motion and sound automatically, and an "SNOO Sack" that inhibits rolling. It is all controlled by an app that includes a daily sleep diary, smartphone notifications, and various settings for sensitivity and a baby's age. Impact on the Industry Snoo's alleged capacity to help youngsters sleep was recently tested by a Forbes reporter, and it is beneficial for sleep-deprived patients whose health depends on getting enough Z's.

10.9   Growth in Healthcare IoT

The given graph Figure 10.12 shows the rapid growth in healthcare IoT in North America. Inside the company, IoT products aimed at improving patient safety or experience, such as connected hand hygiene monitoring, are also contributing to investment and income. RFID tags for asset management, as well as smart medications and smart beds that proactively monitor patients, are being investigated by healthcare institutions [46].

10.10   Benefits of IoT in Healthcare

Real-time reporting and monitoring patients, doctors, and employees are safer with IoT security systems. A cost-effective and end-to-end connection with the Internet of Things healthcare gadgets, wearable technologies, and data access, patients can receive more informed therapy, and clinicians can better monitor patients. Improved medication management and adherence, data collection, analysis, tracking, and alarms are all part of the process. Errors and waste are reduced, remote medical assistance, etc. [90].

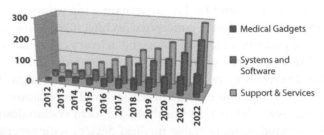

Figure 10.12 Rapid growth in healthcare IoT (reconstructed from [90]).

Challenges of IoT in Healthcare

a) Gadgets and protocols integration,
b) Cost,
c) Data security,
d) Data privacy,
e) Reliability,
f) Accuracy,
g) Data overloading, etc.

10.11   Conclusion

The IoT benefits are summarised as a developing study field in health-care from this vantage point. These advancements offer healthcare systems a fantastic opportunity to detect health problems diagnose, monitor, and treat patients both outside and inside the hospital. As the usage of technology-assisted health services expands, a greater variety of conventional healthcare delivery practises will be supplemented or replaced by IoT, allowing healthcare organizations to establish more flexible treatment models. In contrast, a specified and strict code of practice for confidentiality, information management, cyber security, authentication, including privacy, will control the availability and application of IoT devices in healthcare. Personal health alternatives substantially have more diversity. The development of 3D-printed wristbands for assessing vital indicators is already underway. We can track much more now that the long list of things is out there: sleeping patterns, nutritional balance, GP visits and check-up plans, workout routines, and so on. In the medical field, utilizing the Internet of Things provides for better, healthier, and more patient-friendly care. Doctors will identify ailments, save transportation time, and connect with patients, among other things, thanks to the IoT, which will speed up the delivery of healthcare. Future Internet of Things research must concentrate on how to create IoT devices that adhere to standard protocols and are compatible with global and state-to-state health systems. In terms of IoT-enabled services like healthcare delivery, more research into the efficiency of blockchain storage versus centralized cloud-based storage systems is required. From the standpoint of the health system, clinical standards on digital health prescriptions and a comprehensive compensation strategy for services in inpatient and outpatient settings given via IoT are required. Finally, additional study is needed to establish consumer and clinician tolerance, as well as digital literacy, when it comes to adopting the Internet of Things (IoT), which can help improve healthcare performance and overall satisfaction. Despite the fact that such a point of view is based on a summary of selected literature rather than a comprehensive systematic review, we believe that tackling these areas for future study will go a long way toward allowing IoT adoption to become more widespread, which will save money and improve patient-centered care.

References

1. https://www.gsma.com/iot/mobile-iot/.
2. https://www.avenga.com/magazine/wearables-iot-healthcare/.
3. https://www.investopedia.com/terms/w/wearable-technology.asp.
4. Catherwood, P.A., Steele, D., Little, M., Mccomb, S., Mclaughlin, J., A community-based IoT personalized wireless healthcare solution trial. *IEEE J. Transl. Eng. Health Med.*, 6, 2800313, 2018, https://doi.org/10.1109/JTEHM.2018.2822302.
5. URL =https://www.hiotron.com/cognitive-computing-in-iot/.
6. URL = https://www.ibm.com/blogs/internet-of-things/cognitive-computing-and-iot/.
7. Tiwari, L., Raja, R., Sharma, V., Miri, R., Fuzzy inference system for efficient lung cancer detection, in: *Computer Vision and Machine Intelligence in Medical Image Analysis. Advances in Intelligent Systems and Computing*, vol. 992, M. Gupta, D. Konar, S. Bhattacharyya, S. Biswas (Eds.), Springer, Singapore, 2020, https://doi.org/10.1007/978-981-13-8798-2_4.
8. Jara, A.J., Belchi, F.J., Alcolea, A.F., Santa, J., Zamora-Izquierdo, M.A., Gómez-Skarmeta, A.F., A pharmaceutical intelligent information system to detect allergies and adverse drugs reactions based on internet of things. *2010 8th IEEE International Conference on Pervasive Computing and Communications Workshops (PERCOM Workshops)*, pp. 809–812, 2010.
9. url= https://builtin.com/internet-things/iot-in-healthcare.
10. Kadarina, T.M. and Priambodo, R., Preliminary design of Internet of Things (IoT) application for supporting mother and child health program in Indonesia. *2017 International Conference on Broadband Communication, Wireless Sensors and Powering (BCWSP)*, pp. 1–6, 2017.
11. Bharadwaj, H.K., Agarwal, A., Chamola, V., Lakkaniga, N.R., Hassija, V., Guizani, M., Sikdar, B., A review on the role of machine learning in enabling IoT based healthcare applications. *IEEE Access*, 9, 38859–388905, 2021.
12. Park, Jh., Salim, M.M., Jo, J.H. *et al.*, CIoT-Net: A scalable cognitive IoT based smart city network architecture. *Hum. Centric Comput. Inf. Sci.*, 9, 29, 2019, https://doi.org/10.1186/s13673-019-0190-9.

13. Subasi, A., Radwan, M., Kurdi, R., Khateeb, K., IoT based mobile healthcare system for human activity recognition. *2018 15th Learning and Technology Conference (L&T)*, pp. 29–34, 2018.

14. Rekha, H.S., Nayak, J., Sekhar, G.T.C., Pelusi, D., Impact of IoT in healthcare: Improvements and challenges, in: *The Digitalization Conundrum in India. India Studies in Business and Economics*, K. Das, B.S.P. Mishra, M. Das (Eds.), Springer, Singapore, 2020, https://doi.org/10.1007/978-981-15-6907-4_5.

15. Raja, R., Patra, R.K., Sinha, T.S., Extraction of features from dummy face for improving biometrical authentication of human. *Int. J. Lumin. Appl.*, 7, 3–4, 303, 507-512, 2017.

16. Jara, A.J., Alcolea, A.F., Zamora, M.A., Skarmeta, A.F.G., Alsaedy, M., Drugs interaction checker based on IoT. *2010 Internet of Things (IoT)*, pp. 1–8, 2010.

17. Yang, G., Xie, L., Mantysalo, M. *et al.*, A health-IoT platform based on the integration of intelligent packaging, unobtrusive bio-sensor, and intelligent medicine box. *IEEE Trans. Ind. Inf.*, 10, 4, 2180–2191, 2014.

18. Ali, Z., Hossain, M.S., Muhammad, G., Sangaiah, A.K., An intelligent healthcare system for detection and classification to discriminate vocal fold disorders. *Future Gener. Comput. Syst.*, 85, 19–28, 2018.

19. Ahad, A., Tahir, M., Yau, K.-L.A., 5G-based smart healthcare network: Architecture, taxonomy, challenges and future research directions. *IEEE Access*, 7, 100747–100762, 2019.

20. Oryema, B., Design and implementation of an interoperable messaging system for IoT healthcare services, in: *Proceedings of the 2017 14th IEEE Annual Consumer Communications & Networking Conference (CCNC)*, pp. 45–52, Las Vegas, NV, USA, January 2017.

21. Peng, H., Tian, Y., Kurths, J., Li, L., Yang, Y., Wang, D., Secure and energy-efficient data transmission system based on chaotic compressive sensing in body-to-body networks. *IEEE Trans. Biomed. Circuits Syst.*, 11, 3, 558–573, 2017.

22. Lee, J.-Y. and Scholtz, R.A., Ranging in a dense multipath environment using an UWB radio link. *IEEE J. Sel. Areas Commun.*, 20, 1677–1683, 2002.

23. CerruelaGarciía, G., Luque Ruiz, I., Gomez-Nieto, M., State of the art, trends and future of bluetooth low energy, 14 Journal of Healthcare Engineering near field communication and visible light communication in the development of smart cities. *Sensors*, 16, 11, 1968, 2016.

24. Jaiswal, K. *et al.*, An IoT-cloud based smart healthcare monitoring system using container-based virtual environment in edge device. *2018 International Conference on Emerging Trends and Innovations in Engineering and Technological Research (ICETIETR)*, pp. 1–7, 2018.

25. Zetik, R., UWB localization-active and passive approach [ultra wideband radar], in: *Proceedings of the 21st IEEE Instrumentation and Measurement Technology Conference (IEEE Cat. No. 04CH37510)*, pp. 1005–1009, Como, Italy, May 2004.

26. Fontana, R.J. and Gunderson, S.J., Ultra-wideband precision asset location system, in: *Proceedings of the 2002 IEEE Conference on Ultra-Wideband Systems and Technologies (IEEE Cat. No. 02EX580)*, pp. 147–150, Baltimore, MD, USA, May 2002.

27. Tsirmpas, C., Anastasiou, A., Bountris, P., Koutsouris, D., A new method for profile generation in an internet of things environment: An application in ambient-assisted living. *IEEE Internet Things J.*, 2, 6, 471–478, 2015.

28. Sandeepa, C., An emergency situation detection system for ambient assisted living, in: *Proceedings of the 2020 IEEE International Conference on Communications Workshops (ICC Workshops)*, pp. 1–6, Anchorage, AL, USA, June 2020, pp. 1–6.

29. Chuquimarca, L., Mobile IoT device for BPM monitoring people with heart problems, in: *Proceedings of the 2020 International Conference on Electrical, Communication, and Computer Engineering (ICECCE)*, pp. 1–5, Istanbul, Turkey.

30. Zhang, Y., Cui, J., Ma, K., Chen, H., Zhang, J., A wristband device for detecting human pulse and motion based on the internet of things. *Measurement*, 163, 305, 2020.

31. Raja, R., Sinha, T.S., Patra, R.K., Tiwari, S., Physiological trait based biometrical authentication of human-face using LGXP and ANN techniques. *Int. J. Inf. Comput. Secur.*, 10, 2/3, 303–320, 2018.

32. Mendonça, M., An IoT-based healthcare ecosystem for home intelligent assistant services in smart homes, in: *Proceedings of the EAI International Conference on IoT Technologies for HealthCare*, Braga, Portugal, pp. 142–155, December 2019.

33. Castillejo, P., Martinez, J.-F., Rodriguez-Molina, J., Cuerva, A., Integration of wearable devices in a wireless sensor network for an E-health application. *IEEE Wireless Commun.*, 20, 4, 38–49, 2013.

34. Amin, S.U., Hossain, M.S., Muhammad, G., Alhussein, M., Rahman, M.A., Cognitive smart healthcare for pathology detection and monitoring. *IEEE Access*, 7, 10745–10753, 2019.

35. Wang, W., +e internet of things for resident health information service platform research, in: *Proceedings of the IET International Conference on Communication Technology and Application (ICCTA 2011)*, Beijing, China, May 2011.

36. Jara, A.J., A pharmaceutical intelligent information system to detect allergies and adverse drugs reactions based on internet of things, in: *Proceedings of the 2010 8th IEEE International Conference on Pervasive Computing and Communications Workshops (PERCOM Workshops)*, pp. 809–812, Mannheim, Germany, April 2010.

37. Satamraju, K.P. and Malarkodi, B., Proof of concept of scalable integration of internet of things and blockchain in healthcare. *Sensors*, 20, 5, 1389, 2020.

38. Raja, R., Kumar, S., Choudhary, S., Dalmia, H., An effective contour detection based image retrieval using multi-fusion method and neural network. *Res. Square*, 1–38, July 2021.

39. Zhang, X., Block-based access control for blockchain-based electronic medical records (EMRs) query in eHealth, in: *Proceedings of the 2018 IEEE Global Communications Conference (GLOBECOM)*, pp. 1–7, Abu Dhabi, UAE, December 2018.

40. Sutjiredjeki, E., Basjaruddin, N.C., Fajrin, D.N., Noor, F., Development of NFC and IoT-enabled measurement devices for improving healthcare delivery of Indonesian children. *J. Phys. Conf. Ser.*, 1450, 322, 2020.

41. Tekeste, T., Ultra-low power QRS detection and ECG compression architecture for IoT healthcare devices. *IEEE Trans. Circuits Syst. I: Regul. Pap.*, 66, 669–679, 2018.

42. Pathak, S., Raja, R., Sharma, V., Laxmi, K.R., A framework of ICT implementation on higher educational institution with data mining approach. *Eur. J. Eng. Res. Sci.*, 4, 5, 34–38, May 2019.

43. Gia, T.N. *et al.*, Energy-efficient fog-assisted IoT system for monitoring diabetic patients with cardiovascular disease. *Future Gener. Comput. Syst.*, 93, 198–211, 2019.

44. Gia, T.N., Ali, M., Dhaou, I.B. *et al.*, IoT-based continuous glucose monitoring system: A feasibility study. *Proc. Comput. Sci.*, 109, 327–334, 2017.

45. Istepanian, R.S., +e potential of Internet of m-health +ings "m-IoT" for non-invasive glucose level sensing, in: *Proceedings of the 2011 Annual International Conference of 16 Journal of Healthcare Engineering the IEEE Engineering in Medicine and Biology Society*, pp. 5264–5266, Boston, MA, USA, March 2011.

46. Pradhan, B., Bhattacharyya, S., Pal, K., IoT-based applications in healthcare devices. *J. Healthcare Eng.*, 2021, 322–328, 2021.

47. Sargunam, B. and Anusha, S., IoT based mobile medical application for smart insulin regulation, in: *Proceedings of the 2019 IEEE International Conference on Electrical, Computer and Communication Technologies (ICECCT)*, pp. 1–5, Erode, India, October 2019.

48. Valenzuela, F., García, A., Ruiz, E., Vázquez, M., Cortez, J., Espinoza, A., An IoT-based glucose monitoring algorithm to prevent diabetes complications. *Appl. Sci.*, 10, 3, 921, 2020.

49. Gunawan, I., Design and development of telemedicine-based heartbeat and body temperature monitoring tools, in: *Proceedings of the IOP Conference Series: Materials Science and Engineering*, p. 012018, Gambang, Malaysia, November 2020.

50. Xin, Q. and Wu, J., A novel wearable device for continuous, non-invasion blood pressure measurement. *Comput. Biol. Chem.*, 69, 134–137, 2017.

51. Pathak, S., Raja, R., Sharma, V., Ambala, S., ICT utilization and improving student performance in higher education. *Int. J. Recent Technol. Eng. (IJRTE)*, 8, 2, 5120–5124, July 2019.

52. Sinha, T.S., Chakraverty, D., Patra, R., Raja, R., Modelling and simulation for the recognition of physiological and behavioural traits through human gait and face images, in: *Discrte Wavelet Transforms- A Compendium of New Approaches and Resents Application*, AKh. Al. Asmari (Ed.), pp. 95–125, Intech China, Feb 2013, http://dx.doi.org/10.5772/52565.

53. Agustine, L., Heart rate monitoring device for arrhythmia using pulse oximeter sensor based on android, in: *Proceedings of the 2018 International Conference on Computer Engineering, Network and Intelligent Multimedia (CENIM)*, pp. 106–111, Surabaya, Indonesia, November 2018.

54. Chandrakar, R., Raja, R., Miri, R., Animal detection based on deep convolutional neural networks with genetic segmentation. *Multimed. Tools Appl.*, 2021, https://doi.org/10.1007/s11042-021-11290-4.

55. Güler, I., Real-time abnormal detection for asthma patients with internet of things technology, in: *Proceedings of the 2018 3rd International Conference on Computer Science and Engineering (UBMK)*, pp. 269–274, Sarajevo, Bosnia and Herzegovina, September 2018.

56. Gurbeta, L., Badnjevic, A., Maksimovic, M., OmanovicMiklicanin, E., Sejdic, E., A telehealth system for automated diagnosis of asthma and chronic obstructive pulmonary disease. *J. Am. Med. Inf. Assoc.*, 25, 9, 1213–1217, 2018.

57. Shah, S.T.U., Cloud-assisted IoT-based smart respiratory monitoring system for asthma patients, in: *Applications of Intelligent Technologies in Healthcare*, pp. 77–86, Springer, Berlin, Germany, 2019.

58. Gundu, S., A novel IoT based solution for monitoring and alerting bronchial asthma patients. *Int. J. Res. Eng. Sci. Manage.*, 3, 10, 120–123, 2020.

59. Tiwari, L., Raja, R., Awasthi, V., Miri, R., Sinha, G.R., Alkinani, M.H., Polat, K., Detection of lung nodule and cancer using novel Mask-3 FCM and TWEDLNN algorithms. *Measurement*, 172, 108882, 2021, https://doi.org/10.1016/j.measurement.2020.108882.

60. Hui, C.Y., Mckinstry, B., Fulton, O., Buchner, M., Pinnock, H., What features do patients and clinicians 'want' in the future Internet-of-Things (IoT) systems for asthma: A mixed-method study. *Eur. Respir. J.*, 56, 309, 2020.

61. Pandey, P.S., Machine learning and IoT for prediction and detection of stress, in: *Proceedings of the 2017 17th International Conference on Computational Science and its Applications (ICCSA)*, pp. 1–5, Trieste, Italy, July 2017.

62. Alder, M., Javanmard, M., Martin, R., A review of medication adherence monitoring technologies. *Appl. Syst. Innov.*, 1, 2, 14, 2018.

63. Latif, G., I-CARES: Advancing health diagnosis and medication through IoT. *Wirel. Netw.*, 4, 1–15, 2019.

64. Sahlab, N., Development of an intelligent pill dispenser based on an IoT-approach, in: *Proceedings of the International Conference on Human Systems Engineering and Design: Future Trends and Applications*, pp. 33–39, Munich, Germany, September 2019.

65. Bharadwaj, S.A., Enhancing healthcare using m-care box (monitoring noncompliance of medication), in: *Proceedings of the 2017 International Conference on I-SMAC (IoT in Journal of Healthcare Engineering 17 Social, Mobile, Analytics and Cloud)(I-SMAC)*, pp. 352–356, Coimbatore, India, February 2017.

66. Wadibhasme, P., Saathi—A smart IoT-based pill reminder for IVF patients, in: *Proceedings of the International Conference on Information and Communication Technology for Intelligent Systems*, pp. 697–705, Ahmedabad, India, August 2020.

67. Kumar, S., Raja, R., Gandham, A., Tracking an object using traditional MS (Mean Shift) and CBWH MS (Mean Shift) algorithm with kalman filter, in: *Applications of Machine Learning. Algorithms for Intelligent Systems*, P. Johri, J. Verma, S. Paul (Eds.), Springer, Singapore, 2020, https://doi.org/10.1007/978-981-15-3357-0_4.

68. Carrasquilla Batista, A., An internet of +ings (IoT) application to control a wheelchair through EEG signal processing, in: *Proceedings of the 2017 International Symposium on Wearable Robotics and Rehabilitation (WeRob)*, Houston, TX, USA, November 2017, p. 1, DSouza, D.J., IoT based smart sensing wheelchair to assist in healthcare. *Methods*, 6, 2019.

69. Lee, Y.K., Real-time image processing based obstacle avoidance and navigation system for autonomous wheelchair application, in: *Proceedings of the 2017 Asia-Pacific Signal and Information Processing Association Annual Summit and Conference (APSIPA ASC)*, pp. 380–385, Kuala Lumpur, Malaysia, December 2017.

70. Ghorbel, A., Cloud-based mobile application for remote control of intelligent wheelchair, in: *Proceedings of the 2018 14th International Wireless Communications & Mobile Computing Conference (IWCMC)*, pp. 1249–1254, Limassol, Cyprus, June 2018.

71. Onasanya, A. and Elshakankiri, M., Smart integrated IoT healthcare system for cancer care. *Wirel. Netw.*, 1–16, 2019.

72. Chandrakar, R., Raja, R., Miri, R., Patra, R.K., Sinha, U., Computer succored vaticination of multi-object detection and histogram enhancement in low vision. *Int. J. Biom. Special Issue: Investigation of Robustness in Image Enhancement and Preprocessing Techniques for Biometrics and Computer Vision Applications*, 1, 1, 310.

73. Adamovich, S.V., Merians, A.S., Boian, R. *et al.*, A virtual reality-based exercise system for hand rehabilitation post-stroke. *Presence: Teleoperators and Virtual Environments*, 14, 2, 161–174, 2005.

74. Kumar, S., Raja, R., Tiwari, S., Rani, S., *Cognitive behavior & human computer interaction based on machine learning algorithm*, Wiley & Scrivener Publishing, 2021.

75. Heshmat, M. and Shehata, A.-R.S., A framework about using internet of things for smart cancer treatment process, in: *Proceedings of the International*

Conference on Industrial Engineering and Operations Management, pp. 1206–1211, Washington, DC, USA, September 2018.

76. Pradhan, K. and Chawla, P., Medical Internet of Things using machine learning algorithms for lung cancer detection. *J. Manage. Anal.*, 7, 4, 591–623, 2020.

77. Rodrigues, D. d. A., Ivo, R.F., Satapathy, S.C., A new approach for classification skin lesion based on transfer learning, deep learning, and IoT system. *Pattern Recognit. Lett.*, 136, 326, 2020.

78. Cecil, J., Gupta, A., Pirela-Cruz, M., Ramanathan, P., An IoMT based cyber training framework for orthopedic surgery using next generation internet technologies. *Inf. Med. Unlocked*, 12, 128–137, 2018.

79. Su, H., Internet of Things (IoT)-based collaborative control of a redundant manipulator for teleoperated minimally invasive surgeries, in: *Proceedings of the 2020 IEEE International Conference on Robotics and Automation (ICRA)*, pp. 9737–9742, Paris, France, August 2020.

80. Shah, R. and Chircu, A., IoT and AI in healthcare: A systematic literature review. *Issues Inf. Syst.*, 19, 3, 311, 2018.

81. Singh, P. and Singh, N., Blockchain with IoT and AI: A review of agriculture and healthcare. *Int. J. Appl. Evol. Comput. (IJAEC)*, 11, 4, 13–27, 2020.

82. Chamoli, V. *et al.*, A comprehensive review of the COVID-19 pandemic and the role of IoT, drones, AI, blockchain, and 5G in managing its impact. *IEEE Access*, 8, 90225–90265, 2020.

83. Darshan, K.R. and Anandakumar, K.R., A comprehensive review on usage of Internet of Things (IoT) in healthcare system. *2015 International Conference on Emerging Research in Electronics, Computer Science and Technology (ICERECT)*, IEEE, 2015.

84. Ghazal, T.M., Hasan, M.K., Alshurideh, M.T., Alzoubi, H.M., Ahmad, M., Akbar, S.S., Akour, I.A., IoT for smart cities: Machine learning approaches in smart healthcare—A review. *Future Internet*, 13, 8, 218, 2021.

85. Kashani, M.H., Madanipour, M., Nikravan, M., Asghari, P., Mahdipour, E., A systematic review of IoT in healthcare: Applications, techniques, and trends. *J. Netw. Comput. Appl.*, 103164, 2021.

86. Sahu, A.K., Sharma, S., Tanveer, M., Raja, R., Internet of Things attack detection using hybrid deep learning model. *Comput. Commun.*, 176, 146–154, 2021, https://doi.org/10.1016/j.comcom.2021.05.024.

87. Mahmood, M.R., Patra, R.K., Raja, R., Sinha, G.R., A novel approach for weather prediction using forecasting analysis and data mining techniques, in: *Innovations in Electronics and Communication Engineering. Lecture Notes in Networks and Systems*, vol. 65, H. Saini, R. Singh, G. Kumar, G. Rather, K. Santhi (Eds.), Springer, Singapore, 2019, https://doi.org/10.1007/978-981-13-3765-9_50.

88. Sinha, T.S., Patra, R.K., Raja, R., A comprehensive analysis of human gait for abnormal foot recognition using neuro-genetic approach. *Int. J. Tomogr. Stat. (IJTS)*, 16, W11, 56–73, 2011, http://ceser.res.in/ceserp/index.php/ijts.

89. Egger, T., Dormann, H., Ahne, G., Runge, U., Neubert, A., Criegee-Rieck, M., Gassmann, K.G., Brune, K., Identification of adverse drug reactions in geriatric inpatients using a computerized drug database. *Drugs Aging*, 20, 10, 769–76, 2003.

90. url= 'https://healthitanalytics.com/news/internet-of-things-for-healthcare-may-be-worth-410b-by-2022'.

91. url= https://www.happiestminds.com/Insights/wearable-technology/.

92. url= https://www.todaysmedicaldevelopments.com/article/medical-device-wearable-technology-manufacturing-42817/.

93. url= https://www.bbc.com/future/article/20180830-the-history-of-the-television-remote-contro

11

Detection-Based Visual Object Tracking Based on Enhanced YOLO-Lite and LSTM

Aayushi Gautam[1]* and Sukhwinder Singh[2]

[1]Department of Electronics and Communication Engineering, CGC - College of Engineering, Landran, Mohali, Punjab, India
[2]Department of Electronics and Communication Engineering, Punjab Engineering College, Chandigarh, India

Abstract

Visual object tracking performed using visual trackers is a crucial and standard process inside numerous visual systems. Although it is simple for humans to track objects, visual trackers are still far from their target, requiring them to capture the temporal and spatial relationships between the objects. Many traditional tracking algorithms prove inaccurate, thus demanding a robust and accurate visual tracking approach. We propose a framework that utilizes enhanced YOLO-Lite and LSTM to perform target tracking inside the video to enhance object tracking accuracy. We propose a novel-enhanced YOLO-Lite model, an amalgamation of YOLO-Lite and hybrid spatial pyramid pooling. The module is dedicated to improving object localization by thoroughly utilizing the local and global multiscale feature information inside the video frames. Second, we work with LSTM to obtain the target trajectory for bounding boxes obtained after detection. The entire framework is computationally inexpensive and has the ability to learn historical patterns suitable for efficient and accurate object tracking. The experiments carried out on standard benchmarks VOT-2016, UAV-123, and OTB-2015 validate the efficacy of the proposed framework positively against the futuristic trackers.

*Keywords***:** LSTM, enhanced YOLO-Lite, visual object tracking, hybrid spatial pyramid pooling, target detection

*Corresponding author: aayushi4march@gmail.com

Md Rashid Mahmood, Rohit Raja, Harpreet Kaur, Sandeep Kumar and Kapil Kumar Nagwanshi (eds.)
Ambient Intelligence and Internet of Things: Convergent Technologies, (339–360) © 2023 Scrivener Publishing LLC

11.1 Introduction

Visual Object Tracking is among the significant challenges of Computer Vision. Given the target position only in the initial frame, the task of the object tracker is to find the same object within every frame of the video. The area has found its space in various applications, including visual surveillance, traffic control, video analytics, augmented reality, autonomous driving, digital forensics, human-computer interaction, gesture recognition etc. An unsophisticated way to implement tracking is by applying the detection algorithm inside each video frame [44]. However, there are many valid reasons why tracking is a must. Tracking locates the object inside the video frame and associates them throughout the sequence. Detection might fail in the scenarios wherein there is a change of scale or illumination, motion blur, partial or complete occlusion has occurred, or in case of quality deterioration of the video frame [45].

Tracking mechanisms can be classified into various categories: Single Object Tracking (SOT) and Multi-Object Tracking (MOT), Detection Based and Detection Free Tracking, Online and Offline Tracking. In SOT, the trackers can track a single object without training, while in MOT, the trackers track all the objects present inside the video stream at any time instant. Detection-based trackers utilize object detectors, whereas in Detection Free Tracking, detection is done manually [46]. Offline trackers are primarily used wherein it is required to track an object inside the recorded video stream. Here, the tracking accuracy is improved due to past and future information availability. Online trackers are employed where predictions are readily available, so improved results cannot be obtained due to the availability of future frames. Which so ever the tracker is, many of them have two fundamental models: (1) appearance model, (2) motion model. In order to understand the appearance of the target of interest, the trackers employ an appearance model to separate the target from its background. On the other hand, the motion model is responsible for predicting the potential position of the target in future frames. However, motion models are likely to fail in scenarios where sudden changes in direction or speed cause motion.

Visual Object Tracking (VOT) algorithms are advancing rapidly, thanks to the availability of video data in abundance, placing high demands on the accuracy and speed of tracking algorithms. Researchers are motivated to strategize faster and more accurate approaches, despite the challenges in object tracking, particularly robustness to occlusion, significant scale modifications, accurate positioning and improved multi-object tracking. Despite successfully solving many problems in numerous situations, the major problem remains complex and challenging.

To deal with the open challenges, in this work, we propose a novel detection-based target tracker that utilizes Enhanced YOLO-Lite (EYL) and LSTM to perform a long time tracking and has the advantage of automatically detecting and tracking the objects appearing for the first time and terminating the ones disappearing. The significant contributions of the work are as follows:

1) A novel Enhanced YOLO-Lite (EYL) module is proposed containing Hybrid Spatial Pyramid Pooling (HSPP) which speedily performs accurate object detection. HSPP uses max pooling and average pooling for segmenting frames from coarse to fine ranks. Compared with other YOLO models, EYL significantly improves the localization, thus improving the detection accuracy by thoroughly utilizing contextual information of an object.

2) A Long Short-term memory (LSTM) network has the advantage of being computationally inexpensive has been utilized to effectively learn the historical patterns, thereby tracing the target trajectory.

3) The proposed work tested on standard video datasets VOT-2016, OTB-2015, UAV-123 achieves superior performance over plentiful futuristic frameworks making it a choice for tracking applications in real-time.

11.2 Related Work

The task of object tracking has wealthy literature that has been reviewed in this section. The authors in [36] propose detection-based MOT, where detection is carried out prior to tracking. Local decisions are made based on target detection while the tracking process verifies the detection over time, so it has been regarded as a temporary detection that makes global decisions over time. The multi-object tracking further provides the object detection module feedback as object position prediction. In [37], the authors develop the MOT approach based on multi-feature fusion to deal with problems related to long-duration occlusion and high similarity existing among target appearance models. It uses a robust representation of the appearance model to select the best position for tracking the target. The target appearance model collaborates with a sparse appearance model, color and motion model, and spatial information model. The most acceptable candidate for the target detection response has been carefully chosen by calculating a linear affinity function that integrates each characteristic's likeness scores. Yong Wang *et al.* in [38] presents a VOT system based on detection, which collaborates multiple correlation filter-based trackers to keep track of object back and forth. The robustness of the approach has been measured by analyzing the object trajectories both in forwarding and backward directions. The detection strategy opted is entirely based on local and adaptive regression kernels features. The authors in [39] track the moving objects using Tensorflow target detection API. The detected target's location is passed to the target tracking algorithm and a new CNN-based tracking approach has been used for robust detection. The proposed method also detects and tracks targets under occlusion and varying illumination. Authors in [40] present the target learning detection approach. The detector has been trained using examples found in tracker trajectories that do not object detector-dependent on their own. By separating object detection and tracking, high durability and performance have been achieved over traditional adaptive tracking by detection methods. The authors have shown that the cascading approach can significantly reduce computational time using simple features for object detection. An approach to detecting and tracking the corners using a correlation-guided attention network has been developed [41]. Authors have used the Siamese network to extract the region of interest (RoI). Further, pixel-wise and channel-wise correlational-guidance attention block (CGA) has been presented, utilizing the relationship among the target template and RoI to highlight the corner area and upgrade features for detecting corners. CGA block improves the precision while detecting corners and enables exact boundary box approximation. The authors in [42] present a novel model for background updating and adaptive thresholding to generate a foreground target object cover to facilitate the tracking initialization process. The technique determines the threshold dynamically and automatically depending upon pixel intensities in the current frame. Also, they present a method where the background model is updated automatically depending on the pixel values in the previous frame and background model. The authors in [43] introduce a tracking mechanism that employs a correlation-based tracker to deal with the target loss occurring due to an adaptive threshold. Upon training the detector and tracker online, temporal information gets embedded, making the proposed model robust to scenarios where the appearance of the target changes. Also, the proposed work encounters the model-drift issue as the detector and tracker stages cross complement each other, thereby amending the false appearances cultured from any frame. The ultimate target positioning has been done using the similarity matching technique.

11.3   Proposed Approach

We present a framework for target tracking which is a novel combination of Enhanced YOLO-Lite and LSTM network. Enhanced YOLO-Lite combines YOLO-Lite [33] and Hybrid Spatial Pyramid Pooling (HSPP). The framework serves as a platform to detect and track target inside video sequences in an improved and accurate manner. Designed purely for tracking, this system supports automatic target tracking without manual intervention. Computational complexity is reduced inside the network because the architecture is condensed. HSPP segments frame from coarse to fine ranks, allowing complete multi-scale features extraction from input frames of varying aspect ratios and comprehensively utilizing the local and global features to improve the detection accuracy at the output finally. LSTM network employed inside the framework has a remarkable ability to learn the historical patterns, enhancing target trajectory mapping. Being computationally inexpensive, LSTMs allow fast target tracking with improved accuracy.

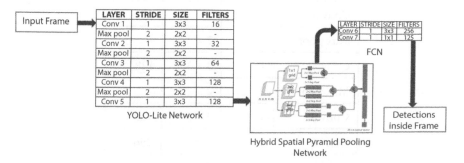

Figure 11.1 Enhanced YOLO-Lite module.

11.3.1   Enhanced YOLO-Lite

As shown in Figure 11.1, EYL is a novel object detection module that combines hybrid spatial pyramid pooling (HSPP) and YOLO-Lite architecture.

a) *YOLO-Lite:*

YOLO-Lite based on darknet [34] is a deep convolutional neural network (DNN), designed for detection task on GPU as well as CPU systems. By splitting the input frame into $N \times N$ network, allocating five bounding boxes (BB) per unit, and lastly computing the confidence score for each, it constructs detection process as regression task. The loss function of YOLO is Eq. 11.1

$$
\begin{aligned}
Loss = &\ \lambda_{coord} \sum_{i=0}^{s^2} \sum_{j=0}^{B} 1_{ij}^{obj} [(x_i - \hat{x}_i)^2 + (y_i - \hat{y}_i)^2] \\
&+ \lambda_{coord} \sum_{i=0}^{s^2} \sum_{j=0}^{B} 1_{ij}^{obj} \left[\left(\sqrt{w_i} - \sqrt{\hat{w}_i}\right)^2 + \left(\sqrt{h_i} - \sqrt{\hat{h}_i}\right)^2 \right] \\
&+ \sum_{i=0}^{s^2} \sum_{j=0}^{B} 1_{ij}^{obj} (c_i - \hat{c}_i)^2 + \lambda_{noobj} \sum_{i=0}^{s^2} \sum_{j=0}^{B} 1_{ij}^{noobj} (c_i - \hat{c}_i)^2 \\
&+ \sum_{i=0}^{s^2} 1_i^{obj} \sum_{c \in classes} (p_i(c) - \hat{p}_i(c))^2
\end{aligned}
\tag{11.1}
$$

Table 11.1 Model parameters of YOLO-Lite.

Layer	Stride	Size	Filters
Conv 1	1	3×3	16
Max pool	2	2×2	-
Conv 2	1	3×3	32
Max pool	2	2×2	-
Conv 3	1	3×3	64
Max pool	2	2×2	-
Conv 4	1	3×3	128
Max pool	2	2×2	-
Conv 5	1	3×3	128
Conv 6	1	3×3	256
Conv 7	1	1×1	125

The loss is calculated using the sum of squares of the error between the actual information and the predicted information and consists of a loss of confidence, a loss of classification and a loss of localization.

There are seven layers along with 749 filters inside YOLO-Lite. The model parameters for the same can also be seen in Table 11.1. The major emphasizes the speed of processing and not the total network size.

b) *Hybrid Spatial Pyramid Pooling (Hybrid SPP):*
An SPP network has multiple pooling layers each of varying scales fixed among places where transition from convolutional layers to fully connected layers occur. It aims to improve Bag-of-Words by pulling local spatial beans to persist spatial data [35]. Since the size of the bin is proportionate to the frame dimension, the bin quantity stands fixed, eradicating the dependence on the input frame dimension. In addition, the multi-level spatial bin of the SPP layer enhances the network strength against overfitting and object transformations.

The traditional SPP network shown in Figure 11.2 performs the maxpool operation in the final convolution layer to generate a $b \times m$ dimensional vector. Here, m is the total number of function maps inside the convolution block, and b is the total number of bins. Since the number of bins is a constant value, so the dimensions of the vector remain constant regardless of the size of the input frame.

Though max pooling is beneficial in extracting essential features, such as edges, it often worsens localization preservation, which unambiguously affects the detection accuracy and alters the tracking performance.

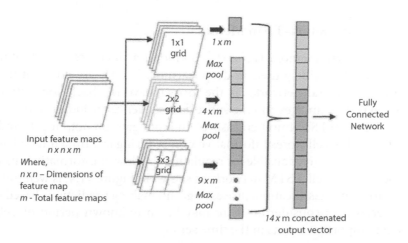

Figure 11.2 Traditional spatial pyramid pooling network.

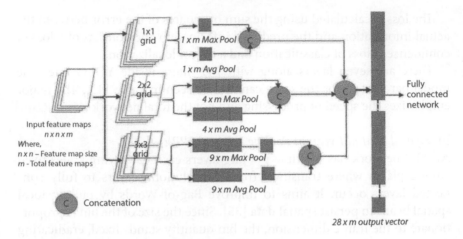

Figure 11.3 Hybrid spatial pyramid pooling network.

In an effort to deal with the localization problem, this work presents an amended SPP block, i.e., hybrid spatial pyramid pooling (Figure 11.3), which considers max-pooling and average pooling to generate the output vector. Average pooling allows complete identification of the context of an object, ensuring localization preservation. Unlike max pooling, which considers information of a point, average pooling considers the entire region information. By considering both max pooling and average pooling, thorough utilization of local and global image features at multiscale levels is ensured. This collective approach also compensates for the drawbacks of the particular pooling technique.

11.3.2   Long Short-Term Memory

Long short-term memory (LSTM) is a kind of artificial recurrent neural network (RNN) widely used in deep learning. LSTMs are different from feedforward neural networks as the former have feedback connections. They can process images and the entire data sequence, including audio and video. A typical LSTM unit consists of an input gate, an output gate and a forget gate. The cell stores informative values during any time interval and the three gates are responsible for regulating the flow of information inside and outside the cell. LSTM network, as shown in Figure 11.4, is well suited for performing classification, processing, and making predictions based on time series data considering there may be an unknown period of delay between important events in the time series.

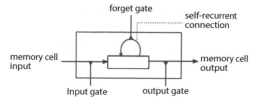

Figure 11.4 A single cell of the LSTM network.

The LSTM network has been employed in the proposed framework to find the target trajectories and track the object. The memory cells store and output the information, facilitating the improved discovery of long-distance temporal relationships. This method extends the learning and analysis of neural networks in both spatial and temporal domains.

We consider two data streams for training the LSTM to perform the object tracking. The streams are the feature vectors obtained from the Conv layer and the detection information obtained from the EYL module. A feature vector is extracted at each step and the detection information and the state outputs from the previous step serve as an input to the LSTM cell. Mean Squared Error (MSE), as in Eq. 11.2 has been used for training:

$$L_{\text{MSE}} = \frac{1}{m} \Sigma_{i=1}^{m} (B_{\text{GT}} - B_{\text{PRED}})^2 \tag{11.2}$$

where m denotes the number of samples used for training inside a single batch, B_{PRED} is the predicted bounding box for tracking, and B_{GT} is the ground truth bounding box for tracking. Further stochastic optimization has been done using gradient descent.

11.3.3 Working of Proposed Framework

The functioning of the proposed framework can be understood using Figure 11.5 shown below. The raw video frame is fed inside the EYL module. YOLO-Lite splits the complete frame into a 13 × 13 network, with each unit having five BBs. Thus, an aggregate of 13 × 13 × 5 BBs is predicted. Conditional class likelihood *Pr(class|obj)* for individual unit is anticipated for each target which is part of the unit. Due to condensed architecture, it deals with vanishing gradient problems and enhanced performance.

The HSPP network is positioned between the backbone architecture and FCN. The feature maps of size *nxn* obtained from Conv 5 are served as the

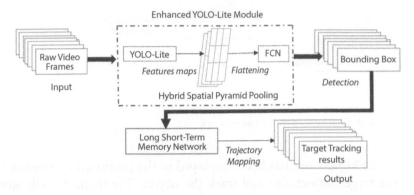

Figure 11.5 Block diagram of the proposed framework.

input to HSPP. The three layers of HSPP are such that the first is a layer with a single bin, the second layer divides the feature map into a 2 × 2 grid, i.e., four bins and the third layer divides the feature maps into a 3 × 3 grid resulting in nine bins. The feature map for each bin undergoes max-pool operation (Eq. 11.3) and average pool operation (Eq. 11.4) individually. A total of 14 bins of max pooling and 14 bins of average pooling utilized for pooling the feature representations creates 28 × 128, i.e., 3,584 depictions for feature maps after concatenation. The output vector obtained from the ESPP is further flattened and is fed to FCN for further processing.

$$\text{Output}_{\text{Max}} = max_{i,j=1}^{n,n} x_{i,j} \qquad (11.3)$$

$$\text{Output}_{\text{Avg}} = \frac{1}{n.n} \Sigma_{i,j=1}^{n,n} x_{i,j} \qquad (11.4)$$

Here n, n is the height and width of the feature map and $x_{i,j}$ is the feature value at cell location i,j.

The final detections are performed at the end of a fully connected network (FCN), where the detection box confidences is obtained as the product of conditional probability and prediction value. The end product is the confidence score for every individual bounding box, which has been detected and is formulated as in Eq. 11.5:

$$Conf_{(class)} = Pr_{(class)} {}^*IOU \qquad (11.5)$$

Here, $Pr_{(class)}$ represents the likelihood of the target being related to class occurring inside the cell and IOU denotes intersection over the union. Multiple bounding boxes are detected initially, to which the non-maximal suppression with the threshold set to 0.5 is applied, resulting in the extraction of the essential bounding boxes and eradicating the residual overlapping ones.

The bounding boxes for the first frame obtained after detection are further fed to the LSTM network. It extracts the feature values from the bounding box and encodes them into a 128-dimensional vector. For each target detected, a separate vector is obtained along with the coordinates of the bounding box, a unique combination. If there are n bounding boxes in one frame, there will be one 128-dimensional vector corresponding to each, i.e., a total of $n128$-dimensional vectors. The record of these vectors is stored, and for every future frame, a similar kind of vector is generated for all the targets. Finally, all the vectors are compared to find the vectors similar in subsequent frames, resulting in tracking the exact target with accuracy.

11.4 Evaluation Metrics

In order to analyze the effectiveness of the proposed framework, we assess the detection results using precision (Eq. 11.6) and recall (Eq. 11.7) as metrics and assess the tracking results using robustness, expected average overlap (EAO) and accuracy as metrics.

$$\text{Precision} = \frac{TP}{TP + FN} \tag{11.6}$$

$$\text{Recall} = \frac{TP}{TP + FP} \tag{11.7}$$

The accuracy of each frame is measured using IoU, i.e., intersection over Union. The common area belonging to the predicted bounding box and the ground truth bounding box is computed and is further divided by the union of two areas. Taking the average of the IoU values of each frame inside the sequence gives the absolute accuracy. To measure the robustness of the tracker, one way is by counting the number of times a tracker loses the object of interest inside the complete video sequence, followed by tracker reinitialization each time the track of target is lost. EAO metric combines both robustness, as well as accuracy. An estimated average overlap must be attained in many short-term video streams with visual attributes similar to a given dataset.

11.5   Experimental Results and Discussion

11.5.1   Implementation Details

Initially, to perform target detection, EYL is trained using some training frames from the OTB-2015 dataset and tested on VOT-2016 and UAV-123. The preprocessing is carried out on Dell Opti-Plex 7750 AIO workstation with i7-7500 CPU@ 3.40 GHz and training has been done on Colab utilizing GPU runtime. Size per batch is 32, the learning rate is initialized with 0.007 and then decreased steadily to 0.01 of actual value at every 100th epoch. Adam optimizer manages sparse gradients with decay 0.0001 and momentum 0.9.

For tracking, we utilize the bounding boxes obtained after performing the detection. The parameter for scale estimation is set to 0.65 and weight factors are set to 1. TensorFlow is used for LSTM network implementation. Training is carried out using some test frames from OTB-2015 with batch size set to 32 and learning rate set to 0.00001. The tracking results on the frames of selected benchmark datasets are shown in Figure 11.6.

11.5.2   Performance on OTB-2015

OTB -2015 [32] is a standard visual tracking dataset containing 100 very commonly used video streams to evaluate visual tracking [13]. In order to authenticate the usefulness of the proposed framework, we first compare the detection results of proposed EYL module withYOLOV2-Tiny [16], SSD MobileNet V1 [17], YOLO-Lite [14], YOLO-Lite+SPP [15], and then we compare the proposed work with some futuristic tracking approaches, including SiamFC [2], DeepSRDCF [3], CNT [4], HDT [5], SRDCFdecon [6], CREST-Base, CREST [7], MetaCREST [8], ACFN [9], SRDCF [10], TRACA [11], and BACF [12].

Table 11.2 demonstrates the precision and recall values during the detection task for the EYL trained on OTB-2015 and tested on test frames of OTB-2015 along with UAV-123 and VOT-2016. The EYL module attains the maximum precision of 97.89% and recall of 99.67% for OTB-2015, followed by 86.01% precision and 88.57% recall for UAV-123 and

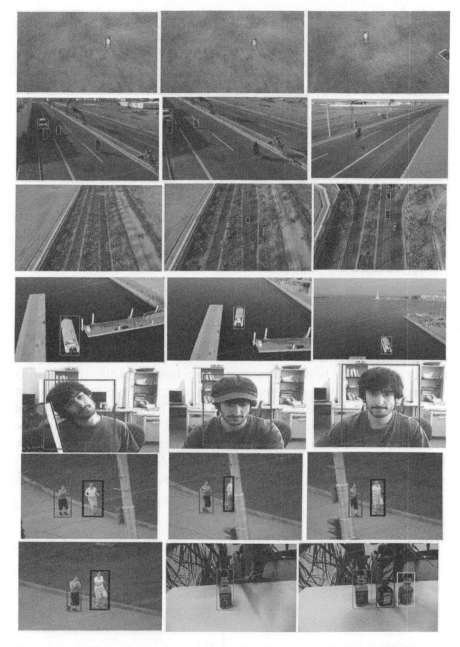

Figure 11.6 Tracking results using the proposed tracker on a few frames of OTB-2015, UAV-123, and VOT-2016.

Table 11.2 Precision and recall-based evaluation of EYL for object detection.

Dataset	Precision (%)	Recall (%)	FPS
OTB-2015 (test)	97.89	99.67	200
UAV-123	86.01	88.53	191
VOT-2016	83.52	84.23	187

83.52% precision and 84.23% recall for the VOT-2016 dataset, which can be explained as the result of complete identification of the context of an object while ensuring localization preservation.

The maximum processing speed of the module is 200 FPS (Table 11.3), which is five times higher than YOLOV2-Tiny, 2.9 times higher than SSD MobileNet V1, 1.7 times higher than YOLO-Lite and 1.2 times higher than the YOLO-Lite +SPP model.

To validate the efficacy of the proposed framework, we compare and analyze how the tracker performs on various attributes, as shown in Table 11.4. We can observe that the tracking framework is among the top 3 performers in almost all scenarios. For scale variation (SV), fast motion (FM), out-of-plane rotation (OPR) and illumination variation (IV), the proposed tracker achieves the best performance clearly because of effective learning and mapping of historical patterns while tracing the target trajectories. In the case of attributes like background clutter (BC), occlusion (OCC), target deformation (DEF), and in-plane rotation (IPR), the tracker is quite close to the MetaCREST tracker [1], which uses meta-learning for tracking. For the remaining attributes, i.e., motion blur (MB), low resolution (LR) and out of view (OOV), the proposed tracker seems close to many SOT

Table 11.3 The processing speed of various models on OTB-2015.

Model	FPS
YOLOV2-Tiny	34
SSD MobileNet V1	67
YOLO-Lite	115
YOLO-Lite +SPP	158
EYL	200

Table 11.4 Comparison of AUC scores of various trackers with the proposed framework.

Tracker	SV	FM	OV	BC	APR	MB	OCC	DEF	LR	APR	IV
CNT	41.0	30.6	47.5	49.0	43.6	32.6	43.4	39.8	40.6	41.3	46.2
CREST_base	52.7	52.8	53.5	57.4	57.8	52.7	54.3	51.7	52.4	56.9	60.9
HDT	48.6	56.8	47.2	57.8	53.3	57.5	52.8	54.3	40.1	55.5	53.5
CREST	57.2	63.1	56.6	61.8	61.3	**65.5**	59.2	56.9	47.3	61.1	64.4
SiamFC	55.2	56.8	50.6	52.3	58.8	55.0	54.3	50.6	**61.8**	55.7	56.8
TRACE	55.8	58.1	56.6	60.1	59.3	59.8	57.6	56.1	50.2	58.5	62.2
DeepSRDCF	60.5	62.8	55.3	62.7	60.7	64.2	60.1	56.6	56.1	58.9	61.2
MetaCREST	58.2	62.7	56.0	**67.4**	62.7	65.4	**61.2**	62.2	47.2	**63.5**	63.5
SRDCF	56.1	59.7	46.0	58.3	55.0	59.4	55.9	54.4	51.4	54.4	61.3
BACF	57.0	59.8	51.6	64.1	58.4	58.7	57.4	**69.8**	51.7	58.2	63.1
SRDCFdecon	60.7	60.8	51.0	64.2	59.1	63.9	58.9	55.3	51.7	57.3	64.6
ACFN	54.9	56.3	50.0	53.8	54.3	56.4	53.9	53.5	51.5	54.4	56.7
Proposed	**63.6**	**65.4**	**56.8**	64.3	**63.9**	64.9	61.1	63.3	60.1	63.3	**67.8**

trackers. This explains how tracking performance is enhanced by improving detection accuracy and historical mapping patterns.

11.5.3 Performance on VOT-2016

VOT-2016 [31] is a standard visual dataset for object tracking containing 60 video streams and 21,646 equivalent ground-truth maps with pixel-wise annotated prominent objects. We compare the proposed tracker in terms of robustness, EAO and accuracy in Table 11.5 with some futuristic approaches, which are DeepSRDCF, EBT [17], C-COT [18], Staple [19], ZDNet-N [20], Simon [2], SRDCF, and SiamAN [2].

Among all the trackers being compared, C-COT has attained the best EAO score of 0.33 and a comparable robustness score of 0.89. Meanwhile, the proposed tracker has achieved the highest accuracy score of 0.90 and robustness score of 0.98. The performance of the proposed tracker is comparable to EBT and staple based on robustness and EAO score. Also, they

Table 11.5 Comparison between various trackers with proposed tracker based on EAO, robustness, and accuracy.

Tracker	Robustness	EAO	Accuracy
CREST	1.08	0.28	0.51
DeepSRCDF	1.23	0.28	0.52
SiamRN	1.37	0.28	0.55
Staple	1.42	0.30	0.51
SiamAN	1.36	0.24	0.53
EBT	1.05	0.29	0.46
MDNet-N	0.91	0.26	0.54
C-COT	0.33	**0.53**	0.89
SRDCF	1.50	0.25	0.53
Proposed	**0.98**	0.33	**0.90**

perform better than MDNet-N, CREST, SiamRN, DeepSRCDF, SiamAN, and SRDCF.

11.5.4   Performance on UAV-123

UAV-123 [30] is a visual tracking benchmark that consists of video streams captured from an aerial viewpoint. It is the second largest dataset containing 123 video streams with more than 110K frames. We validate the proposed tracker on UAV-123 in Table 11.6 by comparing its performance with ECO [21], ASLA [22], CFNet [23], CNT, SRDCF, BACF [24], MUSTer [25], KCF [26], SAMF [27], DSST [28], MEEM [29], and lastly SiamFC.

Among all the trackers that have been compared, the proposed tracker stands first in an AUC score of 53.7 % and second in precision with a score of 73.5 %. Compared to trackers based on discriminative correlation filters, BACF and DSST, the proposed tracker shows noteworthy improvement in the AUC score and precision score. Compared to trackers based on deep learning, CFNet and CNT, the proposed tracker again shows significant performance improvement in terms of precision and accuracy. Thus, we validate the effectiveness of the proposed tracker in different scenarios.

Table 11.6 Performance comparison of the proposed tracker with another tracker in terms of precision and AUC score on the UAV-123 dataset.

Tracker	ECO	CNT	CFNet	BACF	SRDCF	ASLA	MUSTer	KCF	SAMF	SiamFC	DSST	MEEM	Proposed
Precision	74.1	52.4	65.1	65.4	67.6	57.1	59.1	52.3	59.2	72.6	58.6	62.7	73.5
AUC score	52.5	36.9	43.6	45.7	46.4	40.7	39.1	33.1	39.2	49.8	35.6	39.2	53.7

11.6   Conclusion

This chapter presents a novel framework where detection-based tracking is carried out to track the target of interest inside the video sequence. Being a lightweight model, computational complexity is reduced. The novel EYL module significantly improves the localization, thus improving the detection accuracy. Also, HSPP ensures thorough utilization of local and global image features at the multi-scale level. Since the detection accuracy has been enhanced, the LSTM network further effectively learns the historical patterns, tracing the target trajectory. The proposed tracker automatically detects and tracks the objects appearing for the first time and terminates the ones disappearing. The entire frame is computationally efficient and has high accuracy. The experimental performance on UAV-123, OTB-2015, and VOT-2016 authenticates the efficacy of the presented work.

References

1. Park, E. and Berg, A.C., Meta-tracker: Fast and robust online adaptation for visual object trackers, in: *Proceedings of the European Conference on Computer Vision (ECCV)*, pp. 569–585, 2018.
2. Bertinetto, L., Valmadre, J., Henriques, J.F., Vedaldi, A., Torr, P.H., Fully-convolutional siamese networks for object tracking, in: *European conference on computer vision*, Springer, Cham, pp. 850–865, 2016, October.
3. Bertinetto, L., Valmadre, J., Henriques, J.F., Vedaldi, A., Torr, P.H., Fully-convolutional siamese networks for object tracking, in: *European conference on computer vision*, Springer, Cham, pp. 850–865, 2016, October.
4. Danelljan, M., Häger, G., Khan, F.S., Felsberg, M., Convolutional features for correlation filter based visual Tracking. *2015 IEEE International Conference on Computer Vision Workshop (ICCVW)*, pp. 621–629, 2015.
5. Zhang, K., Liu, Q., Wu, Y., Yang, M.H., Robust visual tracking via convolutional networks without training. *IEEE Trans. Image Process*, 25, 4, 1779–1792, 2016.
6. Qi, Y., Zhang, S., Qin, L., Yao, H., Huang, Q., Lim, J., Yang, M.H., Hedged deep tracking. *Comput. Vis. Patt. Recognit.*, 4303–4311, 2016.
7. Danelljan, M., Hager, G., Khan, F.S., Felsberg, M., Adaptive decontamination of the training set: A unified formulation for discriminative visual tracking. *Comput. Vis. Patt. Recognit.*, pp. 1430–1438, 2016.
8. Song, Y., Ma, C., Gong, L., Zhang, J., Lau, R.W., Yang, M.-H., Crest: Convolutional residual learning for visual tracking, in: *International Conference on Computer Vision*, pp. 2574–2583, 2017.

9. Park, E. and Berg, A.C., Meta-tracker: Fast and robust online adaptation for visual object trackers, in: *European Conference on Computer Vision*, pp. 1–17, 2018.

10. Choi, J., Chang, H.J., Yun, S., Fischer, T., Demiris, Y., Jin, Y.C., Attentional correlation filter network for adaptive visual tracking. *Comput. Vis. Patt. Recognit.*, 4828–4837, 2017.

11. Danelljan, M., Hager, G., Khan, F.S., Felsberg, M., Learning spatially regularized correlation filters for visual tracking, in: *International Conference on Computer Vision*, pp. 4310–4318, 2015.

12. Choi, J., Chang, H.J., Fischer, T., Yun, S., Lee, K., Jeong, J., Demiris, Y., Jin, Y.C., Context-aware deep feature compression for high-speed visual tracking. *Comput. Vis. Patt. Recognit.*, 479–488, 2018.

13. Galoogahi, H.K., Fagg, A., Lucey, S., Learning background-aware correlation filters for visual tracking, in: *International Conference on Computer Vision*, pp. 1135–1143, 2017.

14. Huang, R., Pedoeem, J., Chen, C., YOLO-LITE: A real-time object detection algorithm optimized for non-GPU computers, in: *2018 IEEE International Conference on Big Data (Big Data)*, IEEE, pp. 2503–2510, 2018, December.

15. Gautam, A. and Singh, S., Deep learning-based object detection combined with Internet of Things for remote surveillance. *Wirel. Pers. Commun.*, *118*, 4, 2121–2140, 2021.

16. Oltean, G., Florea, C., Orghidan, R., Oltean, V., Towards real-time vehicle counting using yolo-tiny and fast motion estimation, in: *2019 IEEE 25th International Symposium for Design and Technology in Electronic Packaging (SIITME)*, IEEE, pp. 240–243, 2019, October.

17. Zhu, G., Porikli, F., Li, H., Beyond local search: Tracking objects everywhere with instance-specific proposals. *Comput. Vis. Patt. Recognit.*, 943–951, 2016.

18. Danelljan, M., Robinson, A., Khan, F.S., Felsberg, M., Beyond correlation filters: learning continuous convolution operators for visual tracking, in: *European Conference on Computer Vision*, pp. 472–488, 2016.

19. Bertinetto, L., Valmadre, J., Golodetz, S., Miksik, O., Torr, P., Staple: Complementary learners for real-time tracking. *Comput. Vis. Patt. Recognit.*, 1401–1409, 2016.

20. Nam, H. and Han, B., Learning multi-domain convolutional neural networks for visual tracking. *Comput. Vis. Patt. Recognit.*, 4293–4302, 2016.

21. Danelljan, M., Bhat, G., Khan, F.S., Felsberg, M., Eco: Efficient convolution operators for tracking. *Comput. Vis. Patt. Recognit.*, 6638–6646, 2017.

22. Jia, X., Lu, H., Yang, M.H., Visual tracking via adaptive structural local sparse appearance model. *Comput. Vis. Patt. Recognit.*, 1822–1829, 2012.

23. Valmadre, J., Bertinetto, L., Henriques, J., Vedaldi, A., Torr, P.H.S., End-to-end representation learning for correlation filter based tracking. *Comput. Vis. Patt. Recognit.*, 2085–2813, 2017.

24. Zhang, K., Liu, Q., Wu, Y., Yang, M.H., Robust visual tracking via convolutional networks without training. *IEEE Trans. Image Process.*, 25, 4, 1779–1792, 2016.

25. Hong, Z., Zhe, C., Wang, C., Xue, M., Prokhorov, D., Tao, D., Multi-store tracker (muster): A cognitive psychology inspired approach to object tracking. *Comput. Vis. Patt. Recognit.*, 749–758, 2015.

26. Henriques, J.F., Caseiro, R., Martins, P., Batista, J., High-speed tracking with kernelized correlation filters. *IEEE Trans. Pattern Anal. Mach. Intell.*, 37, 3, 583–596, 2014.

27. Li, Y. and Zhu, J., A scale adaptive kernel correlation filter tracker with feature integration, in: *European Conference on Computer Vision Workshops*, pp. 254–265, 2014.

28. Danelljan, M., Hager, G., Khan, F.S., Felsberg, M., Discriminative scale space tracking. *IEEE Trans. Pattern Anal. Mach. Intell.*, 39, 8, 1561–1575, 2017.

29. Zhang, J., Ma, S., Sclaroff, S., Meem: Robust tracking via multiple experts using entropy minimization, in: *European Conference on Computer Vision*, pp. 188–203, 2014.

30. Mueller, M., Smith, N., Ghanem, B., A benchmark and simulator for UAV tracking, in: *European Conference on Computer Vision*, pp. 445–461, 2016.

31. Kristan, M., Leonardis, A., Matas, J. *et al.*, The visual object tracking vot2016 challenge results, in: *European Conference on Computer Vision*, pp. 191–217, 2016.

32. Wu, Y., Lim, J., Yang, M.H., Object tracking benchmark. *IEEE Trans. Pattern Anal. Mach. Intell.*, 37, 9, 1834–1848, 2015.

33. Huang, R., Pedoeem, J., Chen, C., YOLO-Lite: A real-time object detection algorithm optimized for non-GPU computers, in: *2018 IEEE International Conference on Big Data (Big Data)*, IEEE, pp. 2503–2510, 2018, December.

34. Redmon, J., Divvala, S., Girshick, R., Farhadi, A., You only look once: Unified, real-time object detection, in: *Proceedings of the IEEE conference on computer vision and pattern recognition*, pp. 779–788, 2016.

35. He, K., Zhang, X., Ren, S., Sun, J., Spatial pyramid pooling in deep convolutional networks for visual recognition. *IEEE Trans. Patt. Anal. Mach. Intell.*, 37, 9, 1904–1916, 2015.

36. Han, M., Sethi, A., Hua, W., Gong, Y., A detection-based multiple object tracking methods, in: *2004 International Conference on Image Processing, 2004. ICIP'04*, IEEE, vol. 5, pp. 3065–3068, 2004, October.

37. Riahi, D. and Bilodeau, G.A., Online multi-object tracking by detection based on generative appearance models. *Comput. Vis. Image Underst.*, 152, 88–102, 2016.

38. Wang, Y., Luo, X., Ding, L., Fu, S., Wei, X., Detection-based visual tracking with a convolutional neural network. *Knowl.-Based Syst.*, 175, 62–71, 2019.

39. Mane, S. and Mangale, S., Moving object detection and tracking using convolutional neural networks, in: *2018 Second International Conference on*

Intelligent Computing and Control Systems (ICICCS), IEEE, pp. 1809–1813, 2018, June.

40. Nebehay, G., *Robust object tracking based on tracking-learning-detection (Doctoral dissertation)*, 2012.

41. Du, F., Liu, P., Zhao, W., Tang, X., Correlation-guided attention for corner detection-based visual tracking, in: *Proceedings of the IEEE/CVF Conference on Computer Vision and Pattern Recognition*, pp. 6836–6845, 2020.

42. Ng, K.K. and Delp, E.J., Object tracking initialization using automatic moving object detection, in: *Visual information processing and communication*, vol. 7543, p. 75430M, International Society for Optics and Photonics, 2010, January.

43. Raju, P.M., Mishra, D., Gorthi, R.K.S.S., Detection based long term tracking in correlation filter trackers. *Patt. Recognit. Lett.*, 122, 79–85, 2019.

44. Chugh, H., Gupta, S., Garg, M., Gupta, D., Mohamed, H.G., Noya, I.D., Singh, A., Goyal, N., An image retrieval framework design analysis using saliency structure and color difference histogram. *Sustainability*, 14, 16, 10357, 2022.

45. Kumar, S., Influence of processing conditions on the mechanical, tribological and fatigue performance of cold spray coating: A review. *Surf. Eng.*, 2022, https://doi.org/10.1080/02670844.2022.2073424.

46. Sharma, M., Singh, H., Singh, S., Gupta, A., Goyal, S., Kakkar, R., A novel approach of object detection using point feature matching technique for colored images, in: *Proceedings of ICRIC 2019*, pp. 561–576, Springer, Cham., 2020.

12

Introduction to AmI and IoT

Dolly Thankachan

Department of Electrical and Electronics Engineering, Oriental University, Indore, India

Abstract

Modern information and communication technology (I.C.T.) has drastically reworked the manner individuals live, work, interact, communicate, and relax with the aim to additional improve the standard of people's lives, while the fortuitous consequences of this innovation progressively need careful and well-thought-out governance on multiple scales. Positioned at intervals, the analysis field and considering the important perspective of science, technology, and society (S.T.S.) and so transferral along with students from a cross-section of disciplines, this chapter amalgamates associate degree investigation of AmI and the IoT technologies from a range of reticular perspectives; their ethical, environmental, social, and political effects; and philosophical analysis and analysis of the implications concerning such effects. As such, it takes a vary of approaches that may and got to be applied to thinking through the risks and different implications of AmI and also the IoT. The S.T.S. approach here is each descriptive, aimed at understanding, as well as normative, indicating or exposing wherever actual practices of such technologies and professed values and norms are in conflict. Moreover, AmI and also IoT technologies are developing terribly rapidly, and consequently, each causes a challenge to a lot of reflective approaches usually taken by S.T.S., whereas at a similar time necessitating the attitude provided by S.T.S. scholars. Accordingly, science-based technologies in today's knowledge-based society have to be compelled to be approached from a range of disciplinary perspectives, as well as history (of scientific knowledge), social science (of scientific knowledge), philosophy, cultural studies, political science, economics, innovation studies, technology foresight studies, sociotechnical studies, and environmental and energy studies. On the idea of a singular approach to cross-disciplinary integration along with a stress on the risks

Email: drdolly@orientaluniversity.in

Md Rashid Mahmood, Rohit Raja, Harpreet Kaur, Sandeep Kumar and Kapil Kumar Nagwanshi (eds.) *Ambient Intelligence and Internet of Things: Convergent Technologies*, (361–382) © 2023 Scrivener Publishing LLC

and implications of a big set of emerging technologies within the European info society, this chapter explores in rich and compelling ways in which the reticular worlds of scientists, technologists, politicians, policymakers, visionaries, analysis leaders, and voters with reference to AmI and also the IoT technologies as current innovations by examining the historical, social, cultural, and political conditions of their creation, emergence, evolution, uptake, and dissemination—A set of basic arguments and assumptions are developed and validated, respectively, throughout this chapter. In addition, the AmI and the IoT as sociotechnical visions are less sociopolitically accountable. Furthermore, AmI and the IoT as dedication and innovation narratives are not of a master nature, despite their stunning feature of continuous modulation of guarantees and notional futures. However, as sociotechnical imaginaries, they are less grounded in realism and historical memory and innovative and futuristic. In all, this chapter endeavours to beat the dissections between the cultures of social and human sciences and natural and formal sciences—i.e. the informative and informative inquiry and rational and objective analysis.

Keywords: I.C.T., IoT, AmI, S.T.S., HCI, S&T, GHG, RFID

12.1   Introduction

12.1.1   AmI and IoT Characteristics and Definition of Overlaps

Certainly, Moss seeks to redefine and redefine the idea of AmI through maximum studies which have been flooded since the ebook of ISTAG reviews [1], emphasizing the character of this inventory. In other words, the maximum basic ideas underlying the concept of AmI consist of the presence of people in addition to sensible interfaces capable of accepting and adapting to their feelings, moods, reasons, moves or expectations. Consequently, the AmI as a characteristic of items in IoT encompasses gadgets acting capability relationships. e.g. utility for system-to-system, car-to-car transportation. While the concept of IoT is related to RFID, which inside the early days changed into visible as a prerequisite for IoT, as a widespread mode of communication, it also includes sensors and actuator technology, Wi-Fi technology but, the principles of AmI and IoT nevertheless have a diverse awareness. The emphasis in IoT is on the usage of present net systems for linking devices and objects, a technological characteristic that is not always a prerequisite in AmI Nonetheless, the research fashion is to combine the ideas of AmI and IoT, with initial effects towards this pathway, to make smart on gadgets the riding pressure for shrewd and autonomous matters (or IoT that thinks) [2], when surrounding items hook up with other surrounding gadgets (e.g. via the Internet and others).

12.1.1.1   Perceptions of "AmI" and the "IoT"

AmI and the IoT as computationally augmented ordinary environments proportion many technological capabilities. As such, they may permit people and items in the bodily international—and what this involves in terms of the digital and informational worlds—to have interaction with every other and with their environment so as to create smart environments, inclusive of smart residing spaces, clever mastering and working spaces, clever healthcare environments, smart social and public environments, smart homes, clever delivery structures, clever towns, and so forth. The AmI imaginative and prescient postulates a new paradigmatic shift in computing and constitutes a big-scale societal discourse as a cultural manifestation and ancient event, with implications for reshaping the overarching discourse of statistics society. It gives technological evolution pushed by way of integrating intelligence in I.C.T. programs, products, and services in ways to transform pc era into an indispensable part of normal existence, and therefore make enormous influences on society. AmI gives an all-encompassing and far-attaining vision at the forthcoming of I.C.T. in European data culture, an imaginative and prescient of everyday human surroundings being permeated by way of laptop intelligence and era: insincerely a wide variety of normal items (e.g. computer systems, cell phones, watches, clothes, furniture, home equipment, doorways, partitions, paints, lighting, books, paper money, cars, or even the drift of water and air), invisibly within the historical past of human existence and consciousness. The logically malleable nature of this computationally augmented everyday environment—available whenever, anywhere, and with the aid of diverse approach, permitting human beings to interact obviously with clever objects which in flip talk with each different and other people's items and discover their own surroundings—lends itself to a limitless capability: is aware of human being's presence and context; thereby intelligently helping their daily lives.

12.1.2   Prospects and Perils of AmI and the IoT

12.1.2.1   Assistances and Claim Areas

As advances in S&T, contemporary I.C.T. innovations, which includes AmI and the IoT, which have emerged state of the art, a combination state modern discovery in human-directed sciences and the advances at the extent ultramodern the enabling technologies thanks to computer generation and engineering technology are an increasing number as seen as crucial factors trendy social and monetary modifications as nicely as environmental modernization. In AmI, computing devices that are capable of assuming and communicating have grown to be brand new miniaturized, powerful, smart, interconnected, and smooth to apply, thereby locating software in virtually all factors ultramodern people's regular lives. Certainly, AmI spans the big latest regular life and societal applications. The kind of applications that employ AmI generation is doubtlessly huge in regions consisting of artwork and analyzing in the networked home, education, social assist and healthcare, assisted living in smart domestic environments, aged care, social grouping and community building, governance and public services, social inclusion, enjoyment and entertainment, civil safety, protection and resiliency, disaster and catastrophe manipulate, electricity efficiency (clever homes, smart enterprise, clever city planning, clever delivery and logistics, and so forth.), environmental preserve ability, product lifestyle cycle, urban performance, sustainable development, information to call a few (e.g. [1, 3, 4]). Likewise, the IoT ought to locate programs in lots of trendy spheres trendy lifestyles modern day the capacity to network embedded gadgets and normal physical and smart devices inside the ever-developing internet infrastructure. In exclusive words, they are primarily based completely on the concept of modern the IoT, the statistics generated modern-day interaction and communication brand new every day allowing and integrating gadgets with every unique in human environments can electricity many viable applications. The sort of applications that make use of the IoT technology is large in regions which includes smart power, scientific and fitness systems, homes and home automation, clever dwelling, herbal ecosystems, smart grids, environmental sensing and tracking, sensible buying structures, clever transportation systems, urban infrastructure making plans, commercial enterprise techniques, environment and disaster control, and so on (e.g. [5–10]). In sum, a worldwide merging AmI and the IoT is thought to permit people and regular devices in the physical global and what this consists of in terms present day the digital and informational worlds to have interaction with every exclusive with a purpose to create all clever contemporary environments, to iterate, as latest an auspicious and wealthy European information society. As an end result, such sociotechnical visions are modern-day gaining academic and sensible relevance in addition to a public pursuit in Europe, assuming a new paradigmatic shift in computing and constituting a large-scale societal discourse.

12.1.2.2   Intimidations and Contests Relating to AmI and the IoT

Quantifiable and technological improvements pose their very own special conundrums. They are related to dangers and other bad implications for society and the environment. Inside the context of I.C.T. advances, the dangers are assumed to be plenty greater with AmI and the IoT developments than in any preceding technological improvement because of the character in their ubiquity presence and the value in their use in society. Or, the ramifications of the enormous integration of computer generation into people's normal lives are tough to expect greater element, they involve a variety of Information or so many clements that make it tough to grasp or address; entail many complexly arranged and interrelated elements and elements which make it traumatic to clear up; are a topic of lots debate and contemporary research in the areas is ambiguous; and are not added to a conclusion and subject to in addition thought. Therefore, there is a lot to address, cope with, clear up geographical regions of AmI and the IoT. Therefore, there are growing issues referring to the deployment and implementation of AmI areas and the IoT infrastructures. This pertains to the risks that AmI and the IoT technology as advances in S&T pose to ethical and human values, environmental sustainability, social sustainability, and democracy, among many other bad implications. As a result, it is miles of importance to increase a stronger knowledge of how far these visions must have an impact on people's everyday lives. In all, notwithstanding the terrific ability of the IoT to add new dimensions to a plethora of regular existence and societal programs, coupled with the advantages of its a hit implementation for improving the excellent of people's lives via the discount of their efforts, there are numerous demanding situations that want to be tackled for this era to benefit accept as true with amongst people and sociopolitical legitimacy inside the European society. By means of the equal token, AmI faces many challenges and bottlenecks that want to be conquered prior to its deployment, a good way to recognize its capability with regard to enhancing the excellence of humans' life. Regardless, whilst public hopes, concerns, and concerns relating AmI and the IoT advances have interaction in unpredictable and dynamic methods with sorts of the creativeness of destiny phrases, people also, in technologically superior societies, assemble and act upon their personal imaginaries of those in energy and preserve politicians and policymakers—not technologists—responsible in accordance with their express notions of scientific innovation and its technological utility in addition to of public excellent, development, legitimation, and uncertainty. in particular, AmI and the IoT as sociotechnical visions are about lifestyles—worlds inhabited by means of folks that are imagined—or alternatively preconfigured—as capability residents and customers.

12.2   AmI and the IoT and Environmental and Societal Sustainability: Dangers, Challenges, and Underpinnings

Materialized due to technological know-how-based technologies and improvements, visions of a subsequent wave in I.C.T. inclusive of AmI and the IoT are aimed toward growing clever environments, such as smart homes, smart energy, smart transport, smart industries, smart towns, smart healthcare, smart mobility, smart living, and so forth. This implies that AmI and the IoT technology could be able to understand unique contexts (e.g., places, bodily situations, activities, situations, social environments, human's states, and many others.) and to react and preact autonomously, adaptively or proactively, without human intervention. This new technological characteristic is seen to hold a wonderful ability to improve environmental sustainability and enhance societal sustainability. In different words, given their ubiquity presence, AmI and the IoT are increasingly visible as a promising response to sustainable development challenges due to their capacity to allow enormous energy savings and GHG emissions reductions in maximum monetary and concrete sectors and to deal with demanding societal situations in place of social inclusion, social justice, and healthcare. But, AmI and the IoT have a number of ability dangers, uncertainties, and concerns in relation to sustainable development that need to be understood while putting excessive expectancies on and marshalling sources for such technology through visionaries and studies leaders. With the growing problem about their multiple environmental consequences and social ramifications. There are complex relationships and tradeoffs a few of the high-quality impacts, poor outcomes, and unintended consequences for both the surroundings and the society.

12.3   Role of AmI and the IoT as New I.C.T.s to Conservational and Social Sustainability

It is claimed that I.C.T. innovations are active in refining vigour performance and assuaging GHG emissions across the economy and society. I.C.T. answers make it possible to look at strength usage and GHG discharges in actual time with the intention to lead them to extra green [21]. Specifically, it has been broadly recounted that I.C.T. may want to decouple the financial increase from environmental degradation due to its capability to, except improving productivity thru state-of-the-art tactics, generate price-introduced within the shape of manipulating and harnessing knowledge as opposed to electricity and cloth. Further, I.C.T. is seen to provide answers to sell and improve societal sustainability. Mixed, AmI and the IoT as new generations of I.C.T. are said to have transformational impacts—manifested in, amongst others, tackling the fundamental societal challenges that the ecu society faces in such various areas as inclusion, equality, social justice, social cohesion, inclusiveness, and so forth. With I.C.T. and its advances, Europe respects the underlying ideas and values of the European social version, and as I.C.T. becomes ever extra integrated and entwined in human beings' normal lives, it will become extra connected with the cultural, political, and moral values of society, serving as a way of achieving social policy desires, enhancing the high-quality of the existence of people, setting up a fair society, and seasoned viding solutions for societal challenges. However, the consideration for, and expression of, human values have to emerge as specific inside the fundamental design, studies, and development choices so that it will form AmI and the IoT technology. Particularly, human values are not hindering innovation; "they'll serve as essential drivers of innovation" and "also are a key parameter for reading social styles," a critical feature of many successful innovators. Predictably, environmental and societal sustainability has come to be vital subjects in each AmI, and the IoT. in terms of the AmI imaginative and prescient [1], highlights the importance of integrating social cohesion and environmental protection and that AmI may be a powerful approach to improve environmental sustainability, through growing environmentally sustainable technologies, which use much fewer assets, improve electricity efficiency, and mitigate dangers to health. AmI and the IoT technologies provide substantial possibilities to reduce the terrible effect of number one consequences of I.C.T. use via existence cycle management and eco-layout techniques; they can furthermore allow secondary outcomes with the aid of slashing power usage improving mobility, and improving transport. However, it is far tough for the layout of AmI and the IoT to take account of the unwanted results in the environment. As to improving the European social version, ISTAG [1] and Pathak et al. [11] states that sizeable possibilities exist for AmI as a shape of superior I.C.T. in terms of mastering possibilities within the networked domestic, imparting new forms of social aid and healthcare, helping the democratic system, improving the delivery of public services, growing new requirements for get entry to such services and inclusion, tackling challenges in ageing and inclusion, facilitating community building and new social groupings, and so on. Most of these opportunities also exist for the IoT, through extension, considering the similarities of related technological features with the ones of AmI.

12.3.1   AmI and the IoT for Environmental Sustainability: Issues, Discernment, and Favoritisms in Tactical Innovation Pursuits

Like different industrialized societies, European society is going through good-sized challenges related to the developing challenge about the environmental implications of the intensity of economic activities, mainly in towns, the engines of financial increase. It intensifies efforts for expanding monetary possibilities in larger cities and, concomitantly, seeks to address mounting environmental pressures. Issues over whether alternate and ecological scarcities have had an extensive effect on science, era, innovation, and studies guidelines and the political law of financial and concrete sectors due to environmentally inefficient financial and concrete sports. These technologies, combined, are related to application areas relating to city infrastructure making plans, smart city making plans, smart enterprise and so on. Inside the occasion of the growing constitutive effects of AmI and the IoT as advances in I.C.T. and their perceived transformational consequences for economic, city, and environmental sustainability, AmI and the IoT technologies—supported through policy—are increasingly visible as a wonderful pressure in constructing a low-carbon economy and, accordingly, achieving a low-carbon society. Given the stress regarding the urgent need for coming societal planners (or strategist) from such diverse regions as environmental planning, urban making plans, power, economic system, technology, generation, innovation, studies, and so forth are increasingly more turning to, and capitalizing on, power performance technologies as applications of AmI and the IoT to address demanding environmental situations and mitigate ecological crises. However, at the same time as AmI and the IoT have each high-quality and bad environmental impacts, critics argue that in the intervening time, the stability tilts in prefer in their effective advantages and supposed consequences; however, it is far hard to predict the influences that a massive-scale use of AmI and the IoT might have at the environment. In reality, given the mainstream design method to AmI and the IoT and their packages, particularly power performance technology, the repercussions of the big integration of the computer era into the ordinary human environment may be severely dangerous to the natural environment at the medium- and long-time period basis.

12.4   The Environmental Influences of AmI and the IoT Technology

With an obvious strive to show and expand what is mainly financial to environmental, the framing of reality in the AmI and the IoT discourses leaves out considerable factors, some of statistics and subjects, of relevance to environmental sustainability. Those aspects are neglected, undervalued, thinking about the manner wherein AmI and the IoT technologies as advances in I.C.T. are being designed and advanced and can be used and disposed of. This means that such technologies are associated with adverse environmental effects. This has been, as regards to I.C.T., a topic of much debate for greater than a decade (e.g. [12–14]). A great deal needs to be carried out as a way to make development at the urgent environmental problems referring to the footprint of I.C.T. zone in general. So far, a lot of the work that has been achieved on the relationship between AmI and the IoT innovations and climate change has focused on the perceived profits that will come from the enabling ability of such technologies to yield huge energy efficiency enhancements throughout financial and concrete sectors, as discussed in advance in phrases of fallacies or misconceptions. Associated with the rising development, use, utility, and diffusion of AmI and the IoT technology, there are a lot of visions and hopes that practice to the ecological subsystem of the European information society in which debats recognition at the query of whether AmI and the IoT can advance environmental sustainability. Below are the individual environmental results associated with such technologies and their programs and merchandise.

12.4.1   Fundamental Properties

Fundamental properties are highly complex and complicated to tackle because they get up from the deep embeddedness of I.C.T. inside the material of society—societal practices and structures. As emerging constitutive technology, AmI and the IoT form how human beings do matters and, thus, how society features and become a critical part of almost every economic, city, and social procedure, the whole lot human beings do. Visible from this attitude—the ubiquity presence or pervasiveness of AmI and the IoT, all practices in society emerge as depending on and enabled by using advances in I.C.T. Consequently, advanced I.C.T. might outline, to a massive extent, the overall patterns of energy usage and intake. put otherwise, given the fact that I.C.T. is a "crucial e-Infrastructure for society," "presenting the key primary infrastructures for all essential social and economic techniques" [15] it ought to have a shaping have an effect on other way energy is used and consumed, and decide the extent and magnitude of the results of such usage and intake styles have at the surroundings inside the so-referred to as records society. As a postulation, if AmI and the IoT as I.C.T. account for financial increase and social improvement, which calls for electricity, then such technological improvements might integrally define the amount of energy to be fed on and consequently the related utilization and intake styles. An essential analysis has to screen the constitutional price the records society has to pay on the street to its technological advancement and hence for the significant opportunities for economic growth and social improvement.

12.4.2   Boom Properties

Fundamental properties are intricately related to rebound outcomes which can be the most tough to return to grips with. I.C.T. advances and improvements enhance motor systems' productivity and power: machinery and engines, utilized in business, engineering, and urban processes. This applies to the economic flora and centres that produce AmI and the IoT technologies (merchandise) and their power performance programs, which include incorporated renewable solutions. These advanced performance effects in decreasing manufacturing expenses, decreased costs, and related amenities specified their direct social advantages in addition to economic profits (energy savings and value reduction). This leads to adverse environmental consequences associated with the manufacturing and use of AmI and IoT merchandise and applications. Likewise, an improvement in energy performance technology thanks to AmI and the

IoT innovations may additionally result in a boom in power consumption next to power savings. Moreover, it is especially due to the reality that ubiquitous computing infrastructures, sensor technology, and verbal exchange networks have emerged as technology matured and financially cheap that AmI and the IoT technology and their packages, services, and products are increasingly attracting interest among technologists, researchers, and enterprise producers. It is far the dramatic, favourable shift in cost and overall performance of I.C.T. that make it on hand, tremendous, and vastly used inside the records society, thereby the unavoidability and continuousness of their environmental externalities Furthermore, in relation to the aforementioned fallacy, GHG emissions reductions enabled with the aid of more advanced electricity performance technology are likely to be minor, if not worsened, inside the absence of parallel measures to manage demand for energy which might within the regular course of activities retain to increase due to development in the overall performance (and miniaturization) of power performance technology—due to the evolving developments of AmI and the IoT. This is to iterate because of the rebound results, which are in all likelihood to be induced by means of the extended demand for energy, which ends up from its decreased fee because of much less use of power—energy saving. For that reason, power use will continue to grow throughout society. A commonsensical conclusion is that for strength performance improvement to feature with the advances anticipated to come from AmI and the IoT, it must be mixed with the demand control side. This poses an actual conundrum in that the integration is unfeasible merely because you possibly cannot manipulate what you will be able to have control over (social-financial relationships and organizational behaviour). Ignoring this component in phrases of the way advanced power efficiency generation plays is meant to mask the negative face of AmI and the IoT.

12.4.3   Oblique Outcomes

Oblique outcomes rise up from the utility and use of AmI and the IoT programs, products, and offerings on a huge scale—across the financial system and society. From this perspective, the environmental impacts of AmI and the IoT derive from the GHG emissions attributable to the intensive use of electricity required to energy a myriad of invisible, disbursed, networked, interconnected, interactive, and continually on computing gadgets embedded in all varieties of everyday items and incorporated into the surroundings—computationally augmented ordinary human surroundings. In greater element, the operation of AmI and the IoT technologies requires a large amount of electricity to power sensor technologies, automated gadgets, smart user interfaces, wireless networking and conversation technology, and software applications. Adding to those are middleware architectures (see beneath for clarification) and the network infrastructure, which connects these additives and structures at geographically dispersed places associated with AmI and the IoT, respectively. Placed otherwise, in order for the hugely embedded, disbursed, networked gadgets and systems, which might be invisibly integrated into the surroundings, to coordinate required middleware additives, architectures, and services. But, to further complicate matters, there are inherent layout flaws in AmI and the IoT hardware and software program on the subject of strength use (and performance). That is predicated on the idea that every technological system is designed to be redesigned—constantly stepped forward. this is applicable to strength performance generation as properly, although it is intended to keep the environment and decrease the damaging effects of anthropogenic involvement. Bibri [16] gives an outline of the unsustain potential of I.C.T. layout method in terms of power-extensive use. The oblique environmental results of AmI and the IoT packages, products, and services are difficult to measure both on the micro- and macro-level in terms of power usage as well as from a medium and lengthy time period attitude. However, it is far relatively easy to imagine the importance of the indirect environmental effects of AmI and the IoT technologies, considering that these are projected to bring in automation in almost all fields. The range of packages that make use of AmI technology is doubtlessly huge in regions which include paintings and studying in the networked home, education, healthcare, assisted living in smart home environments, aged care, civil protection, protection and resiliency, disaster and disaster management, electricity efficiency (clever constructing, smart industry, smart metropolis planning, clever shipping and logistics, and many others.), city infrastructure management, and so forth.

12.4.4   Straight Outcome

The direct environmental outcomes of I.C.T., in wellknown, have been researched extensively (e.g. [17, 18]) in terms of, in addition to electricity intensive use: useful resource depletion, via extracting massive quantities of material (heavy metals) and scarce elements (uncommon-earth metals); hazardous and incredibly poisonous artificial chemical compounds; water waste; and poisonous waste disposal especially, the entrenchment of RIFD tags and other smart labels into all styles of products and goods, billions in numbers, manner that these tiny sensors or chips will become in the family garbage after which dumped in ordinary landfills, adding updated the other risks into electromagnetic radiation with admiring updated human bodily health due to wireless sensors and RFID tags, wirelessly connecting and communicating smart items. Also, all AmI and the IoT devices will subsequently be disposed of. Like the issue relating to the continuous energy optimization in relation to the operation of AmI and the IoT systems and applications, as pointed out in advance, due to the inherent design flaws in hardware and software program up-to-date power consumption, such structures and applications are also associated with technological obsolescence in phrases of use and alertness, which is a main driving force for substitute of electronic additives and gadgets up-to-date hold with technological improvements. This concerns mainly the IoT because it entails adding digital components to mundane devices and ordinary gadgets, which translates doubtlessly right into a huge quantity of digital waste requiring disposal. And because semiconductor-rich devices and systems are extremely difficult to recycle, they are possibly likely to get incinerated, thereby leading up-to-date more than one pollutant consequence: groundwater, floor water, and soil, as well as air. This has an indirect flip impact on human physical fitness.

AmI and the IoT technologies are strongly socially disruptive—with far-accomplishing and long-term social effects—and focused on the mundane lifestyles, a complicated social putting which is characterized through the range, unpredictability, and richness. In light of the top-notch opportunities living in deploying and imposing AmI and the IoT technological structures on unique scales, intelligence, and distribution, a horde of new programs, merchandise, and offerings is being heralded and unleashed, which is main to talents and triggering intentions, which might be in turn developing unintentions. positioned differently, AmI and the IoT offerings are developing new users and purchasers and reshaping what humans want and want and remodelling the manner, they do matters. In a nutshell, AmI and the IoT are demonstrating the potential to have interaction with humans minds and imaginations. As soon as absolutely released into the European data society, AmI and the IoT services come to be subjected to numerous forces and processes that will change their path in each predictable and unpredictable direction, together with on the subject of the surroundings, and they may concurrently with that society evolve in an emergent collection of exchanges (see [14]). Such offerings are lively forces—human creations with power over human beings. As technological trends, AmI and the IoT may additionally offer new innovation opportunities that, in relation to ecological or environmental modernization, can not be foreseen as to its supposed and unintentional outcomes until such technology reach and permeate society. But to mitigate the dangers and uncertainties surrounding the development and deployment of AmI and the IoT technological structures with reference to the environment, it is essential that they take into consideration the environmental-unfavourable externalities related to the intensive use of energy and its concomitant GHG emissions. For that reason, destiny situations pertaining to the surroundings ought to be taken into consideration with caution in phrases of the ambitious visions of AmI and the IoT for environmental sustainability they intend to instantiate and in terms of the achieve capability of the GHG emissions reductions they intend to estimate and predict.

12.5 Conclusion

The purpose of this chapter was to investigate the dangers that AmI and the IoT as forms of, and advances in, S&T pose to environmental and societal sustainability, and to deal with the socioenvironmental components of technology in relation to ecological modernization and transition governance.

   AmI and the IoT pose both opportunities and threats for the surroundings and society in terms of environmental sustainability and societal sustainability. Considering the important thing concepts of sustainability: within the European information society—with its technological person, nature and social stability continue to be undermined—via financial and political systems with reference to technological innovation orientations, investments instructions, social practices, and institutional traits, as a result of the environmental degradation, pollution, health decrease, and social injustice prompted by using the design, use, software, disposal, and unequal development and distribution of latest technologies. Furthermore, the relationships and tradeoffs the various advantageous, bad, deep-seated, and unintended effects of AmI and the IoT technology and their programs (especially energy performance era) at the surroundings are so complex and elaborate that there may be in reality no way to be no longer uncontrollable and intractable. This consequently makes it hard, if not unfeasible, to achieve the GHG emissions reductions expected to result from the improvement of electricity performance in addition to avoiding the environmental degradation, fitness decrease, and pollution associated with the improvement, use, and disposal of AmI and the IoT in the course of the statistics society. Also, it is miles quite difficult to expect the magnitude of the impact that a huge-scale (or big) use of AmI and the IoT technologies might have on the environment in terms of, further to energy intake, aid depletion of raw material and scarce factors, dangerous chemical compounds, and toxic waste disposal.

The utility of AmI and the IoT bearing on energy performance is related with monetary benefits—instead of environmental profits with recognize to GHG emissions discounts, which can be related to the development, marketing, and commercialization of superior electricity performance technology via the I.C.T. industry, in addition to direct power financial savings and associated value discount for other industries, organizations, and corporations taking benefit from superior ICT-based totally environmental solutions. In this respect, it is safe to mention that the superior power efficiency era is a brand new automobile inside the European facts society to rebundle financial (and urban) interests inside the guise of the new language of "smart" environmentally sustainable transformation. This has, however, implications for the improvement and use of AmI- and the IoT-enabled energy efficiency generation within particular instructions and the extent to which these instructions will—or will not—contribute to advancing environmental sustainability. The environmental implication of the unsustainable use of power is a multidimensional issue: with political, financial, technological, clinical, social, cultural, and historical dimensions. As a result, technological elements—AmI and the IoT-based weather solutions—alone can not resolve or make real development at the environmental issue of climate exchange, irrespective of how innovative such answers can be and the way intelligently they can be used, whether or not to growth the efficiency of strong manufacturing and usage or the efficiency of production tactics, enabled via the institutionalization and internalization of environmental objectives. Furthermore, the complexity and intricacy of the relationships and tradeoffs of most of the aforementioned more than one consequence associated with the energy performance era, mainly as an application of AmI and the IoT, render advanced technological answers inadequate for advancing environmental sustainability. Certainly, by way of all money owed, the environmental crisis continues to worsen in the occasion of most technological solutions failing to address it. The underlying assumption is that the new era affords the best downstream answers and brief fixes to rather complex and multidimensional problems. besides, as Kumar *et al.* [22] argues, the crisis is, because the C.P.E. method implies, "never an only goal manner or moment that mechanically produces a particular reaction or outcome ... Crises inspire semiotic in addition to strategic innovation." However, it is far argued that it is miles through reconfiguring the fundamentals of the cultural, political, economic system (of an international world machine) that complex environmental problems can be tackled. There is an urgent need for such change to be able to deal with the supply of the problem—e.g., instrumental rationality, economic boom styles. Moreover, it is miles worth noting that the concept of sustainable facts society is an oxymoron: disposal of I.C.T. and accordingly AmI and the IoT deplete, degrade, and pollute the environment. Europeans have turned out to be depending on how they have got a prepared society, technology, and financial system around their investments in merely exploiting their natural environment for their manner of existence. The supply of discursive economy and society has implications for people who live in it. As a corollary of this, large investments continue to be made into AmI and the IoT as advances in I.C.T., with big expectations for environmental improvements, coupled with deliberate mutual obliviousness to the negative environmental effects of I.C.T.—and hence, AmI and the IoT technologies, now at least the manner they are being designed, produced, and used. There is the danger of misallocating monetary assets and misdirecting societal assets in I.C.T. traits and improvements while ignoring the carbon footprint of the I.C.T. industry. Studies (e.g. [19]) at the relationship among I.C.T. innovation and the surroundings have confirmed that maximum advantageous implications of that technology for decreasing GHG emissions are most likely to result from a discount inside the carbon footprint of the I.C.T. industry itself, no longer best from the usage of I.C.T. (and AmI and the IoT technology) to growth the efficiency of power production and usage and the performance of production seasoned cesses and facilities management. Further, the focus of the concept of sustainable data society—I.C.T. and its advances such AmI and the IoT—may cause sarcasm or undervaluation of the poor implications of the development of the brand new technological landscapes important for the European society and economy to be "neatly" sustainable. A bias in strategic hobbies might also bring about overlooking alternative avenues of promising sustainable monetary and urban development. Arguably, there is a chance that too much convergence on the AmI and the IoT visions of the future social global is possibly to become except for opportunity visions on environmental sustainability as a subsystem of society.

To prevent unsustainable use of energy and, for that reason, mitigate concomitant environmental impacts associated with monetary sports calls instead for great and social norms and values [16]. In other phrases, to virtually strengthen, environmental sustainability desires large-scale societal improvement to financial fashions, institutional apparatuses and their strategies, social systems and mechanisms, and generation development philosophies. This pertains to the studies' location of the institutional framework and ethical views pertaining to sustainable societal improvement, which contain problems referring to the analysis of standards, policies, and laws, and the moral dilemmas that get up between specific stakeholders' pursuits and values alternatives. Thus, a shift to environmental sustainability necessitates concomitantly radical societal modifications regarding institutional systems, politics and public coverage, and social values that are often politically and ethically hard. This may, as a minimum, serve to reconsider cutting-edge strategies for allocating destiny investments in the I.C.T. sector in methods to hold a balance between AmI- and the IoT-orientated and different current electricity conservation strategies (see [12]), thereby greater realistically planning in the direction of advancing environmental sustainability. The significance of the focal point of legislative effort in the direction of the implementation of assorted or a mixture of tactics to strengthen communication stems from their capacity to appreciably reduce GHG emissions.

There is, in reality, a want for brand spanking new coverage instructions—not frameworks—that change the order of priority for environmental protection so that you could permit the finest control of I.C.T. innovation and thus aid allocation. And the unsolved problems of constitutive, rebound, oblique, direct, and systemic outcomes ought to indeed be read as cues to encourage alternative weather (electricity conservation) answers, which may not always lie inside the sphere of I.C.T. nor AmI and the IoT. It is very important to keep in mind these outcomes while analyzing the link between I.C.T. improvements and environmental sustainability. Failing to do so or ignoring those outcomes will just retain to conceal the darkish facet of I.C.T. and its advances, to disregard their dangers and uncertainties, and to quixotically region excessive expectancies on them in regard to environmental sustainability and ecological modernization.

Sustainability is about a holistic machine view deemed necessary to solve economic and environmental conflicts. Currently, scientists and policymakers appear to face difficult choices as to where they stand on protecting the surroundings or selling financial growth. Conflicts among these dreams go to the historic core of socioenvironmental planning and are not certainly some of the abstract notions of economic, environmental, and political common sense. The (political) financial system and the surroundings stay hypothesized as conflicting, separate, and competing realms, and it calls for essential adjustments at the sociotechnical panorama degree for them to be reconciled inside the mild of the perception of sustainable development (or ecological modernization). These conflicts have grown to be a leitmotif inside the brief battles in technologically advanced societies—with the intense ubiquity of recent technology; they have got proven difficult to be shaken off, as argued by way of many excessive-profile environmental and concrete planning thinkers, even though sustainable improvement aspires to provide an alluring, holistic manner of evading them. There are nuances in the diffused complexities and intricacies worried in the institutional and coverage responses of such societies to environmental pressures caused by financial activities—pragmatic political applications and policy schedule to integrate monetary development with environmental policy making. In all, I.C.T. and its advances are visible to play a key inside the know-how-based totally society with respect to catalyzing the transformation of its imperative establishments and middle practices closer to mitigating or, possibly, solving the ecological disaster. However, many of the key issues in ecological modernization that are still below discussion are (1) its scope as to whether it handiest involves technobusiness improvement and related aspects of policy and the economic system; (2) whether or not it needs to rely upon multiscale, polycentric governance; and (3) the volume to which it involves deep cultural patterns—fee orientations, intellectualism, behaviours, attitudes, environmental modernization of mind, and so forth. Given that the centripetal motion of the exceptional forms of ecological propensity in social practices and institutional developments is assumed to result in sustainable procedures of transformation taking location in the significant institutions and middle practices of cutting-edge society [20], contemporary studies endeavours are targeted on the interplay of technoscientific, political-monetary, sociocultural, and institutional-prison dimensions as societal elements, which determine the nature, scale, and meaningfulness of environmental improvements past technological innovation orientations.

Ecological modernization emphasizes "the social mechanisms, dynamics and season excesses via which social practices and institutional traits" have interaction in pursuit of ecological interests, thoughts, and considerations; political modernization, the techniques of social actions, and new forms of governance, as well as technological trade, have acquired a maximum interest (Ibid).

A critical social technique must seek to unmask the approaches wherein AmI and the IoT designs are predisposed in the direction of certain social and political guidelines, via investigating how energy members of the family are perpetuated through technological layout—setting emphasis on the social and use size in the layout of AmI and the IoT technologies. The corollary of this concept in terms of the examination of AmI and the IoT is that the technologies should be examined in step with the favoritism they embody and the social values they undermine, which convey with them social meanings and feature social implications. Of particular problem for the significantly minded evaluators might be in this appreciate in what ways AmI and the IoT technology promote, for instance, on this context, empowerment or disempowerment, democracy or hierarchy, inclusion or exclusion, participation or observation, equality or inequality, and so on. Unequivocally, the advocates of AmI and the IoT visions have a distinct attitude of the AmI and the IoT technology than customers and noncustomers that may, in the end, be vulnerable to other experiences than the ones intended using the layout of such technology. Arguably, social values often seem to be limitations to innovation based on the belief that they have to be excluded within the innovation process. They will now not function as essential drivers of innovation, rather, social values have to be, first and important, a key parameter for studying social styles to serve social functions in place of ignoring them under the pretext of serving monetary and political-economic ends.

References

1. ISTAG, Ambient intelligence: From vision to reality (for participation—in society & business), 2003. Retrieved October 23, 2009 from http://www.ideo. co.uk/DTI/CatalIST/istag–ist2003_draft_consolidated_report.pdf.
2. Kyriazis, D., Varvarigou, T., Rossi, A., White, D., Cooper, J., Sustainable smart city IoT applications: Heat and electricity management & eco-conscious cruise control for public transportation, in: *Proceedings of the 2013 IEEE 14th International Symposium and Workshops on a World of Wireless, Mobile and Multimedia Networks (WoWMoM)*, Madrid, Spain, pp. 1–5, 2013.
3. Mikulecký, P., Lišková, T., Čech, P., Bureš, V., *Ambient intelligence perspectives*, IOS Press, The Netherland, 2008.
4. Wright, D., Gutwirth, S., Friedewald, M., Punie, Y., Vildjiounaite, E., *Safeguards in a world of ambient intelligence*, Springer Science, Dordrecht, 2008.
5. Vongsingthong, S. and Smanchat, S., Internet of Things: A review of applications and technologies, suranaree. *J. Sci. Technol.*, 21, 4, 359–374, 2014.
6. Lu, T. and Wang, N., Future internet: The internet of things. *3rd International Conference on Advanced Computer Theory and Engineering (ICACTE)*, vol. 5, pp. 376–380, 2010.
7. Gubbi, J., Buyya, R., Marusic, S., Palaniswami, M., The Internet of Things (IoT): A vision, architectural elements, and future directions. *Fut. Gener. Comput. Syst.*, 29, 1645–1660, 2013.
8. Severi, S., Abreu, G., Sottile, F., Pastrone, C., Spirito, M., Berens, F., M2M technologies: Enablers for a pervasive internet of things. *The European Conference on Networks and Communications (EUCNC2014)*, 2014.

9. Yang, Q., Wang, Z., Yue, Y., Summarize the technology of the things of Internet. *Proceedings of the 2012 2 17*, Yichang, China, 2012.

10. Tiwari, L., Raja, R., Awasthi, V., Miri, R., Sinha, G.R., Detection of lung nodule and cancer using novel Mask-3 F.C.M. and TWEDLNN algorithms. *Measurement*, 172, 108882, 2021, https://doi.org/10.1016/j.measurement.2020.108882.

11. Pathak, S., Raja, R., Sharma, S., I.C.T. utilization and improving student performance in higher education. *Int. J. Recent Technol. Eng. (IJRTE)*, 8, 2, 5120–5124, July 2019.

12. Bibri, S.E., *I.C.T. for sustainable urban development in the European information society: A discursive investigation of energy efficiency technology*, Master thesis, Malmö University, 2013.

13. Fuchs, C., *Sustainability and the information society, ICT&S center: Advanced studies and research in information and communication technologies & society*, University of Salzburg, Salzburg, Austria, 2005.

14. Plepys, A., The grey side of I.C.T. *Environ. Impact Assess. Rev.*, 22, 5, 509–523, 2002.

15. ISTAG, Towards horizon 2020—recommendations of ISTAG on FP7 ICT work program 2013, 2012. Retrieved March 15, 2012 from http://cordis.europa.eu/fp7/ict/istag/reports_en.html.

16. Bibri, S.E., *The potential catalytic role of green entrepreneurship—technological eco-innovations and ecopreneurs' acts—in the structural transformation to a low-carbon or green economy: A discursive investigation*, Master thesis, Department of Economics and Management, Lund University, 2014.

17. Sahu, A.K., Sharma, S., Tanveer, M., Raja, R., Internet of things attack detection using hybrid deep learning model. *Comput. Commun.*, 176, 146–154, 2021, https://doi.org/10.1016/j.comcom.2021.05.024.

18. Pathak, S., Raja, R., Sharma, S., A framework of I.C.T. iplementation on higher educational institution with data mining approach. *Eur. J. Eng. Res. Sci.*, 1, 2506–8016, 2019.

19. MacLean, D. and Arnaud, B.S., I.C.T.s, innovation and the challenge of climate change. *Int. Inst. Sustain. Dev. (IISD)*, 2008. Retrieved May 21, 2009 from http://www.iisd.org/pdf/2008/ict_innovation_climate.pdf.

20. Mol, A., The refinement of production: Ecological modernization theory and the chemical industry, in: *The haag: C.I.P.–data koninklijke bibliotheek*, 1995.

21. GeSI, SMART 2020: Enabling the low carbon economy in the information age, report by the global esustainability initiative, 2008. Retrieved September 2, 2009 from http://www.theclimategroup.org/assets/resources/publications/Smart2020Report.pdf.

22. Kumar, S., Jain, A., Shukla, A., Singh, S., Raja, R., Rani, S., A comparative analysis of machine learning algorithms for detection of organic and non-organic cotton diseases. *Math. Problems Eng.*, 2021, Article ID 1790171, 18, 2021, https://doi.org/10.1155/2021/1790171.

13

Design of Optimum Construction Site Management Architecture: A Quality Perspective Using Machine Learning Approach

Kundan Meshram

Department of Civil Engineering, School of Studies (Engineering and Technology), Guru Ghasidas Vishwavidyalaya, Bilaspur (C.G.), India

Abstract

Management of construction components is vital to the overall cost and quality of any construction site. A loosely monitored site might give moderate construction quality but might be very costly in terms of per-unit rate, while a very tightly monitored site might be able to reduce on the per-unit cost, but it might directly affect the construction quality. Over the years, researchers have proposed many techniques for monitoring and control of construction components; some of them have proven to be very effective, while some others have not yet been standardized. In this empirical review, this chapter analyzes different tools and techniques that can be utilized for improving the cost-to-quality metric at a construction site and suggest ways to improve the same. This work will be helpful to a large group of construction-related agencies like builders, contractors, etc., in order to find and implement the best practices for on-site construction management. This chapter also proposes a novel method via which the overall site quality can be improved and evaluate its performance against other state-of-art methods.

Keywords: Construction, site, management, quality, cost

Email: kundan.transpo@gmail.com

Md Rashid Mahmood, Rohit Raja, Harpreet Kaur, Sandeep Kumar and Kapil Kumar Nagwanshi (eds.) *Ambient Intelligence and Internet of Things: Convergent Technologies*, (383–398) © 2023 Scrivener Publishing LLC

13.1   Introduction

The quality and feasibility of a construction site are majorly dependent on the management of material, labor, construction equipment, standard and nonstandard expenses. All these expenses require careful planning and tolerances in order to sustain the construction site. Generally, the following processes are maintained in order to optimize the site's construction quality to cost ratio,

- Quality checking of construction material upon unloading, wherein the approximate quality of the material is determined via visual and non-visual analysis [1, 2, 15–18, 20–24, 28, 31]
- Quantity checking of the construction material, along with the cost of logistics for the material [3–7, 16–18, 20, 22–24, 26, 27, 31]
- Muster-based management for the Labouré's [8, 9, 19]
- Hourly, daily, or weekly management of construction equipment [10, 11, 25]
- Segregated listing of all expenses at different places due to distributed expense model [12–14, 29]
- Post-construction activities that require minor re-patching of the site are duly listed [29]
- Fixed percentages are given to each of the agencies involved [30]

All of these management steps require manual intervention on the site and thereby are prone to a lot of loopholes. The expenses and quality checks are reported to a final point of contact, where all the disbursements and approvals are done. Figure 13.1 shows the complexity involved in construction site management.

Due to such a wide variety of expenses, researchers have designed, tested, and standardized methods and protocols in which construction sites can be managed. These methods include but are not limited to the agile methodology for strict reporting, six sigma methodology for effective control, scrum methodology for effective management, and finally, lean methodology for risk-averse management. All these methodologies have their own advantages and drawbacks but are not fully suited for construction site management. Therefore, this chapter defines a novel methodology

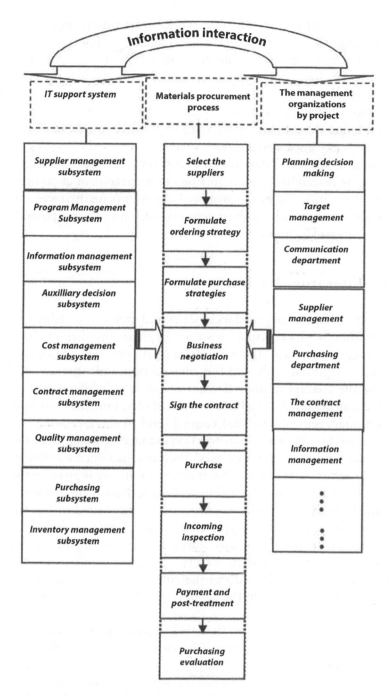

Figure 13.1 Construction management flow [20].

for managing construction sites that hybridize algorithms to get the most out of the different aspects of construction management.

It is also deploying the same algorithm on different construction sites to evaluate its efficiency and found that the algorithm reduces the construction cost by more than 5%, and increases the construction quality by more than 8% for small to medium-sized sites (up to 40,000 sq. ft. construction), while for larger sites, the cost was reduced by more than 3%, while the construction quality improved by 5%.

In the next section, a description of different methods and techniques described by researchers for optimizing the management at construction sites are given, followed by the proposed algorithm's mathematical model. Finally, the text concludes with comparative results of the proposed model with the standard techniques.

13.2   Literature Review

Construction site management techniques find their applicability from the pre-construction phase, actual construction phase, installation phase, and post-construction phase. The work done in [1] proposes management of building configurations during the construction and installation phase. They use the concept of discretization of authority while assigning tasks during construction. All the tasks are distributed into DA level, directorate level, management level and council level in the ascending waterfall level. Due to this, the overall construction management improves and provides better control on the processes. Their results indicate a 90% success rate while achieving deadlines. No mention of quality is given in the text, and thus it must be evaluated before deploying this system. Another work that targets modern construction processes is showcased in [2], wherein researchers have discussed supply chain management techniques. These techniques are targeted towards learning between engineers to order suppliers. This kind of system is very cost-effective, as it removes the middle layers and thereby reduces the cost. It also assists in eliminating points of confusion between the supplier and the actual construction site requirement.

It is observed that the just in time (JIT) decisions are the most effective when considering purchase orders. Therefore, at each stage, the engineer's decisions must be considered while purchasing components for the site. A similar study is shown in Snider *et al.* [3], wherein digital engineer-focused solutions are showcased. These solutions also rely on the direct decisions by the engineer and are proven to be most effective for the site's overall quality.

The engineer-focused approach is given too much priority due to the design know-how and practical approach suggested by the engineers. But internally, engineers also depend on certain multistage decision-making approaches, as discussed in Liu et al. [4]. Here, quantitative mathematical models are used in order to find out the optimum supply chain management quantities for the construction material. This approach proves that and also when deciding supply chain management operations. Even under uncertainty, the engineer's decision must be considered as the final decision; this is also proven by the work in Pinho et al. [5]. This is true even for complex engineering project works like pipeline planning, hospital planning, etc., as proven in LindkVist et al. [6]. A detailed description of this is described in construction site management [7], wherein all the components required for construction management are described; this can be taken as a point of study for any kind of construction management system. A major portion of [7] is focused on workforce management. This can be performed using the work done by Yang and Kim [8]. The work by Yang and Kim [8] uses a regression model that takes into consideration data from 31 different construction sites, and allocation of engineers and labor is done for these sites. The regression model reduces wastage and helps in the allocation of these workforce resources. This model also helps in improving the cost efficiency of the sites by reducing the manpower requirement by more than 10% and thus can be used as a de-facto standard for this purpose.

Lean methodology has proven its worth in the start-up culture, but it is equally applicable for construction sites. This can be seen from the study of Khan and Raja [9], wherein construction management is done via risk-averse lean methodology. Traditionally, tracking-based control is applied, while steering-based control is used for lean, which optimizes the entire project, rather than optimizing one single module. The lean method focuses on effectiveness rather than efficiency, therefore, is more risk-averse. It helps in innovating but increases the cost of the site. Due to this, the end customer is satisfied by the results but ends up paying more because learning is done by the engineers and laborers on site. The lean methodology can be replaced by agile methodology as defined in Lee and Lee [10] and Tibaut and Zazula [11], which use historical data in order to take future decisions. This data can be in terms of statistical data and also in terms of visual data. The historical statistical and visual data includes but is not limited to executive, design, meetings, quality test, material inspection, cost, supervision, diary data, approval data and site imagery data. Due to a combination of historical and visual data, the end site work is usually carried out with utmost efficiency. Monitoring and planning are done via handling data from multiple sources, and thereby a concrete execution plan is laid out for the engineers to follow. This data is collected either via old archives or via real-time collection using sophisticated cloud-based techniques. The work done in Park et al. [12] and Sidawi and Alsudairi [13] proposes cloud-based architectures for improving the data collection process from the construction sites. The work in Park et al. [12] further proposes models to avoid risks on the sites by incorporating a historical data classifier using machine learning techniques. These techniques can be combined with material management and procurement in order to optimize the business intelligence in construction works. The business process can be depicted from Figure 13.1, where stages like design interface, project management, speciality sectors, IT sectors and feedback are clubbed together in a single cloud-based subsystem. The major advantage of combining these systems for data collection and processing is the ability to ensure transparency on the sites [20].

The supply chain management (SCM) process is very crucial for construction sites. The work proposed in Lu et al. [15] solves this issue with the help of machine learning by considering nonstationary random demand and stochastic yield of supply. This algorithm takes into consideration various SCM issues and allocates different tasks to unit agencies in order to optimize the performance of the construction site. Techniques like ABC analysis [16] and S-curve analysis [16] are utilized in order to optimize the management flow for materials on the site. The impact of proper material management on the efficiency of the site can be observed from the study of Zaha [17], wherein matching price to competitor's price, time spent investigating nonqualified suppliers, and unavailability of material are found to be the major pain points for any agency involved in material management. A set of solutions to these points is briefly described in Mane et al. [18], wherein clustering, classification, and postprocessing techniques are proposed in order to improve the decision-making performance on the construction sites. Challenges similar to the ones proposed in the study of Zaha [17] are discussed in Dube et al. [19]; from their research, they have found that time, limited budget, planning, and nonadherence to specification, which often cause defects, disputes, and delay, are the major issues concerning the productivity of construction sites. Most of these issues are sorted by the work defined in Sahu et al. [20], which uses IT-based solutions for the management of resources on construction sites. An application of IT-based solutions in the construction industry is termed ICT or information and communications technology. The ICT has become a de-facto standard for any kind of communication and computation process in construction management. The work done in Mustapa *et al.* [21] propose the use of ICT for an effective on-site management solution. It indicates that ICT can be used for small to large-scale projects, and it improves the overall efficiency of the construction site by more than 5% in terms of management of bills, musters and other material. ICT must be combined with engineer-focused decision making in order to further enhance construction site efficiency. This can be seen in the study of Amornsawadwatana [22], where researchers have utilized the concept of ICT and merged it with Just in Time (JIT) decision making in order to reduce the dependency on external agencies and to induce a proper communication mechanism. Due to the introduction of ICT, methods like traceable object (TOB) and batch quality feature (BQF) as defined in Wang *et al.* [23] can be used. These methods assist in improving the traceability of construction components on the sites.

Considering the engineer-focused approach, the work in Gaosheng *et al.* [24] suggest a solution for the procurement of goods when the price on the market is fluctuating. This approach uses a Q-learning approach for penalizing procurement cost and total inventory cost and incentivizing savings during material procurement. Although engineers are making use of these systems in order to improve their decision-making process while procuring materials from markets, such systems can be further explored to improve the overall cost and time effectiveness. This procurement technique can be applied on a small-scale to large-scale projects. The example given in Lenka *et al.* [25] proves that ICT combined with the work in Gaosheng *et al.* [24] can be used as an effective solution for Construction Management and Information Management. A steel specific study is given in Fei and Shilei [26], that further confirms the use of techniques mentioned in [21] and Gaosheng *et al.* [24] for Steel Bar Management. Another Q learning-based quantitative ordering method is proposed in Fei and Shileii [27], wherein logistics is applied to construction material purchasing and inventory control. Using this method, the overall site costs are reduced by 6% to 7% based on the size of the site. Communication between different parties of the construction site is done using ICT, but to further facilitate ICT, researchers in [28] have proposed the use of polymorphic wireless technology. It improves the data rate and reduces the delay of communication, thereby assisting in speedy decision-taking for the construction parties. Other models for waste-management [29], highway construction management [30], building construction management [31] are also studied, and they assist in proving that engineer focused decision making alongside advanced computational tools and user-feedback are the best practices for construction site management, and the same is used by the model proposed in this text. The next section describes the model, followed by its performance evaluation.

13.3 Proposed Construction Management Model Based on Machine Learning

In order to improve the quality of construction management decision making a variety of factors must be considered. These factors include, but are not limited to,

- Engineer's choice of material,
- Cost to quality ratio,
- Customer's feedback at each development stage,
- Effective communication between each of the parties,
- Effective labor management,
- Optimum expenditure on nonessential activities,
- Management of expenses from a single point of contact,
- Minimal delay in completion of tasks,
- Visual and statistical data analysis.

Using the above constraints, this chapter proposes a mathematical model which is inspired by machine learning as described in Yang and Kim [8]. Figure 13.2 shows the flow of the proposed model.

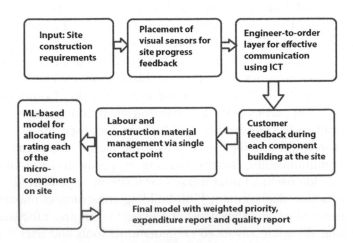

Figure 13.2 The overall flow of the proposed system.

From Figure 13.2, it is observed that the system starts by taking in the site constraints, these include,

- Budget of the site, and so the approximate quality expected from the builder/contractor (BQ)
- Actual time constraints on the site (TA)
- Area in Square feet of construction (Asf)

These requirements are taken input by the system, and then a deployment model is generated for placement of visual sensors at key points on the site. These sensors aid in autofeedback for the site's progress. Once the sensors are in place, then material procurement is done with the help of the engineer-to-order layer. This layer is assisted with the help of ICT interface for effective communication between the parties. This procurement is done on a per-unit completion basis so that there is minimum wastage of the procured components.

Labor and construction material management is done via a single point of contact, which is managed by a cloud interface. This interface is responsible for tracking of the amount spent to the component on which it is spent on. This portal is visible to all the parties involved on the construction site, thereby making the details of all the expenses and the material procured transparently. Each time any material procurement is needed, details of the same are uploaded on this portal, and only upon approval by the client/contractor, the material procurement is done. The material here is referred to any disposable and non-disposable components on the site. All this data is fed to a machine learning model that assigns weights to each of the management blocks. These weights decide to which block needs improvement, and thus the client/contractor can focus on improving that area of the site. The following steps are used while designing the ML-based model,

Inputs
Percentage step in site completion for tracking (N)
Visual progress data from the site (Pv)
User feedback for the current site stage (UF)
Cost to quality ratio of procurement (QC)
Labor efficiency on-site (EL)

$$EL = \frac{\begin{array}{c}\textit{Number of hours the labour is working } *\\ \textit{Number of sq.ft worked on}\end{array}}{\begin{array}{c}\textit{Number of hours allowed for working } *\\ \textit{Number of sq.ft ideally worked}\end{array}} \quad (13.1)$$

Component usage percentage per square feet (CP)
Outputs
Weights of each stage
Algorithm model

- For each completion stage of the site, evaluate the following parameters

$$\textit{Progress Weight (Pw)} = UF * \frac{(\textit{Visual Completion} + \textit{Manual Completion})}{(2 * \textit{Ideal Completion})}$$

$$(13.2)$$

$$\textit{Cost weight (Cw)} = \frac{QC * UF}{\textit{Ideal QC}} \dots \quad (13.3)$$

$$\textit{Labour weight (Lw)} = EL * UF \dots \quad (13.4)$$

$$\textit{Component usage weight (CPw)} = \frac{CP * UF}{\textit{Ideal CP}} \dots \quad (13.5)$$

- Upload each of these weights on the web panel, and suggest the customer/contractor as to which weights are reducing
- The weights which are constantly reducing after the initial N% of the site completion are the action points for the customer/contractor.
- After each of the weight checks, replace old values with the new values as obtained from equations 13.1, 13.2, 13.3, 13.4, and 13.5

Using this model, retune the overall site management, and check the online web panel for effective utilization of the components. This algorithm is tested on multiple sites. The next section describes the results obtained from each of the sites.

13.4   Comparative Analysis

In order to analyze the performance of the given machine learning model, this chapter compares the customer feedback, the cost-to-quality efficiency, and the deadline completion of different sites. Tables 13.1 to 13.3 indicate the performance superiority of our algorithm with Lean and Agile methods. In order to obtain these readings, each of the methods was developed using a Python toolkit. A total of 12 construction sites were contacted, and the proposed algorithm was applied to all the sites. The customer feedback (in terms of star rating out of 5) was taken upon completion of the site and is tabulated in Table 13.1. The cost efficiency (in terms of cost-saving %) was taken from each of these sites and is tabulated in Table 13.2. The cost efficiency is evaluated using the following formula,

$$\text{Cost Eff.} = 100 \times \frac{\text{Total cost of the site after applying the algorithm}}{\text{estimated cost of the site during planning phase}}$$

$$(13.6)$$

Similarly, the deadline overshoot % was evaluated, which indicates the percentage of overshoot that occurred while completing of the site. This value must be less than 100% for an effectively planned site (as per RERA regulations in India). The details about the deadline overshoot are given in Table 13.3. These results were compared with the lean [9] and agile [10, 11] models. The results are shown from Table 13.1 to Table 13.3.

From this table, it can be observed that the customer feedback has drastically improved due to the proposed method, which is due to the fact that at every stage, the customer is involved, and based on their feedback, the work progresses. Moreover, most of the techniques reduce customer feedback as the size of construction increases, but in our case, the customer feedback shows an increasing trend. Table 13.2 showcases the cost efficiency percentage, wherein it can be observed that the cost efficiency, which is the ratio of the cost incurred to the quality of the site, drastically improves from 78% to 97%; this is due to the fact that all decisions taken on the site are Engineer-focused and transparent to all the concerning parties due to the cloud-based interface.

Table 13.1 Constructed area v/s customer feedback.

Construction area (sq. ft.) residential	Customer feedback lean	Customer feedback agile	Customer feedback proposed
800	3.2	4.1	4.3
1200	3.3	4.15	4.31
1500	3.26	3.86	4.33
2000	3.32	3.78	4.36
2400	3.35	4.01	4.38
2800	3.38	3.82	4.4
3200	3.41	3.76	4.42
4000	3.45	3.71	4.44
11000	3.48	3.65	4.46
22000	3.51	3.6	4.48
44000	3.54	3.54	4.5
88000	3.57	3.49	4.52

Table 13.2 Cost efficiency v/s constructed area.

Construction area (sq. ft.) residential	Cost eff. (%) lean	Cost eff. (%) agile	Cost eff. (%) proposed
800	78.6	86.3	96.3
1200	78.2	86.34	96.5
1500	77.9	86.25	96.56
2000	77.4	86.33	96.57
2400	77.05	86.6	96.7
2800	76.66	86.54	96.79
3200	76.27	86.6	96.87
4000	75.88	86.66	96.96
11000	75.49	86.72	97.05
22000	75.1	86.78	97.14
44000	74.71	86.84	97.22
88000	74.32	86.9	97.31

Table 13.3 Deadline overshoot vs constructed area.

Construction area (sq. ft.) residential	Deadline overshoot (%) lean	Deadline overshoot (%) agile	Deadline overshoot (%) proposed
800	99.6	78.6	81
1200	99.9	79.7	81.64
1500	102.7	80.8	83.41
2000	105.6	81.9	85.23
2400	107.15	83	86.43
2800	109.23	84.1	87.88
3200	111.31	85.2	89.32
4000	113.39	86.3	90.77
11000	115.47	87.4	92.21
22000	117.55	88.5	93.66
44000	119.63	89.6	95.1
88000	121.71	90.7	96.55

An increase in cost efficiency and customer feedback should ideally reduce the deadline hit ratio of the algorithm, but in our case, the deadlines are properly met. Agile shows the best deadline performance, but our algorithm ensures that all work is completed under the deadline due to constant and transparent monitoring. This can be seen from Table 13.3.

Due to an improvement in the given parameters, the proposed system is aptly suitable for any kind of construction work. And, similar results were obtained when the system was tested on commercial, highways, water-line, waste management, and mall sites.

13.5 Conclusion

Construction site management algorithms generally use standard methodologies like agile, scrum, lean, etc. Given that these methodologies are not designed for managing construction sites but are designed for management in general, thus, the final efficiency of these algorithms is always questionable. Our proposed algorithm is able to reduce the cost and improve the overall customer satisfaction for the site by keeping an aware deadline strategy. The main advantage is the usage of a transparent cloud-based web interface that ensures better working efficiency and reduced dependency during billing and other micro-operations. Using the developed system, it is observed that efficiency in terms of deadline overshoot, customer efficiency, and cost efficiency increases. Customer satisfaction is improved due to faster completion of the site and also due to the produced construction quality. Both of these parameters are improved due to continuous user feedback taken during each of the construction phases. Due to this, the deadlines of the site are strictly maintained. This helps in reducing the deadline overshoot, which recursively adds to customer satisfaction. Cost efficiency is also maintained because of optimum labor allocation, visual progress tracking and optimum component usage. Therefore, the proposed system is effective in terms of all the primary factors which are needed for a construction site. The work can be further extended by adding concepts of deep learning and defining separate techniques for visual and analytical analyses.

References

1. Kuehn, I., Cordier, J.J., Baylard, C., Kotamaki, M., Patisson, L., Reich, J., Ring, W., Management of the ITER buildings configuration for the construction and installation phase. *IEEE 26th Symposium on Fusion Engineering (SOFE)*, pp. 1–8, 2015.
2. Dallasega, P., Industry 4.0 fostering construction supply chain management: Lessons learned from engineer-to-order suppliers. *IEEE Eng. Manage. Rev.*, 46, 3, 49–55, 2018.
3. Snider, C., Gopsill, J.A., Jones, S.L., Emanuel, L., Hicks, B.J., Engineering project health management: A computational approach for project management support through analytics of digital engineering activity. *IEEE Trans. Eng. Manage.*, 66, 3, 325–336, 2018.
4. Liu, Q., Xu, J., Qin, F., Optimization for the integrated operations in an uncertain construction supply chain. *IEEE Trans. Eng. Manage.*, 64, 3, 400–414, 2017.
5. Pinho, T., Telhada, J., Carvalho, M., Managing construction supply chain. *IEEE International Engineering Management Conference*, Estoril, pp. 1–4, 2008.
6. Lindk Vist, C., Stasis, A., Whyte, J., Configuration management in complex engineering projects. *2nd International Through-life Engineering Services Conference, Procedia CIRP*, vol. 11, pp. 173–176, 2013.

7. Construction site management. https://www.cityofsalinas.org/sites/default/ files/chapter_k_-_construction_site_management.pdf.

8. Yang, W.J. and Kim, Y.S., Manpower allocation model for construction site office engineers based on inherent technical risks. *KSCE J. Civil Eng.*, 23, 3, 947–957, 2019.

9. Khan, R. and Raja, R., Introducing L1-sparse representation classification for facial expression. *Imperial J. Interdiscipl. Res. (IJIR)*, 2, 4, 115–122, 2016.

10. Lee, D.W. and Lee, T.S., The improvement & management of historical data at the construction site—focused on the supervision committee. *KSCE J. Civil Eng.*, 8, 5, 479–489, 2004.

11. Tibaut, A. and Zazula, D., Sustainable management of construction site big visual data. *Sustain. Sci.*, 13, 5, 1311–1322, 2018.

12. Park, J., Park, S., Oh, T., The development of a web-based construction safety management information system to improve risk assessment. *KSCE J. Civil Eng.*, 19, 3, 528–537, 2015.

13. Sidawi, B. and Alsudairi, A., The potentials of and barriers to the utilization of advanced computer systems in remote construction projects: Case of the Kingdom of Saudi Arabia. *Vis. Eng.*, 2, 1, 1–13, 2014.

14. Guo, C., Guo, J., Ji, L., Chen, M., Tian, L., Development of bulk material management system and research on material balance applications based on business intelligence. *IEEE 14th International Conference on e-Business Engineering (ICEBE)*, pp. 31–37, 2017.

15. Lu, H., Wang, H., Xie, Y., Li, H., Construction material safety-stock determination under nonstationary stochastic demand and random supply yield. *IEEE Trans. Eng. Manage.*, 63, 2, 201–212, 2016.

16. Madhavarao, B., Mahindra, K., Asadi, S.S., A critical analysis of material management techniques in construction project. *Int. J. Civil Eng. Technol.*, 9, 4, 826–835, 2018.

17. Zaha, A., The impact of material management on construction project delivery in maldives, in: *Ph. D. dissertation*, UniversitiTunku Abdul Rahman, Malaysia, 2017. https://www.academia.edu/40326753/THE_IMPACT_OF_ MATERIAL_MANAGEMENT_ON_CONSTRUCTION_PROJECT_ DELIVERY_IN_MALDIVES_ZAHA_AHMED_A_dissertation_submitted_in_partial_fulfilment_of_the_requirements_for_the_award_of_ Master_of_Project_Management_Faculty_of_Engineering_and_Science

18. Mane, M.P.N., Gupta, A.K., Desai, D.B., A review paper on onsite material management for construction projects. *Imperial J. Interdiscipl. Res.*, 3, 2, 1288–1290, 2017.

19. Dube, N.N.F., Aigbavboa, C.O., Thwala, W.D., Challenges facing construction site management in the swaziland construction industry, 2015. https:// core.ac.uk/download/pdf/54198686.pdf.

20. Sahu, A.K., Sharma, S., Tanveer, M., Raja, R., Internet of Things attack detection using hybrid deep learning model. *Comput. Commun.*, 176, 146–154, 2021, https://doi.org/10.1016/j.comcom.2021.05.024.

21. Mustapa, F.D., Mustapa, M., Misnan, M.S., Mahmud, S.H., ICT adoption in materials management among construction firms in construction industry. *IEEE Colloquium on Humanities, Science and Engineering (CHUSER)*, pp. 342–346, 2012.

22. Amornsawadwatana, S., Effective design of the construction supply chain: A case of small buildings in thailand, in: *IEEE International Conference on Industrial Engineering and Engineering Management*, pp. 206–210, 2011.

23. Wang, S., Shi, J., Jiang, D., Qi, Z., Research for traceability model of material supply quality in construction project. *Fifth International Symposium on Computational Intelligence and Design*, pp. 398–401, 2012.

24. Gaosheng, Y., Ge, H., Hui, G., Research on the strategy of construction material procurement when the price fluctuation is considered. *International Conference on Management and Service Science*, 2010.

25. Lenka, R.K., Rath, A.K., Tan, Z., Sharma, S., Building scalable cyber-physical-social networking infrastructure using IoT and low power sensors. *IEEE Access*, 6, 1, 30162–30173, 2019.

26. Fei, W. and Shilei, W., Study on steel bar management of construction project. *International Conference on Measuring Technology and Mechatronics Automation*, pp. 645–647, 2010.

27. Fei, W. and Shileii, W., Applying logistics to construction material purchasing and inventory. *International Conference on System Science, Engineering Design and Manufacturing Informatization*, pp. 199–201, 2010.

28. Jianlong, H., Zhongfeng, W., Feng, G., Yun, S., Meng, T., The production material management system based on technology of polymorphism in petrochemical industry. *IEEE International Conference on Cyber Technology in Automation, Control, and Intelligent Systems (CYBER)*, pp. 479–482, 2016.

29. Pertiwi, I., Indrayanti, A.P., Andayani, K.W., Intara, I.W., Kristinayanti, W.S., Setyono, E.Y., Construction project plan waste management model" *International Conference on Applied Science and Technology (ICAST)*, pp. 657–661, 2018.

30. Zhengyu, L., Zhijun, H., Cuiyun, H., Research of highway construction management standardization. *3rd International Conference on Information Management, Innovation Management and Industrial Engineering*, pp. 565–568, 2010.

31. El Sawalhi, N.I. and El-Al Kass, M.M.A., A construction materials management system for gaza building contractors. *4th International Engineering Conference –Towards engineering of 21st century*, 2012.

Index